STEP-BY-STEP
DIY

GUINNESS BOOKS

Executive Editor:
Keith Faulkner

Design & Art Direction:
Jonathan Lambert

Technical Editor:
Mike Lawrence

Contributors:
Mike Lawrence
Ian Penberthy
John Sanders

Illustration:
Hayward Art Group
Andrew Green
Simon Green
David Palmer
Steve Cross
Jeremy Alsford

**Conceived and produced for the publishers
by Keith Faulkner Publishing Ltd.**

**'Guinness' is a registered trade mark of
Guinness Superlatives Ltd**

British Library Cataloguing in Publication Data

Guinness step-by-step DIY. – (Guinness step-
  by-step series)
  1. Interior decoration – Amateurs' manuals
  I. Lawrence, Mike, *1947 –*
643'7   TH8026

ISBN 0 – 85112 – 929 – 3

The producers would like to give special thanks to:
C.E.F. Ltd., Unit 4, May Avenue Industrial Estate.
Perry Street, North Fleet, Kent: Gravesend Electrical
Installation Co. Ltd., 12a Perry Street, North Fleet,
Kent: Fleetway Heating, The Terrace, West Street,
Gravesend, Kent: B.A.F. Smith: Ian Maxwell, Echo
Plumbing & Heating, Unit 10, May Avenue Industrial
Estate, Perry Street, North Fleet, Kent: Drews Oasis
Plumbing, 2 Holborough Road, Snodland, Kent.

Typeset in Great Britain
by Presentia
Printed and bound in Italy
by New Interlitho S.p.a.

STEP-BY-STEP
DIY

Contents

GUINNESS BOOKS

How to use this book

Step-by-Step DIY has been planned, written and designed with one aim in mind – to provide easy-to-find and easy-to-follow information to help you create and maintain an attractive and efficient home.

The book is divided into six main sections, each covering a major area of DIY:

1. **Electrics**

2. **Plumbing**

3. **Decorating**

4. **Central Heating & Insulation**

5. **Indoor Repairs**

6. **Outdoor Repairs**

Each section is a different colour for ease of location and is complete with its own detailed contents list, glossary of technical terms and section index. You'll also find that each section begins with some useful back-up information to give you a general understanding of the subject.

To find any specific information you need, simply turn to the appropriate section of the book, look through the contents list or index and you'll find a project number for the job that you want to know about.

Every project, whether it's mending a window or extending the ring main is self-contained; it has a short introduction to explain the job and a detailed, fully illustrated, step-by-step sequence to guide you through it – just follow the arrows on the boxes.

In addition to the easy-to-follow steps, you'll find plenty of back-up information and helpful tips, all designed to ensure that you spend your valuable time doing the job – not looking for the information.

Electrics

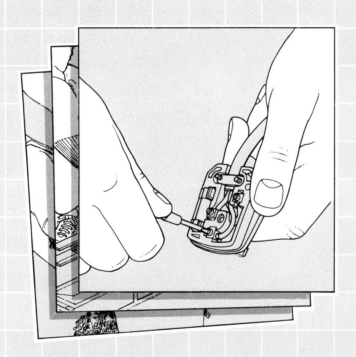

Electrics

Electrics

Of all the jobs tackled by do-it-yourself enthusiasts, home electrics seems to hold the most terrors. Many people admit that they would rather not carry out any work on their house wiring, on the thoroughly sensible grounds that they are afraid to tackle what they don't understand, and know that a mistake could be dangerous . . . or even fatal.

The fact is that carrying out your own electrical work is actually quite straightforward, so long as you know what you are doing and are prepared to work carefully and methodically. You need fewer skills than for any other sphere of do-it-yourself work, and modern electrical wiring accessories and equipment have never been so easy to obtain or so simple to install. This section explains how your wiring system works and how you can go about updating, extending and maintaining it. The advice given complies with the IEE Wiring Regulations.

① The consumer unit

The consumer unit is the most important part of any modern house wiring system. It's a self-contained unit that houses the main isolating switch for the whole system, controls the flow of electricity to each circuit within the building and is fitted with a number of safety devices that are vital to the health of both the system and its users. It's taken the place of the jumble of fuse boxes found in many unmodernised installations (right), but many people still refer to it as the 'fuse box'.

The consumer unit is usually sited close to the point where the supply enters the house. It may be positioned in the hall, the kitchen or an attached garage.

Within the unit will be found fuses or miniature circuit breakers (MCBs) protecting each lighting or power circuit in the house. On the most modern installations the main isolating switch may be replaced by a residual current device (RCD).

On older systems, there are likely to be a number of separate fuse boxes, each feeding an individual circuit. Systems wiring up in this way are likely to be obsolete and in need of replacement.

The fuses in the consumer unit are usually colour coded with the fuse rating.
Green — 45amp, for cooker circuits.
Red — 30amp, for ring mains.
Blue — 15amp, for heaters and small electric showers.
White — 5amp, for lighting circuits.

fuse box

fuse box

distribution box

meter

service fuse

② *Ring circuits*

On modern installations, circuits supplying socket outlets will generally be wired up as ring circuits. The circuit cable runs out from the consumer unit to each socket in turn, and then back again. Within the unit, the two live cable cores are connected to the same 30-amp fuseway; this means that current can flow to any socket on the circuit in either direction. Each ring circuit can serve a floor area of up to 100sq m (1075sq ft).

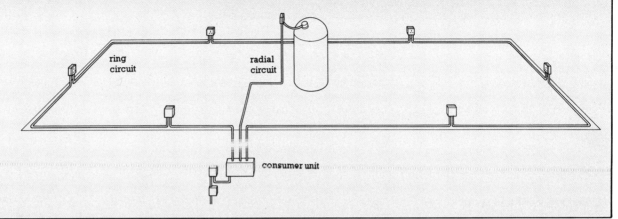

③ *Radial circuits*

On older installations, individual sockets taking round-pin plugs were each fed by a separate circuit (right).

Radial circuits on modern installations feed an unlimited number of sockets. There are two types. One is wired in 2.5mm² cable, protected by a 20-amp fuse and can supply a floor area of up to 20sq m (215sq ft). The other uses 4mm² cable, has a 30-amp fuse and may feed an area of up to 50sq m (540sq ft).

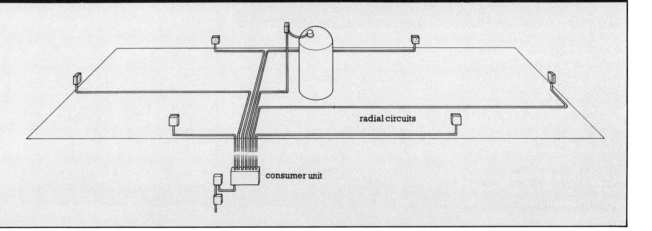

④ *Lighting circuits*

Lighting circuits are wired up in one of two ways. Most modern homes use the loop-in system (left); here the supply cable runs to each lighting point in turn, and the switch cable is wired directly into the ceiling rose, which contains three sets of terminals.

With the junction-box system (right), the cable runs to junction boxes four terminals; from each box one cable runs on to the lighting point, the other to its switch. Many homes contain elements of both systems.

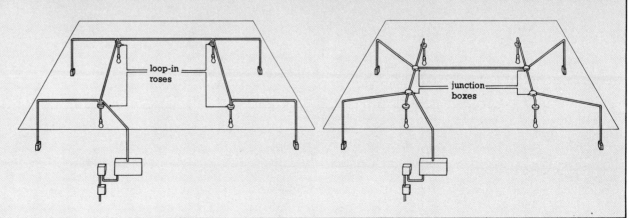

5 Flex

Flex, short for flexible cord, is the vital link between the mains and electrical equipment such as portable appliances and pendant lights. It is flexible because the conductors that carry the current are made up from a bundle of very fine wires, whereas cable (see below) usually has a single thick wire for each conductor and so is much stiffer.

Flex for general-purpose wiring has three cores, each individually insulated in coloured PVC – brown for live, blue for neutral and green/yellow striped for earth. The cores are protected by an outer sheath of PVC or rubber (which is usually covered with a fabric braid). Two-core flex, with no earth core, is used for double-insulated appliances and non-metallic lights.

7 Stripping cable

Cable is used for all the fixed wiring in the house. It runs from the various fuseways in the main consumer unit or fuse box (see Box 1) to individual power and lighting points, and is generally concealed by running it under floors or beneath wall surfaces.

Like flex, most cable contains three conductors. Two are individually insulated in PVC – red for live, black for neutral – while the third, which runs between them, is bare and is used as the earth continuity conductor on each circuit. Where this core is exposed to make a connection at an electrical wiring accessory, it must be covered with a short length of green/yellow striped PVC sleeving to insulate it. The three cores are sheathed in white or grey PVC.

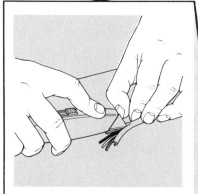

1. Prepare cable by cutting it to length, then slitting it with a knife down the centre line to avoid the cores. Cut off the sheath.

2. Use wire strippers or side cutters to remove about 15mm (⅝in) of core insulation. Slip some earth sleeving on the earth core.

6 Stripping flex

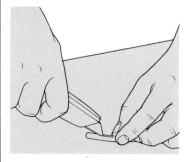

1. Cut the flex to length, then use a sharp knife to make a slit about 38mm (1½in) long in the sheath. Don't damage the core insulation.

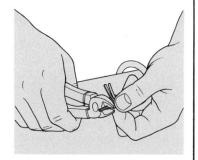

2. Cut away the sheathing, then use side cutters or wire strippers to strip off about 12mm (½in) of insulation. Don't cut the cores.

3. With braided flex, it is a good idea to wrap some insulating tape round the sheath before cutting it to prevent fraying.

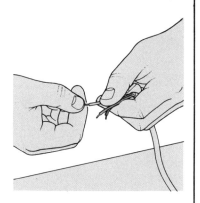

4. Twist the individual strands of each core neatly, ready for connection to the terminals. Solder them too if you wish.

8 Flex & cable sizes

Flex size (mm²)	Current rating (amps)	Weight on twin flex (kg/lbs)	Cable size (mm²)	Current rating (amps)*	Circuit fuse (amps)
0.5	3	2 (4½)	1.0	12	5
0.75	6	3 (6½)	1.5	15	15
1.0	10	5 (11)	2.5	21	20
1.25	13	5 (11)	4.0	27	30 or 45*
1.5	15	5 (11)	6.0	35	45
2.5	20	5 (11)	10.0	48	Service
4.0	25	5 (11)	16.0	64	fuse

To work out which flex to use for any appliance, divide its wattage by 240 to find its current consumption.

*Ratings for circuits with rewireable fuses; increase by one-third if MCBs or cartridge fuses are used instead.

⑨ Making connections

It's vital that connections between flex and plug are properly made; if they're not, sparking, overheating and short circuits may result. Each core must be connected to the terminal so that all the core strands are trapped, and the core insulation should reach the terminal so no bare conductor is exposed. The flex sheathing must be secured in the cord grip.

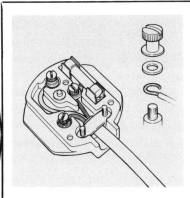

1. With plug open, connect the cores as shown. Wind core clockwise round a stud terminal, then fit washer and stud.

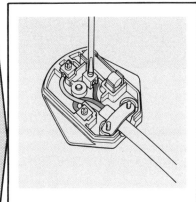

2. With pillar terminals, insert the core in the hole and tighten the screw down to secure it. Double over ends of thin cores.

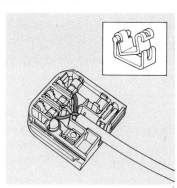

3. With clip terminals, place core in the clamp and snap down bar to secure it. With spring types, retract bar and insert the core.

5
6
7
8
9
10
11

⑩ Running cable under floors

Horizontal cable runs are laid out in the void beneath suspended timber floors, out of sight and harm's way. Where the cable is to run parallel with the floor joists, it is clipped to the sides of the joist (see below) or simply allowed to lie on the surface of the ceiling below where access to the joists is not possible. Where it is to run across the line of the joists, one board is lifted and holes are drilled through the joists to allow the cable to be threaded through. This method is preferable to cutting notches in the top edges of the joists, which could weaken them and also leaves the cable dangerously close the surface where it might be pierced by a floorboard nail. Label the board immediately above a cable run, to avoid any future accidents.

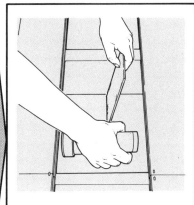

1. To run cable parallel with line of joists, lift a board at each end of run and check for obstructions with a torch and mirror.

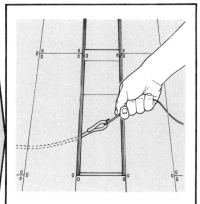

2. Either push cable through the void from one end, or use stiff wire to draw it through – better if the void is obstructed.

⑪ Fixing cables to joists

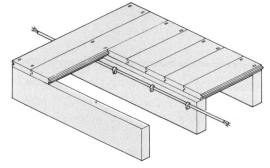

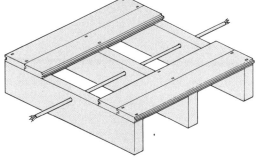

Cables can either cross the line of the floor joists or run parallel with them. In the former case, the cable is threaded through holes drilled in the joists, whilst in the latter it is either clipped to the side of the joist (if access to the whole length of the joist is possible) or allowed to lie on the surface of the ceiling below.

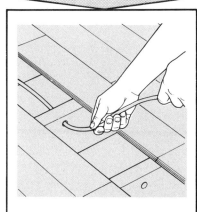

3. To run cable across the line of the joists, lift a board in line with the run and drill a hole through each joist. Then thread cable.

Vertical cable runs across solid walls can be surface-mounted, but it is far less noticeable (and far safer) if they are buried beneath the wall surface. This also allows electrical wiring accessories such as socket outlets and light switches to be recessed into the wall as well. In an existing wall, a groove called a chase is cut in the plaster along the line of the cable run. Where the plaster is less than about

10mm ($\frac{3}{8}$in) thick, the chase is deepened to about 19mm ($\frac{1}{2}$in) by cutting into the masonry too. Then the cable is fixed in place with clips at intervals and is plastered over. Conduit can be laid in the chase first to provide additional protection. Note that cable runs should be vertical or horizontal, never diagonal. This is so that they are easier to locate in the future.

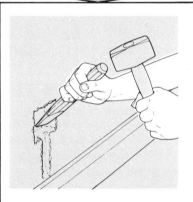

1. Mark out position of flush mounting box and cable run to it, then chip out hole and chase with cold chisel and club hammer.

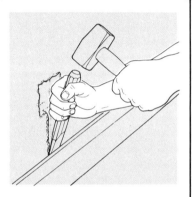

2. Where cable run has to pass behind a skirting board to reach floor void, angle chisel steeply to continue chase downwards.

3. Secure mounting box in its recess after removing a knock-out. Then fit a length of conduit in the chase and feed in cable(s).

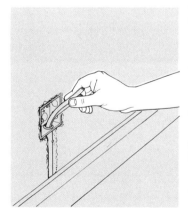

4. Draw in enough cable to allow the connections to be made easily. Then secure the conduit in the chase and plaster over it.

A slightly different procedure is adopted for running cable in stud partition walls – plasterboard sheets fixed to a timber framework of vertical studs and horizontal noggings set betwen ceiling and floor plates. If the wiring is being run in while the wall is being built, holes are drilled in the frame members as required and the cables are fed in before the second skin of plasterboard is nailed in place.

Extra noggings are fitted to allow wiring accessories to be flush-mounted (see below).

If the wall is already built, the cable has to be threaded in from above through a hole drilled in the ceiling plate. Small cut-outs have to be made in the plasterboard at points where the cable run crosses a nogging or stud, to allow a notch for the cable to be cut.

1. On horizontal sections, drill holes through the studs at the required height. Drill both studs at corners.

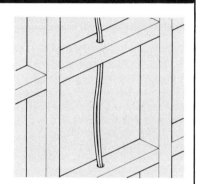

2. Drill holes in horizontal noggings for vertical cable runs, and thread the cables through. Leave a little slack.

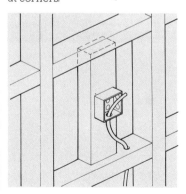

3. Nail a vertical support batten between the existing noggings to support the flush mounting box.

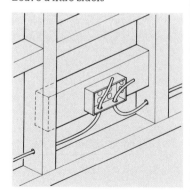

4. Alternatively, you can nail extra noggings in place. Set them back by just a little less than the box depth.

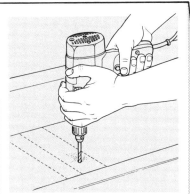

1. To thread cable into the space between the plasterboard skins of a stud wall, drill a hole in the ceiling plate from floor above.

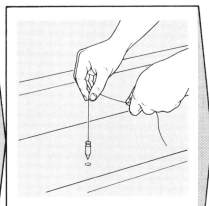

2. Attach a small weight to a line and drop it into the cavity until it stops at a nogging. Draw up the string and note its length.

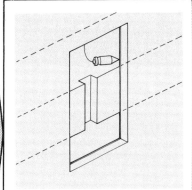

3. Measure that length down the wall and cut the plasterboard to expose the nogging. Notch it to allow the cable to pass it.

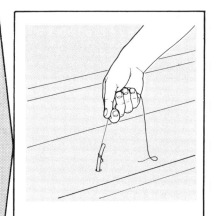

4. Drop the weighted line to the bottom of the cable run, fish it out there and attach the cable. Then draw the string and cable up.

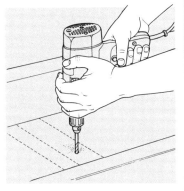

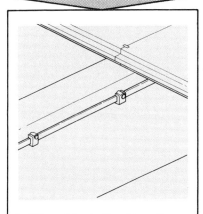

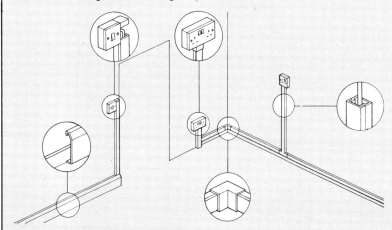

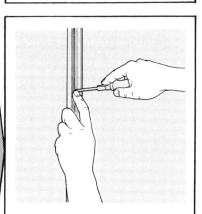

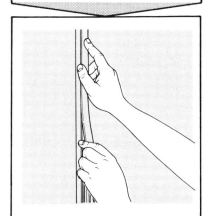

15 Cable in lofts

Perhaps the simplest place in which to lay out cable runs is in the loft, because it's easy to fix the cables to the exposed ceiling joists. Avoid running the cables along or across the top of joists, where they could be damaged by someone walking across the loft. Instead, clip them to the sides of the joints and drill holes through the joists if the cable has to cross them. Don't lay cables underneath loft insulation.

1. Clip cables to the sides of joists so they don't get damaged. It is then possible to floor the loft without disturbing them.

16 Surface-mounting cable

Cable can be mounted on the wall surface instead of being concealed behind it, but exposed cable doesn't look very attractive and could easily be damaged. If cable has to be surface-mounted, it's better to run it in slim protective plastic trunking fixed to the wall surface. This consists of a U-shaped channel which is screwed or stuck to the wall, and a continuous snap-in cover strip which hides the cables when they have been laid in the channel. A variation on this type is designed to resemble door architraves and skirting boards.

Both types are used in conjunction with surface-mounted wiring accessories, and trunking systems include a range of elbow and tee fittings plus neat collars to link trunking to mounting boxes.

Trunking systems incorporate all the fittings needed to take cable runs round internal and external corners, form T-junctions and connect with surface-mounted wiring accessories.

1. To run cable in surface-mounted trunking, mark the position of cable run and screw or stick the channel in position.

2. Lay in the cables, then snap in the cover strip. Use elbow, tee and collar fittings as required to complete the run.

17 Running cable overhead

An overhead cable run is one way of taking power from the house to a garage, garden shed or greenhouse. Ordinary PVC-sheathed cable is used for the run, but must be supported on a catenary wire if the span between supports is more than 3m (10ft). In addition, the cable must be at least 3,5m (11ft 6in) above the ground, and 5,2m (17ft) over drives used by vehicles.

These requirements mean that the cable will normally emerge from the house at first floor level, and will have to be supported at its other end by a post securely attached to the outbuilding.

If the cable is supported by a catenary wire, it must be clipped to it at intervals and should have a drip loop at each end (see below). This is to ensure that water does not run along the cable to the switchfuse unit.

1. Where the cable will emerge through the house wall, fit a screw-in eye bolt. Drill a hole, sloping upwards, for the cable.

2. Run a catenary wire between house and outbuilding. Earth it by running a sleeved earth wire back to the consumer unit.

18 The catenary wire

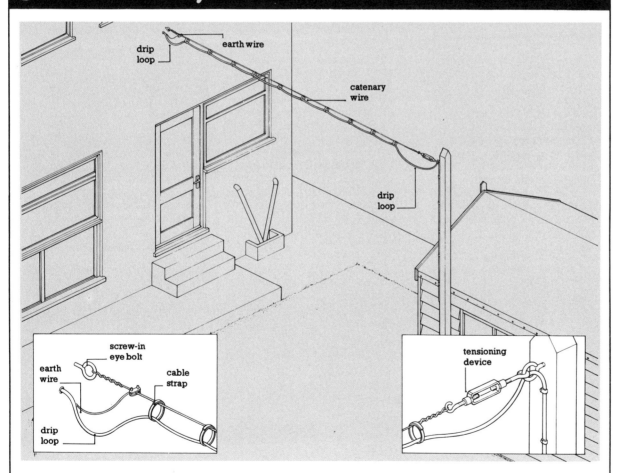

drip loop · earth wire · catenary wire · drip loop

screw-in eye bolt · earth wire · cable strap · drip loop

tensioning device

An overhead cable must be at least 3,5m (11ft 6in) above the ground, and on a catenary wire on spans over 3m (10ft). The catenary must be earthed and the cable should have drip loops at each end.

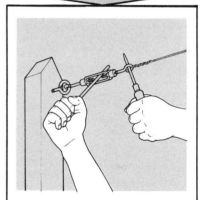

3. At the outbuilding end of the run, fit a tensioning device and turn the eye with a screwdriver until the wire is pulled taut.

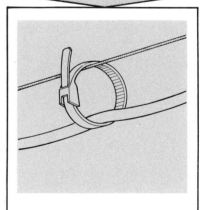

4. Thread the cable into the house and the outbuilding. Then use small plastic clips to attach the cable to the catenary.

As an alternative to overhead cable runs, power can be taken underground to outbuildings and outdoor lighting positions. This has the obvious advantage that the cable is out of sight, and so long as it is buried deep enough to avoid damage from digging it will be safely out of harm's way too. A sensible depth is at least 450mm (18in).

Again, ordinary PVC-sheathed cable can be used, but it must be protected by impact-resistant PVC conduit with solvent-welded connections.

Alternatively, armoured PVC-sheathed cable can be used with no additional protection, but this is more expensive to use than ordinary cable and has to be connected to the house and outbuilding wiring via special connection boxes (see below).

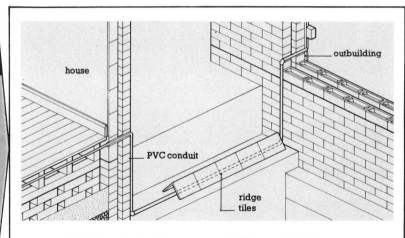

Ordinary PVC-sheathed cable can be used underground if it is laid in conduit. Ridge tiles offer additional protection.

1. Mark out the line the cable run is to take, then dig out a trench to a depth of at least 450mm (18in) across open garden.

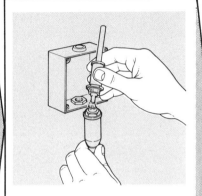

2a. Fit a PVC hood, gland nut, gland and coupler to the end of cable. Mount the conversion box with a backnut in the knockout.

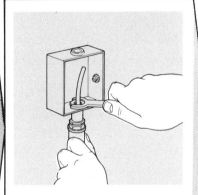

3a. Carefully feed the cable into the box through the backnut, and tighten this with a spanner to pull the coupler up tight to the box.

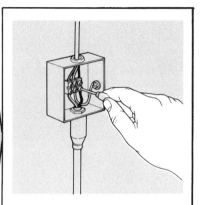

4a. Strip the insulation and attach the live and neutral cores to a connector block. Then link in indoor cable and earth the box.

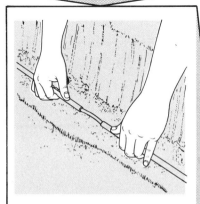

2b. Lay the cable run on a bed of sand in the trench. Then feed lengths of PVC conduit on from one end and slide them along it.

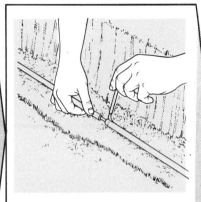

3b. When the conduit is fitted, solvent-weld the joints. Complete the run with elbows at the house and outbuilding ends.

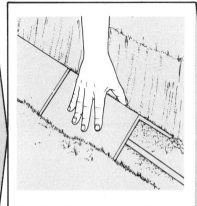

4b. Provide more protection against accidental damage occurring to conduit by laying ridge tiles or paving slabs over it.

5. Complete the wiring and check that the circuit works before backfilling the trench with soil and relaying turf.

20 Surface-mounted accessories

The quickest way of installing electrical wiring accessories such as switches and socket outlets is to surface-mount them. This involves fixing a mounting box on the wall surface to conceal the electrical connections, and then fitting the accessory faceplate to the box. The circuit cables may also be surface-mounted (Project 16), or may be concealed within the wall surface (Projects 12 & 13).

The advantage of surface-mounting accessories is speed of installation, but the drawback is that they protrude from the wall quite noticeably – the projection ranges from just over 25mm (1in) for light switches up to around 70mm (2¾in) with large accessories like cooker control units – and this may make them prone to accidental damage.

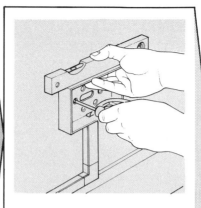

1. Run the circuit cable(s) to the fixing position chosen – either in trunking or concealed – hold the box level. Mark screw positions.

2. Drill holes in the wall to take the box fixing screws, and insert wallplugs (solid walls) or cavity fixings (stud partition walls).

21 Flush-mounting accessories on solid walls

It's safer and neater to flush-mount wiring accessories, by recessing the mounting box containing the connections into the wall surface. The circuit cables are also generally concealed, so the end result is a very neat, unobtrusive installation with the accessory faceplates fitted almost flush to the wall surface.

On walls of solid brick or blockwork, this involves chopping out a recess to match the size of the mounting box required. With some larger accessories such as cooker controls and shaver supply units, the box has to be comparatively deep, so care must be taken on cavity walls not to cut right through the masonry. Some accessory ranges offer special shallow boxes (see right).

22 Flush-mounting boxes

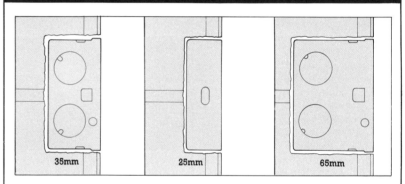

35mm   25mm   65mm

Left: ordinary flush-mounting box. Centre: shallow mounting box for stud walls. Right: deep mounting box for cooker controls.

1. To fit a flush mounting box in a solid wall, hold the box in position on the wall, and draw round it with a pencil.

2. Use a sharp cold chisel and a club hammer to chop out a recess to the required depth. Keep the sides neat and square.

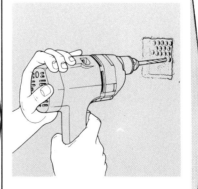

3. You can make the job easier by honeycombing the wall with drill holes before chopping out the waste.

4. Offer up the box to check its fit, and chop deeper or add filler as required. Then mark the positions of the fixing screws.

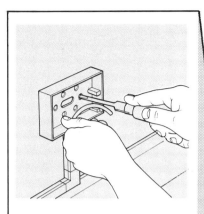

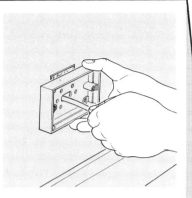

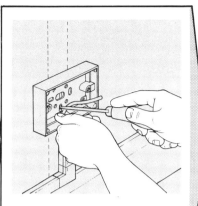

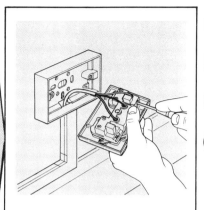

3. Remove one of the plastic knockouts from the box, feed in the cable and screw the box into place. Check that it is level.

4. If converting single socket to a double, mount the new box over the old flush one. Use the old faceplate screws to fix it.

5. On stud partition walls, use woodscrews to fix the mounting box over a stud – more secure than using cavity fixings.

6. With the box securely in place, prepare cable ends and connect them to the terminals. Then attach the faceplate.

23 *Flush-mounting accessories in stud walls*

Wiring accessories can be flush-mounted in stud partition walls too. If they are being installed while the wall is being built, they are mounted on noggings set in the required positions (Project 14). Once the wall has been built, fitting noggings would involve cutting away large areas of the plasterboard cladding, so the usual way of mounting the box is by recessing it into one of the studs.

This involves locating the stud, cutting out a square or rectangle of plasterboard over it to match the size of box being used, and then chopping out the stud to the required depth to allow the box to be fitted flush with the plasterboard surface. To avoid weakening the stud, no more than 25mm of wood should be removed.

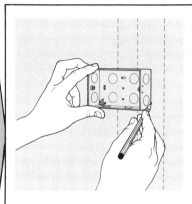

1. Locate the stud by tapping and test drillings. Then hold the box in position directly over it and draw round its outline.

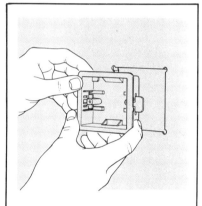

Special cavity fixing boxes *avoid the need for notching studs, allowing the box to be fitted anywhere on the wall.*

5. With the fixing holes drilled and plugged, remove a knockout from the box, fit a grommet to it and feed in the supply cables.

6. Set the box in place in the recess, drive the fixing screws into the wallplugs, then make good round the box with filler.

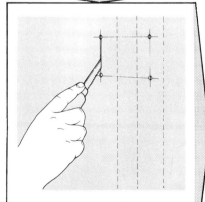

2. Drill a hole through plasterboard at each corner, then cut the hole with a padsaw. Use a sharp knife to cut over the stud.

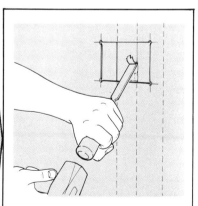

3. Lift out the plasterboard and chisel away the stud until the box fits flush. Feed in supply-cable and screw the box in place.

24. Fitting a conduit (BESA) box

Unless your light fittings are all pendant lampholders connected to ceiling roses (Project 25), you will have to provide a recessed enclosure called a conduit box or BESA box in the ceiling surface to contain the electrical connections. This allows the light fitting's baseplate to be flush with the ceiling; some types are designed to be screwed directly to the box, while others will cover it and be screwed to the ceiling itself.

Conduit boxes, as their name implies, are designed for use with wiring systems using round PVC conduit. However, for this purpose conduit is not used; the lighting circuit cables simply enter the box via the moulded side or rear inlet. The cable is then linked to the fitting flex via small connectors.

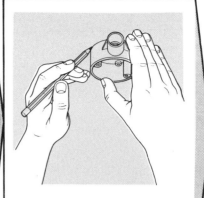

1. Offer up the box to the ceiling at the required position – ideally midway between two joists – and draw round it with a pencil.

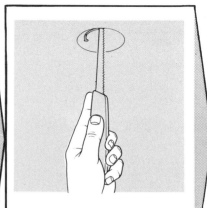

2. Drill a starter hole within the circle, then insert a padsaw blade and cut carefully rond the outline. Remove the waste disc.

25. Making fixings to ceilings

Many light fittings consist of a ceiling rose with a pendant lampholder, connected together by a length of flex. As with a conduit box (Project 24), a secure fitting is necessary to carry the sometimes considerable weight of ornate lampshades, so it is not enough to rely on cavity fixings to hold the rose in place on the ceiling.

The ideal situation is to position the rose so the fixing screws can be driven through the ceiling surface into the underside of a joist. Then the supply cable can be fed along the side of a joist and down through the ceiling surface into the back of the rose itself.

If the position of the light fitting is so critical that it cannot be placed below a joist, a batten must be fitted to support it.

26. Conduit or BESA boxes

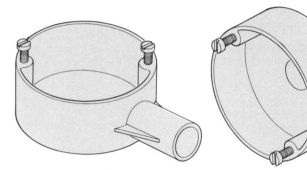

Conduit or BESA boxes come in a range of configurations for use with round PVC conduit.

However, on lighting circuits, only boxes with one side or back inlet are commonly used.

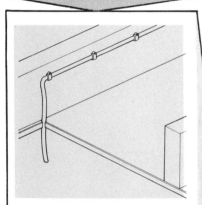

1. Run the circuit cable(s) above the ceiling to the point where the rose is to be fitted and feed them through a hole beside the joist.

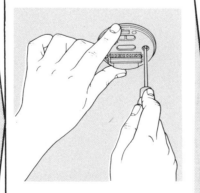

2. Offer up the rose with its centre fixing screw holes in line with the joist, make pilot holes for the screws with a bradawl.

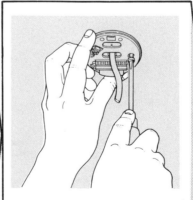

3. Remove the knockout from the rose baseplate, feed in the circuit cable(s) from above and screw the rose to the joist.

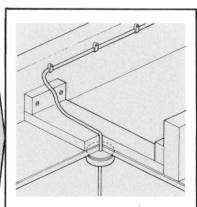

4. If the fixing is not underneath a joist, mount a batten between adjacent joists and screw the rose to it from below.

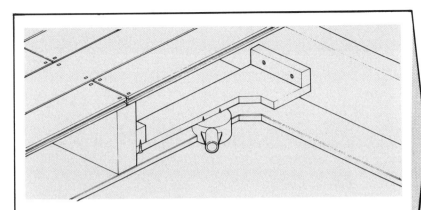

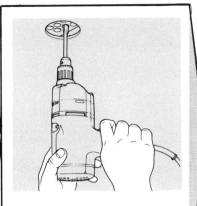

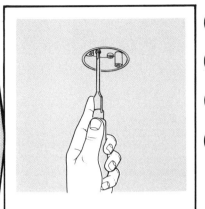

3. To provide a firm fixing for the box (which may have to carry the weight of the light fitting), fix a batten between the joists above the ceiling as shown, to allow the box to be screwed to the batten from below. Lift floorboards in the room above for access.

4. If the light position coincides with a joist, cut away the plaster and then drill and chisel away the joist to the required depth.

5. Offer up the box to check its fit, then screw it in place to the batten or joist. Finally make good the ceiling with plaster or filler.

27 Replacing fuses

Fuses are vital protective links, included in electrical circuits at various points to provide protection against accidental (or deliberate) overloading, and a number of other faults such as short circuits. In modern wiring installations every plug contains a fuse, while circuits are protected by rewireable or cartridge fuses or miniature circuit breakers (MCBs).

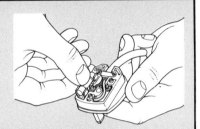

Plug fuses *simply clip into place. Fit 3-amp fuses for appliances rated below 700 watts, 13-amp fuses otherwise.*

Miniature circuit breakers (MCBs) *are switches which are much more sensitive than rewireable or cartridge fuses. If they trip off, reset them to 'on' by pressing a button or small lever.*

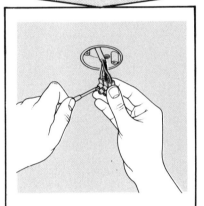

6. Feed the lighting circuit cable into the box, prepare its cores and connect them to a strip of three plastic terminal blocks.

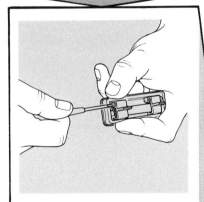

1. To replace a rewireable fuse, switch off the mains, pull out the fuse carrier from its holder and remove the old wire.

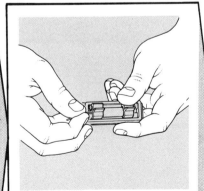

2. Insert new fuse wire of the correct rating, through the ceramic tube or across the central bridge of the fuse carrier.

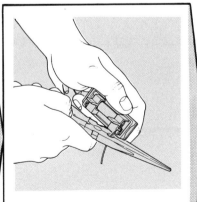

3. Connect the wire to its terminals and trim off any excess. Replace the fuse in the fuse box and restore the power.

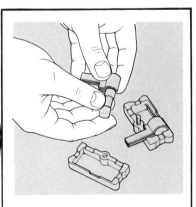

4. With cartridge fuses, remove the fuse carrier and simply replace the blown fuse. Never try to rewire a cartridge fuse.

With a properly-installed and maintained electrical installation, electric shocks should never occur. However it's important to know how to react if they do.

● If an electrical appliance gives a shock, STOP USING IT at once. Switch it off, unplug it and check connections within the plug and the appliance (see A, right). Check and replace the appliance flex too if necessary. If in doubt, have it serviced by a qualified electrical repair agent.

● If a shock is received from any part of the fixed wiring – light switches, socket outlets and so on – see C or get a qualified electrician to check the circuit.

● If someone receives a severe shock and is involuntarily gripping the source of the current, TURN IT OFF IMMEDIATELY. If you can't, DRAG THE PERSON AWAY by their clothing. Avoid touching their flesh or you will get a shock.

● If the person is conscious, lay them down flat with the legs slightly raised, turn the head to one side to keep the airway clear and cover with a blanket. Cool burns with cold water, and cover with a dry sterile dressing. Don't apply ointments to the burns, and don't give the patient any food, drink or cigarettes. Then CALL AN AMBULANCE.

● If the person is unconscious, lay them face down in the recovery position, using the arms and legs to provide support for the body and tilting the head back and bringing the jaw forward to keep the airway clear. Cover with a blanket and CALL AN AMBULANCE AT ONCE. Watch out for signs of breathing or heart stopping; if they do, start artificial (mouth-to-mouth) ventilation and external chest compression.

29 A: Electric appliance won't work

1. If an electrical appliance won't work, plug it in at another socket. If it works, suspect a fault at the first socket (see C).

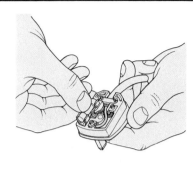

2. If it doesn't work at a second socket, replace the plug fuse with another of the correct rating for the appliance.

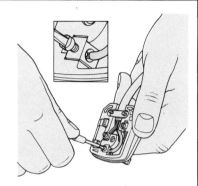

3. Check all the connections and remake any that are loose. If the cores are damaged, cut them back to fresh wire.

4. Unplug the appliance and inspect the connections where flex meets the terminal block. Remake them if necessary.

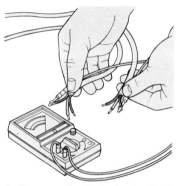

5. Use a continuity tester to check that each core of the flex is continuous. Fit replacement flex if necessary.

6. If these checks fail, suspect a circuit fault (see C) or a fault with the appliance. Call an electrician or service engineer.

30 C: Whole circuit is dead

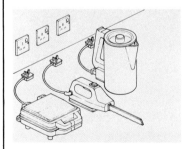

1. If a whole lighting or power circuit is dead, switch off all the lights or disconnect all the appliances on the circuit.

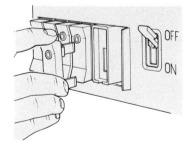

2. Turn off the power at the main on/off switch and replace the appropriate circuit fuse. Reset miniature circuit breakers.

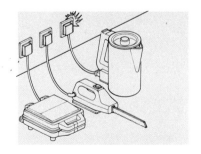

3. Restore power and plug in appliances or switch on lights one by one. Note which (if any) blows the fuse or trips the MCB.

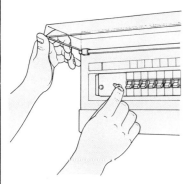 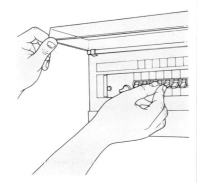

1. If the whole house is without power, check with neighbours to see if there is a power cut (a single-phase fault may affect only

2. If there is a supply fault to your house, call the local electricity authority's 24 hour emergency

one house in three). Then check the consumer unit to see the main RCCB or individual circuit breakers have tripped off.

number. Find it under Electricity in your local directory. Write it down here.

Emergency no.

ELECTRICITY BOARD

ADDRESS: ....
....
....
TELEPHONE NO: ....

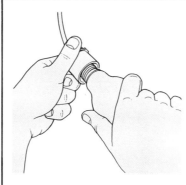 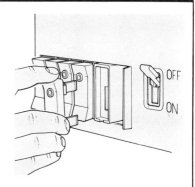

1. If a pendant light won't work, turn off the light switch and replace the bulb. Don't exceed the maximum wattage indicated.

2. If it still won't work, check the lighting circuit fuse after turning off the main switch. Replace the fuse if it's blown — see Project 27.

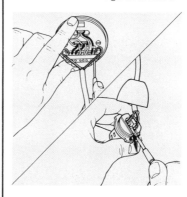 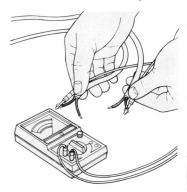

3. With the power still off, open up ceiling rose and lampholder to check for loose connections. Remake them as necessary.

4. Use a continuity tester to ensure that each core of the flex is unbroken. Replace it with new flex if broken cores are found.

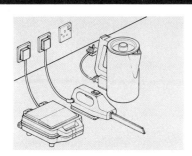 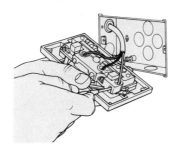 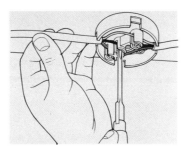 

The Electrical Contractors' Association

NICEIC
APPROVED
CONTRACTOR

4. Isolate the offending light or appliance for repairs. Then replace the fuse or reset the MCB again and restore power.

5. If the circuit is still dead after the fuse has been replaced, turn the power off and open up face plates to check connections.

6. If the fault was caused by damage to a cable, turn off the power and cut out the damage. Reconnect with a junction box.

7. Call in an ECA (Electrical Contractors Association) or NICEIC (National Inspection Council for Electrical Installation Contracting) member.

Fitting a plug to an appliance is one of the most straightforward and common electrical jobs, yet it is surprising how many people do it carelessly – or completely wrong. Badly-made connections will lead to overheating and short circuits, while connecting the cores to the wrong terminals could be lethal.

There are several points to remember when wiring up a plug. Firstly, the core insulation should expose no more than about 15mm ($\frac{5}{8}$in) of the conductors, so it will reach the terminals when connected, and in removing it care should be taken not to damage any of the strands. All loose strands should be twisted together; strays cause short circuits. Lastly, the flex sheath must be securely anchored in the cord grip.

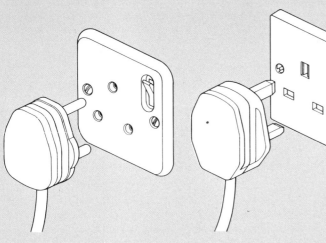

Old round-pin plugs and sockets come in 2, 5 and 15 amp versions, and are unfused. Modern fused plugs have rectangular pins.

As a general rule, flex should run between plug and appliance in an unbroken length. However, there are times when flex has to be extended, and in this case it must be done properly for reasons of safety. Joins should **never** be made by twisting cores together and wrapping them in insulating tape.

A one-piece connector is used for a permanent connection. Two-piece connectors allow the extension to be disconnected when not in use.

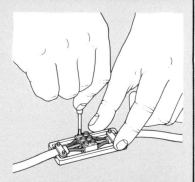

1. Use a one-piece connector to permanently link two lengths of flex. Connect cores at the terminals, and fit both cord grips.

2. To allow disconnection of the flex, use a two-piece connector. Thread the cover onto the flex and connect the cores.

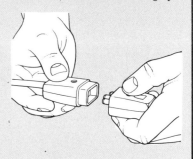

3. Fit the plug part of the connector to the appliance flex, the socket part to the plug flex so the connector pins aren't live.

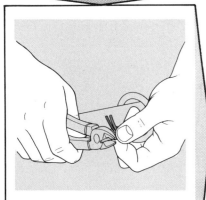

1. Cut back the flex sheath to expose cores and remove 15mm ($\frac{5}{8}$in) of the insulation with wire strippers. Don't damage cores.

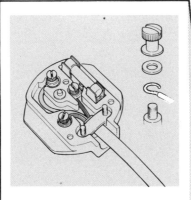

2. With stud terminals, wind the core clockwise round the terminal and fit the washer and screw-on stud.

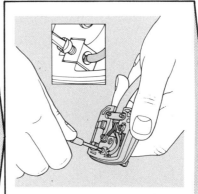

3. With pillar terminals, undo the screw and insert the flex in the hole. Tighten the screw. With thin cores, double over the end.

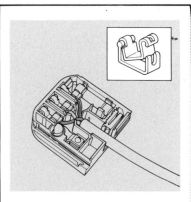

4. With clip-type terminals, lay the stripped end of the core in the jaws of the terminal and snap the cover bar into place.

35 Fitting new flex to a lamp

Flex can become worn and frayed with use, and accidental damage to the sheath could expose live cores. If this occurs, a temporary repair can be made with insulating tape, but new flex should be fitted at the earliest opportunity for safety's sake.

The first step is to choose the correct type of flex for the job. For a table or standard lamp, the most common type to choose is round PVC-sheathed flex, with three cores if the lamp has any metal parts, two cores if it is all-plastic. The 0,5mm² size is adequate for all lamps except extremely powerful fittings containing a number of high-wattage bulbs; here the 0,75mm² size should be chosen. Buy enough flex to allow a socket to be reached easily without causing a hazard.

36 Flex types

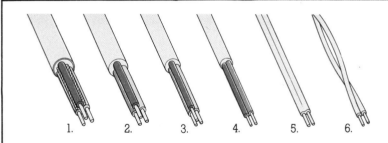

Flex comes in a range of types and sizes. The most common types are: three-core circular braided (1); three-core heat-resistant (2); three-core PVC-sheathed (3); two-core round PVC-sheathed (4); two-core parallel non-sheathed (5); twisted twin non-sheathed (6).

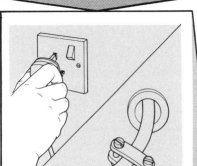

1. Unplug the lamp, open the plug and disconnect the flex cores. Then loosen the flex grip inside the base of the lamp.

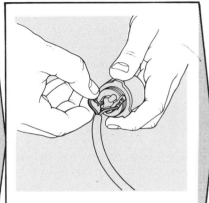

2. Unscrew the lampholder from the body of the lamp. Then disconnect the cores from the lampholder.

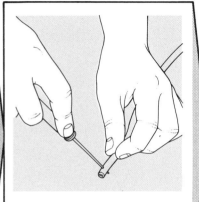

3. On standard lamps make a hole in the old and new flex sheathing, using a bradawl, then link them with strong string.

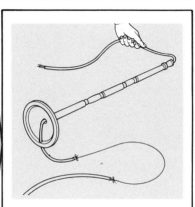

4. Pull the old flex while feeding in the new section so it is threaded through the lamp body. Then connect up the new flex cores.

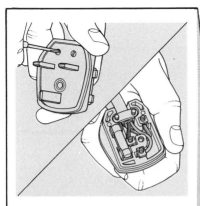

5. To prevent a tug on the flex from pulling out the connections, secure its sheath in the cable grip. Tighten the screws equally.

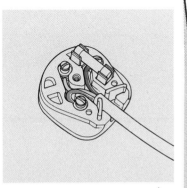

6. Some plugs have nylon jaws that grip flex tightly if it is pulled, and cannot be bypassed – the plug won't close if it's not used.

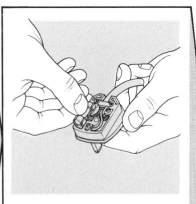

7. Fit a fuse of the correct rating for appliance – 3-amp (colour-coded red) for ratings up to 720 watts, 13-amp (brown) otherwise.

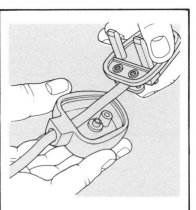

8. Some plugs have an impact-resistant rubber or PVC top. Don't forget to thread this onto flex **before** connecting up cores.

37 Rewiring a pendant lamp

Pendant lamps are less prone to damage than most other electrical wiring accessories, but heat from the lamp itself can cause both flex and lampholder to deteriorate. Also, the swinging to-and-fro motion caused by through draughts on windy days can fray the flex and strain the connections, resulting in short circuits and persistent fuse-blowing. The only solution is to replace the flex and, if necessary, to fit a complete new lampholder.

Start by turning off the power to the circuit the affected light is on – it is NOT sufficient just to turn off the light switch. Then unscrew the rose cover so you can gain access to the flex connections.

Use round two-core flex with plastic lampholders, three-core flex with metal ones.

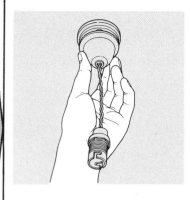

1 After turning off the power to circuit at fuse box, unscrew rose cover and disconnect flex cores from rose terminals.

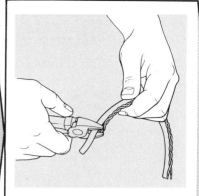

2 Unscrew the lampholder cover and disconnect the other end of the old flex. Use it as a template to cut the new flex to length.

38 Connections at junctions boxes and roses

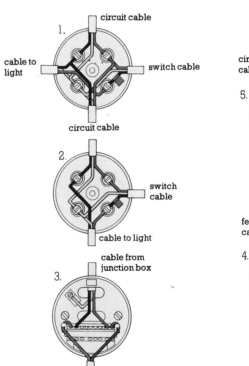

circuit cable

cable to light

switch cable

circuit cable

1.

2.

switch cable

cable to light

cable from junction box

3.

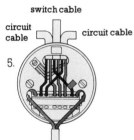

switch cable

circuit cable

circuit cable

5.

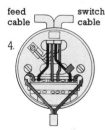

feed cable

switch cable

4.

On a junction box system, the switch cables for each light are connected in to the circuit cables at four-terminal junction boxes. Intermediate boxes have four cables (1), the last one on the circuit only three (2). Roses on this system have just one cable (3). With loop-in roses the switch cable is wired into its rose. The last rose has two cables (4); others have three (5).

39 Replacing a ceiling rose

It's a comparatively simple job to replace an old-fashioned ceiling rose with a modern one, or to replace a damaged rose.

As with all electrical jobs it's essential to turn off the power to the circuit at the main isolating switch box first of all.

If removing the cover of the old rose reveals just one incoming cable, disconnection and reconnection is straightforward. However, if the rose is the loop-in type, there may be up to four cables present if it is an intermediate rose from which a branch cable has been run to feed another light, so its a good idea to study the wiring diagrams given and then to label each cable before disconnecting it. This makes it much easier to reconnect the cable cores to the correct terminals.

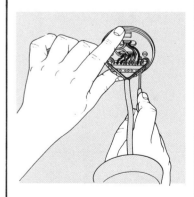

1 Turn off power, unscrew rose cover and disconnect pendant flex cores from their terminals. Set flex and lampholder aside.

2 Unscrew rose backplate and draw it gently downwards. There should be enough slack on the cables to allow this.

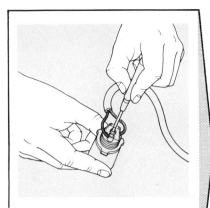

3 Cut back one end of the flex sheathing and strip about 12mm of insulation from cores. Then connect cores to the terminals.

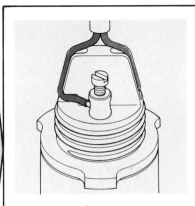

4 To prevent weight of the shade from straining connections, loop each flex core round the small hook moulded into the fitting.

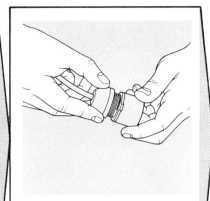

5 Thread lampholder cover onto the flex, screw it on. Then prepare the other end of flex as before, and thread on rose cover.

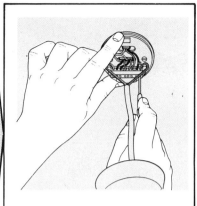

6 Reconnect the flex cores to the ceiling rose terminals. Then loop cores over the flex support hooks, screw rose cover back on.

40 Clip–on rose

The disadvantage of a conventional ceiling rose is that to remove the light fitting for decoration or maintainance, you have to actually open it up and disconnect the flex cores. Clip-on roses allow the light to be unplugged from the rose base. To fit a rose of this type, you simply disconnect the old rose, reconnect the circuit cables and then attach the special plug to the pendant flex.

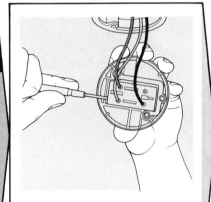

1 Turn off the power, disconnect circuit cables from old rose and connect them to new baseplate, following maker's instructions.

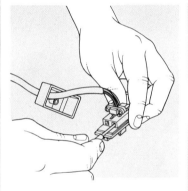

2 Disconnect the flex from the old rose, slip on the cover of new plug connector and then link flex cores to the connector terminals.

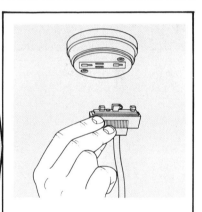

3 Secure new rose cover in place, offer up plug connector to the socket. Make sure it's properly engaged before letting go.

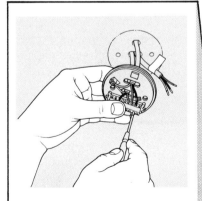

3 Wrap sticky labels round each incoming cable before disconnecting. Then loosen the terminals and free the cables.

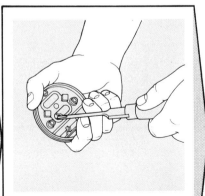

4 Push out the thin plastic from knockout in rose baseplate. If you use a screwdriver, take care not to stab your hand with it.

5 Thread each cable in turn through knockout in baseplate, and reconnect each cable core to its appropriate terminal.

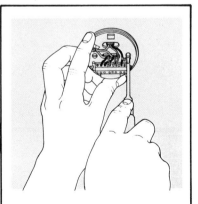

6 Screw the new rose baseplate back on ceiling, using new screw holes if necessary. Reconnect pendant flex and fit cover.

41 Replacing a pull-cord switch

Pull-cord switches are used for safety reasons to control lights and heaters in bathrooms if the switch concerned is within reach of the bath or shower. They can also be fitted where pull-cord operation is more convenient – over a bed, for example. Most are surface-mounted, with the switch mechanism enclosed in a plastic baseplate, but they can be fitted flush with the ceiling over a recessed conduit box if preferred.

Whichever method is chosen, it is important that the fixing is secure; otherwise over-zealous tugging on the pull-cord could bring the switch down with it.

Pull-cord switches are made in three ratings – 5-amp for lights, 15-amp for heaters and towel rails and 30 or 35-amp for showers.

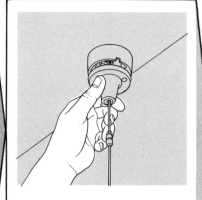

1. To replace an existing pull-cord switch, first turn off power at the main fuse box. Then undo screws holding the switch in place.

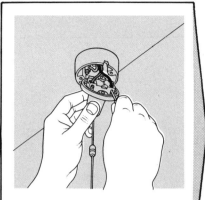

2. Draw the switch assembly gently away from its baseplate, and then disconnect the circuit cable(s) from their terminals.

42 Switch types

Ordinary plate switches come in a range of types. The basic ones are: slim architrave switches (1), one-gang switches (2 and 3) and two-gang switches (4). Those with two terminals per gang are for one-way switching; three are for two-way set-ups.

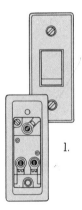

1.

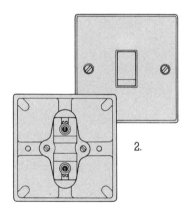

2.

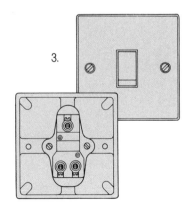

3.

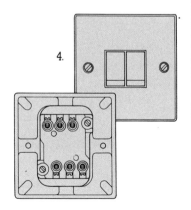

4.

43 Fitting a new plate switch

As with other switches, replacement may be called for if the old faceplate is cracked, or if a new one is wanted for cosmetic reasons. For a switch controlling one or more lights from this switch position only, a one-way switch with two terminals is sufficient, but since a two-way switch costs little more than a one-way type, it seems sensible to use the latter so that two-way switching could be implemented at some future date.

If a metal faceplate is wanted, check first of all that the switch cable has an earth core. This may have been cut off flush with the cable sheathing if a plastic faceplate was originally installed, or single-core live and neutral cables may have been used. In either case, an earth core must be added.

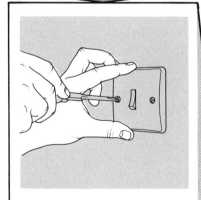

1. Turn the power to the circuit off at the main fuse box, then unscrew the old switch faceplate. Save the old fixing screws.

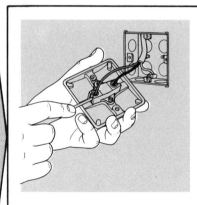

2. Pull the old faceplate away from the box, and disconnect. Check that an earth core is present if fitting a metal switch.

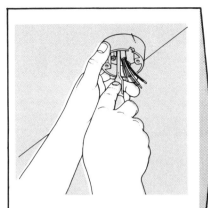

3. Set the old switch assembly aside, and undo the two screws securing the baseplate of the old switch to the ceiling.

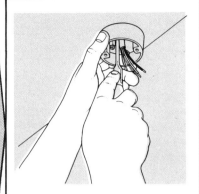

4. Remove the thin plastic from the knockout in the bottom of the new switch baseplate, and screw it in place.

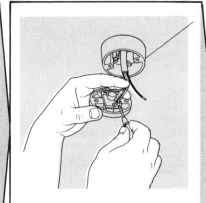

5. Reconnect the circuit cable(s) to the switch baseplate. On power circuits, make sure the correct cables are linked.

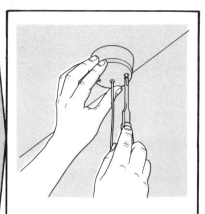

6. Carefully feed the cable(s) up into the ceiling void through the knockout and screw the new switch assembly into place.

44 Replacing a cord pull

Pull-cord switches are usually designed so that the main section of cord can be easily replaced – by unscrewing the acorn coupling and screwing on a new cord. However, if the cord breaks between this acorn coupling and the switch itself, the switch must be dismantled to allow the new cord to be fitted. Since the switch is spring-loaded, this must be done with care to prevent parts flying all over the room.

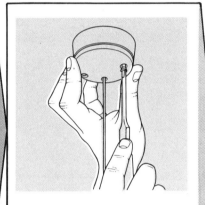

1. Turn the power off, then unscrew the switch from its baseplate and disconnect the circuit cable(s) from the terminals.

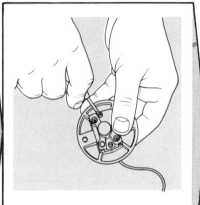

2. Hold the switch mechanism in place while undoing the screws that hold it to the switch casing. Lift the mechanism off carefully.

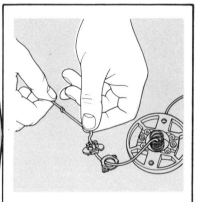

3. Thread in a new piece of knotted cord, then reassemble the switch mechanism and test that it operates before refitting.

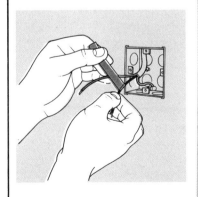

3. If ordinary two-core-and-earth cable has been used, wrap a flag of red PVC tape round the black core to show that it is live.

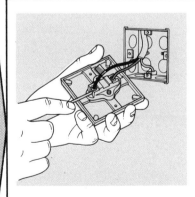

4. Reconnect the cores to the switch terminals. If a two-way switch is used, link the cores to terminals marked C and L1.

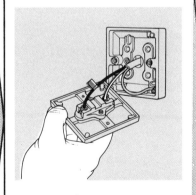

5. With a surface-mounted plastic switch, connect the redundant earth core to the small terminal in the base of the box.

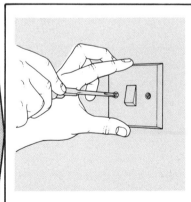

6. Finally, press the new faceplate back into position, taking care not to kink the cable cores, and screw it into place.

45 Replacing a light fitting

Installing a new light fitting can be surprisingly tricky unless you know how the existing fitting has been wired up, since many light fittings are sold without any wiring instructions. Most have a short length of flex emerging from the fitting, and this has to be connected to the lighting circuit wiring by means of small connector blocks. Exactly how this is done depends on whether the lighting point is wired up on the junction-box or loop-in systems.

Start by turning off the power to the circuit at the fuse box. Then unscrew the old fitting so you can see how many cables are present. If there is only one, junction-box wiring has been used; if there are two (or even three), the loop-in system has been used – see below.

1. Where a wall or ceiling light is mounted over a recessed conduit or other box, start by unscrewing the fitting from the box.

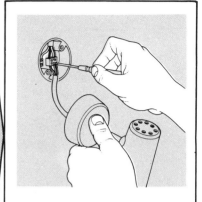

2. Carefully pull the fitting away from the box, and disconnect its flex cores from the terminals of the block connectors in the box.

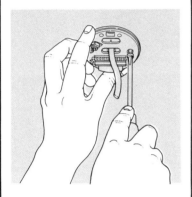

1. To install a flush-to-ceiling light fitting; first disconnect the cable from the old rose and unscrew this from the ceiling.

46 Terminal block connections

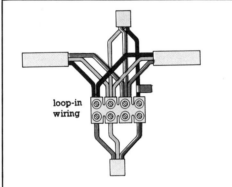

loop-in wiring

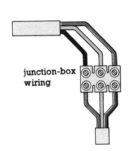

junction-box wiring

Use four connector blocks (left) to cope with loop-in wiring; only three are required for a one-cable junction-box arrangement (right).

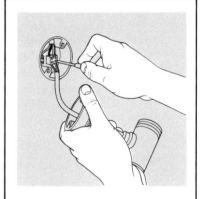

3. Connect the flex cores of the new fitting to the terminals, making sure you copy the original connections precisely.

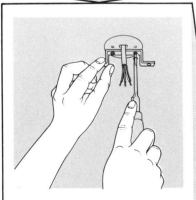

2. Screw the fixing bar to which the baseplate will be attached to the ceiling – either into a joist or to a batten between the joists.

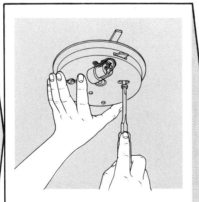

3. Thread the cable cores through the baseplate and connect them to the lampholder terminals. Then secure the baseplate.

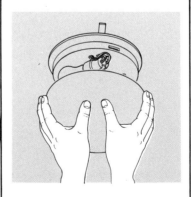

4. Fit a bulb of the appropriate wattage and offer up the fitting's cover. This is often locked in place with a sliding lever.

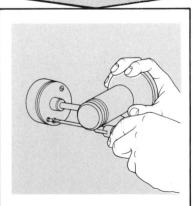

4. Check the connections are correct. Then tuck the connector block and flex inside the box and screw on the baseplate.

Fitting a fluorescent light

Fluorescent lights are ideal for work areas such as kitchens and hobby rooms, where their uniform shadowless lighting is an advantage over ordinary tungsten filament lamps. Their other main advantage is that they give out more light than a filament lamp for the same current consumption, so they are very economical to run.

The light can be fitted in place of any existing light fitting, with one proviso; if a quick-start type or one with a metal casing is chosen, for safety there must be an earth core present at the lighting point.

Older lighting circuits may lack an earth, and it may be easier to fit a plastic-bodied switch-start type with its replaceable starter canister screwed into the baseplate of the fitting.

1. Start by disconnecting and removing the existing light fitting if there was one. Then offer up the baseplate of the new fluorescent fitting to the ceiling and screw it securely either to a single joist or across a run of several joists.

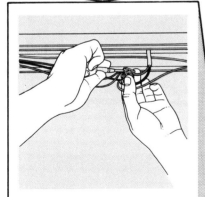

2. Connect the cable cores to the terminal block. If loop-in wiring has been used, replace the block with a four-terminal type.

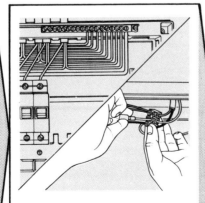

3. If the lighting circuit lacks an earth core, run a single-core earth cable from the main fuse box earthing terminal.

Dimmer switch

Dimmer switches allow the brightness of any filament light fitting to be controlled from the merest glimmer up to almost full power. A range of types is available, with conventional rotary or sliding controls, or sophisticated touch-sensitive or remotely-controlled action, and there are versions with one, two, three and even four gangs. When choosing one, make sure its wattage range is suitable for the lights to be controlled.

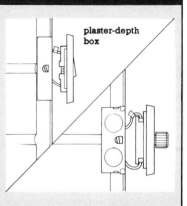

plaster-depth box

1. Some dimmers are designed to fit within an existing shallow plaster-depth mounting box (top); others need a deeper box (bottom).

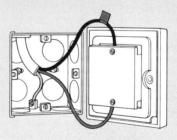 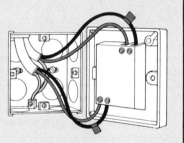

2. To fit a dimmer switch, simply unscrew and disconnect the old plate-switch and connect the cores to the terminals of the new dimmer.

3. With two-gang dimmers, connect the switch cables as recommended by the switch manufacturer. Don't use dimmers with fluorescent lights.

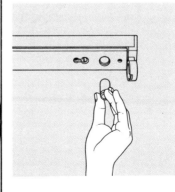

4. With a switch-start type, insert the replaceable starter canister into its recess on the baseplate and twist it to lock it in place.

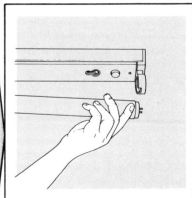

5. Insert one end into its terminals, then pull back the other spring-loaded block to allow the tube to be clipped into place.

49 Fitting wall lights

Wall lights are an attractive addition to any lighting scheme, and the range of fittings now available makes it easy to match any furnishing or colour scheme.

The major difference between installing wall and ceiling lights is the need to conceal the wiring leading to the light position – surface wiring would look very untidy, although could be installed as a temporary measure until the room was next redecorated. In stud partition walls it may be possible to feed the cables down inside the partition – see Project 13 – but on masonry walls recessed conduit and a conduit box provide the neatest solution.

Various wiring arrangements are possible (see below), and one switch can also be used to control several lights.

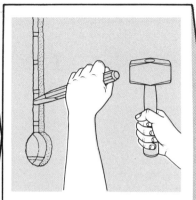

1. Mark the position of the cable drop down to the light position, and chop out the chase and conduit box recess with a bolster.

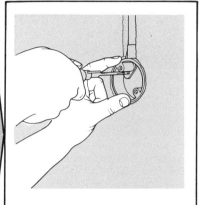

2. Fit lengths of round PVC conduit in the chase from the ceiling to the light position. Then screw the conduit box in place.

50 Switching options

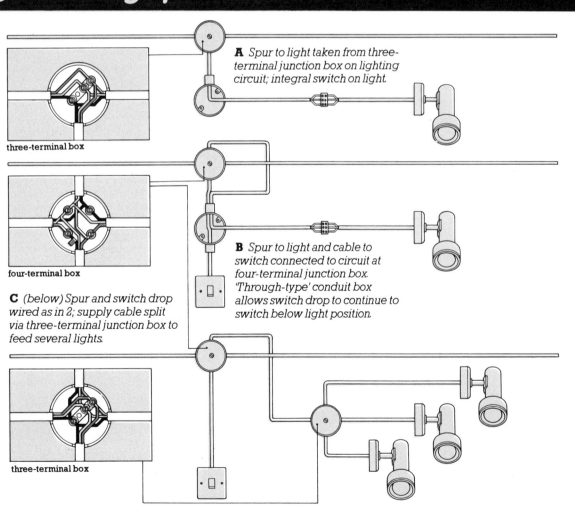

three-terminal box

A *Spur to light taken from three-terminal junction box on lighting circuit; integral switch on light.*

four-terminal box

C *(below) Spur and switch drop wired as in 2; supply cable split via three-terminal junction box to feed several lights.*

B *Spur to light and cable to switch connected to circuit at four-terminal junction box. 'Through-type' conduit box allows switch drop to continue to switch below light position.*

three-terminal box

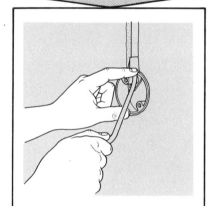

3. Thread in the spur cable to the light position from above. Draw enough cable through to allow connections to be made easily.

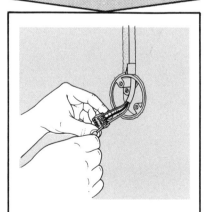

4. Strip and prepare the cable cores, and connect them to the terminals of a strip of three small block connectors.

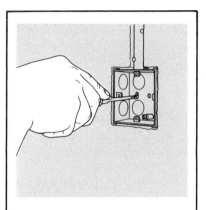

1. With arrangements A and B opposite, cut a chase down to the switch position and secure the light's mounting box in its recess.

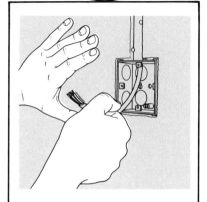

2. Feed in the switch cable from above. If using arrangement B opposite, drop the cable straight down through the conduit box.

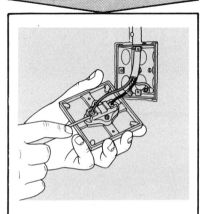

3. Strip the insulation and connect the live, neutral and earth cores. Flag the neutral core with red PVC tape to show it is live.

Two-way switching means being able to control one light from two different switch positions – a boon in situations such as lights in stairwells which can be controlled from hall and landing, or bedside lights which can be switched from the room door or beside the bed.

The principle is very straightforward. A two-way switch (with three terminals on the rear of its faceplate) is installed at each switching position. Then a conventional two-core-and-earth switch drop is run from the light concerned to the nearest of the two switches, and is wired in as shown below. The two switches are then linked with special three-core-and-earth cable, which has cores colour-coded red, yellow and blue for ease of identification.

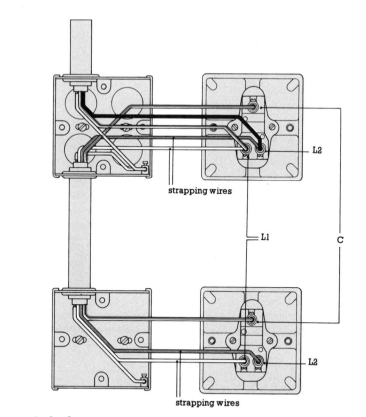

strapping wires

L2

L1

C

L2

strapping wires

The terminals of a two-way switch are labelled C (for common), L1 and L2. The switch drop from the light itself is connected to terminals L1 and L2 of the first switch; then the switch terminals are connected as shown — red to the C terminal, yellow to L1 and blue to L2.

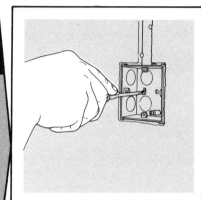

1. To convert an existing one-way switch to two-way operation, start by installing a mounting box at the new switch position.

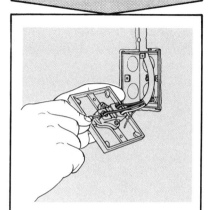

2. Connect the cores of a length of three-core-and-earth cable to the new switch and run the cable back to the original switch.

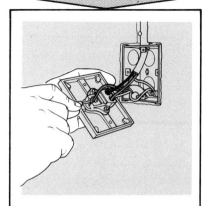

3. At the original switch position, replace the old one-way switch with a two-way one and connect up the switch drop and cable.

Two-way switching for stairwells

Two-way switching arrangements are particularly useful in stairwells, allowing lights to be controlled from both hall and landing. Many homes have only partial two-way switching, however; usually, the landing light is switched from both hall and landing, but the hall light is controlled from the hall only.

A better arrangement is the full two-way switching set-up shown below. Here each light can be controlled from either hall or landing, and the only alterations to the existing wiring required are the replacement of the existing one-gang two-way on the landing with a two-gang two-way switch, plus the addition of an extra run of three-core-and-earth cable linking the hall and landing switch positions.

54 Wiring arrangement

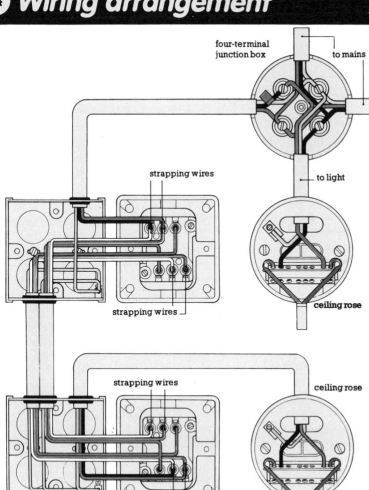

four-terminal junction box

to mains

strapping wires

to light

strapping wires

ceiling rose

strapping wires

ceiling rose

strapping wires

55 Fitting lights out of doors

Outdoor lighting can bring several benefits. For a start, it enables you and your visitors to find their way to your front door easily and safely. It will also deter unwelcome callers, who would far rather approach in complete darkness. And on the pleasure side, it can allow you to sit out on your patio after dark, and can light up attractive features of your garden such as trees and garden ponds.

Two points must be borne in mind when installing outside lights. First of all, any fittings chosen must be suitable for outdoor use, and should be marked as such. Secondly, unless the light fittings are mounted directly on the external wall of the house, separate circuits must be provided if they are to run at mains voltage.

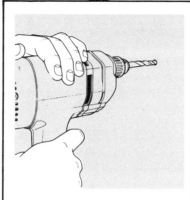

1. To install a light fitting on the exterior of the house, start by drilling a hole for the cable. Angle it slightly up to keep rain out.

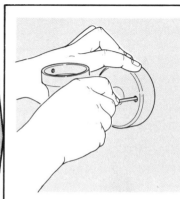

2. Mark the positions of the fixing screws on the wall through the fitting's baseplate, then drill and plug the screw holes.

56 Low-voltage wiring

One of the simplest ways of providing outdoor lighting remote from the house is to install a low-voltage set-up from a small transformer. This gets round the need to run in new circuits from the main fuse box or consumer unit, and since the low-voltage cable can be laid on the surface instead of being buried in the ground or carried overhead, installation is extremely quick and simple. The transformer is simply plugged into a convenient socket outlet within the house or an outbuilding.

A range of fittings is available, including ground fittings on spikes and 'chains' that can be suspended from trees. It is also possible to have pond lights using low-voltage lighting – intrinsically safer than using mains-voltage fittings.

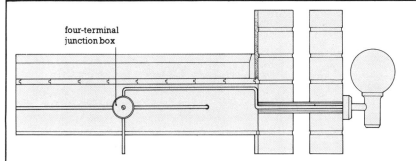

four-terminal junction box

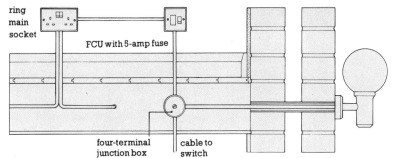

ring main socket

FCU with 5-amp fuse

four-terminal junction box

cable to switch

To provide power for the outside light from a nearby lighting circuit, locate the circuit cable and

cut in a four-terminal junction box. From this run in new cables to the light and its switch. Or connect

into a power circuit. Run 2.5mm² cable to a fused connection unit with a 5-amp fuse, then use

1.0mm² cable for the rest of the wiring to the four-terminal junction box, light and switch.

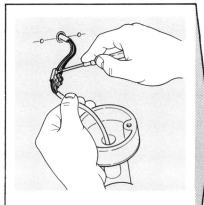

3. Feed in the circuit cable – ideally through a length of PVC conduit – and connect it to the fitting using a connector block.

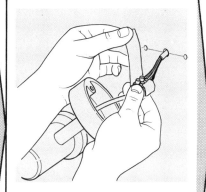

4. Wrap the connector block tightly in PVC insulating tape to keep moisture out of the electrical connections.

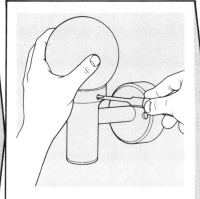

5. Screw the fitting to the wall and fit the bulb and cover. Seal the join between baseplate and wall with non-setting mastic.

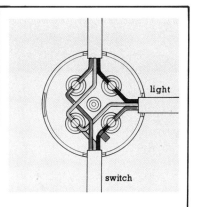

light

switch

6. Connect the cable indoors – via a fused spur off a power circuit, or with a four-terminal junction box on a lighting circuit.

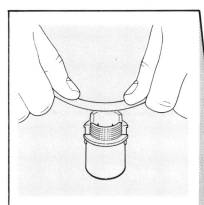

1. Most low-voltage installations have 'spike' connections within each fitting. The flex is simply pressed in to make connections.

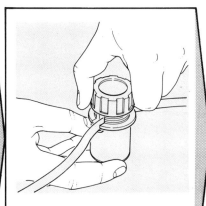

2. With the flex laid in place, screw on the cap of the fitting so that the spikes pierce the flex sheathing and make the contacts.

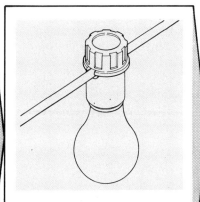

3. Repeat the operation to add other lamps to the circuit. Don't exceed the transformer rating, though, by fitting too many lights.

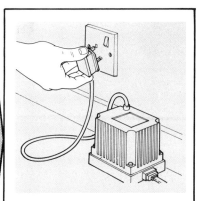

4. Connect the house end of the cable to the transformer terminals, then simply plug the lead in at a socket.

58 Converting single sockets

Many homes, even those that have been recently rewired, have a number of single socket outlets on the various power circuits. It's a simple matter to convert these into double (or even triple) outlets to increase the number of power points available. This is also a far safer choice to make than overloading your existing sockets with too many adaptors.

There are several ways of carrying out the conversion, and which route is chosen depends on whether the existing socket is flush or surface-mounted, and on how the new socket is to be fitted. Surface-mounting is certainly quicker, and means less disruption to decorations; it could be chosen as a temporary measure, with the new socket being flush-mounted when the room is next redecorated.

59 Changeover options

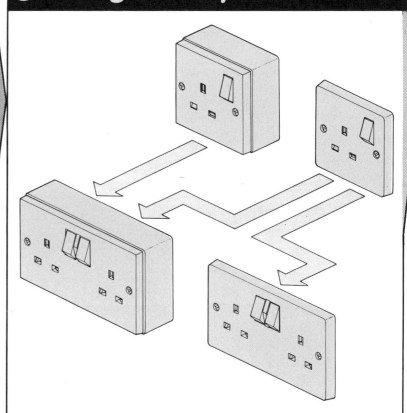

How you tackle the changeover from single to double socket depends on what's there and what you want. The simplest conversion is surface-mounted single to surface-mounted *double. A flush-to-surface mounted conversion involves fitting a new box over the existing flush box. The flush-to-flush option means enlarging the recess in the wall.*

60 Replacing broken faceplates

If the faceplate of an electrical wiring accessory is accidentally damaged, it is essentail that it is replaced as soon as possible. If this is not done, there is a risk that live parts may be exposed and anyone using the accessory could receive an electric shock.

Faceplates can also be replaced for cosmetic reasons – during redecoration, for example, where ornate brass types are being used in place of existing plastic ones.

In either case, the opportunity should be taken to inspect the state of the wiring. If the circuit cables are the PVC-sheathed and insulated type, everything should be well, but if old rubber-sheathed cables are found they should be tested by an electrician to see if they are safe to use.

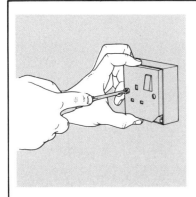

1. As with all electrical work, turn off the power and isolating the circuit you're working on. Then unscrew the damaged faceplate.

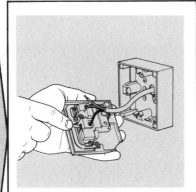

2. Pull it away from its mounting box, to disconnect the cable. If there is more than one, note which cores went where.

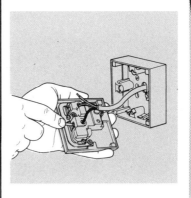

3. Reconnect cable cores to appropriate terminals on new faceplate. Sheath bare earth cores in green/yellow.

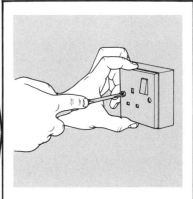

4. Press cable back into mounting box and screw on new faceplate. Use original screws on an old box so the threads match.

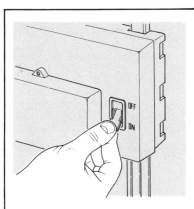

1. Start by turning off the power at the consumer unit and then isolating the circuit you will be working on.

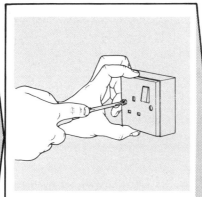

2a. If your single socket is surface-mounted and your new double one will be too, start by unscrewing and disconnecting.

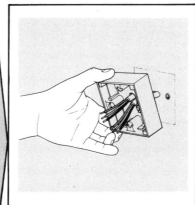

3a. Next, straighten out the cable cores and undo the screws holding the box to the wall. Don't untwist pairs of cores, though.

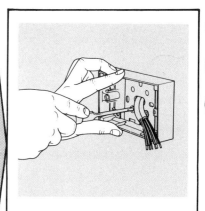

4a. Secure new surface-mounted double box to the wall after removing a knockout to admit the cables. Check that it is level.

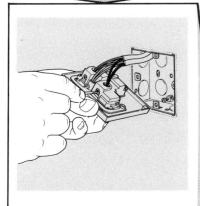

2b. If the single socket is flush-mounted, unscrew the faceplate and disconnect the cables. Save the faceplate fixing screws.

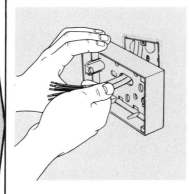

3b. Remove one of the thin plastic knockouts from the base of the new surface-mounted double box and thread in cables.

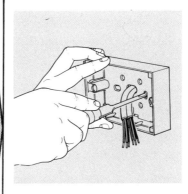

4b. Screw the new box to the fixing lugs of the old flush box, use original faceplate fixing screws so the threads match.

5a/b. With the mounting box in place, reconnect cable cores to their appropriate terminals. Sheath the earth cores.

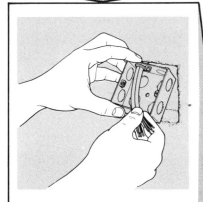

3c. For a flush-to-flush conversion, unscrew and remove the old box. Cut round it with an old knife to free it.

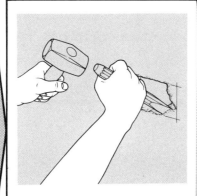

4c. Outline new box on the wall, and enlarge the hole with a cold chisel and club hammer. Keep the outline neat.

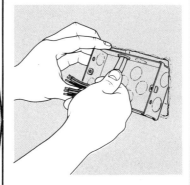

5c. Thread cables into the new box through a knockout fitted with a rubber grommet. Mark, drill and plug to secure the box.

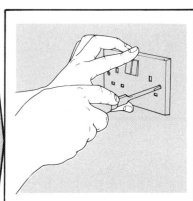

6c. With flush boxes, make good the wall and connect up cables. Compress them neatly into the box and screw on the faceplate.

61 Extending a power circuit

You can extend a ring main circuit or a modern radial circuit in one of two ways — by running a spur cable directly from the terminals of an existing socket, or by connecting a three-terminal junction box into the circuit cable.

In either case the spur can feed only one single socket, one double socket or one fused connection unit; spurs feeding two or more separate outlets are no longer allowed.

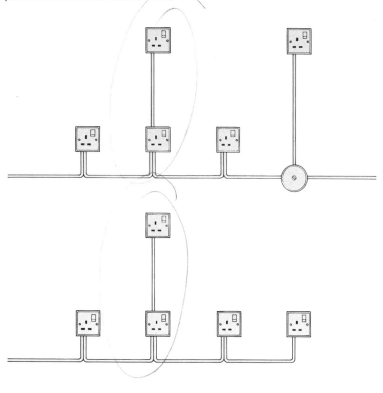

62 Adding a new socket

There are no restrictions on the numbers of socket outlets which a modern power circuit can supply, since you are highly unlikely to be using them all at the same time. The only restriction is on the total floor area of the house served by the circuit.

A ring main can serve a floor area of up to 100sq m (1075sq ft); a radial circuit can serve a floor area of up to 20sq m (215sq ft) if it's wired in 2.5mm² cable and protected by a 20-amp fuse of any type, and up to 30sq m (320sq ft) if it's wired in 4mm² cable and protected by a 30-amp cartridge fuse or miniature circuit breaker. It's important, therefore, to check this point if the new socket will be sited in a room not already served by the circuit you will be extending.

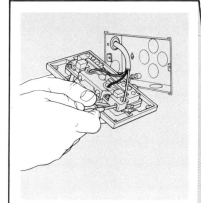

1. Decide on the position for new socket, install its mounting box and the run spur cable back to the socket that will supply it.

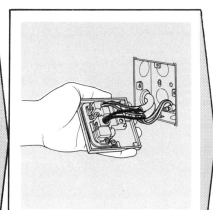

2. Open up this socket to see whether it can supply a spur (see below). If two cables are present, check it's not itself a spur.

63 Checking sockets

Spur cables can only be connected to existing sockets that are on a ring or radial circuit; you cannot take a spur from a socket that is itself already on a spur, since the Wiring Regulations state that a spur may feed only one supply outlet. It is therefore important to be able to indentify the status of any socket from which a spur cable is to be run. The first step is to turn off the power at the main consumer unit and isolate the circuit you will be working on.

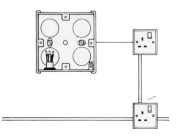

1. If there is only one cable feeding the socket, it is likely to be on a spur and cannot be used.

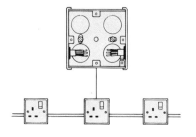

2. If there are two cables present, the socket could be on a ring circuit, so it can be spurred off.

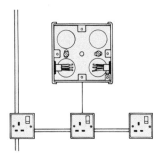

3. It could be an intermediate socket on a two-socket spur. If it is, no spur is allowed.

64 Extending a ring main

It is often possible to make use of an existing ring main circuit to serve a relatively large new floor area such as a home extension. This is prefereable to wiring in a host of new spur cables or adding a whole new circuit. Provided that the total floor area served by the extended circuit does not exceed 100sq m (1057sq ft), the circuit extension can go ahead.

The diagram (right) explains the principle. The existing circuit is cut at two convenient points, which are then linked to a new cable loop running round the new rooms. The new cable can be linked to the existing circuit either at a socket or by means of a three-terminal junction box. The section shown by dotted lines is discarded, or rewired as spurs off the new ring main circuit.

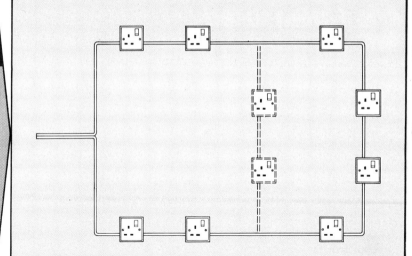

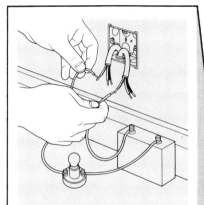

3. Do this by using a simple continuity tester to link the live cores. If the bulb lights, the cables are part of a ring circuit.

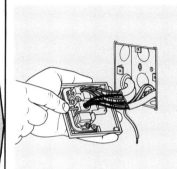

4. Connect spur cable cores to the terminals of existing faceplate. Replace it and restore power to the circuit.

65 Using a junction box

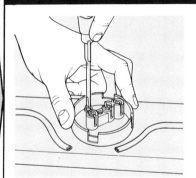

1. Mount three-terminal junction box on a joist near the cable, or on a batten fixed between joists. Cut cable with power off.

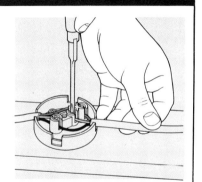

2. Strip off sheathing and prepare the cores. Connect to the terminals, linking live to live, neutral to neutral, earth to earth.

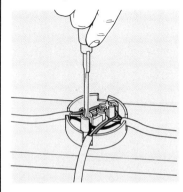

3. Strip and prepare the end of the spur cable in the same way, and connect it to the terminals. Fit the box cover securely.

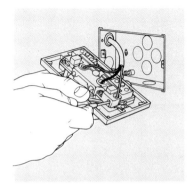

4. Run the spur cable to chosen position for the new socket. Fit a mounting box, connect the spur cable and fit faceplate.

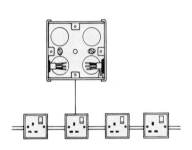

4. It could be an intermediate socket on a radial circuit. A spur could be connected in this case.

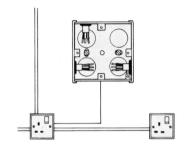

5. If three cables are present, the socket is already supplying a spur and another cannot be used.

Fused connection units are used in two main ways. The first is as an alternative to a socket outlet for connecting an appliance to the mains which should not be accidentally unplugged – a freezer, for example, or a central heating controller. The supply cables are connected in the same way as for a socket outlet; then the appliance itself is connected to it by flex or cable, depending on the arrangement being used. A fuse is housed in a small carrier in the unit's faceplate; this serves the same purpose as a fuse in a 13-amp plug.

The second use is when wiring lights from power circuits, to provide a lower level of fuse protection for the lights. Here the unit acts as the starting point for the lighting spur.

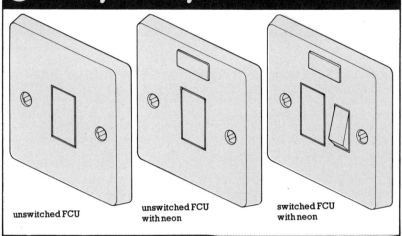

unswitched FCU

unswitched FCU with neon

switched FCU with neon

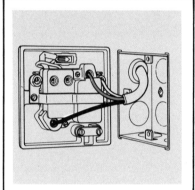

1. To wire up a fused connection unit, run in the cable(s) as for a socket. Then connect the cores to the terminals marked 'FEED'.

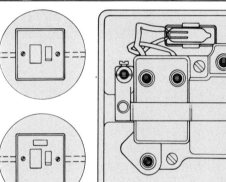
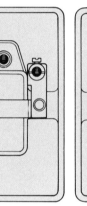
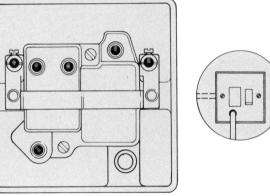

Fused connection units (FCUs) are available with or without a neon indicator. They can be connected into the circuit via knockouts in a mounting box. Alternatively, some have a flex outlet on the faceplate, for connection of fixed appliances such as freezers or electrical showers.

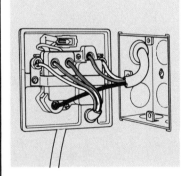

2. Fused connection units are available for side or rear connection; the cores are linked to 'LOAD' terminals.

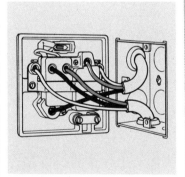

3. With the type having a front flex outlet hole, feed in the flex, prepare the cores and connect to the terminals marked 'LOAD'.

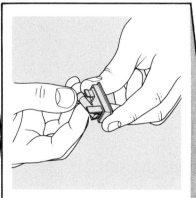

4. Fit a cartridge fuse of correct rating for the appliance (3 or 13 amp) or the wiring spur (5 amp for lights) in the front fuseholder.

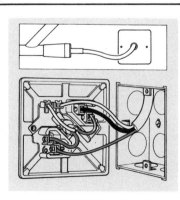

5. For a remote appliance, run cable to a flex outlet plate (inset) and then connect the appliance flex to the outlet's terminals.

If you want to add an extra circuit to your existing house wiring, you may be lucky enough to have a spare fuseway already in place but unused in your consumer unit, or else a blanked-off space where an extra fuse could be fitted. If this is the case, it is a comparatively simple matter to connect in the new circuit cable and if necessary, to install an additional fuse.

When adding a new circuit in this way, remember that the circuit fuses should be arranged so that the one with the highest rating is fitted to the main isolating switch. If the circuit to be added is of comparatively high current rating, check with your local electricity board to ensure that your supply cable and service fuse can cope with the extra load.

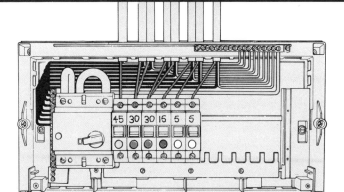

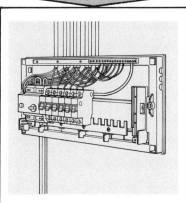

1. To check whether there's a spare fuseway in your consumer unit, turn off power at main switch and remove the unit's cover.

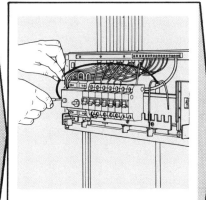

2a. If there's a fuseway of the right rating for the circuit required, connect the new cable's neutral core to neutral terminal block.

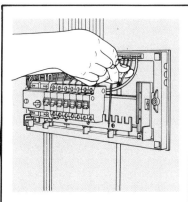

3a. Protect the cable's bare earth core with a length of green/yellow PVC sleeving, and connect to earthing terminal.

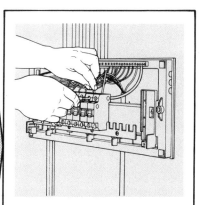

4a. Connect the cable's live core to the top terminal of the spare fuse carrier or MCB. Fit the unit's cover and restore the power.

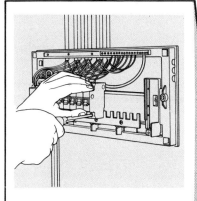

2b. If there is space for a new fuse carrier or MCB, loosen the screws securing the existing fuses or MCBs to the live busbar.

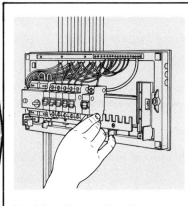

3b. Move the existing fuses or MCBs along the busbar to create space at the appropriate point in for the new fuse/MCB to be fitted.

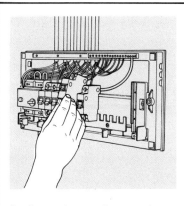

4b. Insert the new fuse carrier or MCB in the space. Fuse carriers are usually slotted into place. MCBs may clip over the busbar.

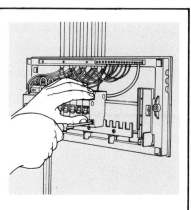

5b. Connect up cores of the new circuit cable as in 2a – 4a above. Secure the fuse carrier or MCB and insert fuse holder if needed.

If you need an additional circuit and you do not have room in the existing fusebox or consumer unit for an extra fuseway, you will have to install a second fuse box or mini-consumer unit alongside the existing one. Extra units like this usually contain from one to four extra fuseways, and are known as switchfuse units because they also contain a separate main switch.

A switchfuse unit is mounted on the same baseboard as the existing unit if space permits, on a new baseboard alongside otherwise. The meter tails are disconnected from the existing unit and linked instead to a distribution box to which both old and new units are then connected. This section of the job must be carried out by your local electricity board.

1. Remove the outer casing of the new switchfuse unit and screw it in place it on the existing baseboard if there is room.

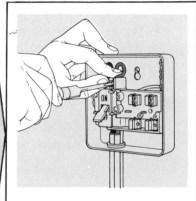

2. Connect the new meter tails to the terminals of the switchfuse unit's main isolating switch. Use same size as the existing tails.

Many electric cookers are wired up from what is known as a cooker control unit. This is a heavy-duty double-pole switch (the switch action breaks both the live and neutral sides of the circuit) with an integral socket outlet, and is wired up on its own circuit from the consumer unit or fuse box. The unit may be flush or surface-mounted; flush boxes are generally around 55mm $(2\frac{1}{8}in)$ deep, so care has to be taken in chopping out recesses in cavity walls not to cut through into the cavity itself.

From the control unit, cable is run on direct to built-in hobs and ovens. With a free-standing cooker, it is taken instead to a special connection unit behind the cooker, and the cooker is linked to this with a short length of cable.

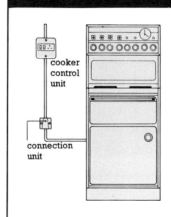

cooker control unit

connection unit

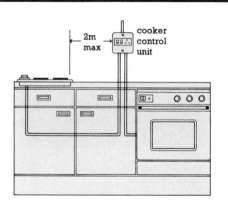

2m max

cooker control unit

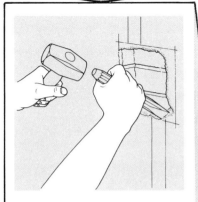

1. Mark out the position for a flush box and the cable runs, and chop them out carefully with a cold chisel and club hammer.

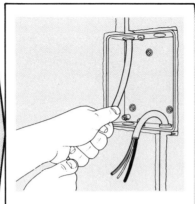

2. Screw the box in place, then lay in the supply cable and the feed cable to the connection unit below.

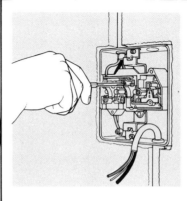

3. Mount the main body of the switch loosely within the box, and connect the main circuit cable to the feed terminals.

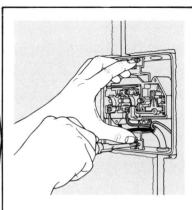

4. Connect up the cores of the cable leading on to the connection unit. Then tighten the fixing screws holding the switch body.

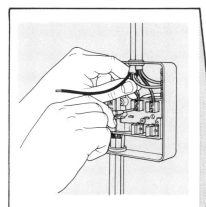

3. Connect in the new circuit cables, taking neutral and earth cores to their terminal blocks and live cores to the live terminals.

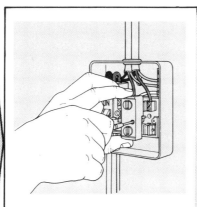

4. If the switchfuse unit has re-wireable or cartridge fuses, mount the fuse carrier in place over the fuseholder terminals.

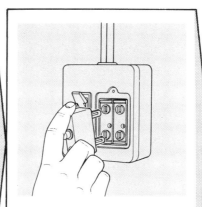

5. Replace the cover of the unit and insert the fuses in their carriers. MCBs are generally clipped in place on the live busbar.

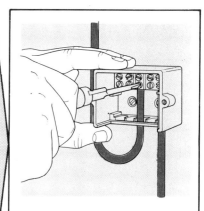

6. Mount the new distribution box close by on the baseboard, and connect the new live tail to the inner terminal block.

73 The completed switchfuse arrangement

The addition of a switchfuse unit to provide additional circuits result in an arrangement looking like this. The existing meter tails have been disconnected from the consumer unit (by the electricity board) and reconnected to the new distribution box. New tails have then been run from this box to supply both the existing consumer unit and the new switchfuse unit. It is not permissible to supply a new switchfuse unit by direct connection to the terminals of an existing consumer unit.

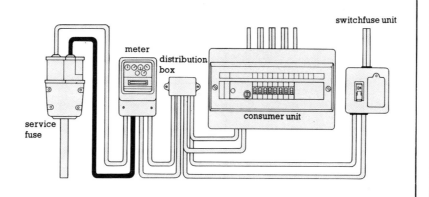

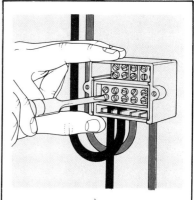

7. Connect the neutral tail to the outer block. Then call in the electricity board to reconnect the existing meter tails to the box.

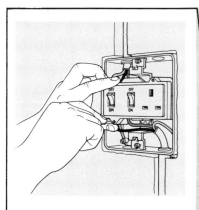

5. Attach the terminal cover to shroud all the connections. Then make good round the mounting box and fit the unit's cover.

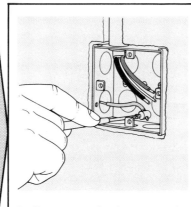

6. Cut a recess for the connection unit's mounting box. Fit the box in the hole and add a short earth core.

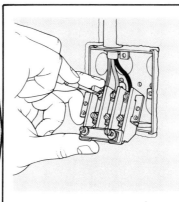

7. Connect the feed cable from the cooker in to the unit's terminal block. Link the short earth core to the block too.

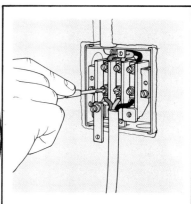

8. Lastly, connect a length of the same size cable to the terminal block, fit the cable clamp and connect the other end to cooker.

74. Wiring an electric shower

Electric showers have grown enormously in popularity in recent years, thanks to improvements in flow rates and temperature control. The reason is that they are extremely easy to install from both the plumbing and electrics point of view. However, they are highly-rated appliances and are used in the riskiest area of the home, so it's important that the circuit wiring is correctly carried out.

The circuit wiring uses 6mm² cable, which has a current rating of 35 amps when protected by a rewireable fuse, more if protected by a cartridge fuse or MCB. The shower itself is controlled by a 30-amp double-pole switch, ceiling-mounted for safety unless it is out of reach of the bath or shower. For more powerful 8kw showers, a switch rated at 35amps should be used.

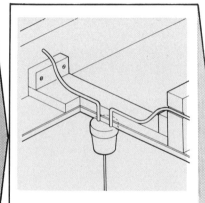

1. Start by deciding on the best position for the ceiling-mounted switch, and fix a batten betwen the ceiling joists to support it.

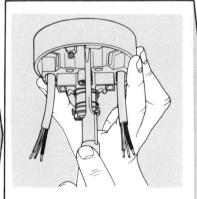

2. Run in the circuit cable and the shower cable above the ceiling, to the switch position and screw the switch base in place.

75. Wiring split-level cookers

Split-level cookers with separate ovens and hobs can be wired up by means of a heavy-duty double-pole isolating switch rather than via a cooker control unit. The circuit wiring is similar in principle to that of an electric shower, with the supply cable running to the isolating switch. Neither oven nor hob may be more than 2m (6ft 6in) away from the switch. Therefore, depending on the relative

positions of the oven and hob, there may be separate cables running from the switch to each component, or one cable running first to one component and then on to the other. The same size cable (6 or 10mm²) must be used throughout the circuit.

Cooker switches are usually rated at 45 amps, and may be flush or surface-mounted.

76. Cooker circuit cables

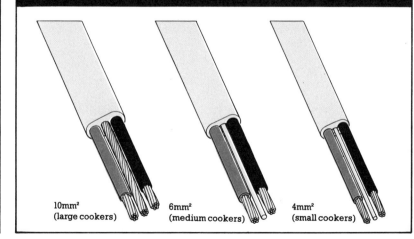

10mm²
(large cookers)

6mm²
(medium cookers)

4mm²
(small cookers)

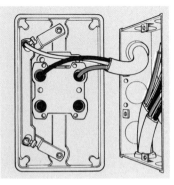

1. For a flush installation, cut the mounting box recess and cable chases.Then run in the cables and connect the supply.

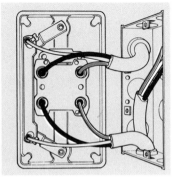

2. Where oven and hob are linked to the switch, connect to the 'LOAD' terminals. Sleeve and connect the earth too.

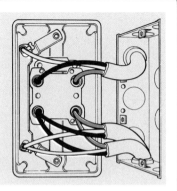

3. Connect in the second cable, making sure that both cores are securely held in the terminals. Connect up the oven and hob.

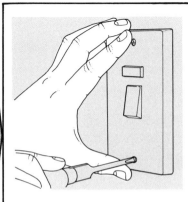

4. Check that the connections are correctly made, then screw on the switch faceplate, restore the power and test.

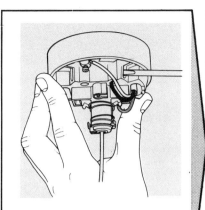

3. Connect the incoming cable to the 'FEED' terminals on the switch base. Cover the earth core in green/yellow sleeving.

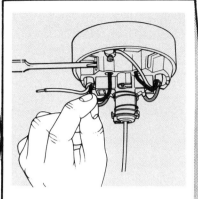

4. Connect the cores of the cable that will run on to the shower to the 'LOAD' terminals. Check that all the connections are secure.

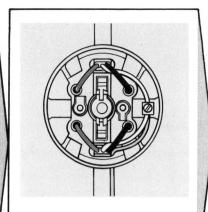

5. Cross-bond the pipework to earth by fitting a clamp and running an earthing core back to the switch earth terminal

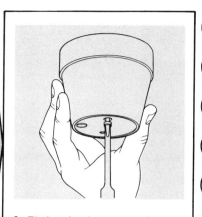

6. Fit the plastic cover to the switch baseplate, and check that the cord pull operates freely. Shorten its length if necessary.

77 Cross-bonding

To guard against the slight risk of exposed metalwork in the house coming into contact with live electrical conductors, cross-bonding is used to link all gas and water pipes to the main earthing terminal at the consumer unit. In bathrooms, additional cross-bonding of all metal is vital for safety.

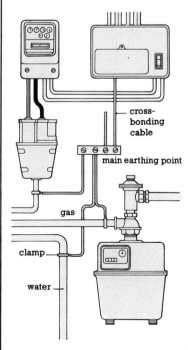

cross-bonding cable

main earthing point

gas

clamp

water

78 Cross-bonding a shower

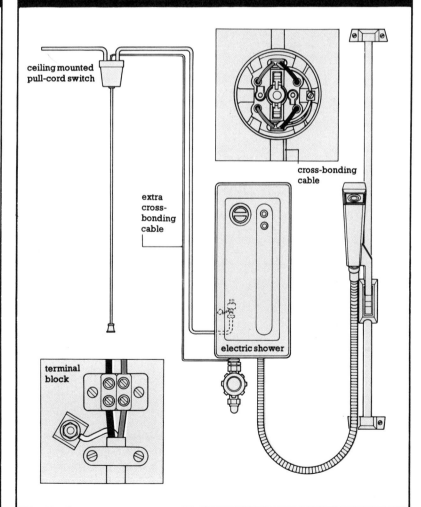

ceiling mounted pull-cord switch

cross-bonding cable

extra cross-bonding cable

electric shower

terminal block

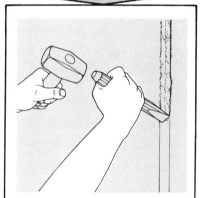

7. Cut a chase in the plaster to allow the cable to run from the switch to be concealed in conduit beneath the wall surface.

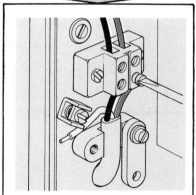

8. Thread the switch cable through the grommet on the shower casing and connect to the terminal block inside.

79 Wiring an immersion heater

Immersion heaters are wired up on their own independent circuit, usually from a 15-amp or 20-amp fuseway or miniature circuit breaker (MCB). The cable size used is 1.5mm² cable on 15-amp circuits, 2.5mm² on 20-amp ones. The cable is run to a point near the hot water cylinder, where it is connected to a double-pole isolating switch with a front flex outlet and neon 'ON' indicator.

From the switch, heat-resisting flex is run to the immersion heater itself.

If required, a time switch can be incorporated in the wiring for automatic control (see below). Dual switches (right) are used to control twin-element immersion heater installations to heat different quantities of water.

80 Connections at dual switch

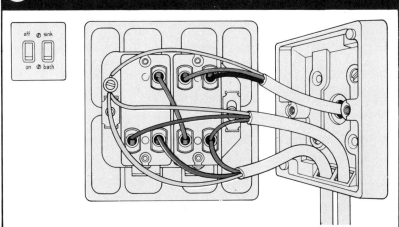

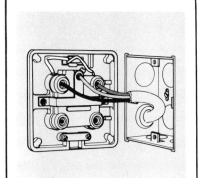

1. Mount the double-pole switch near the heater position, run in the circuit cable and connect up the cable cores.

81 Circuit arrangement

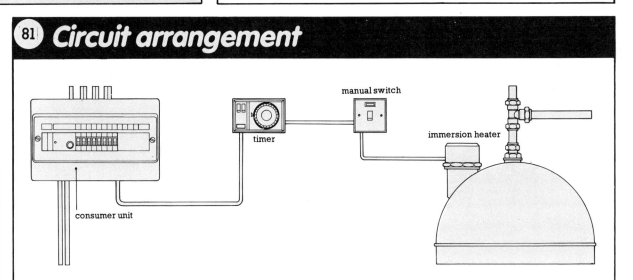

consumer unit

timer

manual switch

immersion heater

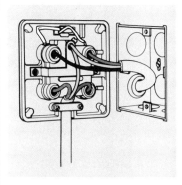

2. Cut a length of heat-resistant flex to reach from switch to heater, and connect it to the 'LOAD' terminals.

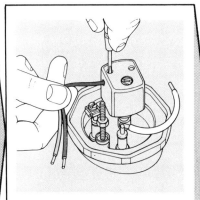

3. Prepare the other end of the flex and connect its live core to one of the terminals on top of the thermostat.

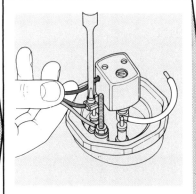

4. Connect the neutral core to the terminal on top of the heating element, and the earth core to its terminal.

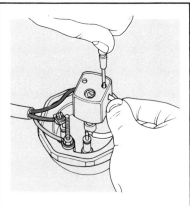

5. Finally, connect the short core fixed to the other heating element terminal to the vacant thermostat terminal.

82 *Wiring up shaver sockets*

There are two types of shaver socket. One is called a shaver supply unit, and contains a transformer that provides an earth-free supply and so is completely safe to use in a bathroom. The other is the shaver socket, which does not contain a transformer and is used in rooms other than bathrooms and washrooms.

Shaver supply units usually offer a choice of output voltages

– 115v for continental shavers, 230v for British ones – and are also available as combined shaver socket and strip-lights, containing a cord-operated fluorescent or tungsten filament light. Both types are may be flush or surface-mounted using a mounting box.

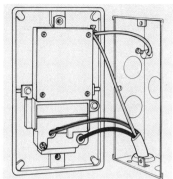

1. Run the supply cable to the point where the shaver supply unit will be installed, and connect it to the terminals.

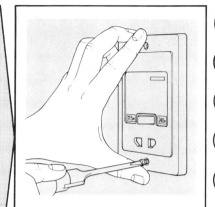

2. With the cable connections complete, screw on the faceplate and restore the power so you can test the unit.

83 *Circuit supply options*

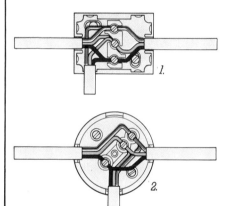

1.

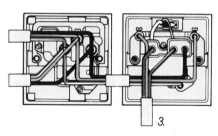

2.

3.

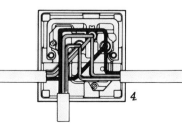

4.

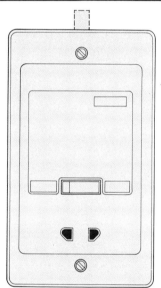

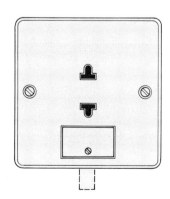

Power can be provided for a shaver supply unit or shaver socket in four ways:

1. via a non-fused spur from a 30-amp junction box cut into a ring or radial power circuit;

2. via a spur from a 5-amp three-terminal junction box cut into a lighting circuit;

3. via a spur taken from a nearby socket outlet on a ring or radial power circuit;

4. via a fused spur using a fused connection unit fitted with a 3-amp fuse (shaver sockets only).

Electric shavers can also be plugged into ordinary socket outlets if a special fused shaver adaptor is used.

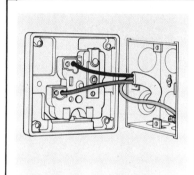

3. Mount the shaver socket box, run in the supply cable and connect its core to the socket terminals.

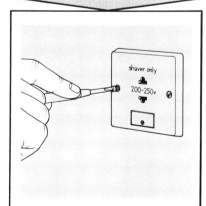

4. Carefully fold the supply cable back into the mounting box, then position the faceplate and screw it into position.

84 Waste disposal unit

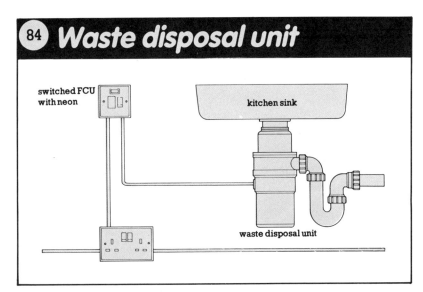

switched FCU with neon

kitchen sink

waste disposal unit

85 Wall heater

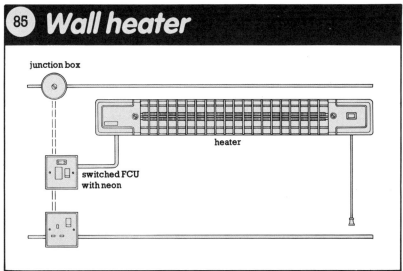

junction box

heater

switched FCU with neon

86 Extractor fan

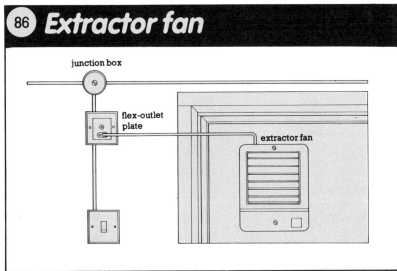

junction box

flex-outlet plate

extractor fan

87 Towel rail

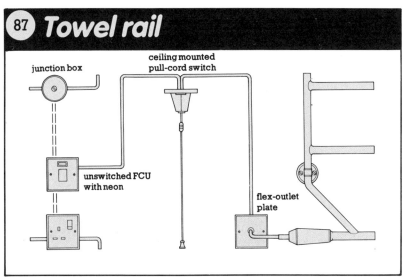

junction box

ceiling mounted pull-cord switch

unswitched FCU with neon

flex-outlet plate

88 Central heating controls

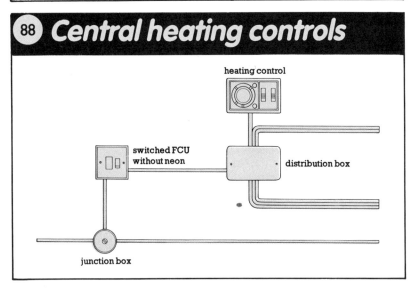

heating control

switched FCU without neon

distribution box

junction box

89 Door bells

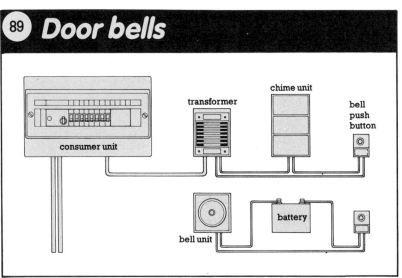

chime unit

transformer

bell push button

consumer unit

battery

bell unit

An outdoor socket outlet can be an extremely useful addition to your house wiring, because it allows appliances and powered garden equipment to be plugged in without the need to trail flexes out through windows and doors. Not only is it more convenient to have an exterior power supply, but it is also much safer.

If the socket will actually be exposed to the elements, a weatherproof type with a screw-on cover must be used.

The Wiring Regulations stipulate that any socket outlet which will power appliances or equipment being used out of doors must be protected by a residual current circuit breaker (RCCB) with a sensitivity of 30 milliamps (mA).

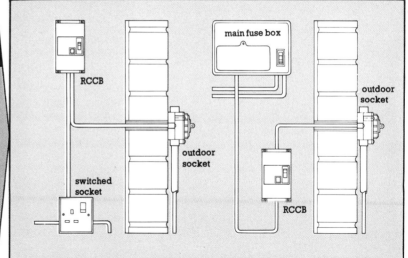

84
85
86
87
88
89
90

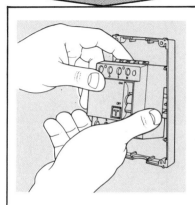

1. Decide on the position for the RCCB inside the house. Mount its baseplate on the wall and fit the RCCB to it.

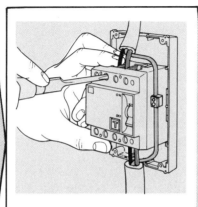

2a. Connect the incoming and outgoing circuit cables to the RCCB's terminals, following the maker's wiring instructions.

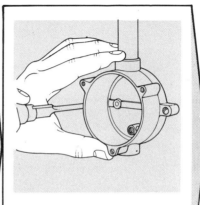

3a. Mount the outdoor socket's baseplate securely on the house wall, and fit PVC conduit for the cable run.

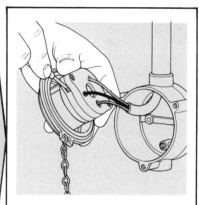

4a. Run in the cable from the RCCB to the socket box, prepare the cable cores and connect them up to the terminals.

2b. If the socket is being installed away from the house, run it in conduit in a trench at least 500mm (20in) deep.

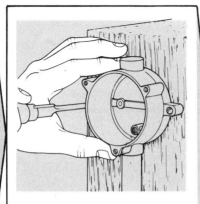

3b. For a post mounting, set the post in concrete and run the conduit up to the position of the mounting box.

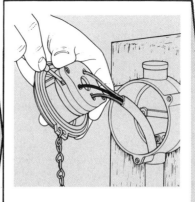

4b. Run in the cable from house to mounting box, prepare the cable cores and connect them up to the switch terminals.

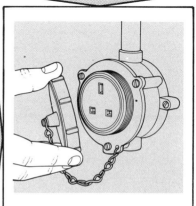

5. Carefully fold the supply cable back into the mounting box and screw the faceplate to it. Then attach the cover.

91 Wiring up an outbuilding

Outbuildings such as garages, greenhouses and sheds remote from the house must have a separate circuit running from the house; they cannot be fed by spurs off the existing circuits. At the house end, the circuit cable orginates either at a spare 30-amp fuseway in the consumer unit or at a new separate switch-fuse unit mounted next to it (see Project 70).

Cable is run to the outbuilding either underground through a conduit or overhead supported by a catenary wire (Projects 17 & 18)

Within the outbuilding itself a second switchfuse unit is fitted, and radial power and lighting circuits are added – the latter can be a separate circuit or a fused spur.

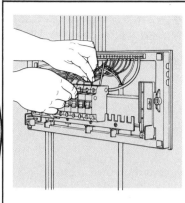

1. If you have a spare fuseway, fit a 30-amp fuse and connect in the end of the cable that will run to the outbuilding.

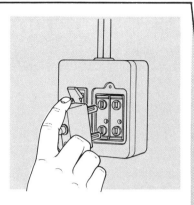

2. If there are no spare ways, mount a small switchfuse unit nearby, ready for connection to a distribution box (Project 70).

92 Wiring at house

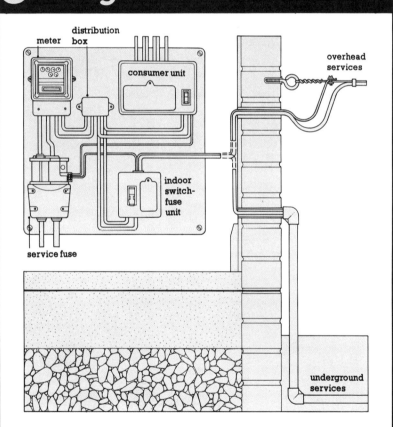

Unless there is a spare fuseway present in the consumer unit, a separate switchfuse unit linked to a distribution box must be fitted to supply the circuit from a 30-amp fuseway. The supply cable can be run to the outbuilding underground or overhead. Catenary wires must be separately earthed.

93 Wiring at outbuilding

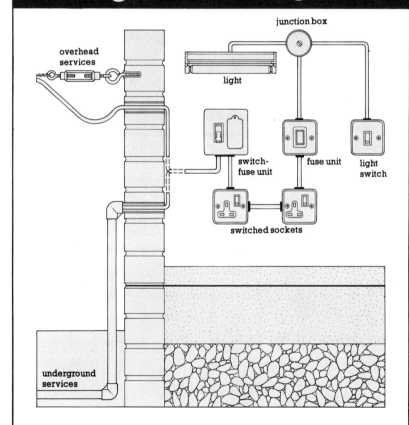

The incoming cable terminates at a second switchfuse unit, fitted with one or two fuseways. If fitted with one fuse way it should be rated at 20 amps, and lights will be run as fused spurs off the power circuit. With two fuseways a separate 5-amp light circuit fuse is also provided.

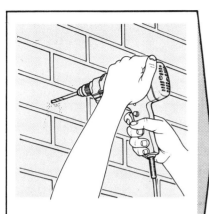

3. Decide on a convenient point for the cable to leave the house, and drill a hole. Enlarge it to accept PVC conduit.

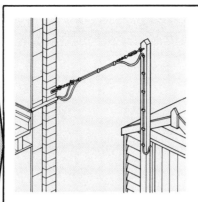

4a. If you want an overhead cable run, make sure it is high enough (Project 17) and has a catenary wire if needed.

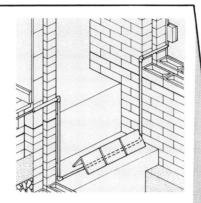

4b. For an underground run, dig a trench between house and outbuilding and run the cable in conduit (Project 19).

5. On a timber outbuilding, run the cable down the main supporting post and then drill an entry hole in the cladding.

94 Switchfuse in outbuilding

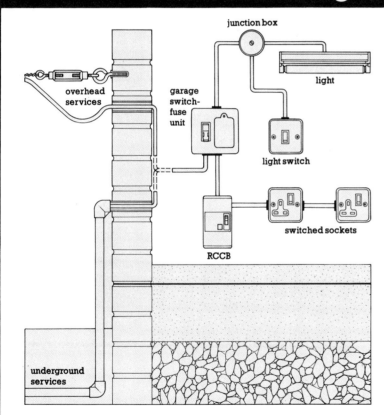

junction box

light

overhead services

garage switch-fuse unit

light switch

switched sockets

RCCB

underground services

If you fit a switchfuse unit in the outbuildings that contains two fuseways separate circuits can be provided for lighting (from a 5-amp fuseway) and power (from a 20-amp fuseway), An RCCB (Project 97) will provide protection when using the sockets for power tools outside.

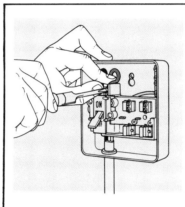

6. Connect the cores of the incoming cable to the terminals of the switchfuse unit. Sleeve the earth core first.

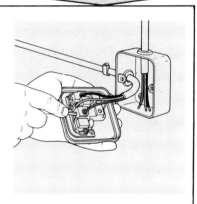

7. Run 2.5mm² cable from the 20-amp fuseway in the switchfuse unit to the first socket outlet in the outbuildings.

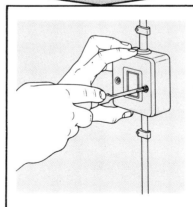

8. For the lighting circuit, run the socket circuit cable on to a fused connection unit fitted with a 5-amp fuse.

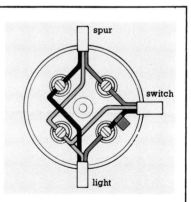

spur

switch

light

9. Then run 1.00mm² cable on to a four-terminal junction box, and wire in the cable to the switch and light fitting.

95 Fitting circuit breakers (RCCBs)

Residual current circuit breakers (RCCBs) are safety devices fitted to electrical circuits to protect both the system and its users from the consequences of certain faults that may occur. They used to be known as earth leakage circuit breakers (ELCBs). They operate by detecting the leakage of current to earth that accompanies faulty insulation or someone receiving an electric shock, and cutting off the supply.

RCCBs can be fitted within a consumer unit to protect all of the house circuits, within a separate enclosure to protect just one circuit, or within a socket outlet.

You can also get self-contained RCCB plugs. These are very useful for protecting individual appliances, especially power tools and electric garden tools such as hedge-trimmers and mowers.

96 Types of RCCB

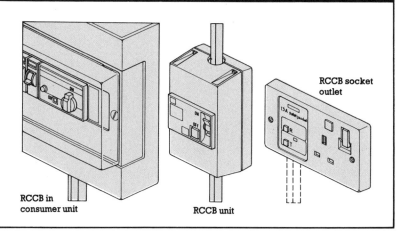

RCCB in consumer unit

RCCB unit

RCCB socket outlet

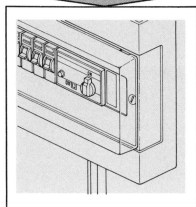

1. You can install an RCCB in a modern consumer unit if there is room. It takes the place of the main isolating switch.

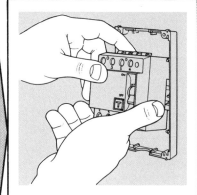

2. If there is no space within the consumer unit, fit the RCCB alongside. Mount its baseplate and clip the RCCB in place.

3. To protect the whole system, connect new meter tails to the RCCB ready for connection to the consumer unit.

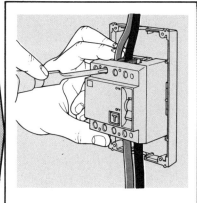

4. Call in the electricity board to disconnect the existing tails from the consumer unit and connect in the RCCB.

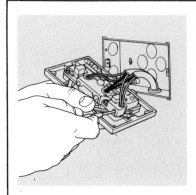

1. You can provide protection for users of outdoor appliances by replacing an existing socket with one containing an RCCB.

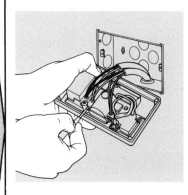

2. With the power off, unscrew the existing socket faceplate and set it aside. Then connect up the RCCB socket.

3. Fit the RCCB socket faceplate in place using the old fixing screw. You may need a deeper box with some models.

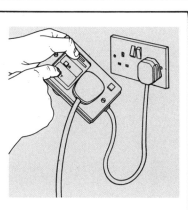

4. You can protect individual appliances by plugging them into a self-contained plug-in RCCB socket and lead.

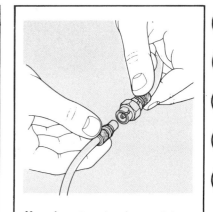
97 IEE wiring regulations

The 15th edition of the IEE Wiring Regulations requires the provision, on all new wiring installations, of a socket outlet protected by a high-sensitivity RCCB for use with appliances being used out of doors. The simplest way of satisfying this requirement is to replace a conveniently situated double socket outlet – perhaps in an outbuilding – with one containing an RCCB.

98 Fitting TV/FM aerial sockets

Gone are the days when you had to run a TV aerial cable down the outside wall of your house and in through a hole in the window frame, ready to plug it directly into the back of the TV set. There is now a wide range of special TV and FM aerial socket outlets which can be used with concealed wiring, just like any other accessory.

One of the neatest arrangements uses a special twin socket to provide TV and FM aerial connections using a single aerial downlead. The aerial is plugged into one outlet in the loft, and the lead is run down to a second socket sited wherever it's needed in the house. By extending the wiring into other rooms and fitting additional sockets, you can move your TV or FM receiver wherever you like.

If you have to extend an aerial lead, connect the two lengths together using proper male and female coaxial connectors.

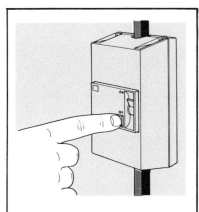

5. When the meter tails have been connected to the RCCB and this is linked to the consumer unit, fit the cover and test.

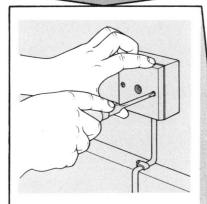

1. Mount the first socket outlet in the loft space, and connect in the aerial cable run down to the house.

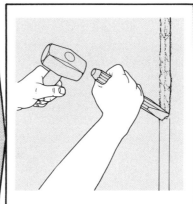

2. Where the cable run crosses a wall surface, cut a chase in the plaster. Then insert round PVC conduit in the chase.

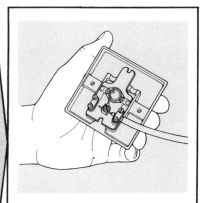

3. Run the aerial cable down the conduit to the downstairs socket position and connect it to the second socket.

5. Similarly, individual appliance protection can be provided by fitting a plug containing an RCCB.

99 Twin aerial circuits

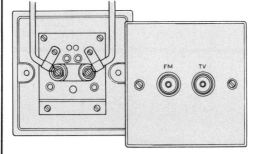
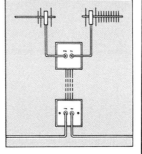

A double TV coaxial socket outlet is used to provide aerial points for both TV and FM radio. Two *downleads are used unless an outlet containing a diplexer is fitted; then only one is needed.*

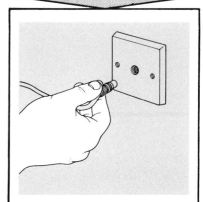

4. Mount the second socket over a flush mounting box, and plug in the TV or FM aerials at each end of the circuit.

Glossary

Amp (A) is the unit of electric current. Divide an appliance's wattage by mains voltage (240) to work out how much current it uses.

Circuits are complete paths round which current flows – along the live conductor to where it is needed, then back to source along the neutral conductor.

Conduit boxes, also called BESA boxes, are round mounting boxes used to contain the connections to light fittings.

Consumer units govern the supply of electricity to all circuits in the house. They contain the system's main on/off switch, and fuses or circuit breakers.

Earthing is the provision of a continuous conductor on circuits to protect the user from certain electrical faults. Earth conductors are insulated with green/yellow striped PVC in flex, and where exposed in cables.

Fuses are protective devices inserted into electrical circuits and plugs to prevent overloading.

Gangs describe the number of switches or socket outlets contained in one wiring accessory.

Grommets are small plastic washers used in metal mounting boxes to stop the cable chafing on the edges of a knockout.

IE Wiring Regulations lay down guidelines for safe electrical installation practice. They are issued by the Institution of Electrical Engineers, but do not have any legal force (except in Scotland, where they form part of the Building Regulations).

Insulation on flex and cable protects users of electrical equipment from touching live conductors.

Junction boxes are used on power circuits to connect in spurs, and on lighting circuits to link the cables to each rose and its switch.

Knockouts are pre-formed weak spots in mounting boxes, designed to be knocked out to admit the circuit cables.

Live describes the cable or flex core carrying current to a wiring accessory or appliance, or any terminal to which this core is connected. Live core insulation is red in cables, brown in flex.

Loop-in light circuits are wired by running cable to each ceiling rose in turn. The switch cable is linked direct to the rose it controls.

Miniature circuit breakers (MCBs) are electromechanical switches which are used instead of circuit fuses in modern consumer units.

Mounting boxes are metal or plastic enclosures over which accessory faceplates are fitted.

Neutral describes the cable or flex core carrying current back to its source. Neutral core insulation is black in cable, blue in flex.

Radial circuits are power circuits originating at the consumer unit and terminating at the most remote socket outlet.

Residual current circuit breakers (RCCBs) are protective safety devices fitted to circuits to detect current leakage which could start a fire or cause an electric shock.

Ring circuits are power circuits wired as a continuous loop, both ends being connected to the same terminals in the consumer unit.

Spurs are cable branch lines connected to a house circuit to supply extra lights or sockets.

Two-way switches are used in pairs to allow control of one light from two switch positions.

Volt (V) is the unit of electrical 'pressure' – the potential difference that drives current round a circuit. In most British homes mains voltage is 240V.

Watt (W) is the unit of power consumed by an appliance or circuit.

Index

Plumbing

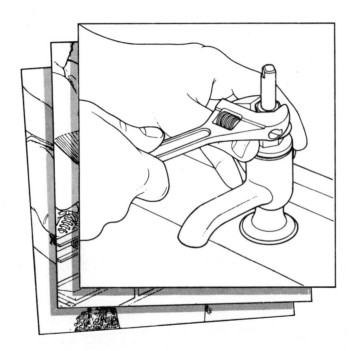

Plumbing

Plumbing

When it comes to repairing or altering a plumbing system, most people will automatically call in a plumber; the thought of tackling the work themselves and the possible consequences should anything go wrong are enough to provoke nightmares. But often this fear is unjustified. Modern plumbing systems are quite easy to understand and modern materials are simple to work with. They are readily available and require few special tools to assemble.

Not only is it possible to make repairs and carry out regular maintenance on your system, but it can also be altered or extended to suit your particular needs. Old, broken or unsightly fittings can be replaced, and appliances added that will make life that much more pleasant for all the family – all at a considerable saving when compared with the cost of employing a professional plumber to carry out the work for you.

① Cold water supplies – indirect & direct

Water, supplied by the local water authority, reaches the house through an underground 'service' pipe. This usually enters the house in the kitchen, at which point it is called the 'rising main'. A stopvalve in the rising main allows the supply to be cut off in an emergency. From here, the system may be of the indirect-feed or direct-feed type.

An indirect-feed system is the most common. Under this system, the rising main supplies a storage cistern which, in turn, provides a gravity feed to the taps, WC cistern and hot water cylinder. However, water from a storage cistern is not fit for drinking, so the kitchen cold tap is connected directly to the rising main.

In a direct-feed system all the taps and the WC cistern are fed from the main. However, a storage cistern is still needed to supply the hot water cylinder.

The indirect cold water system (left) has most outlets under gravity feed, unlike the direct-feed system (right).

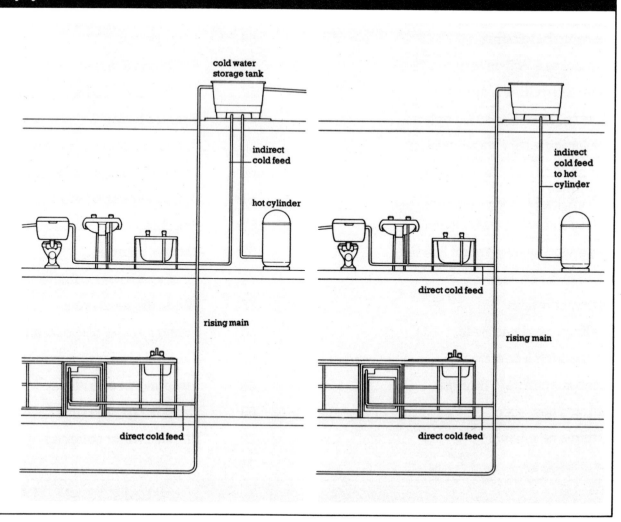

cold water storage tank

indirect cold feed

hot cylinder

rising main

direct cold feed

indirect cold feed to hot cylinder

direct cold feed

rising main

direct cold feed

The most common method of providing domestic hot water is to incorporate a storage cylinder in the system which feeds the hot taps under gravity. A boiler may be used to heat the water by the indirect or direct method.

In an indirect system, a 'closed' primary circuit runs from the boiler, through a coiled heat exchanger in the cylinder and back to the boiler. This heats the water in the cylinder which is drawn off from the top. With this system the water in the primary circuit is constantly recirculated, reducing corrosion in the boiler.

In a direct system, water flows from the cylinder to the boiler and is returned to the top of the cylinder where it is drawn off.

An indirect system (left) with closed circuit between boiler and cylinder, and (right) a direct system.

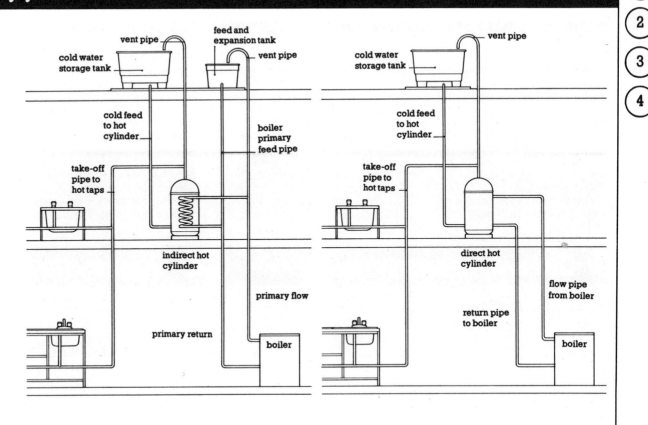

③ Single-point water heaters

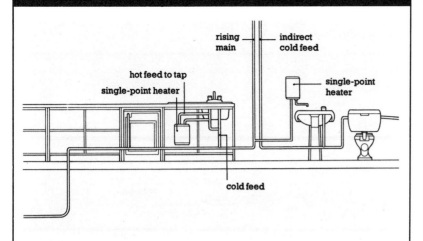

When it is difficult to arrange a hot-water supply to a particular outlet, a single-point gas or electric heater can be used. They are normally connected to the rising main.

④ Multi-point water heaters

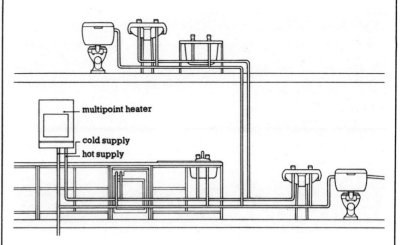

If a gravity-fed hot water system cannot be installed, a gas-fired, multi-point heater can be employed. Like the single-point unit, it is plumbed into the rising main.

5 — Waste disposal: Two pipe systems

A house may have one of two drainage systems. An older house will have a two-pipe system where the soil waste from the WC is kept separate from the waste water from basins, baths, etc. The former is taken directly to a large, vertical soil stack that runs up the outside of the house and is connected to the underground drain.

Waste water from other fittings may discharge over a gully if they are on the ground floor or into a hopper head at the top of a second vertical pipe if they are on an upper floor.

The gully, which is connected to the underground drain, incorporates a water seal in the form of a U-bend in the pipe, called a trap. Rainwater usually discharges over a separate gully.

7 — Waste disposal: Single-stack system

The modern waste drainage system is the single-stack design where the waste pipes from all fittings are connected directly to the single, vertical soil stack. If they are on the ground floor, however, they may still discharge over a gully.

In new houses, the soil stack is invariably installed inside to provide protection against freezing, but it may still be seen on the outside where an old two-pipe system has been updated.

In the single-stack system, rainwater is still dealt with separately, the pipes discharging into gullies or being connected directly to an underground drain. This may run to the sewer, but it is more likely to be connected to a separate storm drain or a soakaway.

6 — Old waste systems

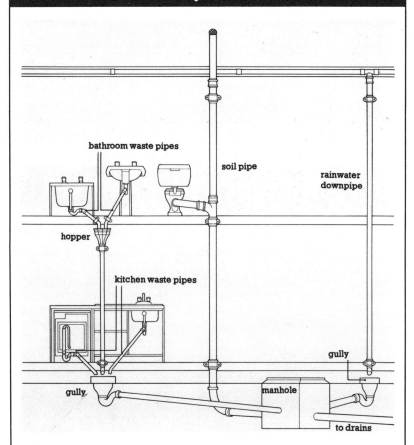

In an older two-pipe waste system, the WC alone is connected to the vertical soil stack and the waste water from basins, baths, etc, either discharges into a hopper head at the top of a second pipe or into a gully.

8 — Single-stack system

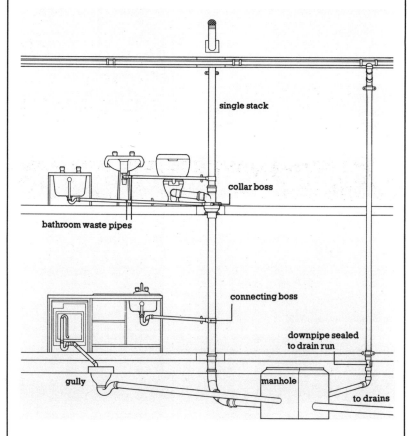

In the more modern single-stack arrangement, the WC, basins, bath, sink, etc, are connected to a single vertical soil stack. Some appliances downstairs may still discharge into gullies. In many houses, the stack is housed within the building.

When considering domestic plumbing, the central heating system must not be forgotten, for if it is a 'wet' system it will be assembled from the same pipe and fittings, and probably share a common heat source — the boiler.

Most modern wet central heating systems employ a two-pipe arrangement where water flows from the boiler to the radiators through one circuit of pipes and returns to the boiler through another circuit. In this way, water reaches all the radiators at the same temperature. An electric pump circulates the water through the system.

The boiler is linked to a separate feed-and-expansion cistern in the loft. This keeps the heating circuit topped up and will catch any overflow should the water in the boiler become overheated. Normally, a separate circuit is run to the hot water cylinder.

The layout of a typical two-pipe 'wet' central heating system showing how it is connected into the normal domestic plumbing system.

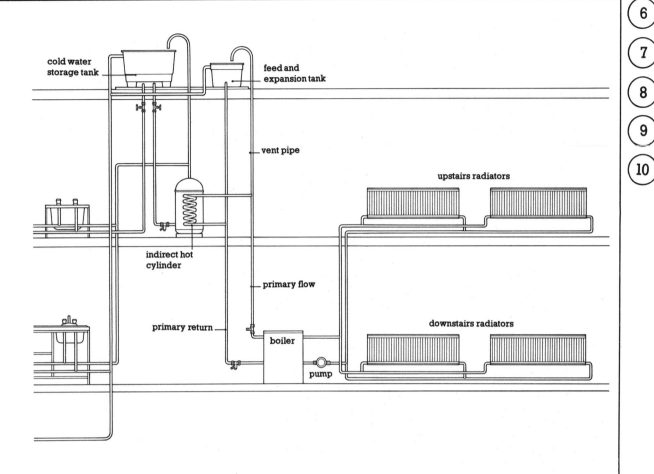

⑩ Microbore systems

A microbore heating system employs very narrow copper pipe to form individual feed and return circuits for each radiator. These are connected to 'manifolds' which are linked to the boiler by normal small-bore pipework. Microbore systems need special valves and pumps.

A microbore system makes use of small-diameter pipes to aid installation. Conventional pipework feeds the manifolds.

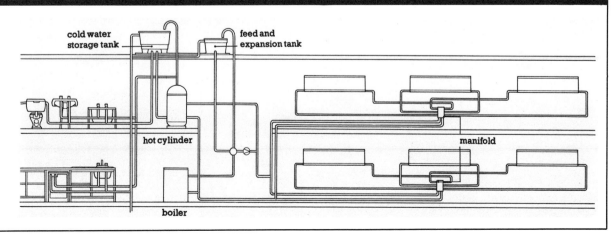

11 Cutting copper pipe

Despite recent advances in the development of plastic plumbing systems, copper pipe continues to be the favourite material for domestic use; it is readily available, easily worked and there is a full range of fittings available.

Copper pipe comes in 15, 22 and 28mm outside diameters. However, systems installed before 1970 are more likely to be in imperial-sized pipe with internal diameters of $\frac{1}{2}$, $\frac{3}{4}$ or 1in. This is no longer available, so special fittings are needed when connecting new pipe into old systems.

Accurate marking out is necessary when cutting copper pipe. The ends must be cut square to ensure watertight joints. It can be cut with a hacksaw, but if a lot of work is envisaged it is better to buy a pipe cutter.

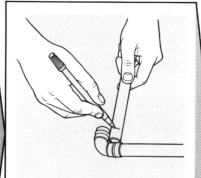

1. When marking out a length of pipe, make allowance for the amount that will fit inside the joint. Mark this off first.

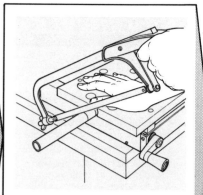

2. For a square cut end, wrap stiff paper round the pipe so that its edges align to provide a guide for the saw blade.

12 Bending copper pipe

While changes in pipe-run direction can be achieved with elbow fittings, it could prove an expensive solution if a lot are used. Moreover, even soldered fittings will spoil the appearance of an exposed pipe run, and in some cases it may not be possible to buy a fitting that provides the exact angle of bend required. Fortunately, copper pipe is easy to bend.

One method of bending copper pipe is to use a bending spring, either internal or external. The former fits inside the pipe to support its walls as it is bent, while the latter fits over the pipe for the same purpose. If a major job is being tackled, or if large-diameter pipe is being bent, it is better to hire a plumber's pipe bender.

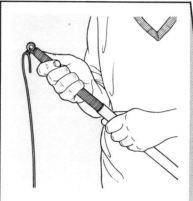

1. Tie a cord to an internal bending spring and insert it into the pipe. Position it at the centre of the bend.

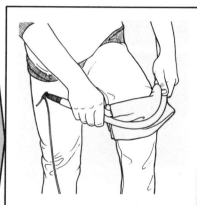

2. Bend the pipe by pulling evenly on both ends until the required degree of bend is achieved.

13 Plumber's pipe bender

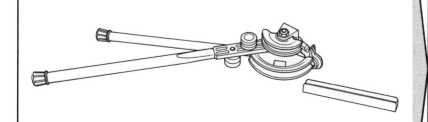

A plumber's pipe bender will take the effort out of the job. It comes with formers to fit the common sizes of domestic copper pipe: 15, 22 and 28mm. Hire it rather than buying.

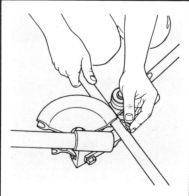

1. Insert the pipe in the machine, setting it on the correct curved former with the end placed under the pipe hook.

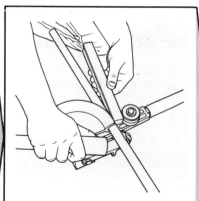

2. Select the appropriate straight former and slide it in on top of the pipe and under the roller on the handle.

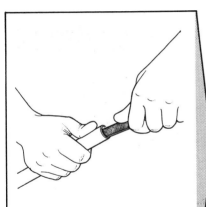

3. All the burr must be removed from the cut pipe end. Use a half-round file inside the pipe and its flat face outside.

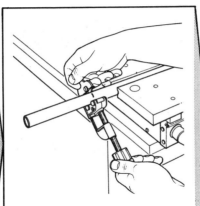

4. A pipe cutter will ensure a square cut end. Place it over the pipe and tighten the clamping screw.

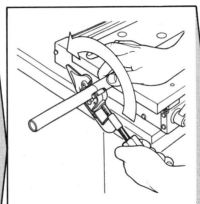

5. Rotate the pipe cutter about the pipe, gradually tightening the clamping screw as the blade bites into the metal.

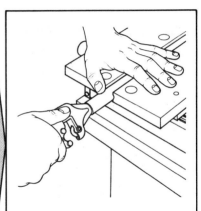

6. The cutter does not produce a burr around the outside, only on the inside. Remove the latter with the integral reamer.

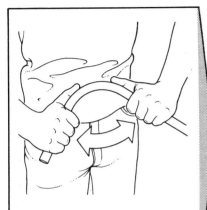

3. The pipe will spring back slightly after bending, so bend it a little more than necessary and gently pull it back.

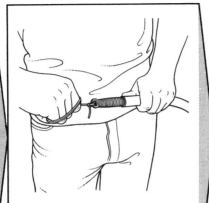

4. Remove the spring. If it will not move, insert a bar through the eye and rotate it clockwise to reduce its diameter.

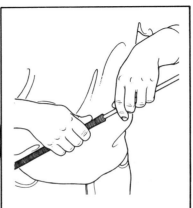

5. With microbore pipes use an external spring. Again, centre it over the bend position before pulling on the ends.

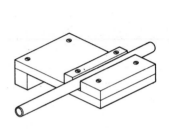

7. Rather than clamping the pipe in a vice for cutting, which might crush it, hold it on a bench hook with a batten.

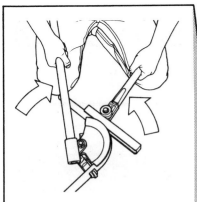

3. Pull the handles together so that the pipe is forced round the curved former until the desired angle is achieved.

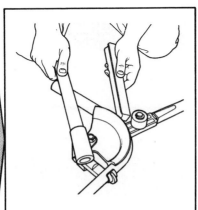

4. Release the machine's handles and remove the straight former. Then release the pipe from the curved former and pipe hook.

⑭ *Corrugated copper pipe*

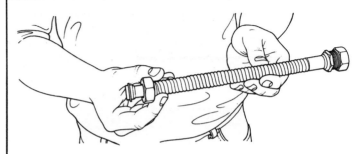

If you are working in tight corners you will find that pliable corrugated copper pipe is the ideal solution. It is easily bent by hand, but care should be taken not to overwork it in case it splits. This type of pipe is often supplied in tap connection kits.

15 · Making compression joints

One method of joining copper pipes is with a compression joint. Made from brass, they come in a wide range of configurations including straight couplers, elbows, tees and special reducer fittings to allow pipes of different diameters to be connected together.

There are two types of compression joint, known as manipulative and non-manipulative. The latter is easier to use. The pipe ends fit inside its body, and as the capnuts are tightened on to the ends of the joint they compress copper or brass rings called 'olives' against the pipe to provide a watertight seal.

In a manipulative joint, the ends of the pipe must be 'flared' with a special tool to fit over an internal copper ring seal.

16 · Compression fittings

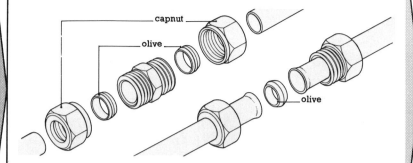

Types of compression joint: manipulative (right) and non-manipulative (left). Brass or copper olives make a leak-proof seal when the capnuts are tightened with wrenches.

17 · Making capillary joints

The second method of joining copper pipes is to use a capillary joint, which has a soldered seal. Capillary joints are made of copper and come in the same range of fittings as compression joints. Unlike the latter, which are easily unscrewed, a capillary joint is a more permanent fixture. However, they are much neater in appearance.

There are two types of capillary joint: Yorkshire and end-feed. Yorkshire fittings have an integral ring of solder at each pipe socket. After inserting the pipes, the sockets are heated with a blow torch until the solder melts and flows around the pipe end by capillary action. End-feed joints must have solder added separately as heat is applied.

1. Clean the pipe end and inside of the joint socket with wire wool and apply flux with a brush or sliver of wood.

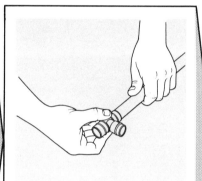

2. Insert the pipe fully into the fitting, twisting it slightly as you do to distribute the flux evenly in the joint.

18 · Acorn fittings

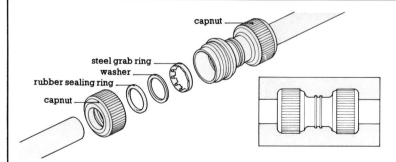

Acorn plastic push-fit joints may also be used with copper pipe. Each contains a toothed metal ring to stop the pipe pulling out and a rubber O-ring seal to prevent leaks.

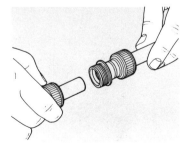

1. After cleaning the pipe end with wire wool, smear it and the joint's rubber O-ring with silicone lubricant.

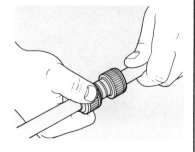

2. To make the joint, simply push the end of the pipe into the fitting until it comes up against the pipe stop.

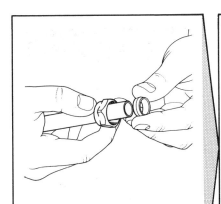

1. To make a compression joint, cut the pipe ends square, clean them with wire wool and slip on the capnut and olive.

2. Insert the pipe into the body of the fitting so that it butts up against the pipe stop and tighten the capnut by hand.

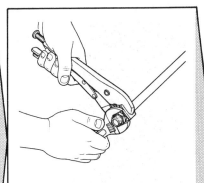

3. Hold the body of the joint with one wrench while tightening the capnut approximately 1½ turns with another.

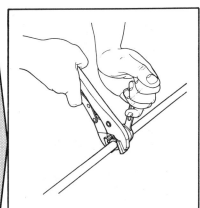

4. Fit the capnut and olive to the second pipe, insert the end in the joint and tighten the capnut as before.

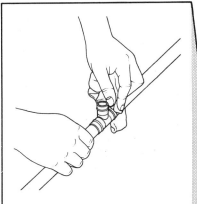

3. Treat the ends of the other pipes in a similar manner and insert them into the fitting. Wipe off any excess flux.

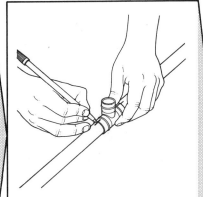

4. Pencil marks where the fitting sockets overlap the pipes will help keep everything in alignment when soldering.

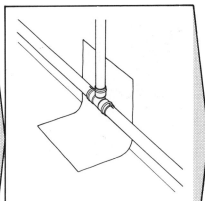

5. If making the joint in situ, protect the wall, skirting and floor from the blow torch with a flame-proof glassfibre pad.

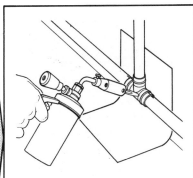

6. Apply heat evenly with the blow torch to all the sockets of the fitting at the same time to melt the solder.

(19) Capillary fittings

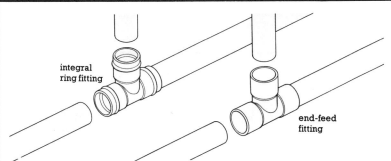

integral ring fitting

end-feed fitting

Capillary fittings may be of the Yorkshire type (left) which has integral solder rings in their

sockets, or the end-feed type (right), which must have solder added to them.

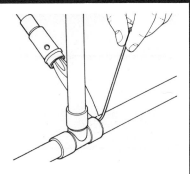

When solder wire touches the heated pipe, it melts and flows between the pipe and joint.

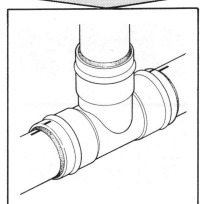

7. Continue heating the joint until bright silver rings of liquid solder appear around the lip of each socket.

⟨20⟩ Joining into existing pipes Compression fittings

Installing any new water outlet will require laying in a new supply pipe, and in most cases it will take its feed from an existing pipe. This involves cutting a short section from the original pipe, inserting a tee joint and adding the new pipe.

Compression joints are better suited to the job than capillary joints and they are easier to use. After 1970 copper pipes went over to metric dimensions and this must be taken into account when breaking into a pipe run. Imperial ½in and 1in pipe can be connected directly to metric 15mm and 28mm pipe with standard 15mm and 28mm tees, but ¾in imperial can only be connected to 22mm metric with a 22mm tee fitted with larger olives.

⟨21⟩ Proprietary connectors

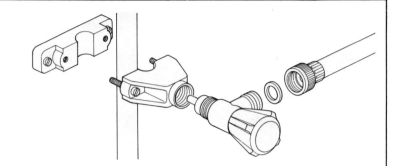

Washing machines can be supplied by using a self-boring connector. After fitting the backplate and saddle, the valve body is screwed into place to cut a hole in the pipe.

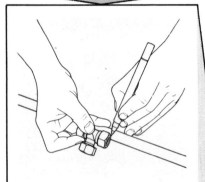

1. Hold the tee joint in position against the existing pipe and mark the pipe stop positions on the pipe.

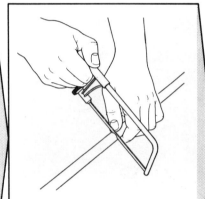

2. After draining the pipe, cut out the section between the pencil marks using a junior hacksaw or a saw file.

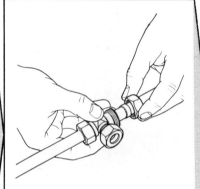

3. Slip the capnuts and olives over the pipe ends and then spring the pipes into the body of the joint.

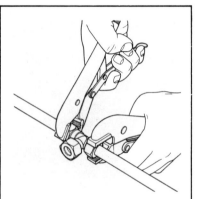

4. Hold the joint with an adjustable spanner and tighten each capnut in turn. Then connect in the branch pipe.

⟨22⟩ Capillary fittings

When connecting into a pipe run with a capillary joint, the procedure is basically the same as with a compression joint. However, the job is slightly more complicated with imperial pipe. The best method is to make up a length of metric pipe with a metric tee in the centre and metric-imperial connectors at each end and solder this in place.

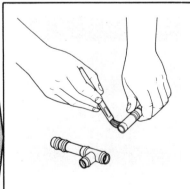

1. Assemble and solder together a capillary tee joint with two short stubs of pipe and a straight connector at each.

2. Hold the assembly against the existing pipe and mark on the pipe stop positions of the straight connectors.

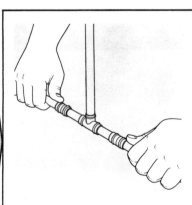

3. Cut the pipe. Then spring the new section into place, solder the straight couplers followed by the branch pipe.

23 Running pipes in walls

When installing a pipe run on a wall, the pipes should be clipped at skirting level or in a corner between walls to make them as inconspicuous as possible; in hollow stud partitions they can be fed through holes drilled in the framework.

Although pipes can be buried in the plaster of a wall, it is not a good idea to do this on an outside wall in case they freeze, or to do it with hot water pipes since their expansion and contraction may cause the plaster to crack.

To prevent the pipes vibrating and knocking, clip them at 1.2m (4ft) intervals.

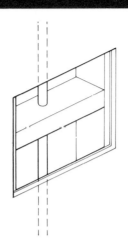

1. In a stud partition, cut access holes in the cladding and drill the noggings with oversize holes for the pipes.

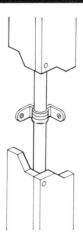

2. Use angled saddle clips to hold a pipe in a corner, and conceal it by fixing two timber battens across the angle.

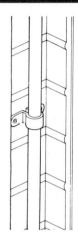

3. Pipes can also be concealed by cutting a chase in the plaster, clipping them in place and replastering the wall.

24 Running pipes in floors

Pipes are easily concealed beneath timber floors, but they must be kept clear of floorboard nails. This means running them at least 50mm (2in) below the tops of the joists and below the centres of the boards.

When the run is parallel to the joists, the pipes may be clipped to their sides, and if it is at right angles to the joists, the pipes can be passed through notches cut in their tops or through holes drilled in them. These should be kept as small as possible to avoid weakening the joist, but they must be at least 6mm (¼in) larger than the pipe to allow for movement and expansion.

Where a pipe is run beneath a timber ground floor or in a roof space, it should be well lagged to prevent it freezing.

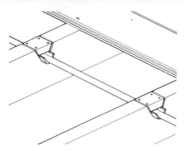

1. Nail the offcuts back after cutting pipe notches.

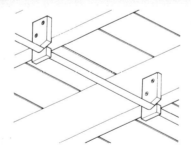

2. Timber pipe 'hangers' can be screwed to ground-floor joists.

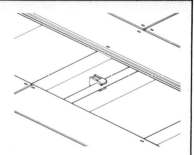

3. Pipes can be clipped to the sides of joists.

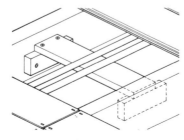

4. Alternatively, support them on battens between the joists.

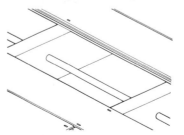

5. Instead of notches, feed pipe through holes in the joists.

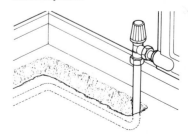

6. Pipes may be buried around the edge of solid floors.

25 Cutting plastic pipe

Waste water systems have long been made from uPVC or ABS plastics, and flexible black polythene pipe is common for cold water supplies in the garden. The development of polybutylene and cPVC pipes has made hot water supply possible too.

Plastic pipes can be cut with a hacksaw; polybutylene pipes can also be cut with special secateurs.

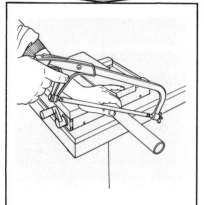

1. Cut plastic pipe with a hacksaw. After cutting, use a file or sharp knife to remove any burrs.

2. Flexible polybutylene pipe can also be cut with a hacksaw or the special cutters available from the manufacturers.

26 Solvent weld pipe

Some types of waste pipe, whether uPVC or ABS, are joined by solvent-weld joints; cPVC supply pipes also have this type of joint.

Though easy to make, solvent-weld joints are permanent, so any pipe run must be trial-assembled first and the various components marked with pencil to ensure correct alignment when assembling for real.

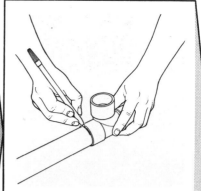

1. Chamfer the end of the pipe with a file and insert it into the fitting. Mark the socket position on the pipe.

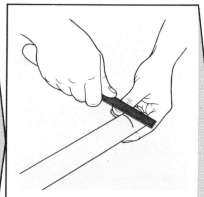

2. Use a file to remove the glaze all the way round the pipe up to the pencil mark. This will aid the solvent.

27 Push-fit connectors

Another method of joining waste pipes is with push-fit joints which contain rubber O-ring seals. The advantage of these joints is that pipe runs are easily disconnected to clear blockages.

When making up waste pipe runs using push-fit joints, it is essential to make allowance for expansion of the pipes when hot water flows through them.

1. Before making a push-fit joint, make sure the rubber O-rings are properly seated in each socket.

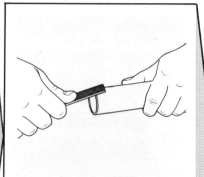

2. Cut the pipe to length, remove the burrs and chamfer the end with a file to ease insertion in the joint.

28 Compression fittings

Polythene and polybutylene pipes can both be joined with ordinary brass compression joints. However, in both cases stainless steel sleeves must be inserted in the pipe ends to prevent them collapsing when the joint is tightened. In addition, polythene pipe will require larger olives.

Polybutylene pipes can also be joined by Acorn push-fit joints.

1. Before connecting a polybutylene or polythene pipe to its fitting, insert a support sleeve in the end.

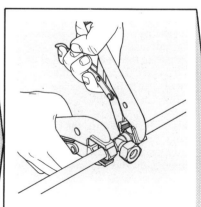

2. When using a compression joint, fit the olives and capnuts as usual and tighten the joint with two spanners.

（25）
（26）
（27）
（28）
（29）
（30）

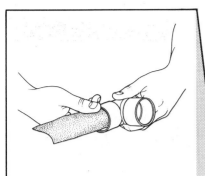

3. Use abrasive paper to 'key' the inside of the joint socket. Treat all the sockets in the same way.

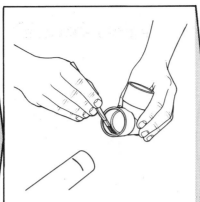

4. Wipe the pipe and joint clean and apply a liberal coating of solvent cement to the pipe and the joint socket.

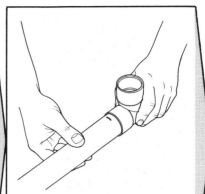

5. Fit the pipe into the joint, twisting it slightly to spread the solvent. Wipe off excess solvent and allow to set.

6 When solvent welding joints in large-diameter soil pipes, work quickly otherwise the solvent will begin to set.

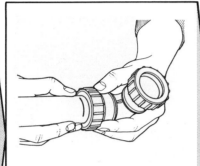

3. Lubricate the pipe with petroleum jelly, push it into the joint fully and mark the socket position in pencil.

4. Pull the pipe back slightly, providing an expansion gap of about 10mm ($\frac{3}{8}$in), using the pencil mark as a guide.

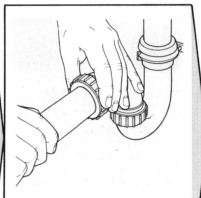

5. Some waste traps have a compression type joint with a threaded capnut and rubber sealing washer.

6. Push-fit connectors are also available, in straight and angled form, for connecting a WC pan to the soil pipe.

3. With an Acorn push-fit joint, smear the pipe and the joint's O-ring with silicone lubricant and push the pipe home.

(29) Plastic pipe restrictions

At one time it was common to earth electricity supplies by connecting them to the cold water supply pipes, but plastic pipes will not conduct electricity. If any part of the plumbing system has been replaced with plastic pipes, the electrical earthing arrangements should be checked by an electrician.

Metal pipes should still be linked to the main earthing terminal in case any are touched by a live conductor.

(30) Earthing & bonding details

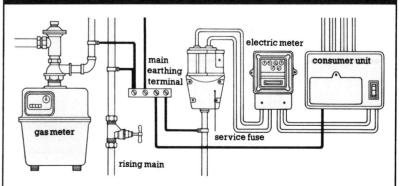

Both water supply and gas pipes should be cross-bonded to the   *main earthing terminal at the consumer unit.*

31 Draining pipework Cold pipes

Any work on the plumbing system will require at least part of it to be drained, and in an emergency this will need doing quickly, so it is important to know where all the stop valves, gate valves and draincocks are.

If the pipes to be drained are fed from the cold water storage cistern, simply close the gate valve on the appropriate pipe leading from the cistern and open all the cold taps on the affected circuit. If there is no valve, tie the ballvalve float arm to a batten across the top of the cistern to keep the valve closed and open the cold taps to drain the pipework and cistern. This will maintain a supply to the kitchen cold tap. If the pipe to the latter needs draining, the rising main stopcock must be closed.

32 Draining pipework Hot pipes

Before draining the hot water system, switch off the immersion heater or boiler.

To drain the water from the pipes between the hot water cylinder and taps, simply close the valve on the feed pipe between the cold water storage cistern and hot water cylinder (or tie up the ballvalve float arm) and open the hot taps on the appropriate pipe circuit.

If the cylinder itself needs draining, this should be done by attaching a hose to the draincock at the base of the cold water feed pipe to the cylinder, running it outside to a gully and opening the stopcock. If no stopcock is fitted, the only way to drain the cylinder is to disconnect the hot water draw-off pipe and siphon out the water.

33 Valves and draincocks

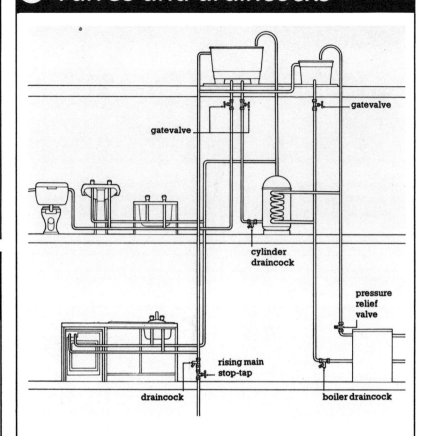

There may be several stop valves, gate valves and draincocks in a plumbing system, allowing individual pipe circuits to be isolated or the entire system to be drained. It is essential to know where they all are in case of an emergency; typical positions are shown above.

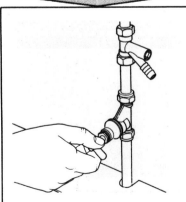

1. If the rising main or kitchen cold tap pipework is to be drained, close the stop valve on the former.

2. Gate valves on the pipes leading from the cold water cistern allow individual circuits to be isolated.

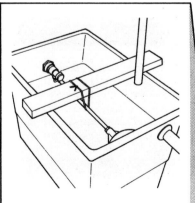

3. If no valves are fitted to the storage cistern outlets, tie up the float arm before draining the pipework.

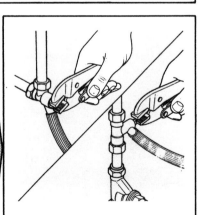

4. Fit a length of hose to draincocks at the hot cylinder and in the rising main and open them with a spanner.

Taps fall into four basic designs: pillar, shrouded-head, shrouded-head with O-ring seals and Supataps. They may leak for various reasons, but none of them are very difficult to repair.

If a tap cannot be turned off fully, or if water drips continuously from its spout, the reason is likely to be a worn washer, which should be replaced. Alternatively, the washer seating may be worn and need regrinding. It may be possible to hire a tool to do this job, but if not washer and reseating kits are available to solve the problem.

If water seeps from around the tap spindle or from under the shrouded head, the cause will be worn gland packing in older taps and worn O-rings in later ones. In both cases the sealing material should be replaced.

Although external design may differ, taps fall into four basic types: pillar, Supatap, shrouded-head, and shrouded-head with O-ring seals.

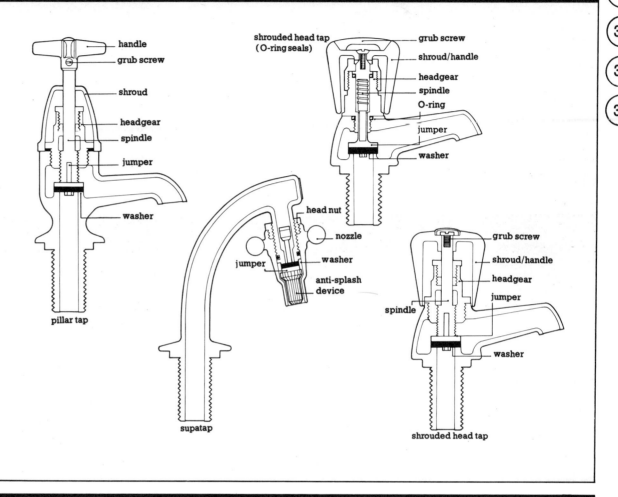

(34) **A: Pillar taps**

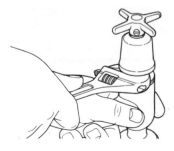

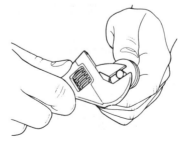

1. Unscrew and lift the cover. Hold the spout to stop the tap turning and unscrew the headgear nut with a spanner.

2. Lift the headgear and cover from the tap body. Then remove the jumper unit which carries the washer.

3. Unscrew the nut holding the washer to the jumper unit, or prise the washer free with a screwdriver blade.

4. Fit a new washer and reassemble the tap. The washer can be turned over and refitted as a stopgap measure.

In a modern shrouded-head tap both the cover and head are in one piece. Although they are not difficult to rewasher, the method of removing the shrouded head may not always be obvious.

The head may be secured by a screw beneath the 'hot' or 'cold' button, or at one side of the head. If no screw can be found the head may simply pull off or need to be unscrewed after turning on the tap fully.

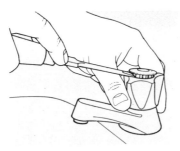

1. After draining the supply pipe, expose the head-retaining screw by prising off the coloured indicator button.

2. Release the screw and lift off the head. Alternatively, the head may be held by a side screw or might be a push fit.

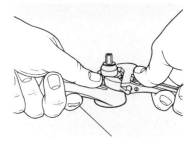

3. Hold the spout to prevent the body turning and release the headgear retaining nut with a spanner. Lift out the headgear.

Supataps are like upside-down pillar taps, the washer being pushed upwards on to its seating to stop the flow of water as the combined head and nozzle unit is turned.

An advantage of the Supatap is that it contains an automatic valve that shuts off the water supply when the head and integral nozzle are unscrewed. Thus, there is no need to turn off the water supply and drain down the pipework.

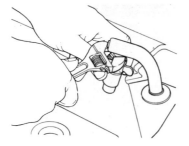

1. When rewashering a Supatap hold the tap nozzle to prevent it turning and loosen the head nut with a spanner.

2. Unscrew the tap head as if turning on the tap — water will flow but will stop when the head comes away.

3. Tap the nozzle on a piece of wood to free the anti-splash device, turn it upside down and remove the device.

Leaks from the hot and cold valves of mixer taps should be treated in the same way as normal shrouded-head taps. However, leaks may also occur at the base of the spout if this is of the swivelling type, in which case the rubber O-ring seals inside will need replacing.

The spout may be secured by a circlip or a grubscrew, but sometimes it may simply pull free after turning it to one side.

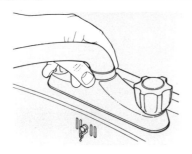

1. Make sure both taps are turned off and unscrew the shroud from the base of the mixer's swivel spout.

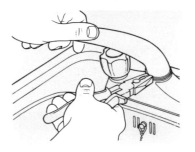

2. Use a pair of pliers to remove the circlip that holds the spout in place and lift the spout from the mixer body.

3. Prise off the old O-ring seals with a small screwdriver. Alternatively, lift them from the grooves inside the body.

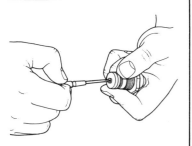

4. Remove the washer from the jumper unit by releasing its retaining screw, fit a new washer and reassemble the tap.

4. The combined washer/jumper unit should be prised from the end of the anti-splash device and a new one fitted.

4. Fit new seals, moisten them with a little water and reassemble the swivel spout to the tap body.

To prevent water leaking past the tap spindle when the tap is turned on, a special sealing material is packed round the spindle where it passes through a gland in the headgear. This gland packing is compressed by a nut to ensure a watertight seal.

If water leaks past the spindle and drips from beneath the head of the tap, the gland packing is no longer doing its job and should be replaced.

Some modern taps have rubber O-ring seals fitted around the spindle instead of gland packing.

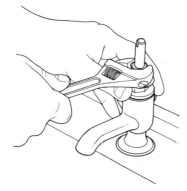

1. Turn off the tap fully and remove the handle and head cover. Try stopping the leak by tightening the gland nut first.

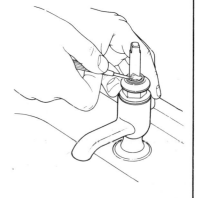

2. If the leak cannot be stopped by tightening the gland nut, unscrew it and pick out the old gland packing.

3. Use graphite-impregnated string to replace the packing, pressing it in with a screwdriver blade.

4. Replace the gland nut and tighten it before reassembling the head cover and handle to the tap spindle.

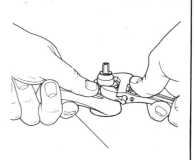

5. On a tap with O-ring seals, turn off the water and remove the headgear as described for replacing a tap washer.

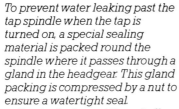

6. Carefully prise out the circlip that holds the spindle in the headgear. Take care not to lose it.

7. Remove the spindle from the headgear and use a screwdriver blade to push off the old O-ring seals.

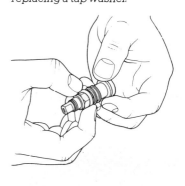

8. Fit new O-ring seals, reassemble the spindle to the headgear and replace the headgear in the tap.

40 Mending burst pipes

Pipe leaks can occur for all manner of reasons: accidental damage leading to fractures or disturbed joints, corrosion causing holes in pipes, or freezing forcing joints apart or bursting the pipes. Therefore, it is a good idea to keep a repair kit for just such an emergency, and there are several proprietary kits to choose from.

When faced with a leaking pipe, it is essential to get the water turned off as quickly as possible and the pipe drained, since even a small amount of water can do considerable damage. Knowing where all the stop valves and draincocks are is a must. Once the flow has been stopped, a temporary repair can be made and the supply reinstated while permanent repairs are planned.

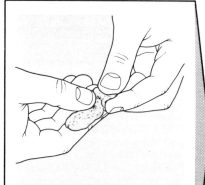

1. When using two-part pipe-repair putty, drain the pipe and mix equal amounts of the putty and hardener together.

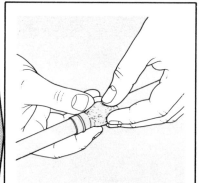

2. Pack the putty around the damage and allow to harden before restoring the water supply. This takes 24 hours.

41 Valve positions

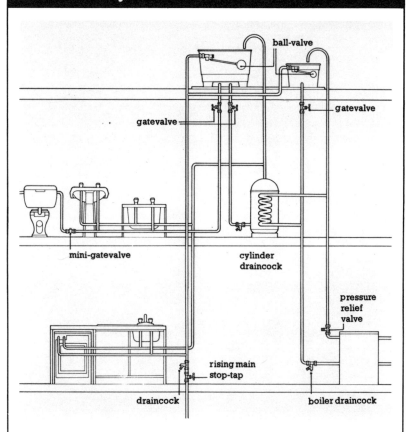

ball-valve

gatevalve

gatevalve

mini-gatevalve

cylinder draincock

pressure relief valve

rising main stop-tap

draincock

boiler draincock

It is important to know where all the stop and gate valves are in the plumbing system so that any damaged pipework can be isolated and drained down quickly. The illustration above shows where they may be found. Draincocks should be positioned so that individual circuits can be drained.

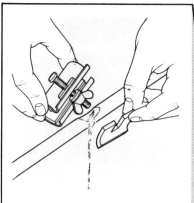

1. The pipe clamp can be used without turning off the water or draining down. Offer up the first section of the clamp.

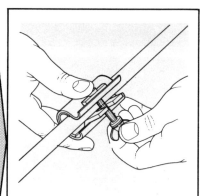

2. Fit the clamp plate and tighten the wing nut to secure it. Unfortunately, the clamp cannot be used on joints.

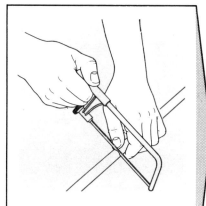

1. For a permanent repair, cut out the damaged piece with a hacksaw, taking care to cut the ends square.

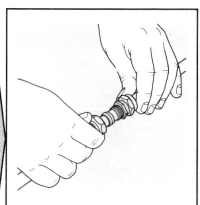

2. Spring the ends of the pipe apart, clean them and join them with a compression joint straight coupler.

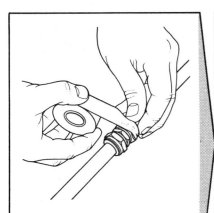

1. Two-part waterproof adhesive tape can also be used. Dry the pipe and wrap the first tape around the damaged area.

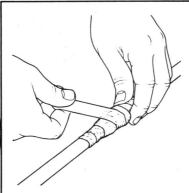

2. Apply the second tape, taking it about 25mm (1in) beyond the first layer of tape and stretching it slightly.

42 Leaking connections

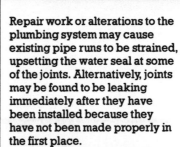

Repair work or alterations to the plumbing system may cause existing pipe runs to be strained, upsetting the water seal at some of the joints. Alternatively, joints may be found to be leaking immediately after they have been installed because they have not been made properly in the first place.

In most cases, repair is a simple matter, particularly if the joint is a compression fitting.

Leaks from these can often be stopped by simply tightening a capnut; there is no need to turn off the water supply or drain down the pipework.

However, in the case of a soldered capillary fitting, the pipes will have to be drained and the area around the joint dried before the joint can be repaired by resoldering.

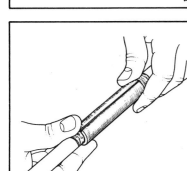

1. For a makeshift repair, bind PVC insulating tape around the pipe, then fit a piece of split garden hose over the tape.

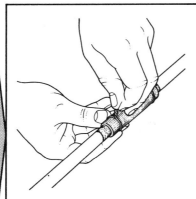

2. Secure the hose by twisting loops of wire around it. Complete the repair by winding more tape over the hose.

43 Fixing leaking connections

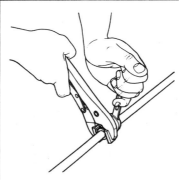

1. If a compression joint is leaking, it may be possible to stop it by tightening the cap nuts a little further.

2. If tightening the joint has no effect, drain down the affected circuit and remake the joint using new olives.

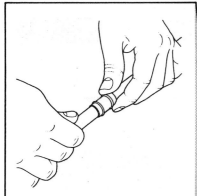

1. Alternatively, slide a shoulderless capillary fitting over one pipe, bring the ends together and solder the joint.

2. Damage repair kits contain flexible corrugated copper pipe and compression couplers to replace the damaged section.

3. Leaks around threaded fittings may be stopped by winding PTFE tape around the thread and remaking the joint.

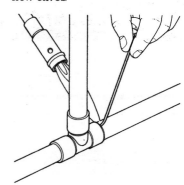

4. If a capillary joint is leaking, drain the circuit, brush on flux, heat the joint and add more solder carefully.

Water storage cisterns and WC cisterns are fitted with ballvalves that control the flow of water into them. High-pressure versions should be fitted to water storage cisterns and low-pressure types to WC cisterns.

Earlier designs of ballvalve are sealed by a rubber washer, whereas later types have a larger flexible diaphragm to shut off the water flow. The valves are operated by a float that rests on the surface of the water and closes the valve as the water level rises. The float position is adjustable to control water level.

A worn washer or diaphragm, incorrectly set float level or damaged float will prevent the valve closing fully and water will continue to flow into the cistern until it runs from the overflow pipe.

Types of ballvalve: Old fashioned Croydon type (right); later Portsmouth pattern (above); and modern diaphragm valve (far right).

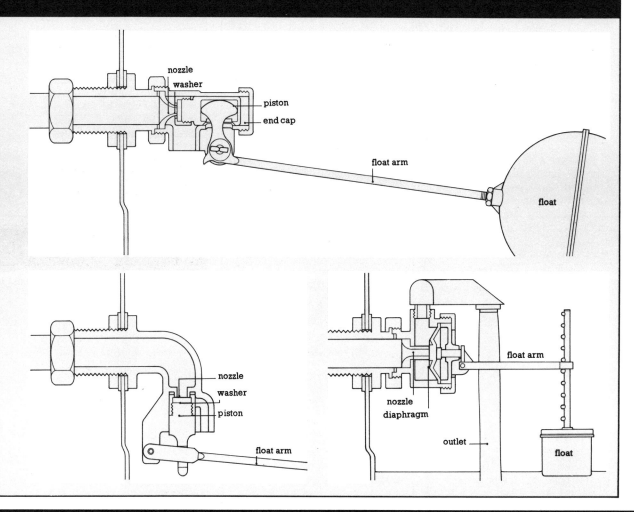

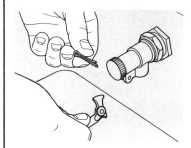

1. To rewasher a Portsmouth valve, turn off the water and disconnect the float arm by removing its retaining pin.

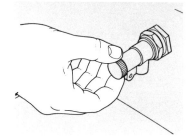

2. Then slacken the knurled cap at the end of the valve's body with a pair of pliers and carefully unscrew it from the body.

3. Remove the piston from the valve by pushing it out with a screwdriver blade inserted through the float arm slot.

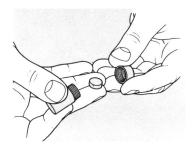

4. Unscrew the piston halves, holding one end with pliers and levering the other round with a screwdriver. Remove the washer.

46 Diaphragm type

1. Note the float position and remove it from the float arm by passing its strut through the float arm.

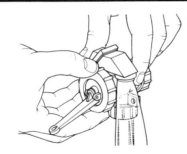

2. Unscrew the large retaining nut from the end of the valve and remove it together with the float arm assembly.

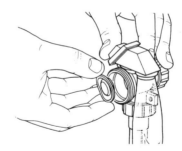

3. Remove the old diaphragm from the body of the valve and fit a new one, making sure it is seated properly.

4. If the nozzle is blocked, remove it by unscrewing the body of the valve. Push a sharp, pointed tool through it.

47 Level adjustments

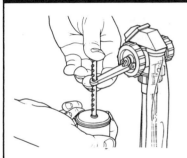

1. Adjust the water level with a diaphragm valve by moving the float up or down at the end of the float arm.

2. With a Portsmouth pattern ballvalve, you can carefully bend the float arm — up to raise the level, down to lower it.

3. Some diaphragm valves have an adjuster screw. Screw it in further to lower water level, or out to raise it.

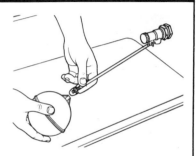

4. If an old metal float develops a leak, remove the arm, unscrew the old float, remove it and fit a new one.

5. Push a new washer into the piston cap, making sure it is seated properly. Then reassemble the piston.

6. If the piston halves cannot be unscrewed, pick out the washer with a screwdriver and work a new one into place.

7. Smear the piston with petroleum jelly and refit it to the valve. Replace the end cap and reconnect the float arm.

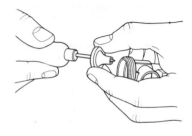

8. To clear dirt from the valve nozzle, unscrew the valve body, remove the nozzle and clean it with a sharp pointed tool.

For the most part WC flushing mechanisms are trouble-free. Any faults that do occur are easily fixed.

A common fault is that the cistern will not flush on the first pull of the flush lever. This is due to worn siphon flap valves. Replace them as shown here.

If water runs into the pan continuously, it indicates that the rubber washer at the base of the siphon pipe needs replacing. On an old high-level metal cistern such a fault indicates wear in the parts, and replacement is the best cure.

In some cases, the rod linking the flush lever with the flushing mechanism may come adrift. In this case, either reconnect it or, if it is broken, replace it with stiff galvanised wire.

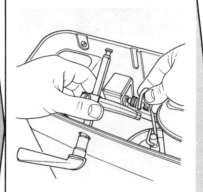

1. Shut off the water supply and flush the cistern to empty it. Disconnect the flush lever from the flushing mechanism.

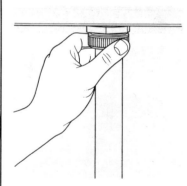

2. Bail out the remaining water in the bottom of the cistern and unscrew the backnut holding the flush pipe in place.

49 *Flush mechanism*

The modern flush mechanism: a standpipe with siphon bend contains a piston linked to the flush lever. The piston usually has rubber flap valves.

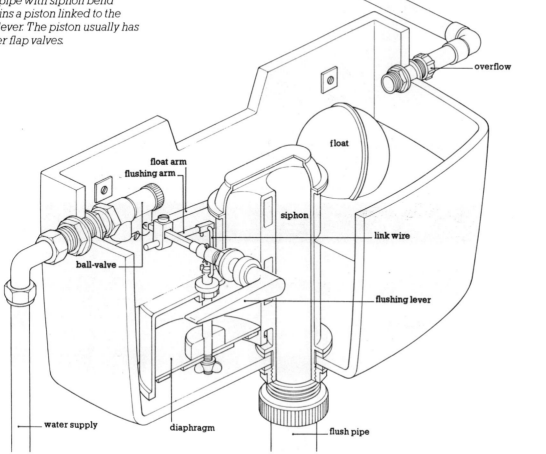

overflow

float

float arm

flushing arm

siphon

link wire

ball-valve

flushing lever

water supply

diaphragm

flush pipe

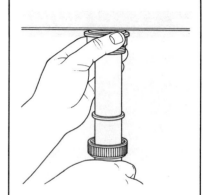

3. Move the pipe to one side to expose the siphon retaining nut. Release this and remove the siphon assembly.

4. Remove the piston from the siphon unit, take off the old flap valves and fit new ones. Reassemble the mechanism.

50 *Freeing jammed stop valves*

Because stop valves are not in constant use like taps, they tend to be forgotten and any problems with them may only be discovered when there is an urgent need to close them to cut off the water supply. What usually happens is that they seize up through lack of use and are impossible to turn off.

It is a wise precaution to open and close all stop valves and gate valves regularly to prevent them seizing up. In addition, it is a good idea not to open them fully but to back them off a quarter turn. This will allow a little movement in both directions for freeing them off.

If a stop valve seems stiff, apply penetrating oil, extra leverage or, in extreme cases, heat from a blowtorch to free it.

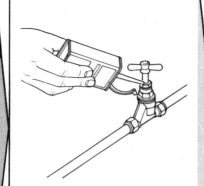

1. If a stop valve is stiff or refuses to move, apply penetrating oil to the spindle, allow to seep in and try again.

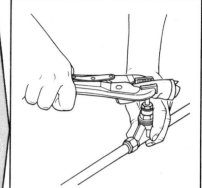

2. If the handle is still difficult to turn, protect it with a cloth and apply extra leverage with a pair of grips.

51 *Clearing airlocks*

If a plumbing system has been properly installed so that all the branch pipes run downhill slightly from the cold water storage cistern or hot water draw-off pipe, air should escape naturally when it is refilled after draining. Faults in the installation may cause air to be trapped in the pipes. This may make taps splutter when turned on or even prevent water flowing completely to some fittings.

Air locks can be cured by connecting the affected pipe directly to the kitchen cold water tap with a length of hose secured by worm-drive clips and opening both taps. Water under mains pressure will force the air out of the system. To prevent airlocks in hot water or heating circuits, fill them from the bottom by connecting a hose between the kitchen cold tap and an appropriate draincock.

Air locks can be cured by connecting the affected circuit to the kitchen cold tap, using mains pressure to force water back up through the system.

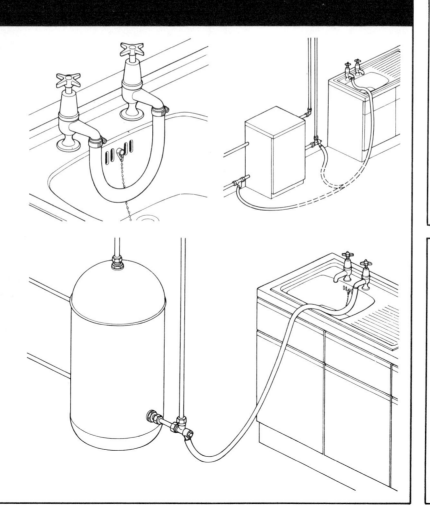

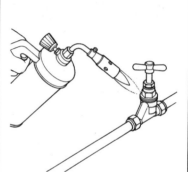

3. Free a stubborn valve with heat from a blow torch. Protect adjacent surfaces. Remember the handle will be hot.

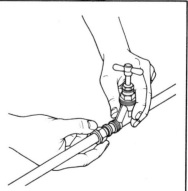

4. If all else fails, turn off the water board's stopcock outside, drain as much water as possible and replace the valve.

52 Fitting stop & gate valves

All plumbing systems should have a stop valve in the rising main; it allows the water to be cut off in an emergency. If there is no stop valve, water supply is controlled by the water authority's underground valve outdoors, but this needs a special key, so it is better to fit a valve to the main.

A stop valve contains a rubber washer to cut off flow; a gate valve has a sliding metal plate.

The former should always be fitted to pipes carrying water under mains pressure and the latter to pipes with a gravity flow.

A stop valve will only stop water flowing in one direction (an arrow on the body indicates this). However, a gate valve will prevent flow in either direction.

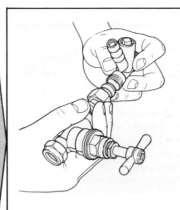

1. Always fit a draincock immediately above a stop valve. Assemble the two to a short length of pipe.

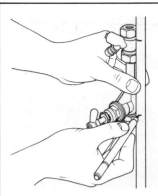

2. Offer up the stop valve and draincock assembly against the rising main and mark the pipe stop positions on the pipe.

53 Inside stop & gate valves

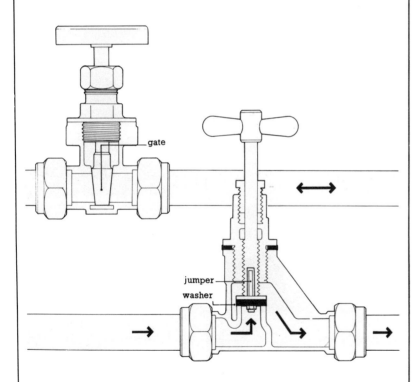

gate

jumper

washer

A gate valve (top) stops water flowing through it by sliding a metal plate across its water passage, whereas a stop valve (below) closes off its inlet with a rubber washer much like a tap. The former will stop flow in either direction, but the latter only in one direction.

54 Stopping water hammer

Water hammer, caused by shock waves passing through the water as the flow is turned on and off, may be due to several reasons including loose spindles or worn jumper units in taps or stop valves, too fast a flow of water and faulty ballvalves. Closing the main stop valve slightly may help to reduce it.

Water hammer may also occur if the float of a ballvalve bounces up and down on the water as a cistern fills. This can be cured by fitting a damper to the float arm – an empty yoghurt pot hung in the water open end up is ideal.

In severe cases the rising main should be continued above the storage cistern ballvalve and terminated in a capped off pipe that forms a shock absorbing air chamber.

55 Clearing blockages

Over a period of time dirt and hair may build up in the waste outlet trap of a sink, basin, bath or shower and block it completely. An early warning that this is likely to happen is a sluggish flow from the outlet when the plug is removed. At this stage it should be treated with a chemical cleaner.

However, there are various methods for clearing a full blockage. A traditional sink plunger can be used with a vigorous pumping action to force the blockage through the pipe or a sink auger can be hired to clear a more persistent blockage. If a rodding eye is provided at the base of the trap, it can be removed and the pipe probed with a stiff wire. A modern plastic trap can be dismantled and flushed out.

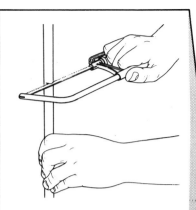

3. Close the water authority's stop valve outside and cut the pipe. Be prepared to catch any spillage.

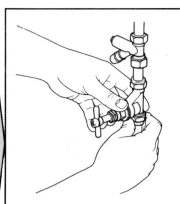

4. Spring the stop valve and draincock assembly into place between the prepared pipe ends and tighten the capnuts.

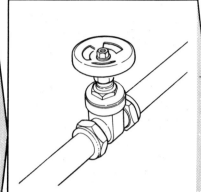

5. Gate valves are easily recognised by their wheel handles. Fit them to low pressure gravity fed circuits.

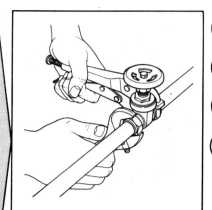

6. Fit a gate valve to a pipe in the same manner as a normal compression fitting, tightening the capnuts with two wrenches.

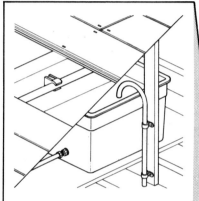

1. Long, unsupported pipes may cause water hammer – clip them at 1.2m (4ft) intervals, adding support battens if necessary.

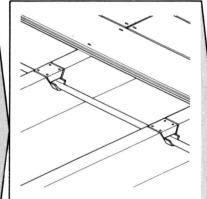

2. Pipes passing through holes in joists may also vibrate; prevent this by laying pads of felt in the holes.

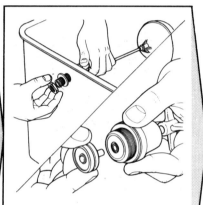

3. Juddering in the system may be caused by worn tap or ballvalve washers – replace them as described previously.

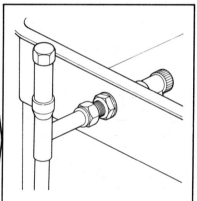

4. An air chamber made from a capped length of 28mm pipe can be added to the rising main to cope with severe cases.

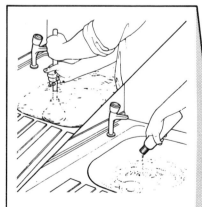

1. Clear a blockage with a sink plunger, closing off the overflow, or bail out the sink and use a chemical cleaner.

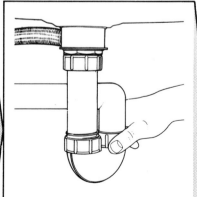

2. If the blockage is stubborn, unscrew the trap and clean it. Be prepared to catch spillage as the trap is removed.

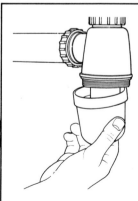

3. In a modern plastic bottle trap, the base can be unscrewed and the blockage cleared by washing it out.

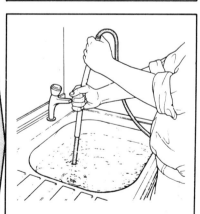

4. An alternative method of clearing a blockage is with a purpose-made sink auger which can be hired locally.

56 Replacing a WC cistern

Replacing an old-fashioned, noisy, high-level WC cistern with a modern low-level cistern is a common job when updating a bathroom.

The new cistern can be connected to the existing pan, but only if a 'flush panel' cistern is used. This will fit on the wall behind the pan, projecting no more than about 115mm (4½in). Such a narrow cistern is necessary because with the high-level set-up, the pan would project too far to allow the seat to be raised.

When removing the old cistern, it may be easier to cut through the pipes rather than struggle to release the connectors. This won't matter since new pipework will have to be installed anyway.

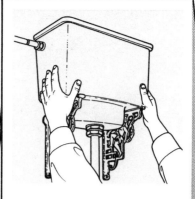

1. Shut off the water, flush the cistern and cut through the pipework. Remove the lid and lift the cistern clear.

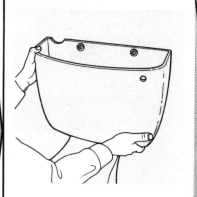

2. Fix the brackets to the wall, position the cistern, and mark, drill and plug its fixing holes. Then screw it to the wall.

57 Cleaning gullies & drains

Gullies are particularly prone to blockage, despite their grids – they may become clogged with dead leaves and dirt. Fortunately, they are easy to clear.

An underground drain is a different proposition since the position of the blockage may not be obvious. Lifting manhole covers is the only way to locate the stretch of drain that is blocked.

Hire a set of drain rods to clear the blockage, inserting them into the pipe and either rodding towards the house or away from it depending on where the blockage is. The last manhole in the run before it enters the main sewer will be trapped. If this is blocked, the rods should be passed through the rodding eye to force the blockage into the main sewer.

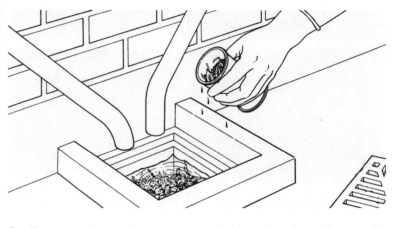

A gully can be cleared by scooping out the debris with an old tin. Wear rubber gloves and rinse the gully well afterwards.

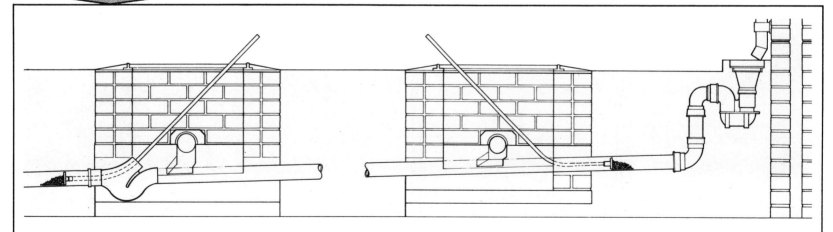

Insert the drain rods into the pipe, working towards the house or away from it as appropriate. Always turn them clockwise to prevent them coming unscrewed. If the blockage is downstream of the last manhole, pass the rods through the rodding eye. Remember to replace its plug.

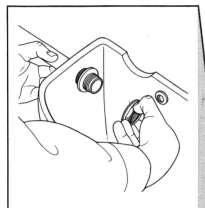

3. Connect the overflow pipe to the cistern, leading it through an outside wall or to a nearby bath or shower tray.

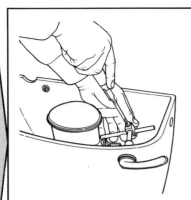

4. Mount the siphon assembly in the base of the cistern. Then fit the flush lever and connect it to the flushing mechanism.

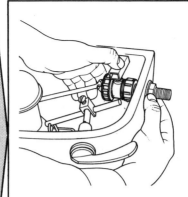

5. Fit the ballvalve assembly to the side of the cistern, making sure the plastic sealing washers are in place.

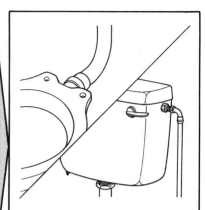

6. Finally, fit the flush pipe between the cistern and pan and connect a 15mm supply pipe to the ballvalve inlet.

58 *Cistern types & position options*

Cisterns have moved steadily downwards as the years have gone by. Many old-fashioned installations still feature high-level cast iron cisterns, often supported on elaborate wall brackets and linked to the WC pan by a metal flush pipe. The flushing mechanism on these old cisterns is primitive and noisy, and the whole assembly is usually ripe for replacement. More recent installations have intermediate or low-level cisterns, often in ceramic or plastic material rather than iron, but still linked to the pan by a flush pipe. Modern WCs usually have the cistern mounted on the rear of the pan — known as close-coupled — or may have a slimline cistern which can be concealed behind a wall panel.

concealed

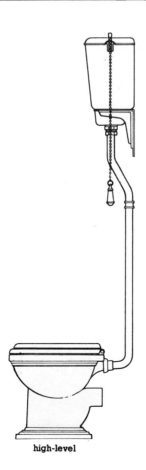

high-level

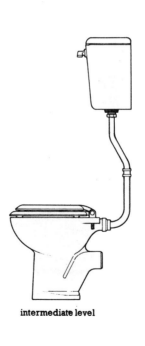

intermediate level

low-level slimline

close-coupled

Many old cold water storage cisterns were made from zinc-galvanised steel and they suffer from corrosion, particularly if the water supply is slightly acidic. This, coupled with copper supply pipes, sets up a chemical reaction that strips the zinc from the tank, leaving it unprotected.

It is better to fit a modern plastic cistern than try to repair a corroded steel item. A capacity of 228 litres (50 gallons) should be adequate for most needs. If a cistern of this size can't be passed through the loft trap, install two smaller cisterns, connecting them in tandem.

An old steel cistern will be bulky and very heavy. Rather than struggle to lower it through the trap, simply push it to one side in the roof.

60 *Connections & 2-tank option*

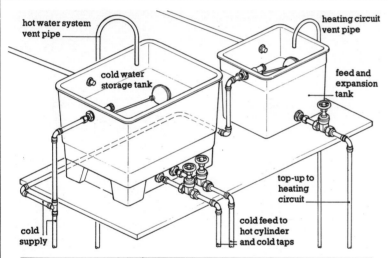

hot water system vent pipe

heating circuit vent pipe

cold water storage tank

feed and expansion tank

top-up to heating circuit

cold feed to hot cylinder and cold taps

cold supply

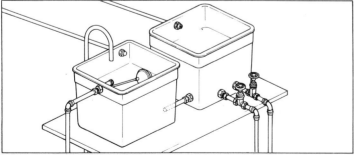

To simplify connections, the smaller central heating header tank should be stood next to the cistern. Two small cisterns can be *connected in tandem to provide the required capacity. Link the two with a 28mm connecting pipe.*

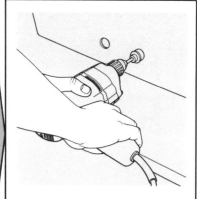

1. After positioning the cistern on a stout wooden base, drill outlet holes 50mm (2in) from the bottom using a hole saw.

2. Wind PTFE tape round the tank connector threads, fit them in the cistern and add the washers and backnuts.

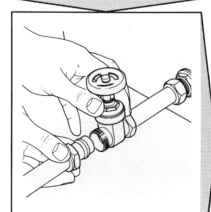

3. Add short pipe stubs to the connectors with compression fittings, then fit gate valves followed by the supply pipes.

There are various reasons why it might be necessary to replace a hot water cylinder; it may have developed a leak, or it may be too small for a growing family – a capacity of 140-160 litres (30-35 gallons) should be adequate for most needs – or it may be necessary to remove a direct cylinder and replace it with an indirect version. The latter is particularly worthwhile in hard water areas.

Whatever the reason for changing a hot cylinder, it is sensible to identify the pipes that connect to it before removing it so that they can be connected correctly to the new unit.

There are various types to choose from including self-priming types that have an indirect heating circuit filled initially from the hot cylinder yet kept separate from the water in the cylinder after that by an airlock. There are also packaged units for single-storey dwellings that incorporate a cold water storage cistern on top.

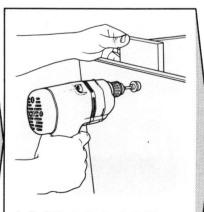

4. Drill the ballvalve hole 25mm (1in) from the top edge. A block of wood held against the side will stop it flexing.

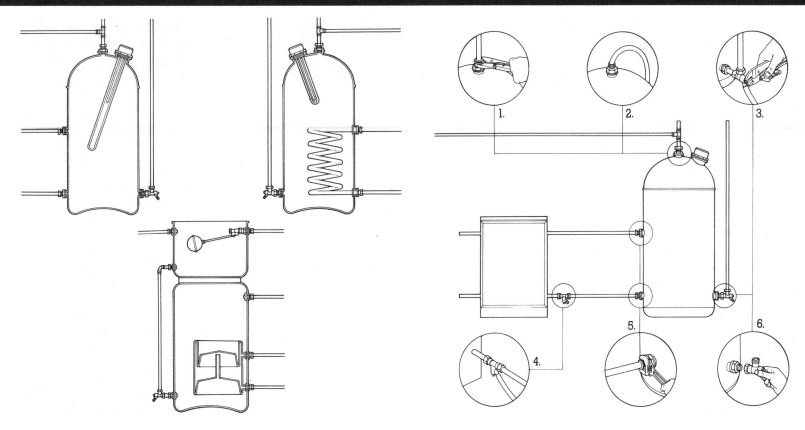

A direct cylinder (left) has no separate heat exchanger, unlike the indirect version (right). An airlock in a self-priming cylinder (below) separates the water in the cylinder from that from the boiler.

Disconnect the draw-off pipe (1) and siphon out the water with a hose (2) or open the draincock (3). Drain the primary circuit between boiler and cylinder (4). Disconnect the primary pipes (5) and the cold feed (6)

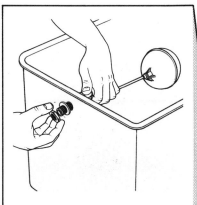

5. Fit a high-pressure ballvalve to the cistern, wrapping its thread with PTFE tape. Connect the rising main to it.

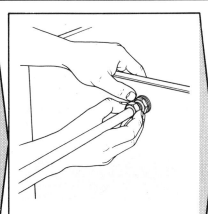

6. Connect the plastic overfow pipe 25mm (1in) below the ballvalve, leading it to discharge at the eaves.

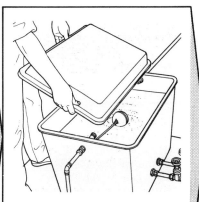

7. All cisterns must have a lid to stop debris falling in. Cut a hole for the expansion pipe from the hot cylinder.

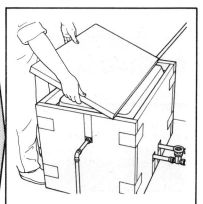

8. Insulate the cistern to prevent it freezing by taping sheets of rigid polystyrene around it to form a box.

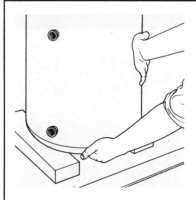

1. Stand the new cylinder on timber battens so that air can circulate around the base to prevent condensation forming.

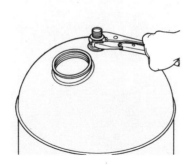

2. Wrap PTFE tape round the threads of the draw-off pipe connector, fit the connector and the draw-off pipe.

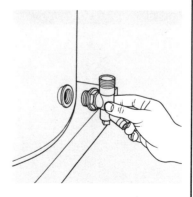

3. Tape the draincock threads and fit it to the base of the cylinder. Connect the cold feed pipe to the draincock.

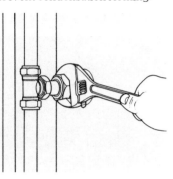

4. Make sure the primary circuit connectors are tight and then connect the flow pipe from the boiler to the upper connector.

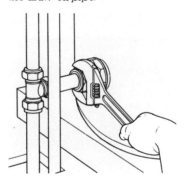

5. Connect the return pipe to the lower connector. It may be necessary to reposition the pipes to meet the new cylinder.

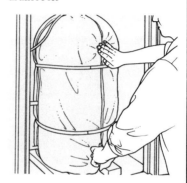

6. Many new cylinders come with insulation moulded on. If not, fit a lagging jacket, keeping it clear of the immersion heater.

Although it may be necessary to replace taps because they have become worn and scruffy, a more likely reason is the desire for a more modern appearance. New styles are constantly being introduced along with new materials that make them more efficient or keep their looks longer.

For all applications there is the choice between individual taps or mixer taps, bath versions of the latter often having a shower attachment. If a mixer is intended for kitchen use, it must have a spout containing separate channels for hot and cold water to prevent the former contaminating the mains supply.

Mixers will usually occupy the holes of individual taps, but it is also possible to buy a single-hole mixer or a three-hole unit with separate spout where all the controls are fitted below the rim of the basin.

Bath taps must be connected to 22mm supply pipes and basins and sinks to 15mm pipework.

Various types of immersion heater are available. Some have a single element that extends the full depth of the cylinder, whereas others have separately-switched dual elements – a short and long one. The former can be used most of the time to heat water at the top of the cylinder and the latter when large quantities of hot water are needed. Some cylinders have tappings in their sides for two short elements, one above the other, which act like a dual-element model.

A heater rated above 3kW must be connected to its own 15A radial circuit through a 20A double-pole switch and heat resisting flex. A heater below 3kW can be plugged into a 13A socket or, preferably, linked to a fused connection unit.

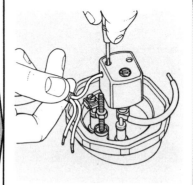

1. Switch off the electricity supply to the immersion heater, remove the top cover and disconnect the flex.

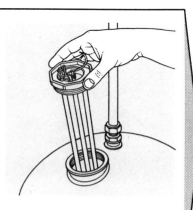

2. Unscrew the immersion heater using an immersion heater spanner (which can be hired). Lift it out.

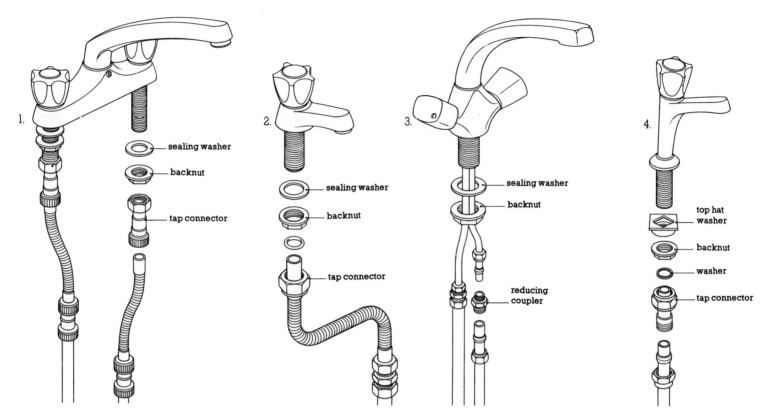

Taps may be connected in several different ways. Tap connecting kits (1) comprise lengths of flexible copper pipe with Acorn push-fit connectors. Flexible pipe can also be obtained with integral brass tap connectors (2).

Single-hole monobloc mixers (3) have 10mm supply pipes that must be connected to the supply pipes with reducing couplers. Rigid copper pipe can be connected with standard brass swivel tap connectors (4).

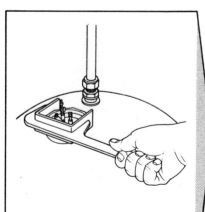

3. Wrap PTFE tape round the threads of the new heater and screw it into its boss, tightening it with the spanner.

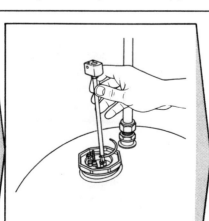

4. Slot the thermostat into the immersion heater, making sure it is seated properly, and connect its link wire.

5. Feed in the flex, connecting the neutral and earth cores to their respective terminals, and the live core to the thermostat.

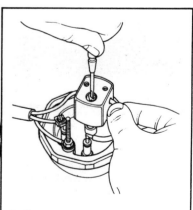

6. Set the water temperature by adjusting the control on top of the thermostat with a screwdriver. Replace the cover.

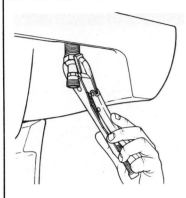

1. Turn off the water, drain the pipes and disconnect them from the tap connectors. Unscrew the connectors from the tap tails.

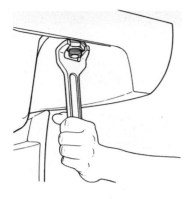

2. Unscrew the tap backnuts, holding the taps to stop them turning. A basin wrench (shown) will make reaching them easier.

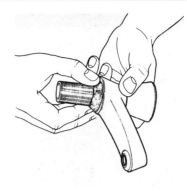

3. If no plastic or rubber gasket is supplied with the tap, press a layer of plumber's putty around its base.

4. Set the tap in place, making sure it is at the right angle and secure it with the backnut. Wipe off any excess putty.

5. Refit the tap connectors and pipes, using tap tail adaptors or lengths of flexible pipe if the new tails are too short.

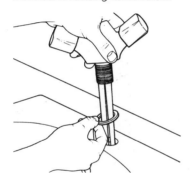

6. A single-hole mixer will need a slightly larger hole than normal. A rubber sealing gasket must be fitted beneath it.

7. With a three-hole mixer, the spout is fitted separately to the water inlet assembly which sits below the basin rim.

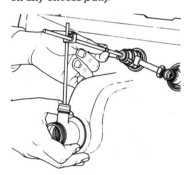

8. A pop-up waste assembly is operated by rods that fit below the basin between the control and waste outlet.

A common problem in the bathroom is getting a good seal between the bath, basin or shower tray and the walls. If allowed to open up, it could cause considerable damage to the wall and floor as water seeps through. Therefore, it is essential to find some means of sealing it permanently.

For gaps up to 3mm (⅛in) wide, silicone mastic should be used. This flexible sealant is squeezed into the gap from its tube and smoothed off with a wet dowel. The mastic is available in white and a range of colours to match bathroom accessories.

If the gap is too wide for mastic, it can be sealed with special strips of plastic or quadrant tiles. These should be bedded on mastic to ensure a waterproof seal.

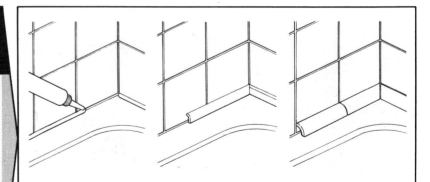

There are three methods of sealing a gap around a bath. Narrow gaps can be filled with a flexible silicone mastic.

Alternatively, plastic strips or ceramic quadrant tiles can be used. They should be bedded on silicone mastic.

Of all the plumbing fittings in the house, the kitchen sink probably works the hardest, often being used for jobs for which it was never intended. Eventually the finish will become scratched and chipped, not only marring its appearance but also making it difficult to keep clean. Inevitably, it will need replacing, as it will if you buy an old house that still has an original earthenware sink.

Modern sinks come in many different styles with single or double bowls, single or double drainers, vegetable preparation bowls, large diameter outlets to accept waste disposal units and other special features. Some are designed for fitting to the top of a kitchen unit, while others are intended to be let into kitchen worktops. They may be made of stainless steel, enamelled steel, plastic or even ceramics.

The kitchen sink should have 15mm supply pipes to the taps and a 38mm waste pipe and trap.

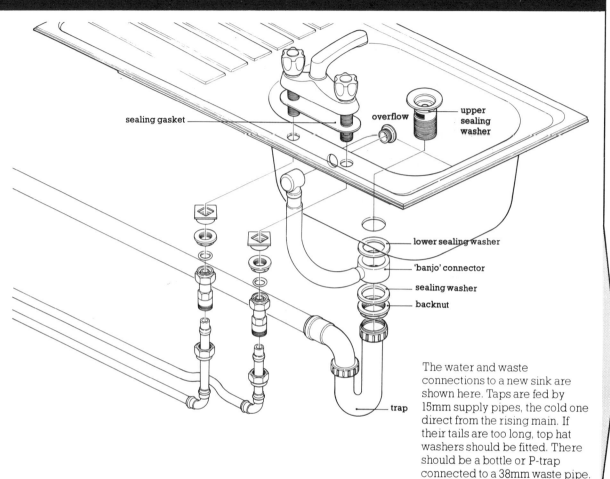

sealing gasket — overflow — upper sealing washer

lower sealing washer
'banjo' connector
sealing washer
backnut

trap

The water and waste connections to a new sink are shown here. Taps are fed by 15mm supply pipes, the cold one direct from the rising main. If their tails are too long, top hat washers should be fitted. There should be a bottle or P-trap connected to a 38mm waste pipe.

68 **Disconnecting old fittings**

Before removing the old sink, turn off the water and drain the supply pipes. Disconnect the waste pipe, cutting through it if it is to be replaced; otherwise unscrew the trap.

Similarly cut through the supply pipes if the tap connectors cannot be reached or are difficult to unscrew. If an old earthenware sink is being removed, it will probably have bib taps screwed to the wall with

the pipes buried in the plaster. Unscrew the taps and expose the pipes.

An earthenware sink will be very heavy; chip away its seal with the wall using a cold chisel and lift it from its brackets. Remove these as well. A later sink should be lifted from its kitchen unit or the entire unit removed.

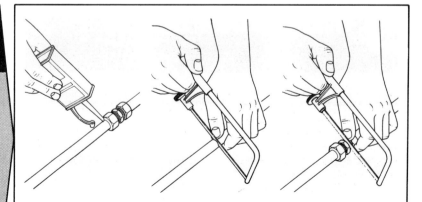

If it is difficult to disconnect the supply pipes to the old sink, soak the tap connectors with penetrating oil; applying heat

with a blow torch may also help. If all else fails, saw through the connectors or the pipes themselves.

1. Wrap PTFE tape around the waste outlet threads and apply plumber's putty to the flange or fit the gasket supplied.

2. Insert the outlet in the sink, bedding it on the putty or gasket. Place the sealing washer over the outlet tail.

3. Set the overflow collar over the outlet tail, aligning it with the slot in the outlet, and add the second sealing washer.

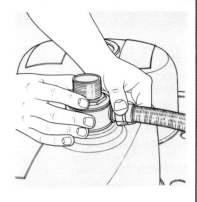

4. Fit the backnut to the waste outlet tail and tighten it with an adjustable spanner. Hold the overflow to prevent it turning.

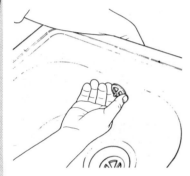

5. Screw the overflow pipe to the rose at the back of the bowl. Then remove excess putty from around the outlet fitting.

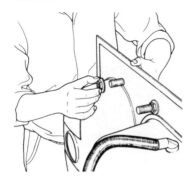

6. Fit the taps, using top-hat washers if the tap tails are too long. Tighten the backnuts to hold them in place.

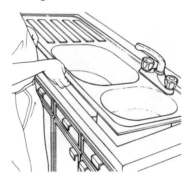

7. Lift the sink top into place on top of the kitchen unit. An inset sink must be bedded on a rubber gasket or clear mastic.

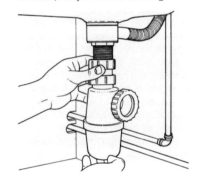

8. Connect the supply pipes to the tap tails, fit a bottle trap (shown) or P-trap to the waste outlet and add the waste pipe.

Simply replacing an old hand basin with a new one is unlikely to cause any problems. However, altering its position or making a new installation will require approval from the local building inspector who will want to know how the waste pipes will be run and connected to the drainage system.

The length of the waste pipe run should not exceed 2.3m (7ft 6in), and if less than 1.7m (5ft 6in)

can be made in 32mm pipe; above that length it must be in 38mm pipe. The waste pipe should have a gradual fall to a hopper head or soil stack if on an upper floor or to a gully if on the ground floor.

The basin should have a P- or bottle trap with a 75mm (3in) deep seal.

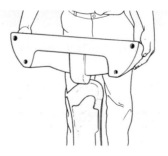

1. Set the basin on its pedestal to determine how the pipes will be run and measure the height of the fixing holes.

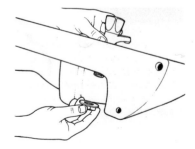

2. Fit the taps with their backnuts, connecting lengths of flexible copper pipe to their tails. Fit the waste outlet.

Basins come in many different styles, sizes and colours in ceramics or plastics. However, there are three basic types: pedestal mounted, wall-mounted on brackets or inset where the basin is mounted in the top of a vanity unit.

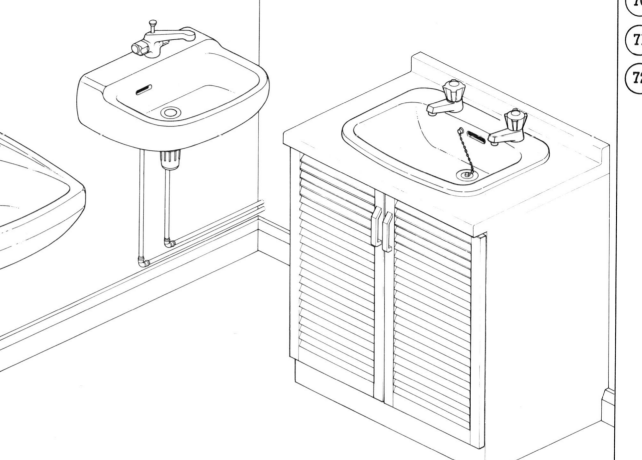

3. After adding the trap, stand the basin and pedestal in position against the wall and check that it is level.

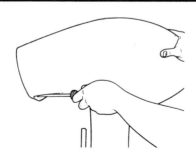

4. Mark, drill and plug the basin fixing holes in the wall. Then replace the basin and screw it in place.

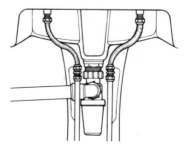

5. Connect the flexible pipes from the tap tails to the rigid supply pipes and the trap to the waste pipe run.

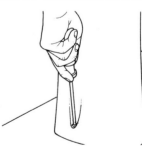

6. Finally, screw the pedestal to the floor, turn on the water and check the pipe connections for leaks.

73 Wall-hung type

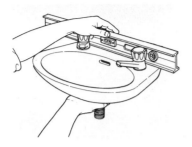
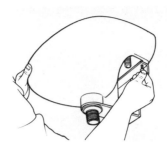

1. Hold the basin bracket on the wall, mark its fixing holes, drill and plug them and screw the bracket to the wall.

2. Set the basin on the bracket and check that it is level. If necessary pack it out with washers.

3. Add the nuts to the upper basin fixings followed by the backnut to the waste outlet to secure it firmly to the bracket.

4. Finally, fit the waste trap and connect it to the waste pipe followed by the supply pipes to the taps.

74 Inset type

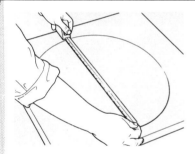
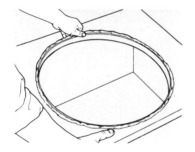
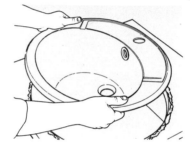
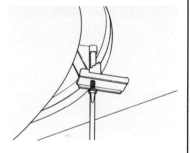

1. Mark the vanity unit for the basin cutout using the template provided — double check the measurements before cutting.

2. Check that the basin fits the hole and apply mastic to the edge for a watertight seal — or use the basin gasket provided.

3. Set the basin in place. Fit the waste and the taps, with flexible copper pipes on their tails, first if you wish.

4. Finally, secure the basin by fitting the retaining clips and tightening them against the underside of the top.

75 Waste connections

The contents of waste pipes from basins, baths, showers and bidets can be discharged in a number of different ways.

Waste pipes from upper floors can be drained into a hopper head in a two-pipe system or connected to a soil stack in a single-pipe system using an existing spare pipe boss or a self-locking or strap boss.

Fittings on ground floors can be drained to a gully or connected to a soil stack.

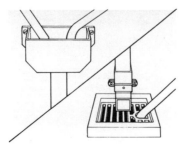
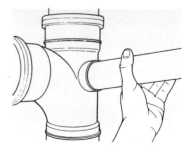

1. Upstairs pipes can be led to a hopper; downstairs they can discharge at a gully — below the grill but above the water.

2. The waste pipe can be solvent-welded to a spare boss in a soil stack in a single-pipe drainage system.

3. If there is no spare boss, use a self-locking or strap boss, solvent-welding the pipe to the boss.

Connecting a new bath

Just as there is a wide range of hand basins to choose from, so the choice of bath styles and colours is considerable. Most modern baths are made of glass fibre and come with a steel supporting frame to keep them rigid. This makes them easier to carry upstairs to a bathroom than to carry down an old cast-iron version. Indeed, the latter are so heavy that it may be preferable to cover such a bath with a thick blanket and break it up in situ with a sledge hammer.

When removing an old bath, it will be easier to cut through the supply and waste pipes than struggle to disconnect them in the cramped space beneath the bath. There will probably be a separate overflow pipe too, running through the wall. This should be cut through and the hole filled in.

The new bath should have 22mm supply pipes and a 38mm waste pipe run; the connections are much the same as for a basin or sink.

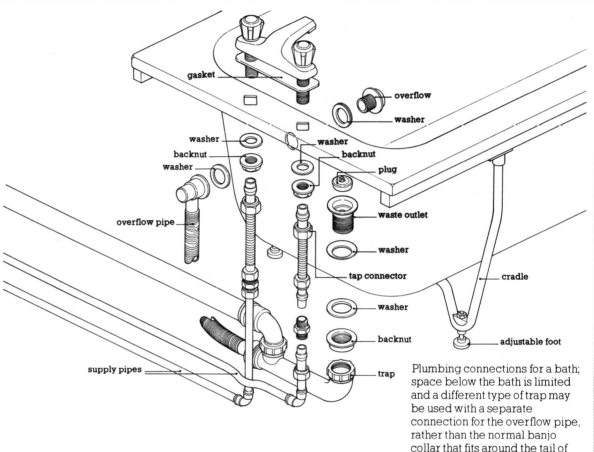

Plumbing connections for a bath; space below the bath is limited and a different type of trap may be used with a separate connection for the overflow pipe, rather than the normal banjo collar that fits around the tail of the waste outlet.

Bath types & sizes

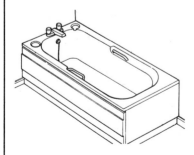

1. The traditional bath has panels to box it in and may come with integral grab handles. Most are of plastic construction.

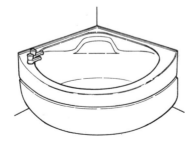

2. A corner bath may take advantage of an odd-shaped bathroom, making the most of the available space.

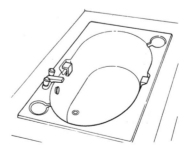

3. Inset baths can be built into a raised section of floor and are ideal for large bathrooms; various shapes are available.

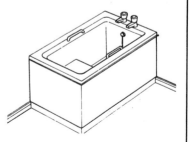

4. A hip bath takes up much less room than a normal bath and incorporates a seat so is ideal for the old or disabled.

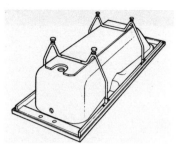

1. Turn the new bath upside down and assemble its mounting cradle as described in the manufacturer's instructions.

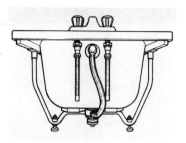

2. Install the taps, waste outlet and overflow. Adding flexible copper pipes to the tap tails will simplify connection later.

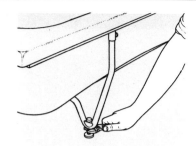

3. Set the bath in position and check that it is level. If necessary, adjust the feet of the cradle to level the bath.

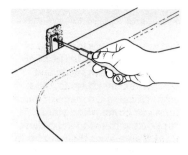

4. If wall brackets are provided, cut away the plaster, drill and plug fixing holes, and attach them to the wall.

79 *Fitting a new WC*

Replacing a WC suite is not difficult if it is to stay in the same position as before. If it is to be moved, or a completely new installation made, the building inspector should be consulted about the waste pipe run.

Modern WC suites are more efficient, more compact and more stylish than their early counterparts. Neatest are the close-coupled suites where the cistern sits on the back of the pan. However, these project further from the wall than those with wall-mounted cisterns, so bear this in mind.

Old pans will be connected to the soil pipe by a mortar seal, which should be chopped away with a cold chisel. The new pan can be fitted with a push-fit connector, making the job much simpler.

80 *WC types & sizes*

Unlike a normal low-level WC suite which relies on the rush of water under gravity to clear the pan of its contents, a close-coupled suite employs siphonic action to draw the contents into the waste pipe.

There are two types of siphonic suite; single trap and double trap. The single trap system is the cheaper and simpler of the two, but the double trap type is particularly silent in operation.

1. Single-trap siphonic: the pan outlet is designed to create a siphonic action.

1. After removing the cistern, break the joint between the old pan and soil pipe with a hammer and cold chisel.

2. Unscrew the pan from the floor. Block the pipe with newspaper and clear the remaining mortar with a chisel.

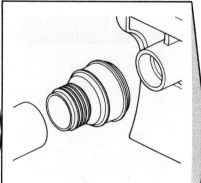

3. Use a push-fit connector to join the pan to the soil pipe. Push it into the pipe before positioning the pan.

4. Position the pan and check that it is level. If necessary, pack underneath with thin strips of wood.

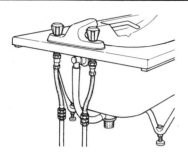

5. Run in the 22mm supply pipes and connect them to the flexible copper pipes with brass compression couplers.

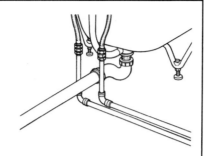

6. Finally, screw the waste trap to its outlet and lay in the waste pipe run, taking it to a hopper, gully or soil pipe.

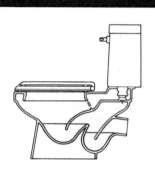

2. Double-trap siphonic: a valve sucks air from between the traps to siphon out the contents.

3. Normal wash-down WC: gravity flow of water forces pan contents into waste pipe.

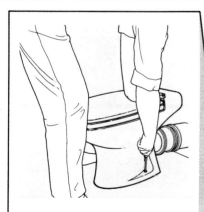

5. Mark the pan fixing holes and remove it temporarily to drill them. Plug the holes and screw the pan to the floor.

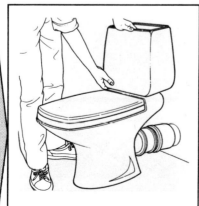

6. Install the cistern and flushing assembly, running in a 15mm supply pipe and connecting an overflow pipe.

There are two types of bidet; over-rim and rim supply with ascending spray.

The over-rim bidet has individual taps or a mixer and can share the water supplies of any nearby basin.

Rim supply with ascending spray bidets are different, having controls that direct warm water around the rim to make it more comfortable for sitting on and then to a fountain-like spray in the bowl. This type must have its own separate supply pipes from the cold water cistern and hot water cylinder.

The bidet should have a 75mm (3in) seal trap and a 38mm waste pipe which can discharge over a hopper in a two-pipe system or a gully. It can also be connected directly to a soil stack in a single-pipe system.

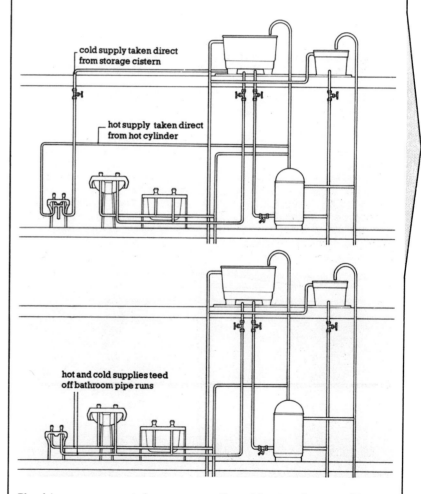

cold supply taken direct from storage cistern

hot supply taken direct from hot cylinder

hot and cold supplies teed off bathroom pipe runs

Plumbing arrangements for a bidet: the rim supply and ascending spray type must have separate supply pipes run from the cold water cistern and hot water cylinder (top); the over rim type may share supplies with nearby taps (bottom).

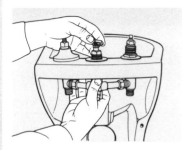

1. Assemble the tap and waste control assembly to the bidet, locking it in place with the backnuts.

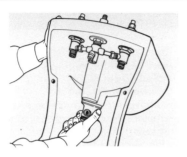

2. Add the waste outlet and spray rose to the bidet, bedding them on plumber's putty and removing the excess.

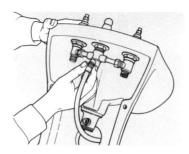

3. Connect the flexible spray pipe between the rose in the base of the bidet and the control on the mixer unit.

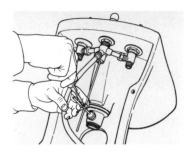

4. Assemble the pop-up waste control rods, attaching one to the waste outlet and the other to the mixer control.

83   Fitting an electric shower

If it is difficult to install a conventional shower, an electric shower is the ideal alternative. It contains powerful elements that heat the water as it flows through the unit.

Electric showers should be connected directly to the rising main with a 15mm supply pipe and require their own 30A electrical circuit with a ceiling-mounted on-off switch. Their waterproof casings allow them to be fitted inside shower cubicles.

Showers of this type have a temperature stabiliser so that if mains pressure fluctuates the temperature remains constant. They also have a sensor that switches off the heating elements if the pressure drops too low, otherwise the hot water might become scaldingly hot.

84   Shower plumbing & wiring

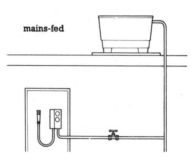

mains-fed

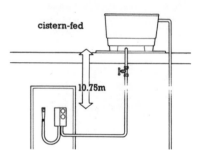

cistern-fed

10.75m

An electric shower should be connected to the rising main. However, it may be fed from a storage cistern provided this is at least 10.75m (35ft) above the shower rose.

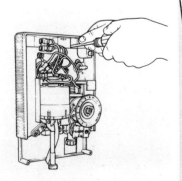

1. Mark and drill the fixing and cable entry holes, run in the cable and screw the shower unit to the cubicle wall.

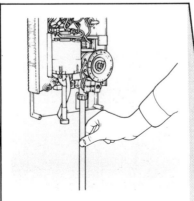

2. Run in a 15mm feed pipe from the rising main, linking it to the shower inlet with a swivel tap connector.

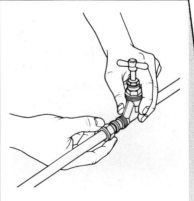

3. Install a stop valve in the shower supply pipe so that the unit can be isolated at any time for repairs.

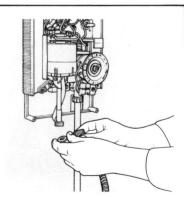

4. Connect the flexible shower hose to the water outlet, making sure the sealing washer is seated in the capnut.

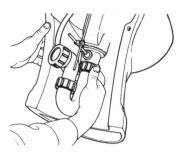

5. Attach a P-trap to the bidet waste outlet, turning it at a slight angle to clear the pop-up waste control rods.

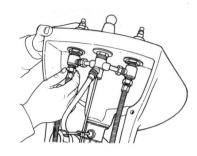

6. Fit flexible copper pipes to the tap tails to simplify connection to the supply pipes and install the bidet.

Supplying hot water by means of a storage cylinder may not always be convenient if space is limited. Nor might it always be easy to run a pipe from an existing cylinder to a remote point in the house. In these situations a gas or electric water heater is the answer.

Gas heaters are usually intended for wall mounting, having balanced flues. Some are single-point (for just one outlet), others multi-point (supplying several outlets). They heat the water instantaneously as it flows through them and must be connected to the rising main. The gas connections must be done by a professional.

Electric heaters come in single-point versions only and usually contain a small storage cylinder fitted with heating elements.

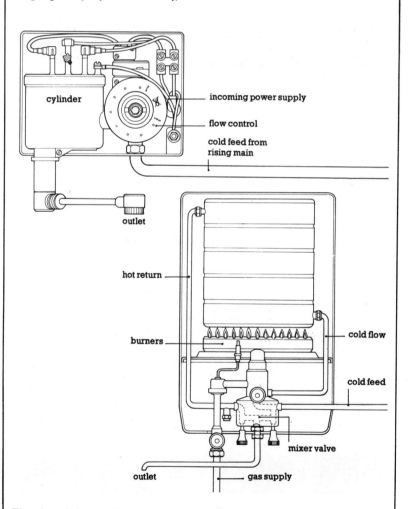

The electric heater (top) has powerful elements that heat the water in a small cylinder. The burners in a gas-fired version (bottom) ignite automatically when the tap is turned on. Some have a cold tap, so that water temperature can be controlled.

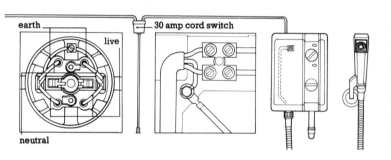

The shower should be controlled by a 30A double-pole cord switch. Connect the cable from the shower to the 'load' terminals and the power cable to the 'feed' terminals.

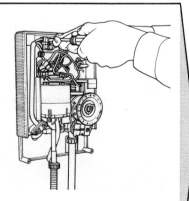

5. Link a 6mm² 2-core and earth cable to the shower's terminals. Take the other end to a 30A double-pole cord switch.

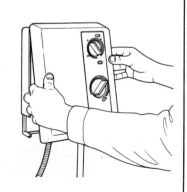

6. Replace the cover. Reinstate the water and electricity supplies and check the shower's operation.

There are many advantages to a shower: it uses much less water than a bath; it is quick to use; it is a hygienic way of washing; and it takes up much less room than a bath, so it can be installed in a bedroom, hallway, under the stairs etc.

The simplest shower is a rose linked to a bath mixer, but this can suffer from pressure and temperature fluctuations when other taps in the house are used.

It is better to fit a separate mixer, above the bath or in a cubicle, with its own supply pipes run from the cold cistern and hot cylinder.

To ensure a decent water pressure in the shower, the cold water cistern must be at least 1m (39in) above the rose; if not, a pump can be fitted to boost pressure.

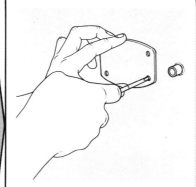

1. With a surface-mounted mixer, decide on the height for the fitting and screw the backplate to the wall.

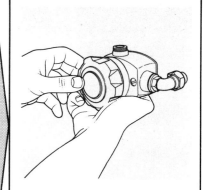

2. Fit the mixer in place to mark the supply pipe positions. Drill holes for the pipes and lay them in position.

87 Shower plumbing

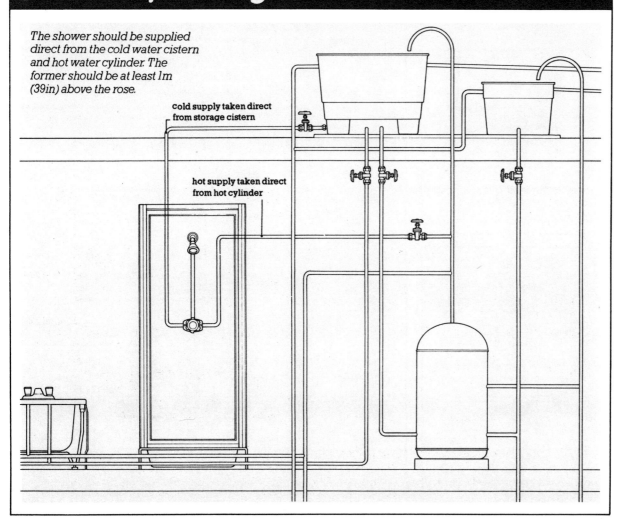

The shower should be supplied direct from the cold water cistern and hot water cylinder. The former should be at least 1m (39in) above the rose.

cold supply taken direct from storage cistern

hot supply taken direct from hot cylinder

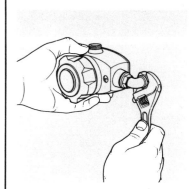

3. Fit the mixer to the backplate and connect the stub pipes to the hot and cold supply pipes.

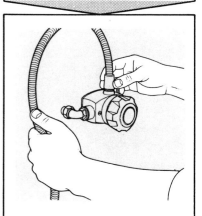

4. Attach the flexible hose to the mixer outlet and connect the other end to the rose (either fixed or adjustable).

If a new shower cubicle is to be installed, the choice is between a cabinet with integral sides and tray or a plastic or ceramic tray with separate side screens.

The screens must be fitted together properly to ensure a watertight seal and they must be sealed to the tray. If an existing wall is used as a cubicle side, it should be tiled.

The tray may need raising on bricks or wooden blocks to make room for the 50mm (2in) shallow seal trap which should be connected to a 38mm waste pipe.

1. Set the shower tray in position and check that it is level. If necessary, you can adjust the feet to set it level.

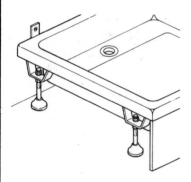

2. If wall brackets are supplied, drill and plug them to the wall. The feet may also fix with screws to the floor.

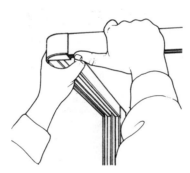

3. Screw the cubicle uprights to the wall and assemble the framework and panels according to the instructions.

4. Use a mastic sealant to seal the joints between the cubicle and the shower tray and between the cubicle and walls.

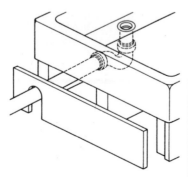

5. If making your own plinth to support the shower tray, incorporate a panel to provide access to the trap.

A waste disposal unit gets rid of a large amount of kitchen waste by grinding it up with water to form a slurry that can be discharged into the waste system. The unit fits between the sink waste outlet and the trap, but needs a larger diameter outlet than normal. This means that it should be fitted in conjunction with a new sink that has the correct outlet, unless the existing sink is of the right type.

The trap should be of the P or S type; not a bottle trap which may become blocked more easily. The unit will also require connecting to a switched fused connection unit for its power supply.

This should be clear of the sink and have a neon indicator to show that the unit has been switched on.

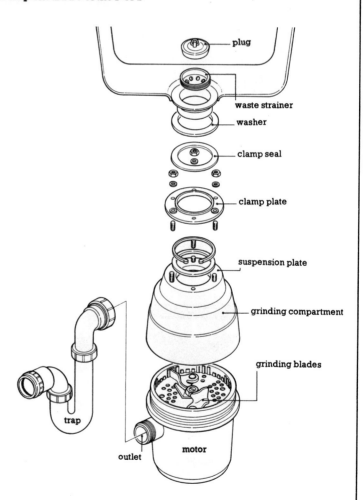

plug
waste strainer
washer
clamp seal
clamp plate
suspension plate
grinding compartment
grinding blades
trap
outlet
motor

The waste disposal unit is held in place by an assembly of clamping plates. The top half incorporates a set of grinding blades which reduce waste to a slurry, while the lower half contains a powerful electric motor to drive the blades.

90 Fitting a waste disposal unit

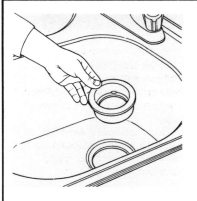

1. Press a layer of plumber's putty around the waste outlet flange and set it in place in the bottom of the sink.

2. Assemble the clamping plates in the correct order and secure them to the waste outlet tail with their circlip.

3. Attach the waste trap to the blade housing, smear its seal with silicone lubricant and bolt it to the clamping plates.

4. Connect the trap to the waste pipe and clip the motor housing to the upper section. Connect the wiring and test the unit.

91 Plumbing in a washing machine

Washing machines are often installed in the kitchen where it is a simple matter to arrange their water supply. The pipes should be terminated with washing machine valves that are threaded to accept the machine's inlet hoses.

The waste pipe should be hooked into a standpipe incorporating a trap to prevent water being siphoned out of the machine when in use. This can discharge over a gully or into a soil stack.

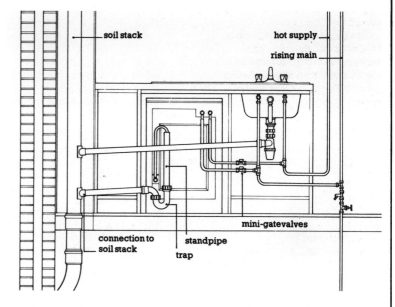

soil stack · hot supply · rising main · connection to soil stack · standpipe · trap · mini-gatevalves

Washing machines are usually near the kitchen sink, so it is convenient to run their branch pipes from the tap supplies.

92 Installing an outside tap

There are many advantages to having a water supply in the garden, and fitting an outdoor tap is simple to do. However, the water authority should be informed before going ahead as it might affect the water rate.

It is usually convenient to supply a garden tap from the rising main, breaking into it just after it enters the house and running a pipe through the outside wall to terminate in a bib tap with hose nozzle. The branch pipe should be fitted with a stop valve so that it can be isolated and drained in winter.

A second tap, connected to the first by a length of black polythene pipe buried underground, can be fitted to the top of a standpipe elsewhere in the garden.

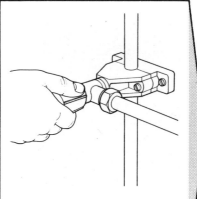

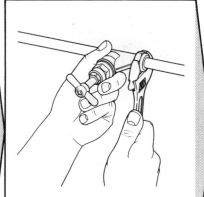

1. A self-boring valve can be used to make the connection between the rising main and branch pipe for the tap.

2. Fit a stop valve in the branch pipe after the rising main connection so that it can be drained in winter.

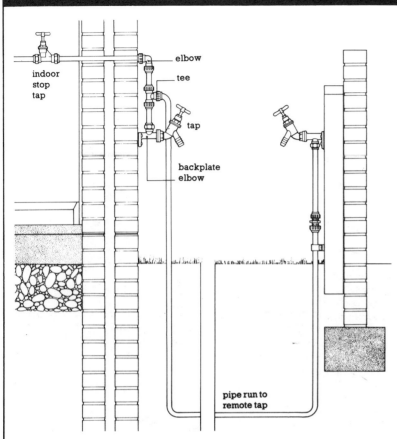

An outside tap should be supplied by a branch from the rising main. Flexible polythene pipe can be connected to the outside pipe with a compression fitting and run underground to a standpipe and tap further down the garden.

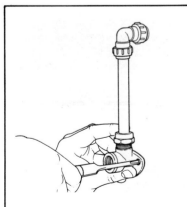

3. Take the pipe through the wall, fit an elbow and run it down to a wall-plate elbow. Fix this in place with screws.

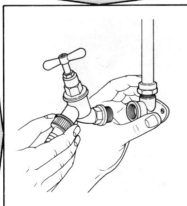

4. Wrap PTFE tape around the tap tail and fit it in place. An inclined bib tap will keep the handle clear of the wall.

Hard water can cause many problems, the mineral salts it contains causing scale build-up on electric heating elements, and inside boilers and radiators. In addition soap will be difficult to lather and baths and basins will need constant cleaning to remove scum marks.

A water softener can prevent the harmful effects of hard water by converting its salts into sodium salts which do no harm. It should be connected into the rising main after the branch to the kitchen cold tap since it is healthier to drink hard water than soft.

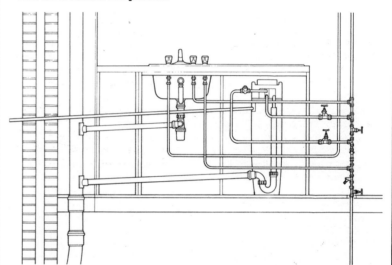

Above: a water softener should be connected into the rising main after the kitchen sink branch. If required, a third tap, supplying softened water, can be fitted at the sink. The overflow pipe is taken through the wall and the waste pipe is hooked into a standpipe and P-trap, the waste pipe running to a gully or soil stack.

Right: water softener fittings. A non-return valve prevents contamination of the kitchen tap supply by water from the softener. A by-pass valve and stop valves in the softener feed and return pipes allow it to be isolated and hard water supplied direct to the cold water storage cistern.

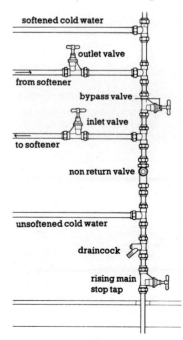

Glossary

Acorn fittings are patented plastic push-fit pipe fittings designed for use with polybutylene and copper pipework.

Ballvalves are valves fitted to storage and WC cisterns to allow them to refill automatically when water is drawn off from them. Various types are available.

Bending springs are flexible springs used to support pipe walls and prevent kinking during pipe-bending operations.

Capillary fittings are copper pipe fittings used to make soldered joints. Most now have integral solder rings; solder has to be added to end-feed types.

Cisterns are storage vessels for cold water – usually in the loft. Small cisterns also supply WCs.

Compression fittings are brass pipe fittings used to make mechanical joints on pipework. They are tightened up with spanners.

Cylinders are storage vessels for hot water, and are supplied in most systems from the loft storage cistern. Most contain a heat exchanger linked to a boiler, or an electric immersion heater.

Drain cocks are small taps fitted at low points on plumbing systems to allow the pipework to be drained for maintenance or repairs.

Gatevalves are valves fitted to low-pressure pipe runs to allow them to be isolated for repair or maintenance. Unlike stoptaps, they can be fitted either way round.

Gullies are in-ground collection points for water from indoor appliances and downpipes. They contain a trap to prevent drain smells from entering the house.

Immersion heaters are electric water heaters installed in hot cylinders to provide a supply of hot water, either on their own or in tandem with a boiler.

Mixer taps have twin inlets for hot and cold water, and one outlet nozzle which may be fixed or moveable. In kitchen mixers the flows are kept separate until the water leaves the nozzle.

Monobloc taps are mixer taps designed to fit a single mounting hole in a bath, basin or bidet. The slim pipe tails are linked to the supply pipework with reducing couplers.

Pillar taps have a vertical water inlet, and are fitted to modern baths, basins, sinks etc.

Pipe clips are made of metal or plastic, and are used to secure pipework to walls or joists.

Rising main is a term used to describe the incoming mains-pressure supply pipe, which enters the house and rises to the storage cistern in the loft.

Single-stack drainage systems take waste water from indoor appliances and WCs direct to the drains via a single stack, which can be installed inside the house.

Solvent-weld fittings are used with a special solvent to make joints in some types of plastic pipework. The special solvent bonds pipe and fitting together permanently.

Stoptaps are fitted to mains-pressure supply pipes to regulate the flow rate and to allow the supply to be shut off for maintenance or repairs. They must be fitted the right way round.

Supataps are taps with a washer and jumper which fall away from the tap seating as the tap is opened. Unlike other types, they can be rewashered without turning off the supply.

Traps are fitted to all water-using appliances to keep drain smells out of the system. Modern traps of plastic can be unscrewed easily for cleaning.

Yorkshire fittings are capillary fittings containing an integral ring of solder, and are simply heated with a blowtorch or special soldering iron to melt the solder and make the joint.

Index

Decorating

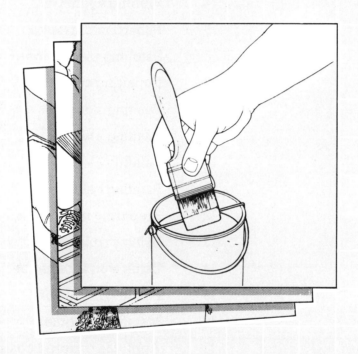

Decorating

Decorating

Thanks to the introduction of modern products and new techniques, home decorating has become a good deal easier in recent years, so much so that even if you have never picked up a paint brush in your life, you can be fairly confident of producing perfectly acceptable results provided you exercise a reasonable degree of care. But that doesn't mean you should forget all the old wisdom and the traditional ways of doing things. Even today a little inside knowledge is frequently essential to produce that really polished, professional finish. And, if you are to avoid a lot of extra unnecessary work – to say nothing of embarrassing mistakes – there are also quite a few 'tricks of the trade' that are well worth picking up. What's more, while modern decorating products are undoubtedly clean and easy to use, it's worth remembering that, in many cases, the old methods are still by far the cheapest.

There are four keys to good decorating – good tools, good materials, thorough preparation, and above all, organization, because working in a muddle is a sure way to a messy finish.

Let's start with tools and equipment. To begin with you need a set of brushes. A pair of flat paint brushes – one 50mm (2in) wide, one 25mm (1in) wide – will cope in most situations,, though a 12mm (½in) brush is handy for fiddly work, and you need a 100 to 150mm (4 to 6in) wall brush for walls and ceilings.

For the preparation, a flat scraper plus a shavehook (a combination type is best) are a must, as are flexible filling knives – one 50mm (2in) or so wide, the other about 25mm (1in) for tight corners. Get either an electric hot air gun or a blowlamp, too, plus abrasive paper, and cleaning equipment: sponges, buckets, and so on.

And access equipment? A step ladder will manage most low-level work, though trestles and scaffold boards are a real boon for some jobs. For high level work, go for an extension ladder, or better still, a scaffold tower. All are widely available for hire.

Materials next, and with paint the usual choice is resin-based gloss for wood and metal; matt or semi-matt emulsion for walls and ceilings. There are other options,

though – resin-based semi-gloss eggshells for walls, and a wide range of special paints for outside walls – so have a good look at what's available before deciding. In particular, look for variations within basic types. For example, there may be a choice between runny paint and jelly-like 'thixotropic' non-drip types.

And, of course, decorating materials don't end with paint. There are wallpapers, vinyl wall-coverings, tiles, wallboards, texturing compounds, floorings – the list could go on and on. Just be sure that, as well as looking good, what you choose wears well and will stand up to conditions such as bathroom dampness.

As for preparation, it's easy. Simply follow any manufacturer's instructions. So long as a surface is clean, dry, and sound, you won't go far wrong.

Which just leaves organization. The trick here is to tackle areas in a sensible order – normally woodwork, ceiling, walls and floor in that order. It also helps to get a clear run at a room by removing all furniture and lifting existing floorings. In practice, though, this is rarely possible, so just move out what you can, and protect the rest with dustsheets, polythene, newspapers and so on, moving furniture into the centre of the room to leave space to work.

① Preparing the room

Empty the room as far as possible, protecting immovable furniture and electrics with dustsheets and polythene, then move in the access equipment – a pair of trestles and a stepladder.

② Preparing paint

Wipe the top of the tin to remove any dust and prise off the lid with, say, an old screwdriver, taking care not to damage it or you won't be able to reseal the tin. Next, cut off any skin that has formed an old paint, throw it away, then stir the paint aiming to blend in any liquid floating on top and any sediment at the bottom. Finally, pour what you need into a clean paint kettle, straining it through old tights to remove lumps. Non-drip paint must be left undisturbed for a while to resume its gel-like consistency.

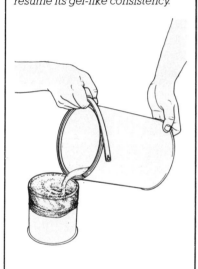

③ Preparing brushes

Before starting work, check that all brushes are clean and in good condition. Proprietary brush restorers may be used to remove paint hardened in the bristles, but there is no guarantee that the result will be fit to use. If the bristles have gone out of shape, the brush is certainly no use for accurate work, so replace it. But don't use a new brush straight away. Wash it out in warm, soapy water to remove dirt, grease and loose bristles. It is also worth 'breaking in' a new brush on priming and undercoating before using it to apply final coats of gloss paint.

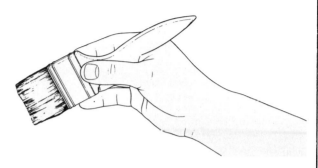

2. It's important to hold the brush correctly. Ordinary flat paint brushes should be gripped pencil fashion with the metal ferrule between the fingers. This gives you much more control than holding the handle, and tends to be a lot less tiring.

1. Flick the bristles between your fingers and work the brush back and forth across your palm to soften it and remove loose hairs.

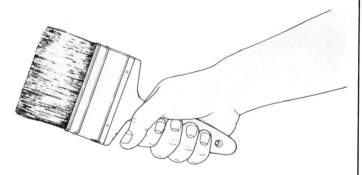

3. Wall brushes tend to be too heavy and unwieldy to grip in this way, so hold them by the handle. This lets you bring all of your arm and shoulder muscles into play, making it easier to achieve the sweeping, strokes needed to paint walls and ceilings.

④ Assessing quantities

To work out how much paint you need, estimate the area to be painted and refer to the chart or to any manufacturer's estimates on the tin. Always buy slightly more than you need, though. The figures are only averages and such factors as surface porosity can have a marked effect on how far paint actually goes. Remember, too, that coverage figures are generally for a single coat, so allow for the fact that most paints need two or three coats for an acceptable finish.

Paint/primer type	Maximum coverage per litre*	
Liquid gloss	16 sq m	(170 sq ft)
Non-drip gloss	14 sq m	(150 sq ft)
Satin gloss	14 sq m	(150 sq ft)
Undercoat	18 sq m	(195 sq ft)
Wood primer	15 sq m	(160 sq ft)
Aluminium primer	15 sq m	(160 sq ft)
Primer/undercoat	15 sq m	(160 sq ft)
Metal primer	16 sq m	(170 sq ft)
Liquid emulsion	15 sq m	(160 sq ft)
Non-drip emulsion	11 sq m	(120 sq ft)
Exterior wall paint	7 sq m	(75 sq ft)
Stabilizing primer	6 sq m	(65 sq ft)

*Depends on roughness and porosity of surface

1 sq m equals: 10-15m (33-50ft) of window stiles, rails and frame. 6m (20ft) of window sill. 15m (50ft) of glazing bars. 10m (33ft) of standard skirting board.

5 Using a brush

Good brush technique is all about obtaining a smooth, even finish using the least amount of paint, and, to that end, there are two major pitfalls to avoid.

First, ensure the section to be painted is clean. If properly prepared it should be free from grease and obvious grime, but any dust that has settled in the meantime must be removed with an old, clean brush or a tack rag – a special cloth obtainable from good decorating suppliers.

Even more important, don't rush things by putting on too much paint in one go. Aim for a fairly thin, even coating, and if that doesn't cover, simply let it dry, rub down lightly with abrasive paper, then re-paint. The one exception here is non-drip paint, this is made to go on fairly thickly, and the finish may be spoilt if it is worked too much with the brush.

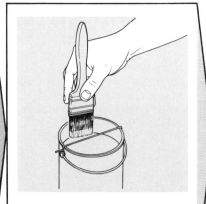

1. To load the brush, simply dip the bristles into the paint so that between a third and one half their length is covered.

2. If using a liquid paint, squeeze the excess from the brush by drawing it over a piece of string stretched across the paint kettle.

6 Painting sequence for doors

Before painting a door, a little extra preparation is called for. Start by removing all the door furniture, including locks and handles, so you will not be slowed up by fiddly 'cutting in' around things you don't want painted. Next, hammer a tapered piece of scrap softwood into the hole left by the door handle. You can then open the door without touching the wet paintwork. Finally, when you are ready to start painting, tap a wooden wedge under the door to hold it slightly ajar.

Large, often complex features such as doors present the painter with something of a problem. If tackled in a random fashion, at least some of the paint will dry around the edges before it can be blended in to the paintwork as a whole. And such 'dry lines' tend to show, even when all the paint has dried, spoiling the finish. To avoid this, mentally divide the door into easy sections and tackle each one in a logical order so that the inevitable 'dry lines' are no longer obvious, being hidden where possible by joints in the woodwork.

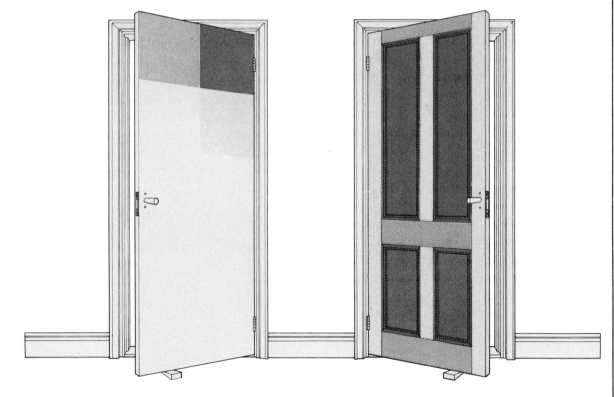

When you are painting flush doors, it is best to tackle them by dividing the area into a series of blocks. As you move on to each successive block, carefully blend the overlap together for a smooth finish.

With a panelled door, start with the mouldings and panels. Then move on to the horizontal cross rails, stopping at the vertical stiles. Finish by painting the stiles and vertical centre rail.

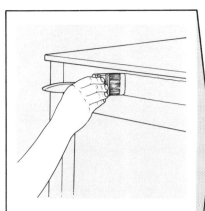

3. Apply the paint to the surface in a series of parallel stripes, working the brush back and forth in the direction of any woodgrain.

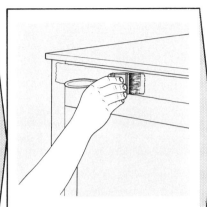

4. When the brush runs dry, work it across the grain to merge the stripes and stop surface defects leaving unpainted 'shadows'.

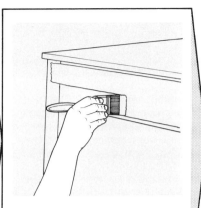

5. Finally, work the brush lightly along the grain for a really smooth finish. You can now reload the brush and paint the next bit.

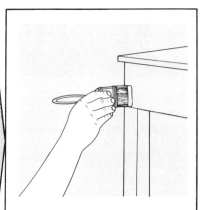

6. Never draw the brush inwards over an edge as this may squeeze out too much paint which could then run.

⑦ *Painting sequence for windows*

Most windows are painted almost like panelled doors, but there is the extra problem of cutting in around the panes. If you don't feel you can manage this neatly, protect the glass with masking tape or a piece of card held next to the brush. Allow a 3mm wide band of paint to stray on to the glass to form a condensation-proof seal. Any other paint that gets on the window should be wiped off with a cloth when wet, or scraped off with a razor blade when fully dry.

Sash windows are especially tricky to paint because one sash always partly covers the other. The trick is to open the window slightly and then paint as much of the both sashes plus the window lining as possible. Once dry, you now simply reposition the sashes to expose the sections you missed. Having painted these you then finish off by painting the window sill and surrounding architraves. There are just two points to watch: don't paint the sash cord pulleys, and don't paint the sash cords themselves because that can weaken them.

1. Position the sashes so the window is partly open with the inner sash at the top. Paint this plus as much of the outer sash and lining as you can see.

2. Reversing the positions of the sashes allows you to complete the outer sash and lining before moving on to tackle the window sill and surrounding architraves.

3. Treat casement windows like panelled doors without panels, leaving the fixed structural frame members, sills and architraves until last.

8 Using a roller

On large, flat areas such as walls and ceilings, paint rollers tend to be both quicker and less tiring than brushes. Most consist of a stout wire frame with a handle at one end and a detachable revolving drum fitted with a roller sleeve at the other, and it is this sleeve that largely determines the finish.

The main options are sheepskin, foam plastic, and synthetic fibre. Traditionally, resin-based paints are applied with natural sleeves, emulsions with synthetic ones, but in practice many modern synthetic fibre sleeves cope well with both. Sleeve choice is also affected by the type of surface being painted – on heavily textured surfaces you need a long piled sleeve to achieve good coverage. Specially durable versions are available to cope with rough exterior walls.

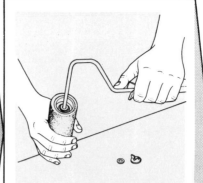

1. As a single integral unit, slide the sleeve assembly on to the frame and secure with a washer and wing nut.

2. With other roller designs, the sleeves come as hollow tubes that you just slip over the roller frame's metal cage.

9 Using a paint pad

Paint pads offer another alternative to brushes. Sold separately or in kits (complete with special loading tray) they consist of a short piled fibre pad on a plastic backing plate complete with handle, and come in a choice of shapes and sizes roughly equivalent to various types of paint brush. They are best used with emulsion – cleaning out resin-based paint tends to be a rather messy job.

1. Having poured a small quantity of paint into the loading tray's reservoir, dip the pad in so that its pile is only just covered.

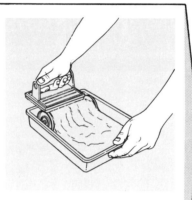

2. Remove excess paint from the pad by running it back and forth across the grooved roller fitted to the tray for the purpose.

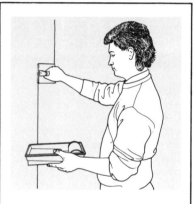

3. Without pressing too hard, apply the paint with smooth downward strokes, in a series of overlapping stripes.

10 Using a spray gun

In theory, there is no faster way to paint than with a spray gun, but since masking off areas you don't want painted is quite time-consuming, you will only reap the full benefits of the technique on large, straightforward areas or small individual items.

Suitable spraying equipment is available from tool hire shops, the choice being between 'scent spray' style guns run off an air compressor, and airless guns which pump paint out as a fine mist. However, the type of paint you intend using must be taken into account, because some (notably for exterior walls) need a special type of gun. Whatever you get, make sure it comes with full operating instructions. Pay special attention to any on thinning down the paint. Most guns cannot spray domestic gloss and emulsion in its natural state – it's too thick.

1. Having thinned the paint as directed, pour it into the gun's detachable reservoir, then screw this back on to the gun.

2. Before starting work, spray a piece of old newspaper to check that the nozzle is clear and that the gun works properly.

3. Pour paint into the deep end of the roller tray until the paint level just starts to creep up on to the sloping section.

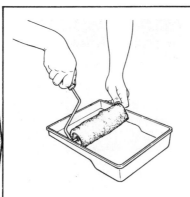

4. To charge the roller, run it into the paint reservoir then remove the excess by rolling it up and down the ramp several times.

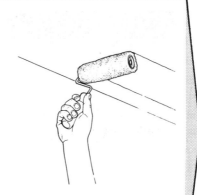

5. Paint a border strip as close to the edge of the area as possible. The unpainted gap may be filled in later with a brush.

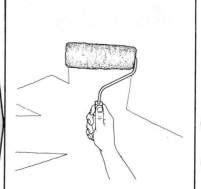

6. Cover the rest of the area with criss-cross strokes, taking care not to work so fast that the roller sprays paint everywhere.

⑪ Viscosity

Accuracy is of the utmost importance when thinning paint for spraying. If it's too thin it may give a poor finish; too thick and the gun may simply refuse to work. To check that you have got it just right, use a viscosity cup — basically a special funnel. Simply pour a measured quantity into the cup and see how long it takes to drain out. Thin paint flows proportionally faster than thick paint.

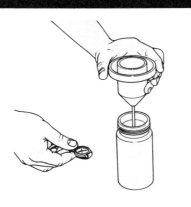

⑫ Masking room for spraying

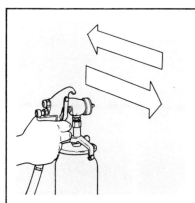

3. Spray a series of overlapping stripes with the gun at a constant distance from the surface. Switch off at the end of each stripe.

4. A box will bring small items up to a comfortable working height. Protect the surrounding area with newspaper.

Before spraying, cover areas you don't want painted with newspaper or polythene and masking tape. On large areas like floors, only mask the edges — modern guns are quite accurate so in a well-ventilated room the spray shouldn't stray too far.

⑬ Paperhanging equipment

For measuring and cutting you need a tape measure, a rule or straightedge, a pencil, a sharp knife, and a pair of long bladed scissors. For pasting, you need a plastic bucket, some suitable paste, and a wall brush. To hang the paper, use a seam roller, a paperhanging brush (or a sponge for ready-pased vinyl), plus either a plumb-line or a spirit-level with a vertical vial. And, of course, you need a pair of steps, ideally paired with a trestle, and a scaffold board.

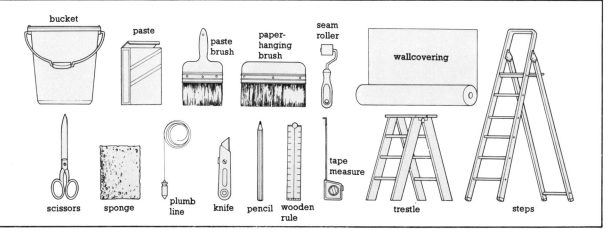

bucket
paste
paste brush
paper-hanging brush
seam roller
wallcovering

scissors
sponge
plumb line
knife
pencil
wooden rule
tape measure
trestle
steps

⑭ Estimating quantities

Most wallcoverings come in rolls about 10m long and 530mm wide. To work out how many rolls you need, simply measure both the average wall height above the skirting board, and the total length of wall to be papered (including doors and windows), then refer to the chart on the right. Add an extra roll or two to the result to allow for wastage if using a paper with a large distance between pattern repeats.

Wall height from skirting in metres	Measurement round room (including doors and windows) in metres												
	9	10	11	12	13	14	15	16	17	18	19	20	22
2.0 to 2.2	4	4	5	5	5	6	6	6	6	7	7	8	9
2.2 to 2.4	4	4	5	5	6	6	6	7	7	8	8	9	9
2.4 to 2.6	4	5	5	6	6	7	7	8	8	9	9	10	10
2.6 to 2.8	5	5	6	6	7	7	8	8	9	9	10	11	12
2.8 to 3.0	5	5	6	7	7	8	8	9	9	10	11	12	13

⑮ Cutting and pasting

The most important point to watch when pasting is that you use the right paste. Ordinary paste is suitable only for fairly light wallpapers. For heavier wallcoverings, use a heavy-duty paste – one containing fungicide if hanging washable or vinyl wallcoverings. All come ready-to-use or as a powder you mix with water.

The second thing to remember is that, once pasted, the paper must be put aside to soak for a few minutes – the thicker it is the longer it needs. The idea is to leave the paper pliable enough to hang easily, yet not so soft that it tears at the slightest excuse. Try to paste in batches so that as you finish pasting the last drop, the first is ready to hang. Similarly, when hanging, try to pace yourself so that as you finish putting up one drop, the next is just ready to go up.

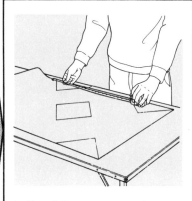

1. Carefully measure the height of the first drop, then add an extra 50mm or so at top and bottom to allow for trimming.

2. Cut the first drop squarely to length, and use it as a guide to cutting the remaining drops, matching the pattern as you go.

You will find pasting much easier if you work on a proper pasting table. These are exactly the right size to hold most of a typical paper 'drop.' Made from hardboard and softwood, they are fairly cheap and normally fold up for easy storage and transport. In most designs, the hinged top forms a sort of case containing the legs, so just open it up, swing the legs into position, and secure them with the hinged stays or stiff wire props provided.

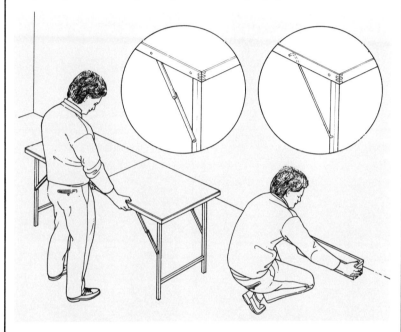

To prepare ready-pasted papers, simply soak them in a purpose-made plastic trough about half full of water. If you are working upstairs, you can soak cut lengths in the bath and use the trough to carry them to the wall where they are to be hung.

It is normally best to start papering at one end of a nice long, uncomplicated wall to get your hand in before tackling any tricky sections. The wall next to the main door is usually a good choice. Where this means cutting the very first drop in around a light switch, simply ignore it and begin by hanging what should be the wall's second drop. You can return to hang the drop containing the light switch when you feel more confident.

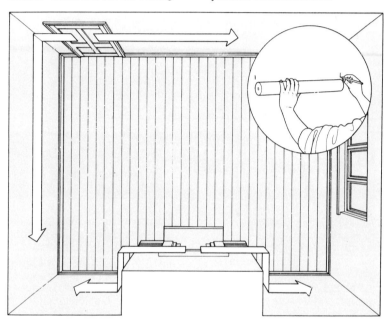

If you're using a plain paper or one with a small pattern, start paper-hanging next to the room door. With large pattern motifs, start by centring the design on the chimney breast. Use a roll of paper as a gauge to ensure that you avoid narrow corner pieces.

3. Starting in the centre of the paper, apply the paste making sure you cover every part with a liberal coating.

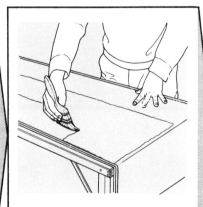

4. To paste the edge, align it with the table edge and work the brush out across it to keep paste off the patterned side.

5. When you have pasted all you can, fold the paper in half, paste side to paste side, and pull the rest of the drop on to the table.

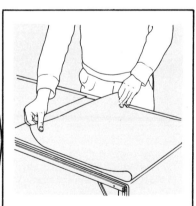

6. Paste this section in exactly the same way, then fold it in half and put the drop to one side in order to soak and soften.

A ruler, soft pencil, and a tile cutter — either a simple tiler's spike or a more complex device that helps you mark out and snap tiles — forms the basic tiling kit. Add pincers, something to measure right-angles, a spirit level, some timber battens, plus a hammer and nails, and you can cope with almost any tiling job. Plastic serrated spreaders for grout and adhesive are often supplied with the pack, and where you need tile spacers, instead of buying you can use matchsticks or thick card.

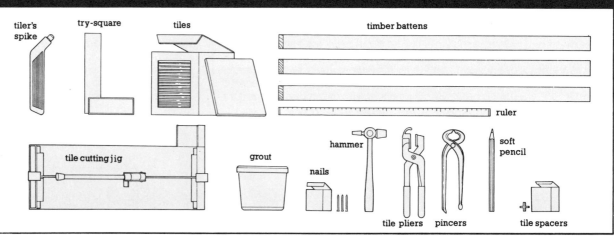

One big difference between professional tiling and the average amateur effort is that professionals take a lot of trouble setting out – deciding beforehand how each tile should fit on to the wall with a fair degree of accuracy.

There are two reasons why this is so important. Firstly, the more symmetrical the arrangement, the better it looks. Secondly, and just as important, setting out shows up potential practical snags – the need for impossibly narrow tiles around the tiled area's perimeter, for example, or the need for intricately shaped tiles to fit round obstacles such as pipes. Having identified the problems, on small tiled areas it is normally easy to avoid them. Just alter the position of the first row of tiles – half a tile width up, down, or sideways often does the trick.

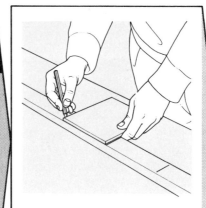

1. For accurate setting out you need a tile gauge – a long timber batten stepped off in nominal tile widths (tile plus 3mm grout).

2. Properly set out, any area of tiling should be symmetrical, and free from awkwardly narrow or awkwardly shaped cut tiles.

In principle, setting out tiled walls is no different to setting out a splashback. Your aim is to find a symmetrical arrangement that avoids difficult cutting. Unfortunately, this is not so easy.

To begin with, whole walls tend to contain more obstacles, and a good arrangement for one obstacle may spoil the tiling around another. Several tiles may be needed to find a compromise. Ensuring cut tiles at the wall's edges are reasonably wide (no less than 25mm) and looking balanced can also be tricky, particularly if the wall is badly out of square.

And when tiling a whole room, you must remember to allow for the affect of such cut tiles at corners. In some cases, using off-cuts from one wall to turn a corner looks best; in others it is better to treat the walls as separate symmetrical entities.

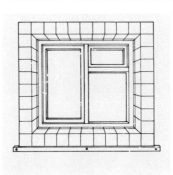

1. Walls containing a window look best with the tiling centred around the window's middle – visually a natural focal point.

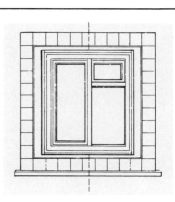

2. Don't forget to work out how the tiling on the wall will affect the practicality and neatness of the tiling into any window recess.

The simplest way to work out how many tiles you need is to measure the height and width of the area to be tiled, not with a tape measure, but with a long timber batten stepped off in nominal tile widths/heights — that's the actual tile size plus a 3mm allowance for grouting. Round up each dimension to the next whole tile to allow for cutting, multiply width and height together, and you have the total number of tiles required. But do buy a few extra — just in case.

Tile size	Area to be covered (sq m)									
	1	2	3	4	5	6	7	8	9	10
100 x 100mm	100	200	300	400	500	600	700	800	900	1000
108 x 108mm	90	175	260	345	430	515	600	690	775	860
150 x 150mm	45	90	135	180	225	270	315	355	400	445
200 x 100mm	50	100	150	200	250	300	350	400	450	500
300 x 300mm	12	23	34	45	56	67	78	89	100	112

All quantities except for 300 x 300mm tiles are rounded up to next 5.

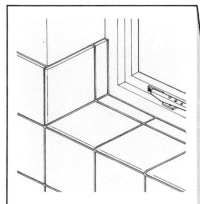

3. For neatness, window sills and reveals need whole edging tiles along the front edge, so arrange for cut tiles to fall at the back.

4. Mark the tiling's centre line using basins and so on as a guide, then measure out from this to find the sides of the splashback.

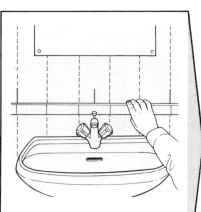

5. Using the gauge, see how the tile columns fit in. Is the tiling better centred around a line of whole tiles or a vertical join?

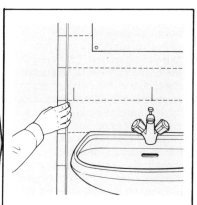

6. Next, set the row positions. It's easier with whole tiles at the bottom, but ensure this doesn't leave awkward cut tiles above.

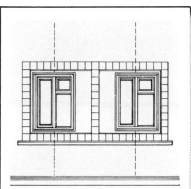

3. If a wall contains a pair of windows, centre the tiling around a point mid-way between their individual centres.

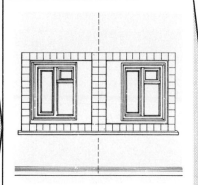

4. In some cases, it may be easier to position a grout line at the centre of the tiling, rather than a column of whole tiles.

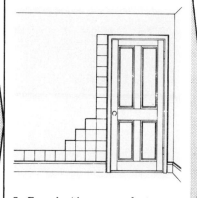

5. Faced with a corner feature such as a door, it is often easiest to start tiling around the feature, then work outwards from there.

6. Support the lowest row of whole tiles on battens until the adhesive sets. Remove and fill in with cut tiles later.

Provided existing paintwork is in good condition, there is usually no need to remove it. Just rub it down with wet-and-dry abrasive paper (used wet), then wash it with warm water and detergent. Where you must remove old paint and varnish – because it is in very poor condition, or because you want a different sort of finish – the basic strategy is to soften it using a blowlamp, a hot air stripper or some form of chemical paint stripper, then to scrape it off.

Hot air strippers (a bit like powerful hair driers) and gas blowlamps are best for general work. They are quick and fairly cheap to use. Where they are not so good is on fiddly items such as furniture and in preparing for a transparent finish such as varnish – blowlamps may leave scorch marks. Here use a chemical stripper. Liquid strippers are normally cheapest, but powder types tend to be better on mouldings. However, do follow the maker's safety instructions to the letter – many contain strongly corrosive chemicals.

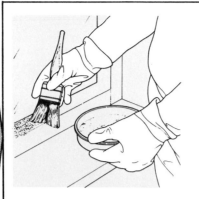

1. Wearing rubber gloves and long sleeves for protection, dab the liquid stripper liberally on to the surface with an old brush.

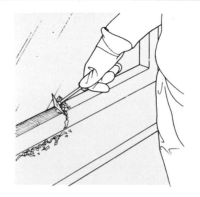

2. Allow the stripper to work before attempting to scrape off the softened paint. Scrub out mouldings with wire wool.

3. Re-treat any paint that's left, then wash the surface to neutralize the stripper using water or white spirit as directed.

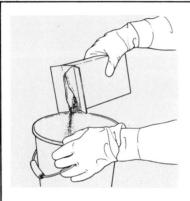

1. Carefully mix the powder with water, following manufacturer's instructions, to form a smooth, fairly thick paste.

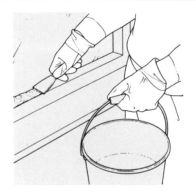

2. Using a filling knife, apply a thick layer of paste to the surface, and leave to soften the paint for an hour or two.

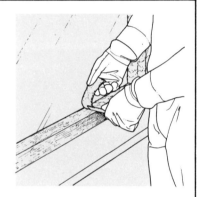

3. The stripper poultice should now peel off in sheets, bringing the paint with it. Wash with water to remove any surface residue.

1. Play the stream of hot air over the surface until the paint softens and bubbles. Fit a deflector shield when working near glass.

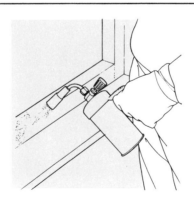

2. Blowlamps are meant to soften paint with the flame's heat, not burn it off, so keep the flame moving lightly over the surface.

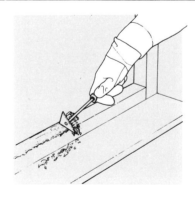

3. Keep the paint soft but avoid burning the wood. Tackle small stubborn patches later with glasspaper.

4. If you're stripping an area with delicate mouldings, tackle these first to avoid charring the surrounding flat surfaces.

23 Stripping wallpaper

Although, theoretically, there are times when you can redecorate over old wallpaper, it is always a risky business, so play safe and strip it off.

The basic technique is to soak the paper with water to soften both it and the paste holding it in place. It should then be a relatively easy (if messy) task to remove it with a scraper. One tip: regularly sweep the peelings into plastic sacks before they get

trodden through the house.

But there is a snag. Washable and painted wallcoverings are impervious to water, so you have to score through the surface to let the water reach the paste. Life is easier with vinyl wallcovering. With this the vinyl surface layer peels off to expose the layer of plain backing paper beneath. Strip this off in the usual way, or leave in place to act as lining paper.

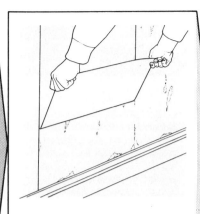

1a. On vinyls, pick away a corner of the top layer, then peel it away in one piece. The paper beneath may be stripped or left.

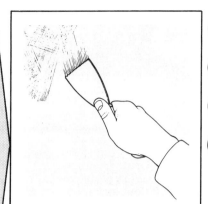

1b. With other washables and painted papers, scratch the surface using a special serrated scraper.

1. Soak the paper with water applied using a brush, sponge or garden spray. The latter gives better penetration.

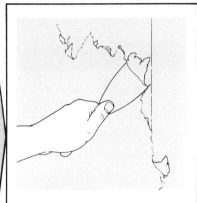

2. Leave the paper and paste to soften then, starting in one corner, scrape off using a stiff, broad-bladed scraper.

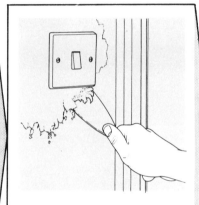

3. Keep water way from electrical fittings. Scrape round these dry, but take care not to damage the surface of the plaster.

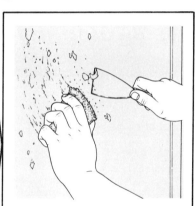

4. Finally, thoroughly wash the wall, scraping off any tiny flecks of paper. Sand off any small bits that still refuse to budge.

24 Steam strippers

If you want to strip a lot of wallpaper very quickly, consider using a steam stripper. In principle, this is rather like a giant steam iron — a portable electric boiler providing the necessary steam via a hose. Not only does steam penetrate paper more efficiently than water, but also it breaks down paste in no time at all. Available from good tool hire shops, the stripper's only drawback is that you do need to strip rather a lot of paper to make renting worthwhile.

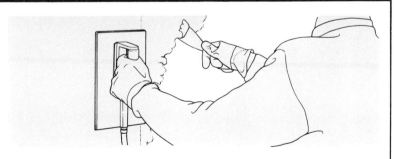

One reason why steam strippers are so fast is that having steamed one section of paper, you can get on with stripping it off while

steaming the next. Alternatively, have a helper take charge of the steaming while you follow on with the scraper.

25 Wetting agents

To speed the soaking process add a proprietary wetting agent or a few drops of washing-up liquid to the water to improve penetration.

26 Filling small cracks

Most small cracks in walls and ceilings are nothing to worry about – they are usually due to small, natural structural movements – but they should be filled before redecorating, particularly if you intend painting the bare plaster.

Proprietary filler is best for this – interior and exterior grades come either ready-mixed or (more cheaply) as a powder you mix with water. However, some defects need a special filler. For cracks between masonry and woodwork (round door frames for example) use flexible mastic or caulking, because such cracks tend to open and close as the wood expands and contracts with the weather. Similarly, ordinary fillers work out too expensive for large cracks and holes. Fill the bulk with a cheap repair plaster, then finish off with ordinary filler.

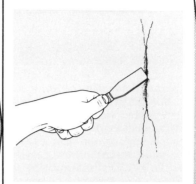

1. Rake out the crack with a filling knife, slightly undercutting the surrounding sound plaster to help the repair grip.

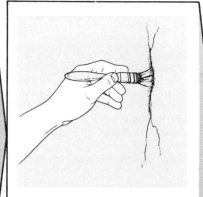

2. Next use an old, clean, dry brush to sweep out any dust and other debris that might prevent the filler adhering.

27 Patching plasterboard

Because plasterboard is just a finish for rough masonry and timber framed partition walls and ceilings, there is nothing behind most sheets but a void. This makes repairing defects quite difficult because, instead of filling the crack or hole, any filer tends to drop straight through. On small holes you can often get round the problem by using tape or mesh to hold the filler in place, but with larger holes it may be necessary to replace the damaged section completely.

A partition wall is constructed on a timber framework of studs and noggins, or plasterboard may be fitted on a framework attached to a solid wall. When repairing larger areas, the damaged section must be cut back to the centres of the vertical studs. You can roughly locate the studs by tapping along the wall. Then punch through with a nail to mark each side of the stud and draw a line between them. To avoid replacing an unnecessarily large area, you may need to screw additional noggins to the exposed studs to support the repair patch.

For small holes in plasterboard, chip off any surface plaster skim. Cover the hole with scrim tape, sticking it in position with filler. You can then apply more filler until it is flush with the surrounding surface.

For larger areas of damage, cut back to the vertical studs. Fit additional noggins to support the patch. Cut the patch to size and nail in place with galvanized nails. Then fill the joint around the edges.

3. It is a good idea to dampen the crack with a plant spray in order to stop the filler drying too quickly and dropping out.

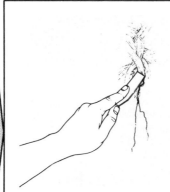

4. Press the filler well into the crack, smoothing it off just proud of the surrounding wall to allow for shrinkage during drying.

5. Once the filler has set hard, complete the repair by rubbing it down with fine glasspaper until flush with surrounding plaster.

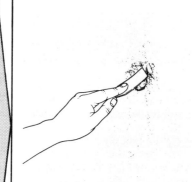

6. Fill deep cracks and holes in two or more easy stages. If you put in too much wet filler in one go it will probably sag.

Repairing corners

While the technique is basically the same as for cracks in flat walls, chipped corners are especially difficult to repair because, as well as leaving the walls smooth and flat, you must ensure they meet at a neat right angle. Fortunately, where the damage is fairly minor, you will probably manage this quite well working free-hand. Just let the filler start to harden before forming the corner, and tackle the final shaping with glasspaper once it has completely set.

Unfortunately, the more seriously damaged the corner, the harder free-hand repairs become – the filler simply sags leaving the corner worse than ever. In most cases, the answer is to use a little temporary formwork – a timber batten, in fact – to both hold the filler in position, and help form a neat corner. On vulnerable, frequently damaged corners, it may also be worth building in a short length of metal reinforcement to preserve the corner. You will find purpose-made strips available from builder's merchants.

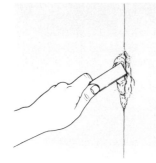

1. If the corner is only slightly damaged, apply filler in the normal way, shaping it as best you can with the filling knife.

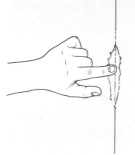

2. Once the filler has begun to harden, start shaping the corner more accurately. You may find this easier using your finger.

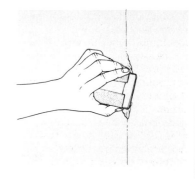

3. After the filler has set hard, use glasspaper to remove any excess and complete the shaping of the corner.

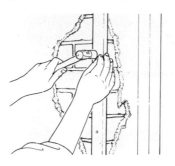

4. Tackle larger repairs one wall at a time. Start by nailing a batten to the the first wall to define the finished edge of the repair.

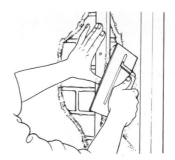

5. Apply filler or plaster to the other wall and smooth it off level with the batten and surrounding plaster using a float or trowel.

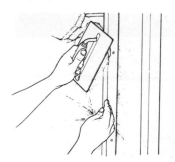

6. Remove the batten once the filler is hard and fill the remaining wall in the same way, using the batten as a guide.

As with all gloss painting, when painting a door it's important to prepare the surface thoroughly. If existing paint is in good condition, simply scrape off any loose flakes, then sand the rest with wet and dry abrasive paper (used wet), before washing it down with warm water and detergent. If, however, the paint is in generally poor condition, or if the sheer thickness of accumulated layers makes the door stick, strip back to bare wood and start from scratch.

Faced with a bare wooden door, start by rubbing the surface down with glasspaper until smooth. Begin with a coarse paper, then work through medium and fine grades for the best results. Rub down mouldings with wire wool. Now for the painting. Seal any knots with proprietary knotting compound, then paint the whole door with a thin coat of wood primer, followed by one of undercoat, and two or three of gloss. Allow each coat to dry thoroughly, before lightly rubbing it down with glasspaper ready for the next.

Having removed any door furniture, wedge the door partly open, and paint the various sections in the order given in project 6. Be sure to paint the edges the right colour. The rule is to open the door, and paint each edge to match the door's face and surround as seen from the room that particular edge faces.

Don't forget to paint the door's top edge. Just make sure the surface is absolutely clean and free from dust first.

Tapping a tapered spike of scrap wood into the hole left by the handle lets you open and close the door avoiding the wet paint.

To hold the door steady while you work, wedge it partly open with a piece of scrap softwood tapped firmly into place.

Divide walls into a series of squares, each of about a square metre (or square yard), and then tackle these one after the other, allowing the paint on each square to slightly overlap with the next. Start in the top right-hand corner of the wall (top left if you are left-handed) and work across and down. When you have finished, neatly cut in the paintwork around the edges using a smaller brush.

Starting in an upper corner, divide the wall into imaginary squares and paint them one at a time, carefully blending each

square into the surrounding new paintwork. At this stage, don't attempt to paint right up to the edges of the wall with the large

wall brush. Leave that until last, carefully cutting in around adjacent walls, ceilings, and woodwork with a smaller brush.

31 Painting a window

In most respects, windows are treated in the same way as any other surface: ensure the surface is clean, dry, and smooth, then build a uniform paint film with primer, undercoat, and two or more coats of gloss. But windows do present a couple of special problems. Firstly, check any putty and replace if unsound. Secondly, pay special attention to preparing the wood around panes of glass – condensation often lifts the paint film there and begins to rot the timber.

For the rest, the process is similar to painting a door. Remove stays, catches, and other window furniture, then prop the window partly open and tackle the various sections in the order given in project 7. Of course, there is the problem of cutting in neatly around the panes of glass, but with care and practice you should be able to manage. To be sure, though, consider protecting the edges of each pane with masking tape, positioned to allow a 3mm wide band of paint on to the glass in order to form a seal against condensation.

Because you must open windows to paint them, work on a reasonably fine day, preferably in daylight. You will be able to see what you are doing much better in daylight, your new paint will not be spoilt by incoming rain, and you won't find the room filled with moths and so on attracted by the light.

Neatly cutting in around panes of glass takes care and practice, so to guarantee perfection protect the pane with masking tape.

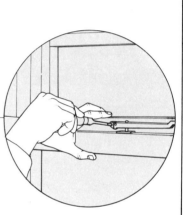

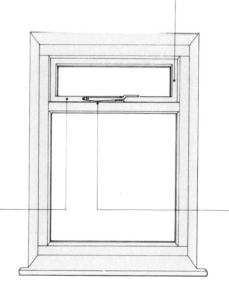

Wedge side-hung casements open as you would a door. Top-hung windows must be propped open with scrap wood.

Remove window stays, catches, and other hardware before painting, refixing them when the final coat of paint is dry.

32 Painting ceilings

For the best results, ceilings should be painted in strips, working outwards from the wall containing the room's largest window. In this way, brush marks, 'dry lines' and so on are less obvious. And try not to get in a mess. Avoid overloading the brush, and don't work it so fast that it flicks paint everywhere, nor so hard that paint works into the metal ferrule – from there it soon trickles down the handle.

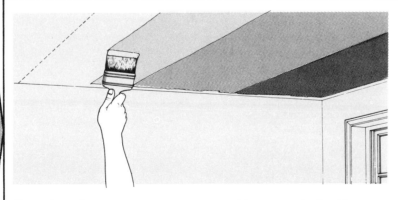

Cover the ceiling in a series of parallel, overlapping strips, starting along the wall containing the room's main window and

working outwards. Any 'dry lines' and brush marks are then less likely to be picked out in daylight. As when painting walls,

finish off by neatly cutting in around light fittings, the edges of the ceiling and so on using a smaller paint brush.

33 Preparing metalwork

When preparing metalwork for painting, the most important thing is to remove all traces of rust. Don't simply confine your efforts to obvious rusty patches. Check for rust beneath the existing paint film – this will generally have started to lift and blister. Scrub off the bulk of the rust with a wire brush, clean up with wire wool or wet and dry abrasive paper, then apply a proprietary rust cure.

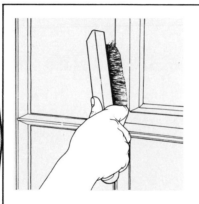

1. Scrape off any blistered or flaking paint and remove as much of the loose rust as you can using a coarse wire brush.

2. Finish cleaning up the metal with wire wool, removing every trace of rust. Fill any noticeable pock marks with car body filler.

3. As soon as you have finished cleaning and repairing the metal, brush on a proprietary anti-rust treatment, then prime.

34 Using varnish

Whether using traditional indoor varnish, a durable exterior one such as yacht varnish, or one of the modern, harder wearing polyurethanes (sold in a variety of interior and exterior grades) the basic application technique is the same. Seal the surface with a coat thinned with a little white spirit, then brush on at least two finishing coats, lightly rubbing down each one before applying the next.

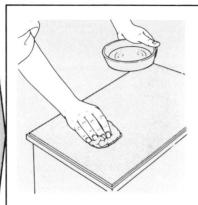

1. Prime the surface using varnish thinned with a little white spirit; working this into the wood grain with a soft, lint-free cloth.

2. Because the priming coat tends to raise the timber grain, sand the surface when dry with medium grade glasspaper.

3. Subsequent coats of varnish (at least two) are applied with a brush. Let each dry, then rub down before applying the next.

35 Using wood stains

Used mainly to improve the look of stripped softwoods, these spirit-based or water-based dyes come in a variety of woody shades (mainly imitating hardwoods) plus a few primary colours. Intermediate shades can be obtained by mixing stains (ideally from the brand range). Colour can also be affected by the way the stain is put on – the more you use, the darker the colour – so take care to apply them evenly. What's more, the wood's natural colour also makes a contribution to the finished results (it shows through all but the thickest, darkest stain), so allow for this when choosing. As a rule, it is best to start off light, and gradually darken the stain to obtain the exact colour you want. Finally, remember that stains have no protective value. When you have finished, the wood must be varnished in the normal way.

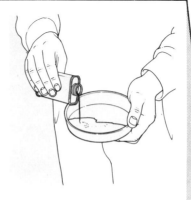

1. Don't attempt to use stain straight from the can. Instead pour a small quantity into an old saucer or similar container.

2. Wearing rubber gloves to avoid staining your skin, lightly charge a wad of clean, lint-free cloth with stain from the saucer.

Wait for a warm, dry day to paint metalwork because of the risk of condensation stopping the paint sticking properly. Even in good weather, wipe the surface with a dry, lint-free cloth before painting, just in case.

You should also take extra care to build up a durable, continuous primer/undercoat/gloss paint film, tricky though that can be on some work. Where paint forms the metal's only protection against rust, severe damage can result if any moisture at all penetrates as the corrosion spreads beneath surrounding paintwork.

Use the correct type of paint. Ordinary resin-based gloss is normally fine as a finishing coat (though on radiators and so on consider a heat-resistant type), but you must be sure to use the correct primer to prevent unwanted chemical reactions.

There is a wide range of primers available for use on metal, and to get good results it's important to choose the correct primer for the metal you're treating. The chart below lists the various types of primer commonly available, and tells you which one goes where.

Note that metals such as copper, brass and lead need no priming before decorating. Copper and brass can be painted directly. Lead should be allowed to weather for several months first.

Type of primer	Used on
Calcium plumbate	Iron, steel, new galvanised surfaces outdoors
Zinc, phosphate	Ferrous and non-ferrous metals, aluminium alloys
Zinc chromate	Aluminium alloys and other non-ferrous metals
	Iron and steel indoors (lead-free finish)
Red lead	All types of iron and steel outdoors
Aluminium spirit-based sealer	Bitumen-coated metalwork

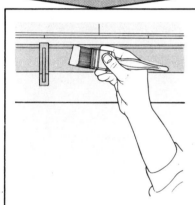

1. Wipe the surface dry, and apply a normal covering coat of the correct primer for the particular metal being painted.

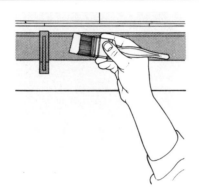

2. Once the primer has dried, lightly rub down with wet and dry abrasive (used dry) before brushing on the undercoat.

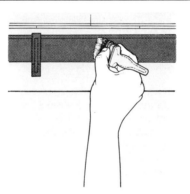

3. Finish off with two or more coats of gloss, allowing each to dry before rubbing down the surface and applying the next.

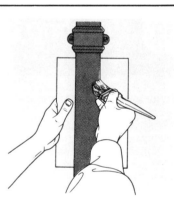

4. Don't forget to paint the backs of pipes fixed to the wall. A piece of scrap card stops stray paint spoiling the wall's finish.

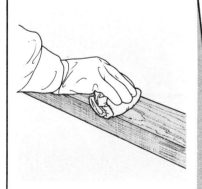

3. Carefully wipe the stain over the surface of the wood, applying even pressure throughout to produce a thin even coating.

4. To avoid smears and local dark patches, wipe off any excess stain with a clean lint-free cloth before it can soak into the wood.

5. Apply subsequent coats in the same way as the first, gradually deepening the finish until the desired affect is achieved.

6. Staining usually swells the grain, roughening the surface, so once the stain has dried, sand down before varnishing.

38 Applying textured coatings

As well as offering a decorative alternative to plain colour and pattern, textured coatings make a very good cover-up for walls and ceilings which, while basically sound, are not in good condition. There are several types to choose from, ranging from plaster-like compounds that come as a powder you mix with water, to what are essentially little more than thickened emulsion paints. The former gives a deeper texture, but normally needs painting to protect it from atmospheric moisture and dirt.

But whatever you use, there is just one snag – removing textured finishes is a difficult, messy job, even with the special stripping agents now on the market. So think carefully before using them, and stick to fairly restrained patterns – you are less likely to get bored with them.

1. Mix up as much as you can apply in a reasonable time, following the instructions, and pour into a roller tray.

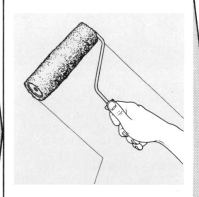

2. Apply a fairly thick coating to the surface using the roller. Don't worry about texturing. Just obtain a good, even coverage.

39 Painting a mural

Murals provide another simple way to give walls a really individual look. Even if you doubt your ability to draw, you can still obtain good results by sticking to straightforward geometric designs, or by copying pictures from photographs. Simply draw a grid over the picture to be copied, draw a scaled-up version of that grid on the wall, then use the grid squares as a guide to transferring the design's main outlines. Alternatively, work from a slide so you can project the image directly on to the wall and trace round it.

Once you have the outline, painting the mural is easy enough. Ordinary emulsion paint (left-overs will do) is quite suitable and is easily mixed to extend the colour range. You may also come across special dyes for tinting emulsion paint.

40 Mural finishes

1. Draw the outlines in soft pencil, black felt tip, or charcoal. The latter is easier to rub out, but may discolour the paint.

2. When you are satisfied, 'fix' the outline by painting it with a coat of clear varnish, thinned with a little white spirit.

1. To copy a picture on to the wall, cover the wall with a grid drawn in pencil with the aid of a long batten and spirit-level.

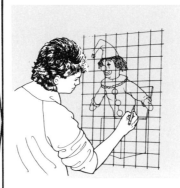

2. Draw a square grid on the picture to be enlarged and use the grid squares as a guide to transfer the outlines on to wall.

3. Use ordinary brushes for large areas; artist's brushes for small ones. Start painting by blocking in the basic shapes.

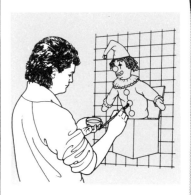

4. Finish off by adding the details and colour variations. An old cup is handy for mixing up small quantities of paint.

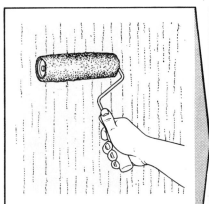

3. For a very simple effect, all you do now is run over the compound with a foam roller, working it in vertical stripes.

4. Use a small brush to 'cut in' around electrical fittings and so on, reproducing the roller's texture as closely as possible.

42 Six common textures

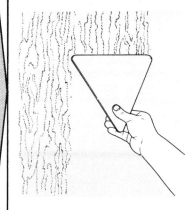

1. Lightly drawing a flat plastic scraper (usually obtainable from the manufacturer) over the surface gives a subtle bark effect.

2. For a traditional rough stucco finish, roughly sculpt the surface with the edge and tip of the triangular scraper.

3. Serrated scrapers can be used to create a variety of ribbed effects including basketweaves, and overlapping arcs.

4. For a stipple finish, just press a sponge on to the surface, then lift it off. Wrap the sponge in plastic for more pronounced peaks.

5. An ordinary sponge can also be used to produce a circular motif — the coarser the sponge the more marked the effect.

6. Special rollers are available for designs such as this diamond pattern. Alternatively, wrap string round an ordinary sponge roller.

41 Drawing up a mural

Draw wall and picture grids as accurately as possible — the smaller the squares the more accurate the results. Squares containing a lot of detail can be sub-divided if required.

There are many differences between painting walls indoors and out. To begin with, you must use the right paint. Those based on exterior emulsion (often with fillers to bridge cracks) are most convenient because you can clean equipment with water. There is the problem of access, too. A scaffold tower normally makes a better working platform than an extension ladder.

The roughness of exterior walls can also give trouble, making it difficult (and tiring) to obtain a good, even coverage, as well as wearing out ordinary brushes and rollers very quickly. Finally, there is the sheer size of the area to be painted. Fast painting techniques are clearly an advantage here, but even so don't try to do too much in one go. Break the job up into small sections so you can spread the work over a number of days.

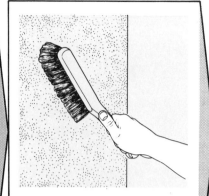

1. Painting with a brush is simplest, but is slow and tiring. Use cheap dustpan brushes on textured surfaces.

2. Roller painting is quicker but can give poor coverage on very rough walls. Use extra durable sleeves – ordinary ones wear out.

Where possible, take advantage of architectural features such as windows, doors, drainpipes and so on when deciding how to split the wall into manageable areas for painting. The various sections are then easier to identify, and the joins between new and not so new paintwork are then less obvious.

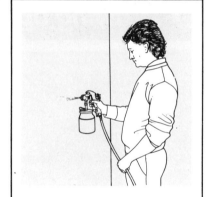

3. Spraying is fastest of all. You can hire the equipment quite cheaply, but ensure it can handle the paint you are using.

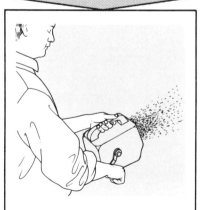

4. Applying an aggregate finish such as Tyrolean is harder and more expensive than painting but will last longer.

The main thing to remember when hanging wallcoverings is that walls are rarely perfect. In most rooms, corners are frequently out of square, door and window frames may be crooked, wall/ceiling and wall/skirting joins will be anything but straight, and so on. Paperhanging technique is therefore mainly about compensating for these defects in order to avoid both unnecessary practical problems as you work around the room, and the strange visual effects that can result when some wallcovering patterns are hung askew.

1. With the aid of a plumb-line, draw a vertical line on the wall 25 to 50mm less than the width of the paper away from one corner.

2. Carry the pasted paper to where it is needed draped over one arm, then open out the fold at what will be the top of the drop.

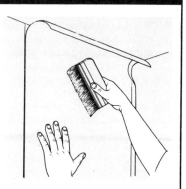

3. Offer the paper to the wall so about 50mm overlaps at the top. Line its edge up with the guide line, then brush firmly into place.

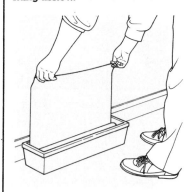

4. With a ready-pasted paper, position the soaking trough against the wall and lift the paper out by its top corners so it unrolls.

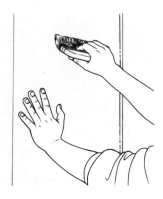

5. Continue smoothing the rest of the paper into place, working the brush towards the edges to avoid trapping air bubbles.

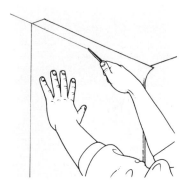

6. To trim the paper to size at the top, run the back of your scissors along the wall/ceiling angle to leave a sharp crease.

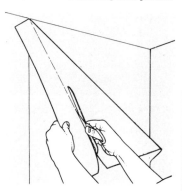

7. Carefully peel back the top of the paper, cut along the crease and brush back into place. Trim the bottom edge in the same way.

8. Hang subsequent drops in the same way, sliding each one until it butts tightly against its neighbour with pattern matching.

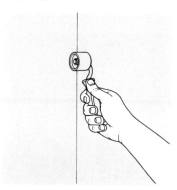

9. For a really neat join between drops, flatten it off with a seam roller. Don't press too hard though, or the paper may mark.

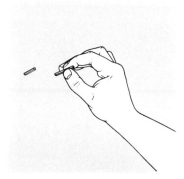

10. Push matchsticks into any wallplug fixings in the wall so you can find them again when they are covered with paper.

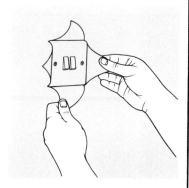

11. To paper round a switch, cut a switch-sized 'X' through the paper, brush into place, and trim off the triangular flaps of waste.

Having mastered the papering of flat walls, the next step is to learn to paper round obstacles. Some, like doorways, need little more than the ability to trim neatly. But room corners are less simple. The fact that they are usually out of true means you cannot simply turn the paper around them. It will finish neither flat nor vertical. Windows in reveals are even trickier, but don't worry – all these problems are normally easily overcome by a few basic tricks of the trade.

However, one problem will remain – difficult papering tends to produce edges that refuse to stick. The answer is to keep a small brush and paste pot handy – in fact, you may need this for straightforward papering using ready-pasted wallcoverings. With vinyls, use household latex adhesive to stick down overlaps.

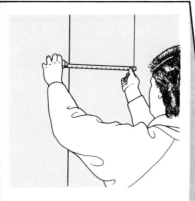

1. At internal corners, measure the gap between the last drop and the adjacent wall at several different heights.

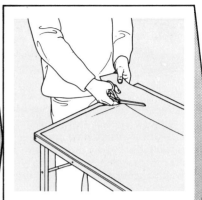

2. Working to the largest of these measurements, cut a drop 25mm wider than necessary – more if the walls are badly out of square.

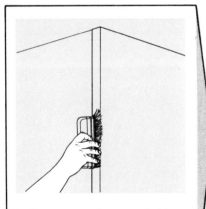

1. At an external corner, finish the first wall with a drop cut to width as for an internal one but with a slightly wider overlap.

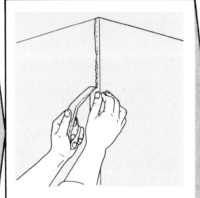

2. Carefully tear off a little of the overlap to feather its edge. This stops it showing through overlaying paper as a ridge.

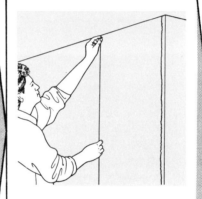

3. As with an internal corner, the next job is to strike a vertical guide line for the edge of the first drop on the second wall.

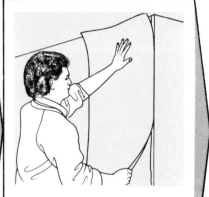

4. Hang this drop so it covers as much torn overlap as possible; match the pattern across the drops as accurately as you can.

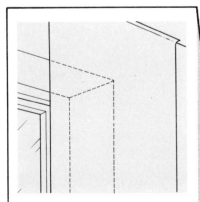

1. Find a symmetrical layout for the drops round the window then start at one side, letting the drop hang over the opening.

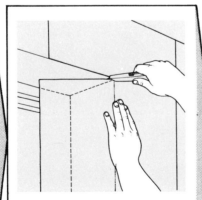

2. Cut through the paper, level with the underside of the soffit, so you can turn the resulting flap on to the side of the reveal.

3. Paper the soffit with a patch, cut about 25mm oversize and turned on to the frame, reveal and wall above the window.

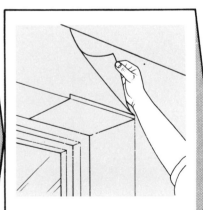

4. Tuck the turned edges of this patch beneath the paper covering the wall and reveal, then trim to fit along the frame.

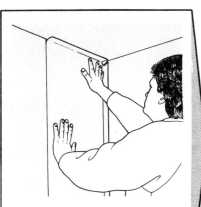

3. Hang the drop in the normal way, so that the side allowance turns on to the adjacent wall, and trim at top and bottom.

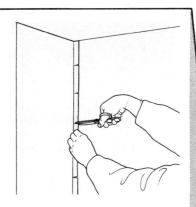

4. Snip through the overlap on the second wall to help it lie flat, then smooth it down, pressing the paper hard into the corner.

5. With the aid of a plumb-line, you now strike a vertical guide line for the first drop to be hung on the second wall.

6. Hang this just as you would the first drop on any wall, pushing it into the corner to cover the previous drop's snipped overlap.

5. Finally, neaten the overlapping join by smoothing it down with a seam roller, taking care not to mark the paper.

(47) Coping with lifting seams

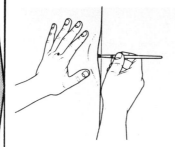

Use a small brush to repaste the edges of paper that have lifted at a butt joint, then smooth down with a brush and seam roller.

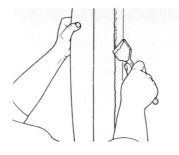

To stick down overlapping joints on vinyl wallcoverings, peel back a section, spread on latex adhesive, then press back in place.

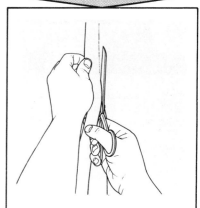

7. Having obtained as good a pattern match as possible, trim at top and bottom then crease and trim its edge to fit into the corner.

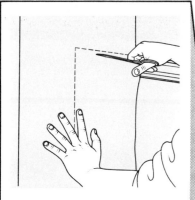

5. To paper round a door, let the drop fall over the frame and cut off most of the waste paper – leave 25mm for trimming.

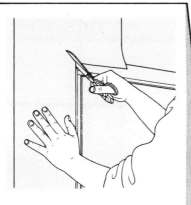

6. Next, cut diagonally through the remaining waste to the corner of the architrave, ending as close to the corner as possible.

7. Push the paper into the angle between wall and architrave by stabbing at it with the bristles of your paperhanging brush.

8. Finally, crease and trim off the flaps of waste in the normal way, taking care the paper does not tear at the corner.

48 Papering a ceiling

You might imagine that your main enemy when papering a ceiling is gravity, but, in fact, if you use plenty of paste and you size the ceiling first – priming it with a coat of paste – the risk of the paper falling off is small.

Failing to gain access to the ceiling along the entire length of the drop is much more likely to cause problems. Working from one step ladder you will be constantly up and down, pulling away the partly hung drops in the process. A step ladder and trestle with scaffold board in between is a much better arrangement. You can then simply walk along the board, brushing the paper into place.

The sheer length of ceiling paper drops can also give trouble. The trick is to fold them carefully when pasting, and to avoid stretching the paper unevenly as you brush it out.

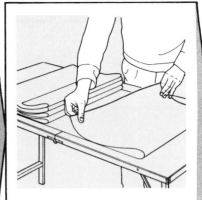

1. As you paste the drop, fold it concertina fashion so it can be supported by one hand holding a roll of scrap paper.

2. Working to a line struck parallel to the starting wall, offer the drop up to ceiling and brush the end folds into place.

49 Papering a stairwell

The problems associated with papering a stairwell are very similar to those encountered on ceilings. You are faced with hanging long drops on fairly inaccessible surfaces.

As with ceilings, good access equipment is certainly a must, but you need a slightly different approach to paper handling since, perhaps surprisingly, the fact that gravity works with you on walls can be quite a nuisance.

The answer is to have a helper support the paper concertina while you unfold the sections and brush them into place. This in itself goes a long way to preventing uneven paper stretch – which can result in it becoming impossible to match patterns – but you still need to exercise care when using the brush to avoid it completely. You should avoid letting the drops soak for too long before hanging them.

1. Start at the bottom of the well, using an assistant to support the concertina of paper while you brush it into position.

2. Cut subsequent drops to the length required on the down side of the stairs in order to allow for the slope of the stair string.

50 Access arrangements

An indoor scaffold tower normally provides the simplest way to reach up into a stairwell. Hire one whose legs can be adjusted to accommodate the stairs. The alternative is to use a combination of ladders, steps, small steps called 'hop ups,' scaffold boards, and a certain amount of ingenuity. Always rope or screw the component parts together, and stop ladder feet slipping by wedging them against a timber batten screwed to the floor.

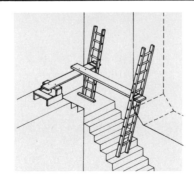

On quarter landings, use scaffold boards, ladders, steps and hop-ups.

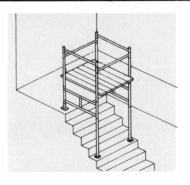

Use a narrow platform tower with special staircase leg frames.

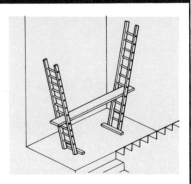

On half-landings, use a scaffold board between two ladders.

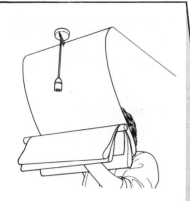

3. Brush out the rest of the drop unfolding it as you go, until you reach either the far wall, or an obstacle such as a pendant light.

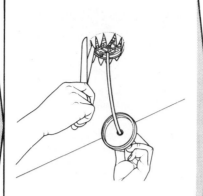

4. Cut a hole for the pendant flex to drop through, then snip outwards until it fits round the ceiling rose. Brush flat and trim.

5. Trim the complete drop to fit as you would on a wall, working round pillars and other angles as you come to them.

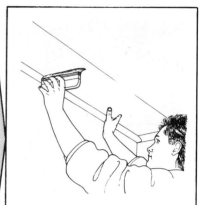

6. To finish off, trim the last length approximately to width before hanging it, allowing about 50mm extra for trimming.

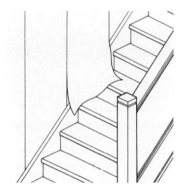

3. Hang these drops so they overlap the stair string, then crease and trim just as you would along a skirting board.

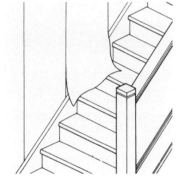

4. Slit the paper lengthways to fit it round bannisters and so on, making ceiling-rose-style 'freeing cuts' for the handrail.

(51) Hanging lining paper

It's lining paper that is largely responsible for the smooth finish characteristic of professional wallpapering. A layer of cheap, plain paper put up before the main wallcovering, it simply smooths out the wall's minor lumps and bumps. There is just one thing to watch – if the seams in the two layers of paper line up, the finish will be weakened. For this reason, lining paper is normally hung horizontally. On very poor walls, two layers of lining paper can be used. In this case, hang the first vertically.

1. Hang lining paper horizontally, starting at ceiling level. Turn one end of the length onto the next wall by about 50mm.

2. Brush out along the length to remove creases and air bubbles. Then brush the end well into any internal corners.

3. Where shallow returns such as chimney breasts are encountered, take the paper round the internal and external angles.

4. Trim off the overlap in internal angles carefully using a sharp knife. Alternatively, peel and trim with paperhanging scissors.

5. At skirtings, the last length of paper will probably be too wide. Trim it off just above the top edge of the skirting board.

52 Hanging friezes and borders

Using paper friezes and borders to alter the proportions of a room by breaking up its wall into smaller areas is not a new trick. But it is one worth remembering, particularly for large, old rooms that have lost their original plaster and wood friezes, picture rails, dados and so on. There is a fair range of designs to choose from – mainly traditional – and they are very easy to put up. Just cut the required length from the roll, paste and brush it into place.

However, there are a couple of points to watch. Don't get the two mixed up. Friezes are meant to hang horizontally on the wall just below the ceiling, while borders form decorative surrounds to doors, windows, and wall panel effects. Remember, too, that many friezes and borders are sold with strips of waste down the edges. Trim them off before hanging.

1. Using a long straight wooden batten and a spirit-level, draw a line on the wall to indicate the edge of the frieze.

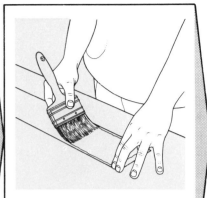

2. Paste the frieze like ordinary paper, folding it into a loose concertina. Avoid getting paste on the table or pattern side.

53 Hanging fabrics

While many household fabrics can be used as wallcoverings, it is best to stick to those made for the job. Hessian is most common (dyed or natural), but there are a number of other possibilities including felts, jute (a sort of coarse hessian), and even silk.

Paper-backed types are more expensive but easier to hang. Using a thick starch or ready-mixed paste, just paste in the same way as wallpaper, taking special care not to get paste on the fabric side. With unbacked fabric wallcoverings the paste is applied to the wall. In both cases, you then smooth the fabric into place with a foam roller, not a brush, using a special 'trick' to butt adjacent lengths together. One point to watch: fabric wallcoverings are often wider than wallpaper (around 915mm), which can cause problems of stretching.

54 Hanging relief paper

Relief wallcoverings like those in the Anaglypta family are used mainly to beautify walls whose plaster is in such poor condition that its faults would show through paint or ordinary wallcoverings. However, they do not form a decorative finish in their own right. They must be painted to keep out dirt and moisture.

The technique for hanging them is the same as for wallpaper, but they do present special problems. First, you need a thick paste, and it's advisable not to soak them for too long – they are very porous. Second, they stretch easily, so take care when hanging or it may become impossible to match the pattern. Finally, because they are embossed, it's not easy to make neat overlapping joins at corners. You cannot use a roller to flatten joins out as it would crush the relief pattern.

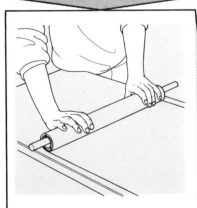

1. With unbacked wallcovering, cut the drops to length and roll them on to a broomstick. This makes them easier to handle.

2. Next brush a thick coating of ready-mixed or starch paste over the wall, covering the area where the drop is to be hung.

3. Smooth the fabric into place with a foam roller, pulling it off the broomstick as you go and taking care not to stretch it.

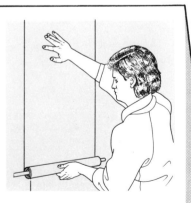

4. Hang the next drop so it overlaps its predecessor by about 25mm, then trim at top and bottom with a knife.

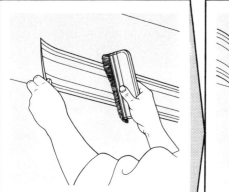

3. Working to the guide line, brush the frieze into place, slowly unfolding the concertina as you work along the wall.

4. If necessary, butt join on an extra length to extend the freeze, taking care to cut both ends squarely so the pattern matches.

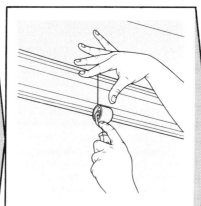

5. Use a seam roller to flatten any joins, making sure you do not damage the frieze in the process – especially embossed designs.

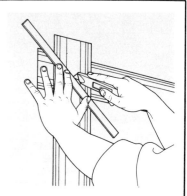

6. At the border corners, overlap horizontal and vertical strips, then cut through both diagonally using a sharp knife.

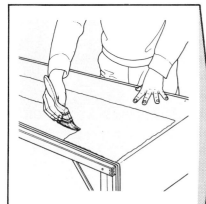

1. Apply a liberal coat of paste to the wallcovering and leave to soak. Don't soak for too long or it will be likely to stretch.

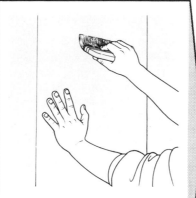

2. Smooth it down by stabbing at it with your brush. Brushing it out in the normal way could damage the relief pattern.

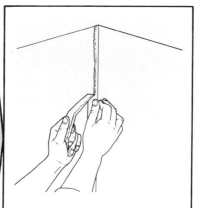

3. At overlapping corner joins, tear the first length to feather its edge and thus reduce the thickness of the seam.

7. Removing the waste from both pieces should produce a neatly mitred corner, though extra paste may be needed to stick it.

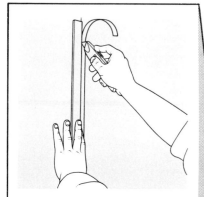

5. Using a straightedge as a guide, run a sharp knife down the middle of the overlap, cutting through both layers of fabric.

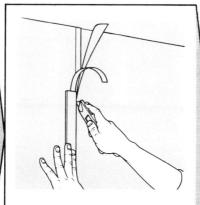

6. Remove the strips of waste from both the top and bottom layers, peeling back the edge of the drop to reach the latter.

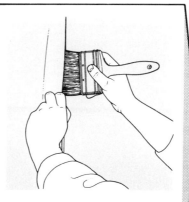

7. The edges of both drops should now match perfectly so peel them back, repaste the wall behind and smooth out.

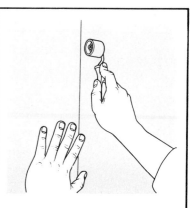

8. Finally neaten the seam by gently running over it with a wooden seam roller. Wipe off any paste with a damp cloth.

So long as you have taken care to ensure the surface being tiled is clean, dry and reasonably flat, actually putting up the tiles should be straightforward.

With a serrated spreader, apply adhesive to the wall, covering about a square metre at a time, then press the tiles into place. Make sure the tiles are correctly spaced though. Unless using a self-spacing type (with angled edges or spacing lugs), push spacers between the tiles as you put them up. Once all the tiles are in place, let the adhesive set, mix up some grout and press it firmly into the gaps between tiles using a plastic spreader; neaten the grout lines with a wet stick or similar tool. When the grout has dried, wash off the excess clinging to the tiles' surface. Use plenty of water and a sponge, repeating the process until only a fine bloom of grout remains. Polish this off with a soft, clean cloth.

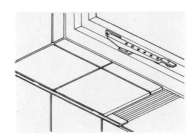

1. Most ranges of tiles for use on worktops offer special edging tiles (L-shaped in section) including mitred pairs for corners.

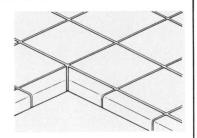

2. With ordinary wall tiles, you may need special edging trims for external corners. These are bedded in the tile adhesive.

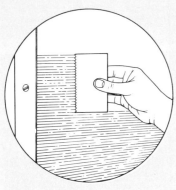

Use a notched spreader to create a bed of adhesive of uniform thickness, be pressing the teeth hard against the plaster.

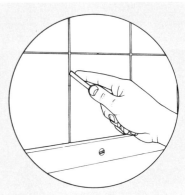

When tiling is complete, use a flexible spreader to force grout into the gaps. Wipe off excess and neaten the joints with a dowel.

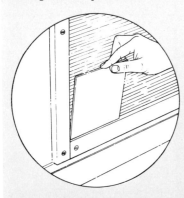

Position each tile by resting its lower edge on the guide batten (or the tile below it) and then press it into the adhesive.

When tiling a wall, always take the trouble to centre the tiles across the width and height, and position guide battens at the bottom and side of the area to ensure that the rows are truly horizontal and vertical. The gaps at the edge are filled with cut tiles later.

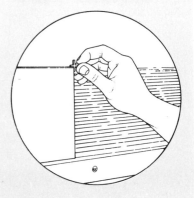

To ensure even spacing between universal tiles without spacer lugs, insert small plastic tile spacers at every intersection.

56 Coping with window reveals

Window reveals are often reckoned to be one of the hardest parts of a room to tile, but so long as you have set out the tiling correctly, you will have overcome most of the real problems before you start. For the rest, the techniques involved are fairly basic. All that is required is the ability to cut and shape tiles with a reasonable degree of accuracy and neatness.

However, there are a few points to watch. Firstly, when cutting tiles allow for walls being slightly out of square. Secondly, remember to use edging tiles along the front of the reveal, sill and soffit so that unglazed edges are not on show. If this means filling the gap along the window frame with cut tiles, avoid making these so narrow they are hard to cut. If necessary, trim a little off the edging tiles to enlarge the gap.

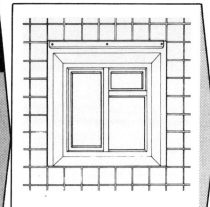

1. Tile as close to the window as you can using whole tiles. Support the row over the opening on a batten nailed in place.

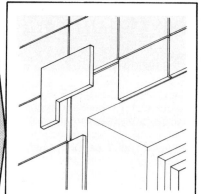

2. Once the adhesive has set, remove the batten and tile up to the reveal using cut tiles. Note the L-shaped tiles at corners.

57 Tiling internal and external corners

The trouble with tiling into an internal corner is that the walls are usually out of square. Cut tiles must therefore be shaped to allow for this. One way to do this is to measure the gap at top and bottom and use the results to angle the cut line on the tile. Alternatively, cover the last whole tile in the row with the tile to be cut, then hold a third whole tile over this with one edge pressed into the corner. The top tile's other edge can then be used to draw the cut line.

You must also allow for walls being out of square when tiling external corners. But here there is another, trickier problem – hiding the cut tiles' unglazed edges. To do this, finish one wall with tiles cut to fit in the usual way. The cut tiles starting the other wall are then placed so that they overlap those on the first. To complete the job, grout over the exposed cut edge when the time comes. For a still neater finish start the second wall with whole edging tiles, though this will work only if the walls are truly vertical.

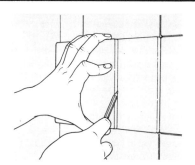

1. Lay the tile to be cut over the last whole tile in the row, and use a spare tile pushed into the corner to draw the cut line.

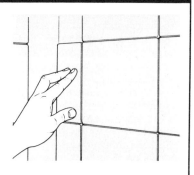

2. To stick narrow cut tiles in place, you will probably find it easier to apply adhesive to the tile back rather than the wall.

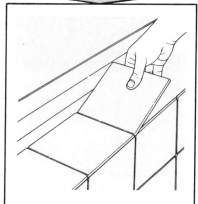

3. Next, tile the front of the sill, reveal and soffit with edging tiles, positioned to cover the edges of the tiles on the wall.

3. A batten held against the corner makes it easier to cut and position the tiles needed to finish off the first wall accurately.

4. Position the tiles on the second wall so they cover the edges of the tiles on the first. Neaten the join later with grout.

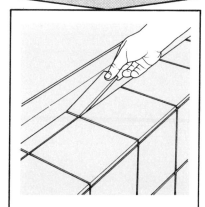

4. Finally, fill in round the frame with cut tiles. Leave a gap between tiles and frame to be filled later with flexible mastic.

58 Cutting tiles

Cutting tiles is largely a matter of confidence. To make a straight cut, first use a tiler's spike, or another tile cutting tool to score along the line of the cut, making sure you go right through the glazing, including any on the edges of the tile. Now, lay the tile on a flat surface, glazed side uppermost, and push a couple of matchsticks immediately under the cut line. If you now press down on the tile, it should snap neatly in two along the line you have just scored. Alternatively, if you prefer, use one of the many tile cutting aids on the market. Most offer some means of snapping the tile for you. Making an L-shaped cut tile is a little harder – you cannot snap along the scored line. Instead, nibble out the waste with pincers, and finish off with a file. For still more complex cut-out shapes, use a saw file in a hacksaw frame.

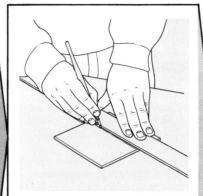

1. Using a straightedge as a guide, score right through the glaze (including any on the tile's edges) along the line of the cut.

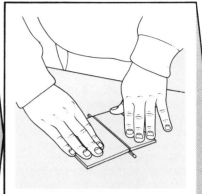

2. Slip a couple of matchsticks under the tile beneath the cut line, and press. The tile should snap cleanly in two.

59 Using mosaics

Modern mosaics are small ceramic tiles sold fixed to backing sheets to speed laying. You will find versions for use on worktops and floors, but bear in mind that the latter are normally thicker, so do not get the two muddled. Be sure, too, that you use the right adhesive and grout. For floor mosaics use floor tile adhesive; for worktop types use a two-part epoxy-based waterproof grout to make cleaning easier.

As for actually tiling with mosaics, treat each sheet as a tile when settling out, bearing in mind that to fill in around the edges of the tile area you can cut through the paper backing, and also cut through the individual tiles. One other tip: on floors, define the area to be covered with whole sheets using battens temporarily nailed in place.

60 Fixing mirror tiles

Walls and panels covered in mirror tiles add a sense of light and space to a room, but they must be put up with care. If not set out squarely on a perfectly flat, stable surface, distorted reflections will ruin the effect. For this reason it is best to line the wall with 12mm chipboard screwed to battens. The tiles themselves can also pose problems – they are not always perfectly square. To get round this, lay them out on a flat surface of the required size, and shuffle them about until you get a good fit. Each tile can then be numbered ready to be placed in the corresponding position on the wall. Lastly, because mirror tiles are fixed using self-adhesive pads, you have little opportunity to adjust their position on the wall, so line them up carefully before pressing them into place.

1. Press the mosaic sheets into place, spacing them out to maintain an even gap between individual tiles.

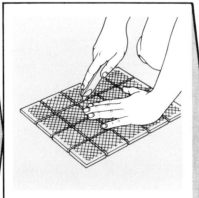

2. To tile round obstacles, start by removing enough tiles from the sheet for it to fit into place. Use a sharp knife or scissors.

3. Final fitting is achieved by cutting and shaping individual mosaic tiles by nibbling away the waste with pliers.

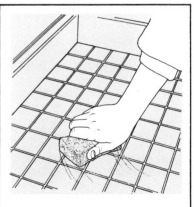

4. Once the adhesive has set, peel off the backing paper, and grout the mosaic just as you would a normal tiled wall or floor.

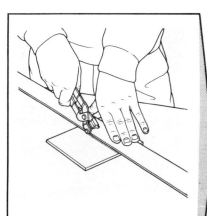

3. To make an L-shaped cut tile, score round the area of waste to be removed, again making sure you go right through the glaze.

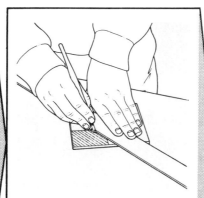

4. Cross-hatch the area of waste tile with additional scored lines to weaken it and make the next stage easier.

5. Finally, removing only a little at a time, nibble away the waste tile with a pair of pincers, then neaten the cut edges with a file.

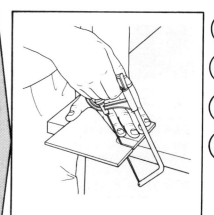

6. To cut out more complex shapes fit a saw file (a thin, round, flexible file) in a hacksaw frame and saw round the cut line.

1. Line the wall with chipboard screwed to timber battens, set about 750mm apart and fixed with screws and wallplugs.

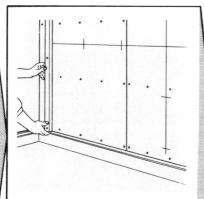

2. Set out the tiles working from horizontal and vertical lines that cross in the exact centre of the wall to ensure symmetry.

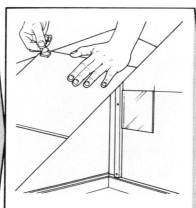

3. Put up as many whole tiles as you can, fixing them with adhesive tabs. A batten provides an accurate starting point.

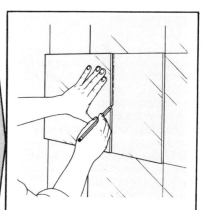

4. Mark out cut tiles in the same way as for ceramic tiles, and cut as you would glass – score with a glasscutter then snap in two.

61 Fixing cork wall tiles

Cork tiles are perhaps the simplest of all wall tiles to put up. Available in a choice of textures and colours, shapes and sizes, just set them out as you would any other tiling; stick them down with a contact adhesive (preferably water-based) and cut them to size with a sharp knife. Once in place, all that remains is to seal the surface (unless they come pre-sealed) with a polyurethane varnish.

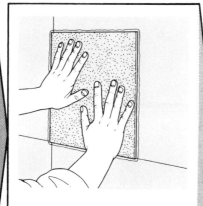

1. Set out as you would for mirror tiles, restriking the guide lines to indicate the positions of the central tile rows and columns.

2. Working out from the centre of the wall, fix as many whole tiles as you can before filling in around the edges with cut tiles.

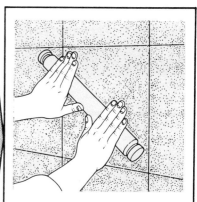

3. Initially, press each tile into place with a cloth. Then use a rolling pin to smooth the tiles out and remove air bubbles.

Expanded polystyrene tiles offer a quick, attractive cover-up for a ceiling in poor condition. What's more, the insulation they provide, though not enough to have any real effect on your heating bills, should help reduce unsightly condensation. Sold in white only, the tiles (normally 305 or 455mm square) come in a wide range of plain and embossed surface finishes, and most ranges including a selection of covings and ceiling centres to complete the effect if desired.

Unfortunately, polystyrene tiles do have drawbacks. They are not easy to keep clean, and can be difficult to remove. Safety is something else to bear in mind – under certain circumstances the tiles can pose a fire hazard. It's true the fire-retardant additives in modern tiles reduce this risk, but you must still take care. Always put up the tiles on a continuous bed of adhesive, and never paint them using a solvent-based paint. It is also a good idea to avoid using them in high-risk parts of your home such as the kitchen.

Find a starting point at or near the centre of the ceiling to give a symmetical arrangement which does not include over-narrow cut tiles around the edges. Apply adhesive to the ceiling with a notched spreader and press the tiles in place using a spare tile or a square of scrap wood fitted with a handle.

Polystyrene tiles are easily cut with a sharp knife, so shaping them to fit round obstacles such as light fittings is straightforward.

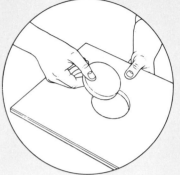

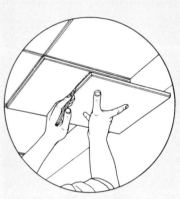

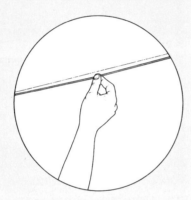

To mark centre guide lines stretch a chalk line between the mid-points of opposite walls, then snap it on to the surface.

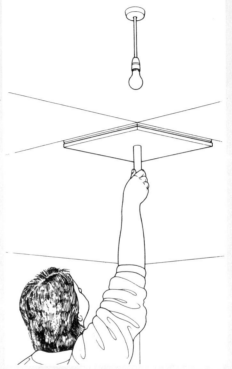

Use a spare tile as a gauge when marking out cut tiles to allow for the fact that most rooms are out of square.

Tongued-and-groove fibre tiles provide one of the most robust cover-ups for a poor ceiling. Set them out as for polystyrene tiles, then fix timber battens along two opposite walls, and at intervals across the ceiling to coincide with the joins between rows of tiles. Ensure the battens are fixed to the ceiling joists and run at right angles to them.

Start tiling out from a corner of the room along two adjacent walls. Cut these border tiles to size so that their grooved edges face into the room and secure to the battens with staples driven through the groove's lower edge. That done, tile the rest of the ceiling, slotting the tongue of each tile into its neighbour's groove before stapling. Complete the ceiling by sticking the last rows of cut tiles to the battens with a woodworking, panel or contact adhesive.

1. Fix battens across the joists, spacing these to match the joins between tile rows. A wooden spacer ensures they are parallel.

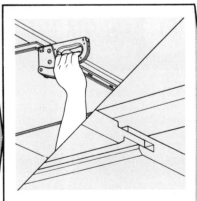

2. Each tile is fixed by slotting its tongue into a neighbouring tile's groove; its own grooved edge is stapled to the battens.

Illuminated ceilings consist of translucent plastic panels hung below the level of the existing ceiling on a grid of alumnium bars. They take their name from the way fluorescent lights fixed to the original ceiling shine through them, effectively turning the ceiling into one giant fluorescent light. Most offer panels in a choice of sizes, colours and textures; many include opaque fibre tiles, allowing ceilings with selected illuminated areas to be made.

Most illuminated ceilings come with full fitting instructions, which should be followed carefully as there are slight differences between brands. In essence, though, all you do is fix L-shaped bars to the room walls, to support parallel T-section bars running the full width of the room. To stop these sagging it is often necessary to tie them to the ceiling at intervals with wire or aluminium hangers. Shorter T-bars are then inserted between these runners, ready for the panels themselves to be simply dropped into place.

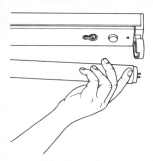

1. Install the necessary lights, fixing them to the original ceiling. If in doubt, have this done by a professional.

2. Nail or screw L-shaped bars to the walls along horizontal guide lines drawn with the aid of a spirit level.

3. Cut T-bars to run the full width of the room, then rest the ends on the wall bars and add some intermediate support if required.

4. Next drop the short cross bars into place, resting these on the main runners. Use a spare tile to ensure the correct spacing.

5. Using a fine toothed saw, cut any border panels needed to fit round the edges of the ceiling and drop these into place.

6. Continue slipping panels into position, adding more T-bars as required. Only the final panel may prove slightly fiddly.

3. Start tiling in a corner, fixing border tiles along two walls, then work out across the ceiling from the angle between these rows.

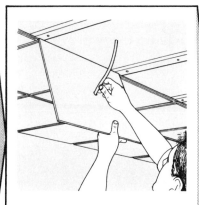

4. Where the tiles meet a ceiling rose, disconnect the cable and thread it through a hole in the tile. Then reposition the rose.

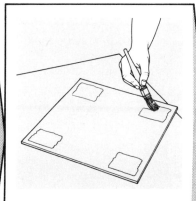

5. For an invisible fixing, stick the last row of tiles in place. Prime their absorbent backs with stabilising or similar primer.

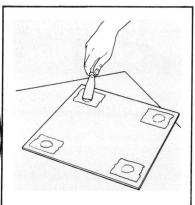

6. Then apply dabs of panel or woodworking adhesive to the primed patches, and press the tiles into position.

Cladding walls with tongued and grooved matchboarding isn't cheap, but it does offer a very attractive way to cover up poor walls. For variety, consider staining it before varnishing, or use a coloured varnish. Fixing it horizontally or diagonally can be very effective, too. What's more, matchboarding provides extra insulation (enough to help cure condensation problems) and can, if desired, be used to cover an insulating layer of glassfibre blanket or rigid polystyrene.

To clad a wall, start by fixing sawn softwood battens to the wall with screws and plugs. Fix one at the top, one at the bottom, and the remainder at 600mm intervals in between. Add extra battens as necessary to support the edges round windows, doors, electrical fittings and so on. The boards themselves are now fixed to these battens with panel pins driven into the tongue at an angle so they emerge through the underside of the board's fence. The next board's groove can then simply slot into place. Alternatively, use proprietary fixing clips.

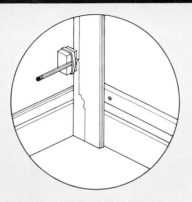

Where the cladding ends in a corner, scribe the board to fit. Fix a pencil to a block of wood and run the block down the wall.

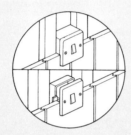

Refix the mounting boxes of electrical fittings to leave the face plates flush with the surface of the cladding.

At a corner, remove the tongue to make a butt joint. Neaten with quadrant beading.

Neaten the top of the cladding with coving or mouldings. If you want to keep an old coving or cornice, use a moulding to merge the cladding with it.

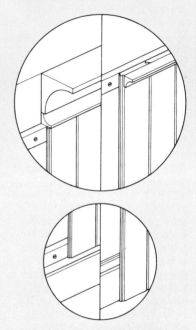

At the bottom of the cladding, stop level with the skirting board or clad over it, fixing a new skirting board on top if desired.

The easiest way to get a wall with a brick or stone finish is to use brick or stone effect tiles or thin slabs of natural stone. All three are usually put up with normal bricklaying mortar or special tile adhesive, and there is no need to be too fussy about setting out. Just ensure the mortar joints are fairly even, and, if using bricks or regularly shaped stones, check that the coarses are horizontal.

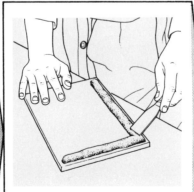

1. Butter adhesive onto the back of the tile rather than onto the wall. With mortar, wet the wall to stop it drying too quickly.

2. Press the tiles into place using a spirit-level to check that brick and dressed stone coarses are level – as they would be in reality.

3. With a small trowel, press a little mortar between each tile (any on the tile face may stain), then neaten with a dowel.

Wallboards offer a much faster way of cladding walls than matchboarding. They are usually cheaper, too. Made from either hardboard or thin plywood, they are available in a wide choice of finishes including natural wood veneers, plain plastic coatings, and coatings printed and embossed to resemble ceramic tiles, timber cladding, brick and stone. All come in standard 2400 x 1220mm sheets. Like matchboarding, wallboards can be used to conceal wall insulation.

There are two ways to put up wallboards. The first is to pin them to a grid of timber battens screwed to the wall. Arrange the vertical battens to coincide with the vertical joints. Space the horizontal battens between them to support any horizontal joins, and give the board some rigidity.

The second option is faster and cheaper, but works well only on reasonably flat walls in good condition. All you do is glue the boards directly to the wall using a special wallboard adhesive. This method can also be used to stick boards to a batten grid.

Provided the wall is in reasonable condition and fairly flat, the simplest way to put up wallboards is to glue them up using a special gap-filling panel adhesive. Simply apply beads of adhesive to the back of the board around the edges of each board, and at intervals across the surface, then press into place.

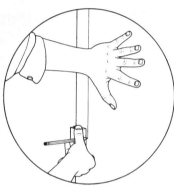
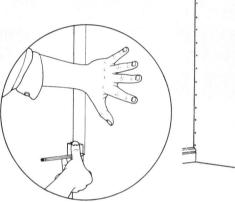

Where the cladding ends in a corner, scribe the edge of the last board to fit the adjacent wall and cut to shape with a tenon saw.

If you use the nail and batten fixing method, punch the pin heads below the surface of the board, then fill and retouch as required.

68 *Plastic laminates*

Plastic laminates come in a choice of plain colours and designs (including wood, and fabric effects), all very tough, making them an ideal covering for worktops, table tops, and the like – they are too thin and brittle to be used on their own. To apply them, just cut a sheet roughly to size with a fine-toothed saw, stick down with contact adhesive, then trim accurately to fit.

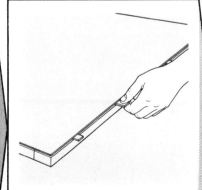

1. Because contact adhesive 'grabs' instantly, use card spacers to lift the laminate clear while you move it into position.

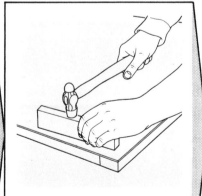

2. Remove the spacers, smooth the laminate down with a cloth, then tap with a wooden block to improve adhesion.

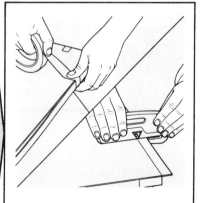

3. Trim accurately to fit with a block plane or special laminate trimmer. Tape strips to the edges until the adhesive is fully cured.

69 Fixing coving

Traditionally, covings were pieces of decorative plasterwork moulded in situ to ornament the angle where wall and ceiling join. Today, they are more likely to be made from foam plastic, glass fibre or pre-moulded plaster, and are used in renovation work, or as a cover-up for unsightly cracks between wall and ceiling.

There are many designs to choose from, ranging from simple modern lines in foam plastic to authentic period reproductions in plaster. All come in straight lengths, and many forms now offer ready-mitred corner pairs. Fixing methods, of course, vary with the material from which the coving is made. Foam plastic versions are usually glued in place, plaster ones are stuck up with plaster or adhesive, and glass fibre is stuck or fixed with a system of clips.

1. For a plaster moulding, clean the wall thoroughly and score the surface with an old chisel to provide a key for the new plaster.

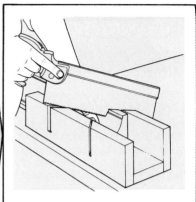

2. Cut the coving to length with a tenon saw, using a mitre box to angle the ends where the coving must turn a corner.

70 Making and fitting a roller blind

The roller blind is a beautifully simple and attractive window dressing. The trouble is that off-the-peg versions come in such a limited range of designs they may not suit your home, and in such a limited range of sizes that they may not fit your windows. But there is a way round the problem – you can make your own, using a kit.

These contain everything you need except the fabric. You get the roller (complete with spring mechanism), fixing brackets, the bottom batten and cord pull. Just as important, you should get an aerosol can of fabric stiffener (most fabrics are naturally too limp to be used as a blind), plus a full set of instructions. Like ready-made blinds, kits still come in a choice of standard sizes, but all you do is buy a size larger than your window and cut it down to fit.

71 Putting up a curtain track

There are now several different types of curtain track on the market designed specifically for diy installation. Available in styles ranging from modern to pseudo-antique, there are simple wooden poles and metal or plastic tracks which oblige you to draw the curtains by hand, and there are more complex cord-operated models, including some designed to resemble curtain poles.

The main thing to take into account when choosing is the weight the track can carry. In general, the cheaper tracks are suitable only for fairly lightweight curtains. However, they are normally easier to cut to size – just saw them to the required length. The heavier, more expensive, corded-tracks tend to come in a choice of standard sizes which cannot be altered without re-cording.

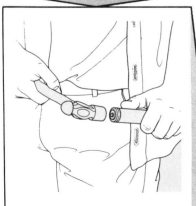

1. Cut the roller to the required width, tap the end cap firmly into place with a hammer, then saw down the bottom batten to match.

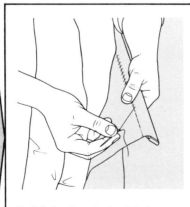

2. Stitch a hem in the fabric along the blind's lower edge and insert the bottom batten, which should be a fairly tight fit.

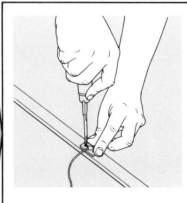

3. Fix the cord pull and anchor plate in the centre of the lower batten, checking that it is on the right side of the fabric.

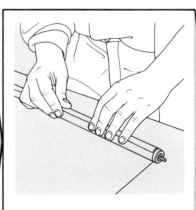

4. Fix the stiffened fabric's top edge to the roller following the instructions – the recommended fixing method varies.

3. Stick the coving in place with blobs of adhesive, then reinforce the join with nails driven through into the wall every 600mm or so.

4. To turn a corner, slide the coving into place until the mitred ends line up. Neaten the join with fresh plaster.

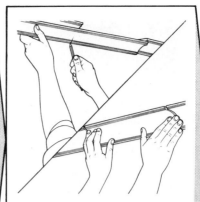

5. To complete a run of coving between two mitred lengths, offer up a new piece and mark off the length with a pencil.

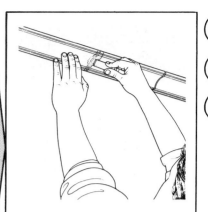

6. Bed the section in place with adhesive, secure with a nail, then neaten the joins between the lengths with fresh plaster.

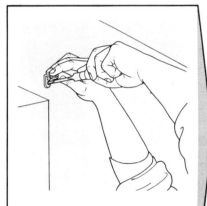

1. Fix the track support brackets to the wall over the window with screws and wall plugs. Check they are evenly spaced.

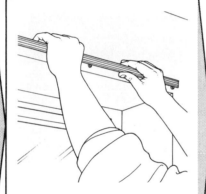

2. Cut the track to length with a hacksaw, then clip on to the brackets. Fit the curtain hooks and any end stops supplied.

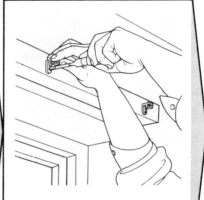

3. If lintels make bracket fixing difficult, just screw and plug a softwood batten to the wall, and fix the track brackets to that.

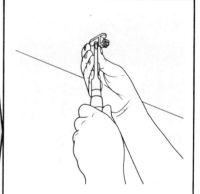

4. Alternatively, it may be easier to fix the brackets to the ceiling, screwing them to joists. Find out if special brackets are needed.

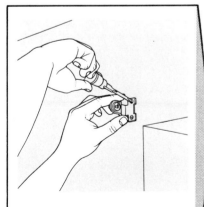

5. Screw the brackets to the wall. Ensure they are level and leave the blind accurately centred over the window opening.

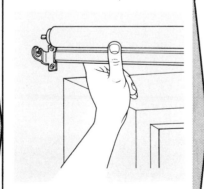

6. Roll the blind up on to the roller and drop this into place on its brackets. Now check that the blind works properly.

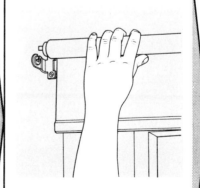

7. If the blind won't stay down or won't roll up as it should, adjust the roller tension, following the manufacturer's instructions.

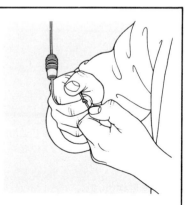

8. Finally, thread the acorn on to the cord pull, securing it by tying a couple of knots in the end of the string.

72. Laying sheet vinyl

If you want an attractive, water-resistant, hardwearing, easy to clean and relatively inexpensive flooring, sheet vinyl is a very good choice. Sold in 2m (and in many cases 4m) widths, there are two main domestic types. The cheapest has a backing, a layer bearing the pattern, and a top wear layer of vinyl. Dearer but more comfortable, cushion vinyls have an extra flexible layer, and are often embossed to look like ceramic tiles, stone, and so on.

Both are quite easy to lay so long as you remember a couple of basic points. First, let the loosely rolled sheet warm up before laying. It will be more flexible. Second, joins between sheets are vulnerable to damage so arrange for them to fall in a 'quiet' part of the room. If possible avoid them altogether by using the wider sheets.

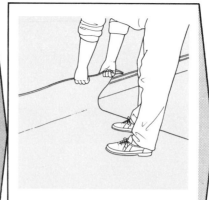

1. Unroll the vinyl and manoeuvre to give the best possible fit, letting at least 50mm turn up each wall for trim.

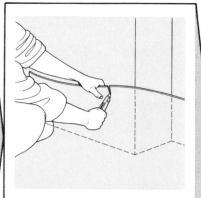

2. Where chimney breasts and so on get in the way, cut through the waste until the vinyl lies flat. This is called a freeing cut.

73. Stripping and sealing floors

The cheapest, simplest way to get an attractive wooden floor is to sand existing floorboards, and then seal them with a protective polyurethane varnish – there are now non-slip, scuff-resistant formulations made specially for the job. Provided the boards are in good condition, the results can be just as decorative as dearer overlaid wooden flooring, and by staining the timber before you varnish you can even create the impression of having a really expensive hardwood floor.

Sanding floorboards is not a job for ordinary diy sanders. Instead, you will have to hire tools designed for the purpose. Widely available at reasonable rates from good tool hire shops, you need two in all: a floor sander (a large belt sander that looks like a lawnmower) for the bulk of the floor; and an edging sander (a heavy-duty disc or belt sander) for the rest. Abrasive paper for both is usually supplied on sale or return. Hire a dust mask, too. Another tip: don't underestimate the time the job will take – it's physically fairly tiring.

Sand the floor in strips, working through coarse, medium and fine abrasives. Start with your back to a wall, let the sander pull you to the far side of the room then, without pausing, drag it back to the starting point. Sand diagonally to flatten warped boards; along the boards to produce a good finish.

Clean up awkward sections with glasspaper or wire wool, using paint stripper to remove any old decorative finish.

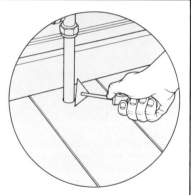

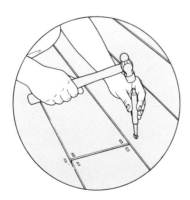

Before sanding, refix loose boards and punch all nail heads below the surface where they cannot damage the sanders.

Floor sanders leave an unsanded strip round the room walls. Sand this with the edging sander. Take care not to scratch the wood.

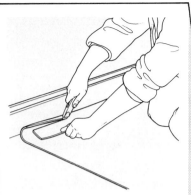

3. To make it easier to trim the vinyl accurately to fit, roughly cut off any large areas of waste turning up the walls.

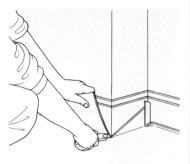

4. At external corners, neaten the freeing cuts, angling them into the waste to allow for the corner being out of square.

5. Press the vinyl into the angle between floor and skirting with a block of wood, then trim accurately using a sharp knife.

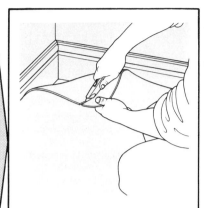

6. At internal corners, cut off the corner of the waste at an angle of 45 degrees exactly level with the corner's point.

74 Finishing vinyl at doorways

Sheet vinyl is very vulnerable to damage at door thresholds. Not only is this an area where it sustains a lot of wear, but also, even when stuck down, there is the risk of someone tripping over the edge and tearing it. For these reasons it is well worth giving the edge here extra protection in the form of a threshold strip — it's safer, too. These are made from wood or metal; simply screw them down to cover the join between the flooring on one side of the door and the other.

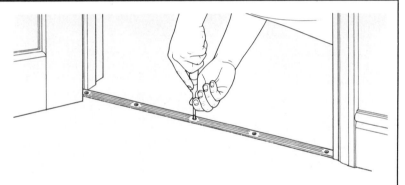

Cut the threshold strip to length, and screw to the floor so it covers *the join where the floorcoverings meet in the doorway.*

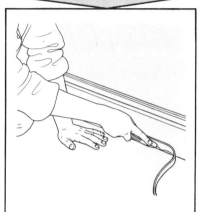

7. You can now trim off the waste along the walls. Crease the vinyl first by running a wooden block along the skirting board.

75 Shaping vinyl using a template

Some obstacles, such as WCs, are too awkwardly shaped for sheet vinyl to be fitted around them using normal methods. The answer is to use a template. Tape two sheets of paper to the floor, roughly shaping them to fit round the obstruction, then draw an oversize image of the outline using a compass as shown. If you now tape the resulting paper template in the correct spot on the vinyl, reversing the process will produce an accurate outline to which you can cut.

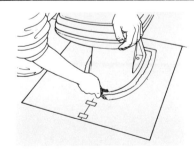

1. Use a compass to transfer the outline of the obstacle on to paper. Keep it at right-angles to the obstacle at all times.

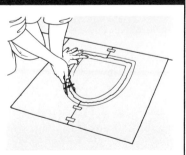

2. Lay this paper template on the vinyl and reverse the process to an accurate image of the outline to which you can cut.

8. After the vinyl has settled for a few days, stick down the edges and all joins with double-sided carpet tape or flooring adhesive.

76 Laying floor tiles

Although rather fiddly, you may find floor tiles easier to lay than sheet flooring, particularly in rooms with lots of obstacles and/or little space to manoeuvre. Cork and vinyl tiles are the most popular choices; the latter are warmer and softer under foot than cold, hard but durable vinyl. Both are normally 300mm square, and laid in much the same way. The main differences are that some vinyl tiles are

self-adhesive (if not, they must be stuck down with flooring adhesive), and that, unless pre-sealed with a plastic coating, cork must be varnished.

As to the actual laying, the main thing is to set the tiles out properly. Strike a cross in the centre of the room, and dry-lay tiles out from there. If this gives very narrow border tiles, move one or both guide lines along half a tile width and try again.

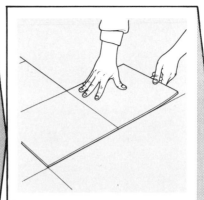

1. Set out along lines between the mid-points of opposite walls, then lay the first tile in the angle between guide lines.

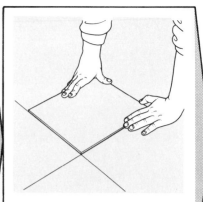

2. Tackling a quarter of the floor at a time, work along the lines, then fill in between with whole tiles. Cut border tiles to fit.

77 Setting out floor tiles

Unless you are laying plain tiles such as cork, always take the trouble to set the tiles out so you get an even border of cut tiles all round the room. Start by fixing chalk lines between the midpoints of opposite walls. Then dry-lay a row of tiles out towards the walls as shown. If the gaps at the ends of the rows are less than a third of a tile width, move one or other string line along by half a tile width. When you are content with the arrangement, strike the chalk guide lines on the floor.

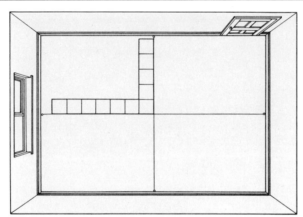

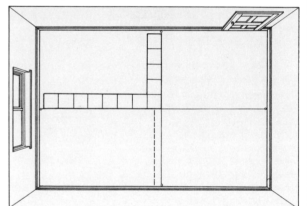

78 Laying ceramic floor tiles

Setting out and laying ceramic tiles on a floor isn't so very different to tiling a wall. The main points to watch are that floor tiles are thicker than wall tiles, making them a little harder to cut, and that there are no self-spacing types – you must separate the tiles as you lay them, using spacers to ensure an even grout lines.

Remember, tiling raises the floor level, so plane down the bottom of the room's doors to provide the necessary extra clearance.

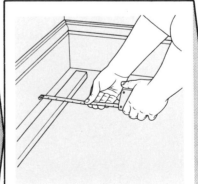

1. Set the first at batten the required distance from the skirting board to allow for the border of cut tiles at the wall.

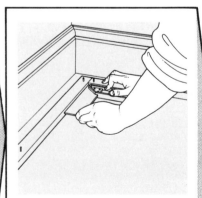

2. Nail a strand batten to the floor to indicate where the edges of the outermost whole tiles fall. Ensure the corners are square.

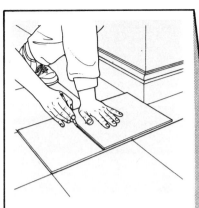

3. As with wall tiling, use a spare tile as a gauge to mark the cut tile. To fit round a corner, first mark up against one wall.

4. Next, taking care not to rotate the cut tile, mark it to fill the gap against the second wall so the two cut lines cross.

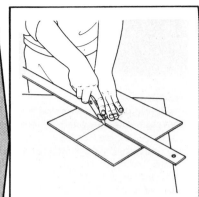

5. Cut out the rectangle of waste using a sharp knife and a straight edge. Work on scrap board to avoid damaging the new floor.

6. The resulting L-shaped tile should now fit perfectly round the corner. The same technique is used on internal corners.

79 Quarry tiles

Quarry tiles and other unglazed tiles are laid in a slightly different way to ordinary ceramic floor tiles. To begin with, they are set in a thick bed of mortar, not stuck down with adhesive. Secondly, they are harder to cut. After scoring, you must tap along the back of the tile with a hammer to make it break. For this reason, accurate setting out is doubly important. Follow the same routine as for ordinary tiling.

1. Use a batten to cordon off the section you are tiling, using a tile gauge to position it against the edge guide batten.

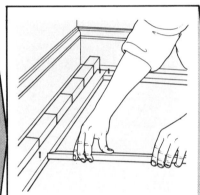

2. Fill this bay with a layer of mortar, and smooth off with a trowel. Bed the tiles, using a spirit level for checking.

3. Tap the tiles down with a wooden block, leave the mortar to harden, then move the side batten along and tile the next bay.

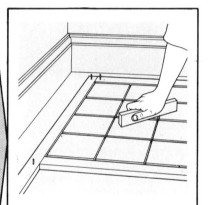

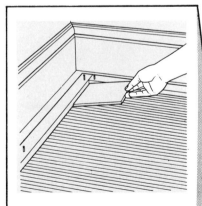

3. Working on roughly a square metre at a time, spread out the adhesive using a notched trowel, and bed the tiles into place.

4. Separate the tiles with pieces of card as you work out across the floor. Check that the tiled surface is level with a spirit-level.

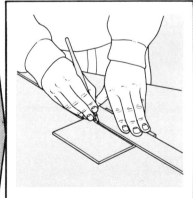

5. With all the whole tiles laid, remove the battens and cut border tiles to fit. Floor tiles are cut in the same way as wall tiles.

6. Allow the adhesive to harden for 24 hours, then remove the spacers and grout the floor. Again this is the same as for walls.

80 Laying foam-backed carpet

Foam-backed carpets are quite easy to lay, but if you have spent a lot of money on a carpet it is best to leave fitting to a professional.

Diy carpet laying is more applicable to cheaper carpets in rooms where mistakes are not too serious – say, a bedroom. The simplest method is known as loose laying. Simply cut the carpet to fit in much the same way as you fit sheet vinyl (see project 72), then secure it around the edges – at at any joins – with double-sided carpet tape. Take extra care to secure it at doorways. A threshold strip is essential here because of the trip hazard. One other tip: cover the floor with special glass fibre underlay or stout brown paper before laying the carpet. This stops dust working its way into the carpet's back, and helps prevent the foam sticking to the floor in heavy-traffic areas.

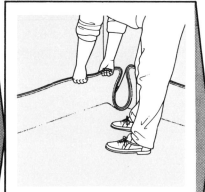

1. Unroll the carpet in the middle of the room and manoeuvre so that a reasonable trim allowance turns up all of the room's walls.

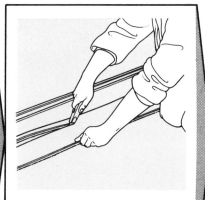

2. Smooth out any wrinkles with your feet, then trim off any large amount of waste to leave the way clear for final trimming.

81 Stair carpets

For obvious safety reasons stair carpets should not be loose-laid. Instead, secure them with special gripper strips, stretching the carpet slightly in the process. On the stair treads you should manage by hand, but on larger areas such as landings, a special tool called a knee kicker is needed – available from good tool hire shops. Don't overstretch the carpet, though, and try to ensure the tension is even.

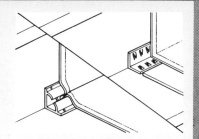

There are two main types of stair carpet gripper – those with teeth and those with sprung jaws.

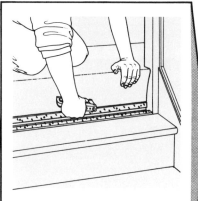

1. Nail the gripper strips in place, then cover the horizontal treads and vertical risers with underlay, held down with tacks.

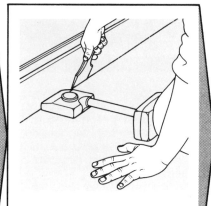

2. Start at the top landing. Stretch the carpet on to the gripper strip and poke down the edges with a bolster chisel.

82 Laying woodblock panels

Parquet and similar woodblock floorings are renowned for being both attractive and hardwearing. Unfortunately, they are also expensive and difficult to lay, but there is an easier way to get the same look – using woodblock panels. Made from veneer-faced plywood, these come in a range of hardwood finishes including teak, mahogany, sapele, oak and walnut, and a choice of pattern, parquet or basketweave.

As for laying the panels, it's easier than many other forms of floor tiling. There's no setting out to worry about, and all you need to cut them to fit is a tenon saw. However, you must leave a gap between panels and skirting to allow for the natural movement of the wood. This can be either covered with some form of wooden beading, or filled with strips of cork – these flex to absorb any expansion.

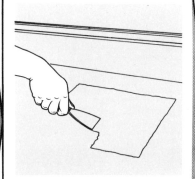

1. Apply flooring adhesive to the floor using a notched spreader, aiming to cover an area equal to three or four panels at a time.

2. Starting along one wall, press the panels into place, leaving a gap of at least 12mm between the flooring and skirting board.

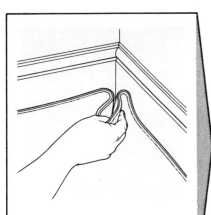

3. Freeing cuts are needed at corners for the carpet to lie flat. Feel through the carpet to find where the cut should end.

4. Mark this point by notching the foam with your knife, then make the freeing cut. Cut the carpet from the foam side.

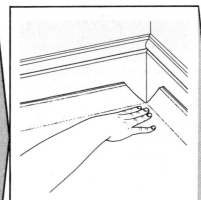

5. Press the carpet back into the corner to check its fit, allowing the waste tongues to lap up the skirting board at each side.

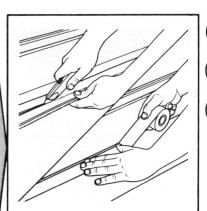

6. Finally trim round all the walls until the carpet fits exactly, then secure its edges using double-sided carpet tape.

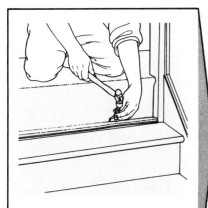

3. Turn the landing carpet over the top riser, fix to the gripper strip, then work down the stairs, fixing the stair carpet as you go.

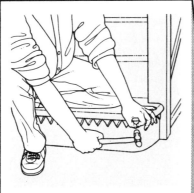

4. Use lots of freeing cuts to fit it round a bullnose tread. Cut the waste into triangles and tack to the bottom riser.

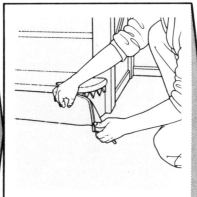

5. Cover the bottom riser with a strip of carpet cut accurately to fit, tacking it in place as neatly as you possibly can.

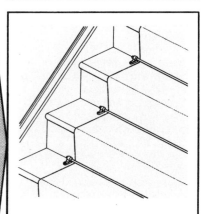

6. Where the carpet is narrower than the stairs, pin it into the tread-riser angle using stair rods and brackets.

3. To mark up a panel for cutting, lay it on top of the adjacent whole tile, and use a second panel, butted to the wall, as a gauge.

4. Cut the panel to size using a tenon saw, holding it right side up to avoid splintering the decorative veneer.

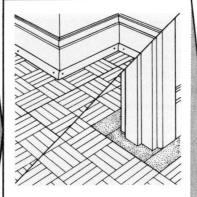

5. With all the panels in place, cover the expansion gap around the walls with beading, or fill with strips of cork tile.

6. Finally seal the surface of the panels (and the cork or beading) with at least three coats of polyurethane varnish.

Glossary

Alkyd resins are used as binders in modern solvent-based paints, in place of linseed oil which gave oil paints their name.

Anaglypta is a trade name for a relief wallcovering made from wood pulp. It's white, is intended for overpainting once hung and comes in a wide range of designs.

Artex is also a trade name, for a textured coating used on walls and ceilings. Original Artex is a powder which is mixed with water; most modern textured coatings are now ready-mixed.

Borders are narrow strips of printed wallpaper, used to highlight features such as window openings.

Cladding describes timber and wallboards used as a surface decoration for walls. It is usually fixed to a network of battens.

Cornices and covings are terms used interchangeably nowadays to describe decorative mouldings of plaster, plasterboard or plastic used to conceal the joint between walls and ceilings.

Cross-lining means hanging lining paper horizontally on wall surfaces prior to hanging another wallcovering over it.

Cushioned vinyls are vinyl floorcoverings with a layer of trapped air bubbles incorporated in their construction to improve comfort and insulation underfoot.

Distemper is an old-fashioned wall paint no longer used, but often found beneath old wallpaper. It must be removed or sealed before being decorated over.

Drop pattern wallcoverings have a pattern which drops by half a repeat across the width.

Efflorescence is a white powdery deposit found on wall surfaces that are damp or which have not dried out after replastering work. It should be brushed off dry.

Eggshell paints are solvent-based paints which dry to a sheen rather than a high gloss.

Emulsion paint is a water-based paint mainly used on wall and ceiling surfaces. It is thinned and washed from tools with water.

Fillers are powder or ready-mixed products to repair minor damage in plaster and plasterboard surfaces. They are applied with a filling knife, which is more flexible than a stripping knife.

Friezes are narrow strips of printed wallpaper, somewhat wider than borders, used to form decorative bands on wall surfaces.

Grout is a powder or ready-mixed product used to fill the narrow gaps left after ceramic tiles have been fixed to floors or walls.

Knotting is a special sealer used to cover knots in woodwork, preventing resin from oozing through and marring the finish.

Laminates are rigid sheets of resin-impregnated paper with a decorative finish, used on surfaces such as worktops.

Lincrusta is a relief wallcovering made from a mixture of linseed oil and fillers, hardened rather like putty and formed into rolls. It's hung with special adhesive.

Lining paper is plain paper hung to provide a stable base for other wallcoverings. Special grades are available for overpainting.

Murals are designs painted on wall surfaces as decoration, usually using emulsion paint.

Novamura is a foamed polyethylene wallcovering, hung straight from the roll. It can be dry-stripped.

Primers are used on many surfaces to seal them and provide a good base for subsequent undercoats and top coats.

Relief wallcoverings are embossed papers designed to be overpainted once hung. Types include Anaglypta, Supaglypta and Lincrusta.

Solvent-based paints are mainly used on wood and metal, and have white spirit as a thinner and cleaning agent. Gloss and eggshell paints are of this type.

Vinyl wallcoverings have the design printed on a PVC layer which is stuck to a paper backing. They can be stripped dry.

Index

Central heating and insulation

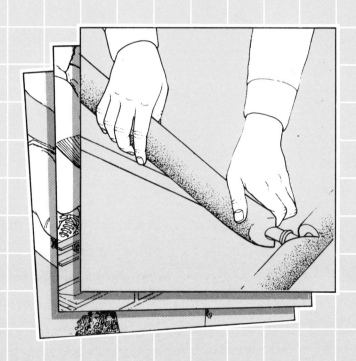

Central heating and insulation

Central heating and insulation

A modern home without a central heating system would be unthinkable, yet central heating has only become commonplace within the last generation or so. There are obvious advantages in having both hot water and heating supplied by one heat source, and modern boilers and controls mean that in many cases the system can be fully automated, with programmers running the system to suit the needs of the family.

The various components of a modern heating system can all be installed or replaced fairly easily by a competent do-it-yourselfer, and the complete installation of a new heating system is perfectly possible with a little careful planning. The most difficult part of the job lies in actually designing a system to suit your requirements, but help is now widely available. Obtaining the actual materials has never been easier.

Central heating is by definition a heating system with a central heat source, from where heat is delivered to wherever it is needed – either as hot water for direct use, or to provide space heating. Houses with night storage radiators or individual balanced-flue gas heaters do not, strictly speaking, have central heating.

Installing a central heating system is one of the most cost-effective do-it-yourself jobs there is. It will certainly add to the value of your house, since purchasers will invariably expect central heating to be present and will be looking for a price reduction if it is not. It will greatly improve home comfort, since

modern system controls can ensure that the correct room and hot water temperatures are reached and maintained automatically. It may save money on your existing fuel bills if insulation is taken into account when the new system is designed, since a smaller boiler and smaller (or fewer) heaters will be required. Last of all, it will save you money if you do it yourself, because the installation is a fairly labour-intensive operation, doing it in your own unpaid time means that you have to pay just for the hardware, and this is generally surprisingly inexpensive. The actual installation techniques are well within the capacity of any

competent do-it-yourselfer . . . although there are times when an extra pair of hands will be useful.

Central heating equipment is now widely available to the home installer, through specialist high-street suppliers, mail-order companies and DIY superstores. The most difficult and involved part of the job is actually designing the system, a job which you may prefer to leave to an expert. You can either call in a heating engineer to do the job, or else rely on your equipment supplier to do the design calculations for you. You have to supply accurate floor plans of the house, complete with constructional details; he can then calculate the heat losses through

individual parts of the structure and work out the size of the various components necessary to maintain the design temperatures you want. It's at this stage that the question of insulation should be brought up, since it is better to upgrade the roof, wall, floor and window insulation first; then a smaller system can be specified.

Whether you plan to do the installation yourself or call in an expert, you need to make some preliminary decisions about what sort of system you want, which fuel to use, which type of boiler to install, what sort of heat emitters to use and where they are going to go. The following pages should help you to find the answers.

① Unvented systems

Most hot water storage systems in the UK are vented — in other words, the system is open to the air at the top (see opposite). Both hot and cold water supplies within the house are at low pressure, fed from a storage cistern in the loft.

Recent changes to the Building Regulations and forthcoming changes to the model water bye-laws now allow the use of unvented hot water storage systems of the type widely used in Continental and American homes, which supply both hot and cold

water at mains pressure.

Unvented systems require the inclusion of a number of safety features such as non-return valves, pressure-reducing valves, expansion vessel, expansion valve and a safety valve to operate as a last resort. At present, only proprietary packaged plumbing units which contain all the safety components and have BBA (British Board of Agrément) approval may be installed, and the layout must be agreed with the local water authority.

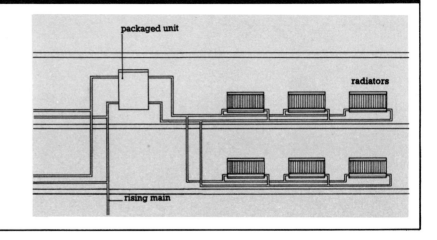

packaged unit

radiators

rising main

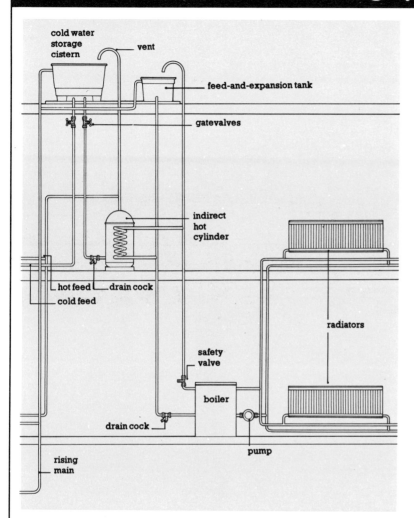

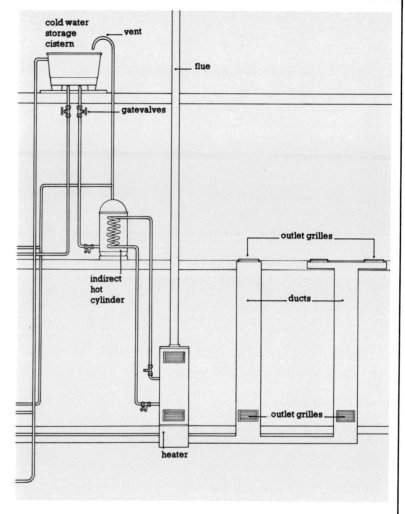

Wet systems

The term 'wet central heating system' is applied to a system where water is heated in a boiler and is then circulated to heat emitters (usually radiators). When it reaches these it gives up its heat to warm the rooms, and is returned to the boiler to be reheated. Most modern heating systems have a pump to push the water round the system, and a series of controls to switch the system on and off as required. The heat emitters can be conventional steel panel radiators, convectors or skirting heaters.

Such a system is also used to heat domestic hot water for washing, bathing and so on. An additional circuit is run to a heat exchanger — in effect, another radiator — inside a hot water storage cylinder; this warms cold water in the cylinder and feeds the hot taps throughout the house.

A cold water storage cistern in the loft supplies the cold taps in the house (except the one over the kitchen sink, which is fed directly from the rising main), and also supplies cold water directly to the hot cylinder to replace that drawn off to the hot taps. The hot water storage system is open to the atmosphere at the top, and a vent pipe runs from the top of the hot cylinder to discharge over the cold cistern and maintain the open circuit.

Such a system usually also has a small feed-and-expansion tank or header tank, which keeps the primary circuit between boiler and hot cylinder topped up with water and accommodates the expansion that takes place within this circuit as the system heats up. It also acts as an escape pipe for steam if the boiler thermostat fails and the system overheats. Some systems do not have this tank and vent pipe; instead the system is sealed, and contains a closed expansion vessel to cope with expansion within the system. This type is popular on the Continent.

Dry systems

So-called dry central heating systems use warm air instead of hot water to heat the rooms. Air is drawn through the boiler and then transferred to the rooms through a series of insulated galvanised sheet metal ducts, emerging through grilles set in the floor or just above the skirting boards. The return air flow to the boiler is usually by means of gaps round internal doors, but sometimes grilles are inserted above doors to provide a guaranteed flow.

Most gas-fired warm air systems also supply hot water via a separate heater linked to an indirect hot cylinder.

③ Types of fuel

Domestic whole-house heating installations can be run using gas, solid fuel, oil or mains electricity. Which one you choose will depend mainly on its availability, but price and storage requirements are also important.

Gas is the first choice for most people, because supplies are generally available to all but remote country areas, you don't have to store it, it burns cleanly and boilers can be automatically controlled.

Solid fuel comes next in the price league, but suffers from two drawbacks when compared with gas; you need considerable storage facilities, and fully automatic control of the system is not possible.

Oil is more expensive than solid fuel, needs storage space but can be automatically controlled.

Electricity, used on the night-rate Economy 7 tariff, costs roughly the same as solid fuel, but does not offer the same flexibility as other systems.

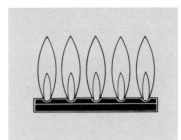

Gas — readily available except in remote areas, needs no storage, burns cleanly and can easily be automatically controlled.

Oil — available everywhere, can be automatically controlled but needs substantial storage facilities. Prices can fluctuate.

④ Types of boiler

Apart from fuel choice, your choice of boiler also depends on where you want to put it and what sort of flue it requires.

Gas-fired boilers come in the biggest range. They can be floor-standing — set in a run of kitchen base units for example, or housed within a chimney breast (known as a back boiler) — or wall-mounted. Some use a conventional flue, others a balanced flue (see opposite) which may be fan-assisted to make positioning more flexible. The latest types,

known as condensing boilers, offer efficiencies of around 90 per cent compared with about 75 per cent for ordinary types, so cost less to run (but rather more to buy).

Oil-fired boilers can also be floor-standing or wall-mounted, and modern types — usually of the pressure-jet type — are much quieter and more compact than the older wallflame type.

Solid-fuel boilers are always floor-standing; free-standing and back boiler types are available.

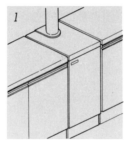

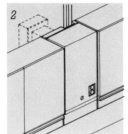

Gas boilers can be floor-standing — often within a run of base units (1) — or wall-mounted, and can use a conventional or balanced flue. The

latter must be sited on an outside wall (2) unless a fan- assisted flue is used (3). Back boilers are sited within chimney breasts.

⑤ Types of heat emitter

Every heating system needs some means of delivering the heat the boiler generates to wherever it is needed, and this is the job of the heat emitters.

Panel radiators are the most commonly used heat emitters, and also the cheapest. The steel panel generally has a corrugated surface designed to increase the contact area, and may also have fins at the back to enhance the heat transfer still further (these are known as convector radiators). Single and double panel types are

available in a wide range of sizes.

Skirting convectors are a variation on the convector radiator idea, and are installed at skirting board level along one or more sides of the room.

Fan-assisted convectors include an electric fan which boosts the air flow over the heated surfaces, and so offer faster warm-up times than plain panel or convector radiators. They may be wall-mounted, or concealed within the kick space beneath kitchen units. Some even fit beneath the floor.

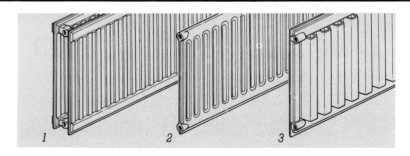

The conventional steel panel radiator is available in single and double versions in a wide range of lengths and heights (1 and 2).

Convector radiators (3) have banks of fins on the rear surface to give increased heat output without a corresponding increase

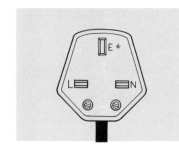

Solid fuel — *available everywhere, but needs substantial storage facilities and control cannot be fully automatic.*

Electricity — *available everywhere, needs no storage, clean to use but not so controllable due to night-time charging period.*

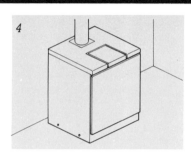

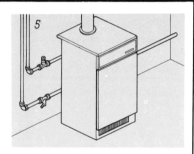

Solid fuel boilers are bulkier than other types, and are always floor-standing — alone, or within a chimney breast. All require a

conventional flue. Oil boilers can be floor-standing or wall-mounted; some use a conventional flue, others a balanced flue.

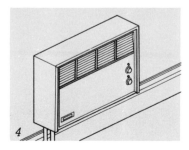

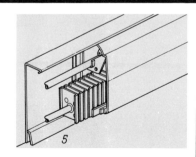

in panel size. Skirting convectors (5) are a compact type designed for fitting to one or more walls of the same room at skirting level.

Fan-assisted convectors (4) can be wall-mounted, fitted into the kick space beneath kitchen base units or housed beneath floors.

Every fuel-burning boiler needs a supply of fresh air to ensure safe and efficient combustion, and also some means of getting rid of the combustion products. Most boilers draw their air supply from the room in which they are sited, so this must have adequate ventilation. Modern gas and oil boilers often have what is known as a balanced flue, and draw their air supply through it directly from the outside air. Other boilers need a conventional flue, which can be an existing chimney (fitted with a liner if necessary) or a prefabricated flue built inside or outside the house.

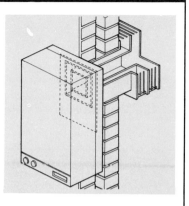

Balanced flues provide a direct fresh air supply and exhaust the combustion by-products through one short stub duct.

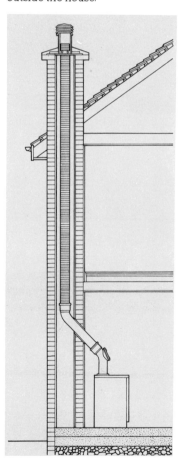

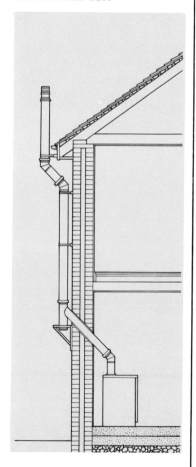

Conventional chimneys can be used with all boiler types, but may have to be lined or insulated to prevent condensation problems.

Sectional prefabricated flues can be built up inside or outside the house. New flues need Building Regulations approval.

⑦ Types of hot cylinder

The hot cylinder stores hot water, which may be heated by a boiler or an immersion heater.

Direct cylinders are so-called because water flows to the boiler and then directly to the hot taps. Indirect cylinders have an internal heat exchanger to keep the boiler and hot water circuits separate. Self-priming cylinders separate water in the boiler and hot water circuits by means of an air bubble; they need no header tank. Combination types have the cold tank on top of the cylinder.

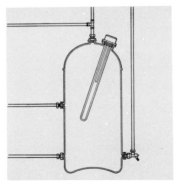

Direct cylinder

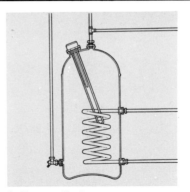

Indirect cylinder

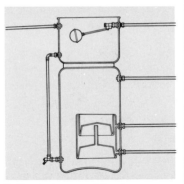

Self-priming combination cylinder

⑧ The pump

Modern central heating pumps are small and generally extremely durable — they will often run for years without the need for any maintenance. They contain a simple electrically-driven impeller, and are connected into the pipework with ordinary compression joints. Many are now sold with integral isolating valves, allowing the pump to be removed easily for maintenance or replacement. Most have variable speeds, and can cope with normal circuit loads.

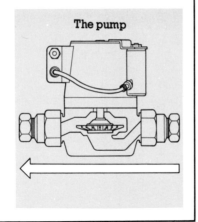

The pump

⑨ Feed-and-expansion tanks

Most domestic central heating systems are the open-vented type, and have a small cistern known as the feed-and-expansion or header tank situated at the highest point in the system. This tops up any losses in the system, accommodates the expansion in volume that occurs as the water in the system heats up and provides a safety valve if the system overheats. The tank is fed by a ballvalve, and must be able to withstand boiling water. It may be round, square or oblong.

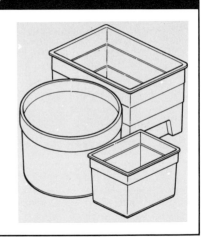

⑩ Types of valve

Valves of various types are used at different points on the heating system to control the flow of water around it.

Motorised zone valves (1&2) are used on the main circuit pipework to divert water to one part of the circuit or another, and are controlled by the system's programmer.

Radiator valves (3&4) control the flow of water through individual radiators, and may be operated by hand or by means of an integral thermostat (5&6)

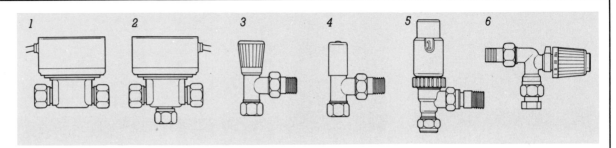

Zone valves are linked to the system's programmer, and are used to switch the water flow — to the hot cylinder or the radiators, or between different heating zones. Radiators are fitted with a handwheel valve for daily on/off control, and a lockshield valve to balance the radiator temperature. The handwheel valve may be replaced by a thermostatic radiator valve (TRV).

Typical modern heating systems may have a variety of different system controls fitted to enable them to run automatically and efficiently. At the heart will be a programmer of some sort; this will switch the system on and off at pre-set times, and will also enable it to provide hot water only or hot water and heating as required. More sophisticated types can offer different programmes for each day of the week, and will be linked to a number of other temperature or flow controls.

Thermostats operate in response to changing temperatures. The boiler thermostat prevents water leaving the boiler from rising above a pre-set temperature.

A room-thermostat switches on the boiler and pump when room temperatures fall below pre-set levels, and turns them off again when the required room temperature is achieved. It may also operate a motorised valve to divert water to the heating system rather than the hot cylinder, or to one heating zone rather than another.

A cylinder thermostat does the same for the hot water cylinder, calling for heat when the stored water temperature drops below a pre-set level.

A frost thermostat is sometimes fitted outside the house to switch on the heating if the temperature drops below freezing point — useful if the house is frequently left unoccupied for long periods.

Thermostatic radiator valves are fitted to individual radiators, and stop water flowing in when the room temperature reaches a pre-set level.

Modern heating systems can be fitted with a range of controls. Which are chosen depends on the type of boiler and programmer, and on the degree of control required by the users.

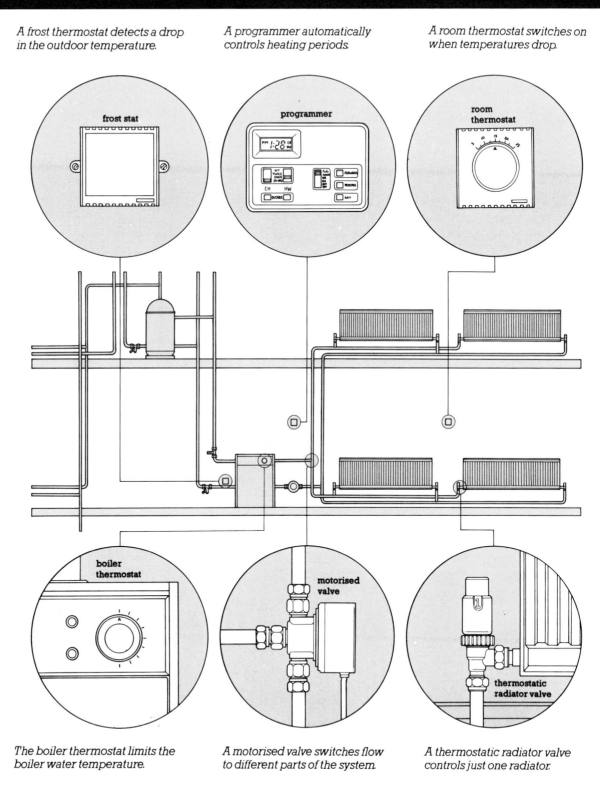

A frost thermostat detects a drop in the outdoor temperature.

A programmer automatically controls heating periods.

A room thermostat switches on when temperatures drop.

The boiler thermostat limits the boiler water temperature.

A motorised valve switches flow to different parts of the system.

A thermostatic radiator valve controls just one radiator.

When designing a central heating system, the first step is to calculate the amount of heat needed to keep each room at its design temperature while taking account of its heat losses. An example of how this is done for one room is shown below. Then all the heat requirements are added up, with an allowance for the hot water supply, to enable the boiler size to be determined.

U-values

Different types of building construction transmit heat at different rates; as a general principle, the thicker and denser the material, the better it acts as an insulator. The rate of heat transfer through a particular material, measured in watts per square metre per degree of temperature difference across the material $(W/m^2°C)$, is known as its U-value. The table below gives U-values for some common building elements.

Building element	U-value
Pitched roof (tiles, loft, plaster ceiling)	2.0
Ceiling (with 140mm insulation)	0.25
First floor (boards, joists, plaster ceiling)	1.45 (up) 1.43 (down)
Ground floor (concrete)	1.15
Ground floor (timber)	1.7
Outside wall (275mm, cavity uninsulated)	1.95
Outside wall (cavity insulated)	0.6
Internal wall (115mm, brick)	2.55
Window (single-glazed)	5.7
Double glazing	2.9

outside air temperature –1°C   ac/h = air changes per hour

ground floor

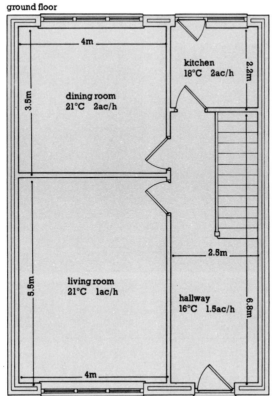

first floor

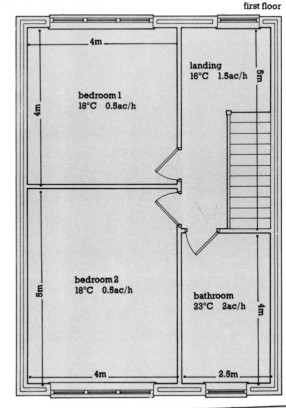

	AREA M²	U-VALUE W/m²°C	TEMP. DIFF °C	LOSS W	GAIN W	TOTAL HEAT COST FOR EACH ROOM	
							WATTS
BEDROOM 1. (18°C / 0.5 AIR CHANGES PER HOUR)						DINING RM	2207.20
WINDOW	2.50 × 5.70 × 19			270.75		LIVING RM	2518.04
EXT WALLS	17.50 × 1.95 × 19			648.38		KITCHEN.	933.19
LAND. WALL	10.00 × 2.55 × 2			51.00		HALL.	1229.17
BED. 2 WALL NO HEAT LOSS – SAME TEMP.						BEDROOM 1.	1634.89
FLOOR *	16.00 × 1.43 × 3				68.64	BEDROOM 2.	1727.95
CEILING	16.00 × 2.00 × 19			608.00		LANDING	1201.37
AIR CHANGE	40m³ × 0.33 × 19 × 0.5			125.40		BATHROOM	2092.66
				1703.53			13544.47
				– 68.64		ALLOWANCE FOR	
			TOTAL LOSS	1634.89		HOT WATER	3000.00
* HEAT GAIN DUE TO HIGHER TEMP. OF ROOM BELOW.						TOTAL HEAT REQUIREMENT	16544.47

Once the heating requirements of individual rooms have been worked out, the next step is to decide on the size of radiator that will be needed to supply it. Radiator manufacturers publish this information in their catalogues, so it is a simple matter to choose a radiator of the required heat output. Choose the height and width carefully to fit the wall space available. Note that the output of double-panel radiators is slightly less than twice that of single-panel types.

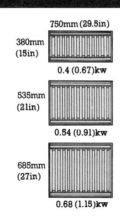
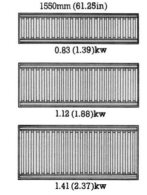
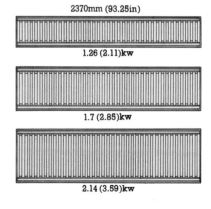

	750mm (29.5in)	1550mm (61.25in)	2370mm (93.25in)
380mm (15in)	0.4 (0.67)kw	0.83 (1.39)kw	1.26 (2.11)kw
535mm (21in)	0.54 (0.91)kw	1.12 (1.88)kw	1.7 (2.85)kw
685mm (27in)	0.68 (1.15)kw	1.41 (2.37)kw	2.14 (3.59)kw

14 Sizing boilers, pipes and pumps

Sizing the boiler

The calculations (explained opposite) of the heating requirements for the house are the basis for choosing the boiler size. Because of the inherent inaccuracy of the calculations, it is usual to add a margin of 10 per cent to the heating requirement in each room to allow for unquantifiable heat losses from pipes and fittings (this will also affect the radiator sizing — see above). A further 10 per cent is added if heating is planned to be intermittent, to ensure that the house warms up quickly from cold. On top of this, an allowance has to be made for providing domestic hot water; this is usually estimated at a nominal 2 or 3kw, rather than the full demand, since for most of the time the boiler will not be satisfying 100 per cent of the heating requirement and so will have some spare capacity.

Once the final figure has been reached, manufacturers' catalogues can be consulted to select a boiler or suitable output for the job. If the heating requirement falls between the outputs of a smaller and a larger boiler, try to find a way of reducing the heating requirement slightly, since it is more economical (in terms of both purchase price and fuel efficiency) to have a small boiler running at nearly full capacity than a large one working at only part-capacity. To give you an idea of the sort of figures involved, typical boiler sizes are likely to be around 8kW for a small terraced house, up to 14kW for a three-bedroomed semi-detached house and about 18kW for a large detached house.

Sizing the pipework

The next important stage is planning the pipe sizes. The aim of the exercise is to ensure that each section of the system can supply the demand for heat, and it usually results in pipework nearest the boiler being run in larger diameter pipework than the sections of the system most remote from it. For a typical domestic system, most of the pipe runs will be in 15mm diameter pipe, with just the main flow and return legs in 22mm pipe; parts of the system that also carry the hot water load may have to be increased in size to 28mm.

The table above gives a rough guide to sizing pipes based on the heating load they have to satisfy; the figures assume a typical temperature drop of 11°C between

Minimum pipe sizes

Total radiator output (watts)	Provisional pipe size (mm)	Heat loss from insulated pipe (W/metre)	Total load possible (watts)
up to 650	6	4	700
650 to 1300	8	6	1500
1300 to 2100	10	7	2500
2100 to 5500	15	10	6000
5500 to 11000	22	12	13000
11000 to 18000	28	14	23000
18000 to 28000	35	15	34000

Note that the insulation thickness required to give the quoted heat losses from pipework is 9mm for 6, 8 and 10mm pipe, 19mm for 22 and 28mm and 25mm for 35mm pipe.

the flow and return pipes. Once they have been used to work out provisional pipe sizes, any that appear to be on the borderline can be checked by working out the local heating load more accurately to take account of losses from the pipework itself. Of course, these can (and should) be substantially reduced by planning to insulate all buried pipe runs from the start.

Sizing the pump

The system's pump has to be capable of pushing water round the system fast enough to deliver the right amount of heat; this depends not only on actual pump speed but also on the amount of resistance the water has to overcome as it circulates. The smaller the pipe diameter and the greater the number of bends and other fittings used on the pipe runs, the greater the resistance becomes. Fortunately, most modern central heating pumps can cope with all normal loads; adjusting the pump speed provides enough fine tuning to achieve optimum performance. Only on large systems, or those involving a lot of microbore tubing, will detailed calculations of pump sizing be necessary.

15 Running pipes in floors

It is of course perfectly possible to install a heating system with all the pipework run on the surface, but the end result would be extremely untidy. For this reason, the circuit pipework is run in floor voids wherever possible so that it is hidden from view, yet is still reasonably accessible if necessary for maintenance or extension work. The only pipework that is visible is the short length rising to connect to the flow and return tappings of each radiator. Where pipes rise vertically – to the upstairs heating circuit, for example, or between boiler and cylinder – they are either hidden beneath the surface or boxed in.

It's a good idea to mark the position of all pipe runs on the floorboards above them, to aid pipe identification during repair or extension work.

16 Making threaded connections

Many of the connections between the circuit pipework and the various pieces of equipment it links up are made by means of threaded joints. These may be 'male' or 'female'; a male fitting or tapping has the thread on the outside, while a female one has the thread on the inside. The thread size is known as BSP (for British Standard Pipe) and fittings are sized in inches, not millimetres; this results in fittings with cumbersome names, such as 22mm copper x ¾in male iron for a fitting that will screw into a ¾in female tapping in the side of a hot cylinder ready for 22mm pipe to be connected to it.

Most threaded fittings can be screwed into place with an ordinary spanner, but radiator couplings need a special hexagonal key. All joints are made with PTFE tape.

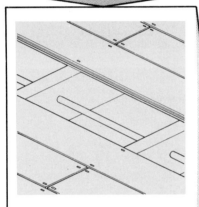

1. On new construction work, feed pipes through holes drilled in the joist centres. This is also possible with plastic pipes.

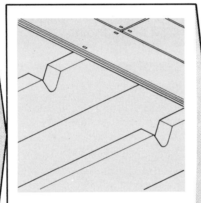

2. It is generally simpler to cut shallow notches in the joists to accept the pipes. Don't notch deeper than ⅙th of the joist depth.

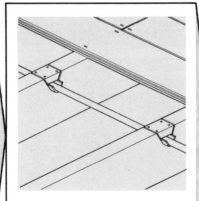

3. Rest the pipe on a pad of insulation to reduce vibration, and replace part of the cut-out if the notch is deep enough.

4. Beneath accessible suspended timber ground floors, support pipe runs using notched brackets nailed to the joist sides.

17 Running pipes in walls

Vertical pipe runs can simply be surface-mounted using pipe clips at 1.8m (6ft) spacings, but this is not particularly elegant. It's far neater to conceal the pipe within the wall – by cutting a chase in the masonry if the wall is solid, or by running it within the timber framework if it is a stud partition. In either case, avoid burying joints if possible, since repairing leaks would mean having to expose the pipe.

In solid walls, cut a chase deep enough to allow at least 12mm (½in) of plaster to cover it, using a cold chisel and club hammer (hire a powered wall chasing machine if you have a lot of pipes to conceal). Then clip the pipe in place and plaster over.

On stud partition walls, cut out panels over noggings and drill holes or cut notches so you can feed the pipe in. Then replace the panel and make good.

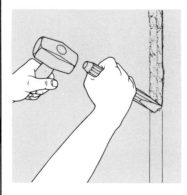

1. Cut a chase in the wall with a cold chisel and club hammer. It should be deep enough to allow 12mm of plaster over the pipe.

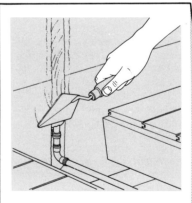

2. Clip the pipe in place in the chase and plaster over it. Avoid burying joints if possible, since leaks could be tricky to repair.

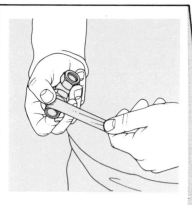

1. Wind PTFE tape round the male thread of the fitting or tapping. Wrap it clockwise when viewed end-on.

2. With radiators, insert the fitting and tighten it into place with a hexagonal key (see 4). Use a spanner on ordinary fittings.

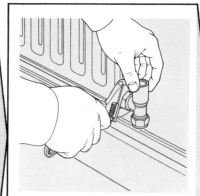

3. Connect the radiator valve to the coupling with an ordinary spanner, holding the valve vertical as you tighten the nut.

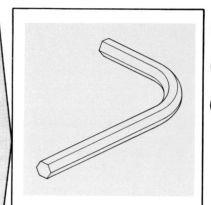

4. Use a special hexagonal key (often called a radiator spanner) to tighten couplings into the radiator's corner tappings.

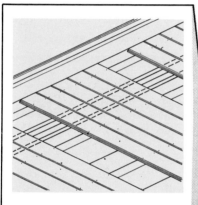

5. Where pipes run parallel to joists, lift floorboards as necessary to allow the pipes to be fed into the void.

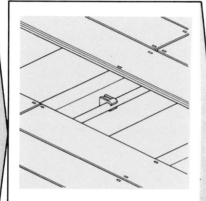

6. Use plastic pipe clips to secure the pipes at 1.2m (4ft) intervals. Aim for a very slight fall from radiators to avoid airlocks.

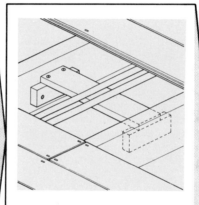

7. Where several pipes share a run between joists, support them on battens fixed between the joists at 1.2m intervals.

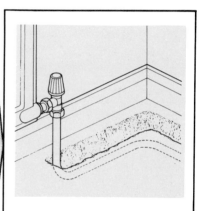

8. On solid floors, cut channels to accommodate the pipes. Damp-proof the channel if they breach the floor's damp-proof membrane.

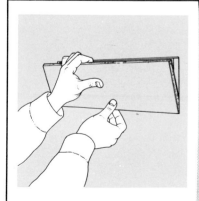

3. With stud partition walls, cut out panels between the studs to expose the noggings, using a sharp handyman's knife.

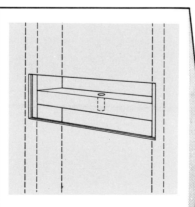

4. Drill holes in the noggings if you are using plastic pipe; cut notches in the face of the nogging for copper pipe.

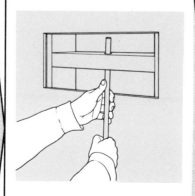

5. Feed the pipe in through the opening and guide it through the holes. Use pipe clips to hold copper pipe in notches.

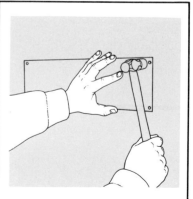

6. When the pipe run is in position, replace the plasterboard panels by nailing them to the studs and noggings.

18 Hanging a radiator

It's best to hang radiators before running in the pipework, since it's easier to adjust the position of the latter. Aim to position it about 25mm (1in) above the skirting board so you can dust this easily, and allow at least 100mm (4in) clearance between the top of the radiator and any sill above it.

On solid walls, fix the brackets with galvanised screws driven into wallplugs. On stud partition walls, you may be lucky enough to find that the bracket positions coincide with the studs. If they don't, the simplest way of mounting the radiator is to screw a piece of 12mm thick plywood securely to the studs and then to screw the radiator brackets to this; it will be hidden when the radiator is hung.

If you plan to use insulating foil behind the radiator, fit it after positioning the brackets.

1. Begin by marking the position of the centre of each hanger on the top edge of the radiator, using pencil or a felt-tip pen.

2. Hold the radiator against the wall and transfer the marks to the wall surface. Extend each line downwards with a spirit level.

19 Installing a flue liner

If you are fitting a gas or oil-fired boiler that will discharge its combustion by-products into an existing chimney, it's usually necessary to fit a flexible stainless steel flue liner. If this is not done, the flue gases may condense on the flue walls, damaging the brickwork, staining the chimney breast and, with oil-fired boilers, leading to boiler corrosion if the condensate runs back down the flue. The liner traps an insulating layer of air between itself and the flue and stops condensation from forming. Make sure the correct liner is used – different types are needed for gas and oil boilers.

Flexible liners cannot be used with solid fuel boilers. Instead, flues built after 1966 must be lined with either a sectional liner (straight flues only) or with a pumped-in lining of lightweight insulating material.

20 Flue terminals

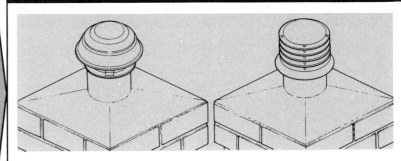

Make sure that you fit the correct type of flue terminal when installing a flexible flue liner; you need a GC1 type (right) with a *gas-fired boiler, a 'core' type (left) with an oil-fired one. Both are fitted to the top end of the liner and are neatly flaunched in place.*

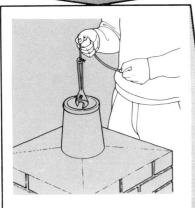

1. To fit a flexible flue liner, drop a weighted string down the flue so you can measure the length of liner needed. Cut it to size.

2. Chip away the flaunching from the top of the stack and lift the old chimney pot clear. Rope it to the stack for extra safety.

3. Lower a weighted string down the flue to a helper below, and attach it to the plug-in nose cone. Lower the liner into the flue.

4. When the liner has reached the bottom safely, secure its top end in the clamping plate and fit the terminal cowl over it.

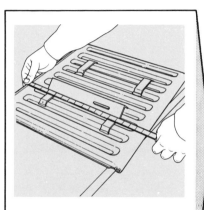

3. Hook the brackets on the hangers and measure the distance from the top of the bracket to the bottom edge of the radiator.

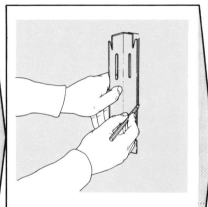

4. Add 25mm for clearance, and mark the position of the top of the bracket on the wall. Then draw round the bracket baseplate.

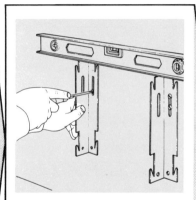

5. Mark the fixing holes, drill and plug them and fit the first bracket. Then fit the second, using a spirit level to check its height.

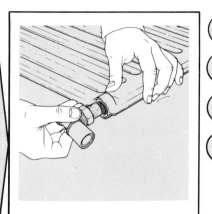

6. At this stage, it's best to attach the valve couplings, the air vent and a blanking plug to the four corner tappings.

21 Radiator fittings

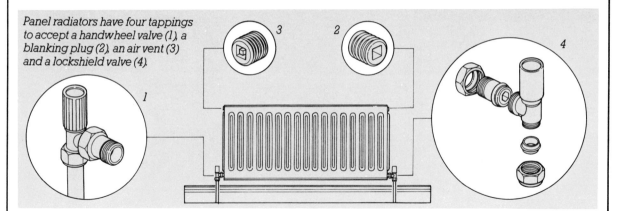

Panel radiators have four tappings to accept a handwheel valve (1), a blanking plug (2), an air vent (3) and a lockshield valve (4).

7. Finally, hang the radiator on its brackets by locating the hangers over the lugs on the brackets. Check that it is secure.

5. Remake the flaunching round the cowl using a 1:3 cement:sharp sand mortar. Slope it smoothly to ensure rainwater runs off.

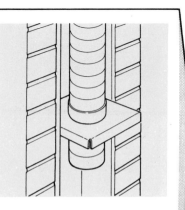

6. Fit the blanking-off plate round the bottom end of the liner just above the boiler position to form an insulated air column.

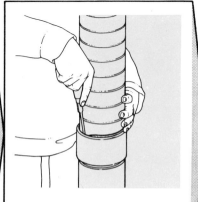

7. Connect the liner into the flue pipe from the boiler using asbestos rope and fire cement to make an airtight joint.

8. With oil-fired boilers, pour vermiculite insulation into the gap between liner and flue before fitting the top clamping plate.

22 Installing a balanced-flue boiler

The main advantage of balanced-flue boilers is that they are comparatively straightforward to fit; for this reason they are particularly appropriate for do-it-yourself installation. Since the balanced flue provides both a guaranteed supply of fresh air for safe combustion and an exhaust duct direct to the outside air, there are no problems of ventilation or flue construction to be overcome. Fan-assisted types do not even have to be sited on an external wall.

Most wall-mounted balanced-flue boilers are designed to be built into a run of kitchen units, and it is important to ensure that there is sufficient ventilation round the boiler casing.

Remember that the final connection of the gas supply must be left to the local gas board, although you can run the pipe back to the new take-off point.

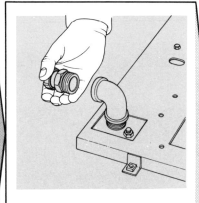

1. With the boiler on its front, attach the various couplings to the flow and return tappings using PTFE tape and jointing compound.

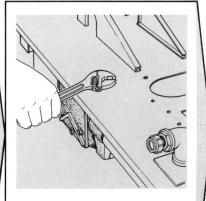

2. If the system will be fully pumped, fit a blanking-off plug to block off the gravity flow for the hot water circuit.

23 Fitting the balanced flue

The balanced flue provides an air supply to the boiler's combustion chamber and also takes away the noxious combustion products, all through a surprisingly narrow duct that protrudes through the house wall immediately behind the boiler. To install it, all you have to do is cut a rectangular hole through the wall and insert the flue lining inside which the inlet and outlet ducting fit. There are no restrictions as to where the flue is positioned indoors, but there are rules about avoiding proximity to windows, ventilators, corners and so on which must be followed (see opposite), and these will have some bearing on where the boiler is sited indoors.

On the outside, a special terminal is fitted over the ends of the inlet and outlet ducts. A protective grille may have to be added if it is accessible.

24 Using a template

Wall-hung boilers are supplied with a template to help in marking the positions of the flue outlet and the fixing holes. Align it with a horizontal line level with the top edge of the boiler.

1. Mark the position of the boiler and flue on the wall using the template provided (see above right), then chop out the flue opening.

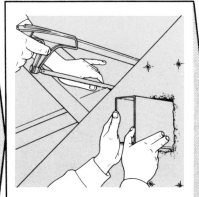

2. Measure the thickness of the outside wall, cut the aluminium flue liner to length and push it into place through the hole.

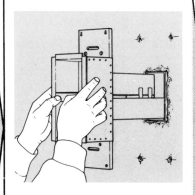

3. Cut the inlet duct to match the wall thickness and screw it to the plenum box. Offer this up and mark the exhaust duct outdoors.

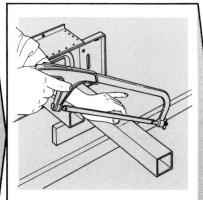

4. Withdraw the duct unit and cut the exhaust duct to length. Then remove the liner and coat inside the opening with plaster.

3. Attach lengths of copper pipe to the various flow and return tappings, ready for connection to the circuit pipework.

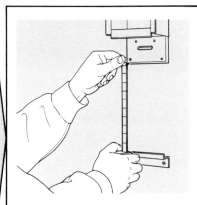

4. Carefully measure the distance from the bottom edge of the plenum box (see opposite) and position the boiler support bracket.

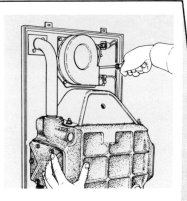

5. Lift the boiler up into position on its mounting bracket. If it's too heavy for you, get help. Then screw it to the wall and plenum box.

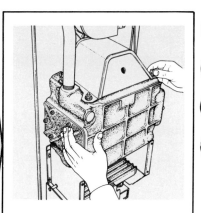

6. Next, fit the boiler's flue hood in position, screwing it to the plenum chamber and bolting it over the waterway.

25 Positioning the flue

Because the flue provides both fresh air for combustion and an exhaust for the combustion by-products, there must be no obstructions near the exterior terminal to impede the air flow. It should not be sited near the corners of the building, or on a wall facing and close to another building, where strong winds could affect its performance. There are also restrictions on how close it can be placed to windows, downpipes, ventilators, eaves and other obstructions.

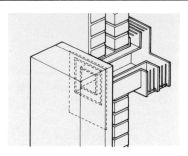

The flue's inlet and exhaust performance depend on the absence of any obstructions near its exterior terminal.

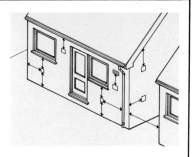

There are several restrictions on where the flue terminal can be placed in relation to eaves, windows, corners and so on.

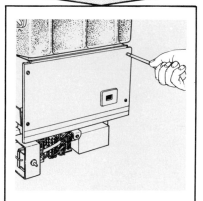

7. Finally, attach the cover over the front of the combustion chamber. This must be a tight fit so that no gases escape.

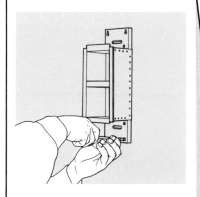

5. Reinsert the liner and make good round it. When the plaster has set, replace the duct unit and screw the plenum box to the wall.

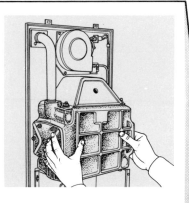

6. Locate the boiler on its support bracket, adding shims if necessary. Then screw it to the wall and to the plenum box.

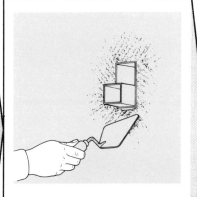

7. Make good the interior wall round the flue liner. Take care not to allow any mortar to get into either of the ducts.

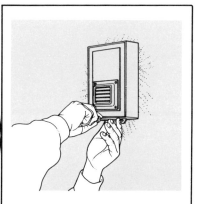

8. Complete the installation by fitting the flue terminal. Add a protective mesh grille if the terminal is within reach.

Back boilers

Back boilers are designed to be installed within a fireplace recess – a useful feature when space is at a premium. Early solid fuel back boilers heated water on a direct system, with the hot cylinder sited either high in the adjoining alcove cupboard, or in an airing cupboard in a bedroom immediately above it.

Modern solid fuel back boilers are linked to an indirect cylinder, and usually have an enclosed solid fuel room heater rather than an open fire. Some are hopper-fed, thermostatically controlled and fitted with a fan and time switch so the heat output can be easily regulated.

Gas-fired back boilers have a completely separate room heater in front of the boiler, and either can be used independently of the other. Full automatic control of boiler operation is provided by a programmer.

Free-standing boilers

Free-standing boilers are usually installed in kitchens or utility rooms, and discharge either into an existing flue or into a new pre-fabricated flue fitted inside or outside the house.

Modern solid-fuel types can be hopper-fed, reducing refuelling to a once-a-day operation, and some incorporate combustion air fans which can rapidly increase the burning rate as required and so give a greater degree of control over heat output.

Free-standing gas-fired types are slim enough to be incorporated into a run of kitchen units; some include the pump and controls within the boiler casing.

Oil-fired boilers are mainly of the pressure-jet type nowadays, and are quiet enough for installation in a kitchen. Controls allow for a fully automatic operation.

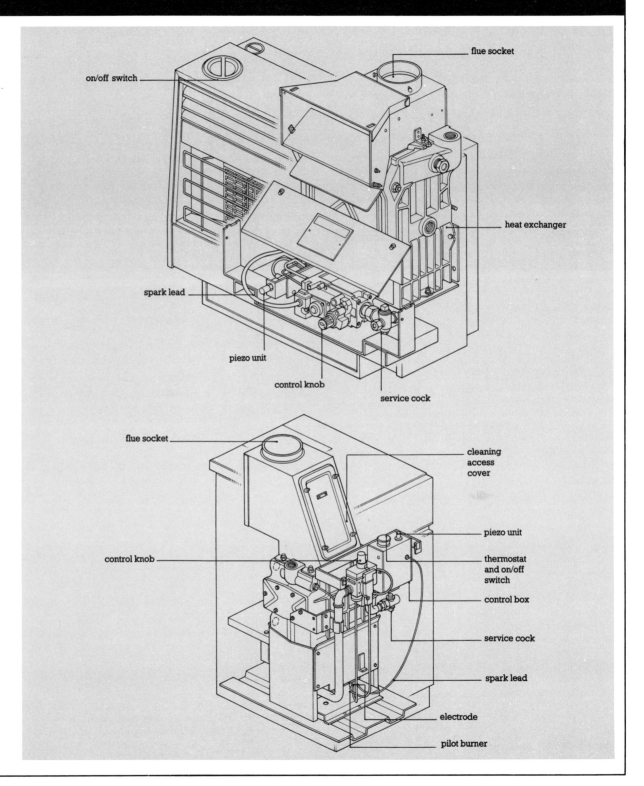

27 Installing a hot cylinder

Whatever type of cylinder you are fitting, you will need to provide the following connections:
- 22mm feed from the cold water storage cistern;
- 28mm pipes to and from the boiler (gravity system) or
- 22mm boiler circuit (pumped);
- 22mm vent pipe running up to the cold water storage cistern;
- 22mm hot water supply pipes running off the vent pipe to supply the hot taps.

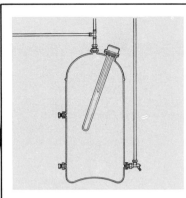

1. Direct cylinders are used nowadays only with immersion heaters, since scale soon clogs the boiler circuit.

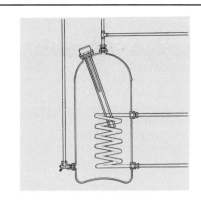

2. Indirect cylinders contain a heat exchanger which heats stored water; the primary and secondary circuits are separate.

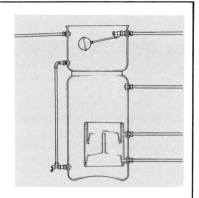

3. Self-priming cylinders need no feed-and-expansion tank; the primary circuit is topped up from the cold supply.

28 Fitting a header tank

Most conventional systems are described as vented, and have a small open tank known as the feed-and-expansion or header tank positioned at the top of the system. This accommodates the expansion in the system's water content as it heats up, tops the primary circuit up if any slight losses occur through leaks or evaporation, and provides a safety vent if the primary circuit overheats for any reason.

The tank must be capable of withstanding boiling water; its body should be stamped to indicate this. It is usually situated close to the cold water storage cistern, and is fed by a 15mm pipe teed off the rising main and connected to a high-pressure ballvalve. The 22mm feed pipe is connected about 50mm above the bottom of the tank, and the 22mm vent pipe terminates just above the overflow level.

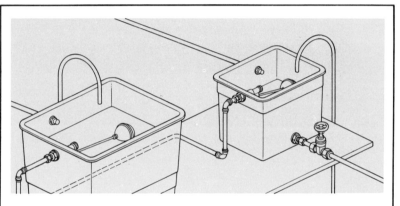

The feed-and-expansion tank is set on a firm platform, usually next to the cold water storage cistern. It's fed from the rising main, and must have a 22mm overflow pipe to the eaves. It should be fitted with a lid through which the vent pipe passes, and an insulating jacket.

29 Adding motorised valves

Motorised valves are used to control the flow of water between the cylinder and heating circuits, or between different parts (zones) of the heating system. Two-port and tree-port types are available. They contain a small electric motor which opens the valve (and closes it too on some types; others close by spring action). Some incorporate switches that can operate other electrical circuits, such as those controlling the boiler and pump, when the valve is operated. They can be operated by means of a programmer, or can be under the control of a thermostat attached to the hot cylinder.

Motorised valves are connected into the circuit pipework where required by the system design, using compression-type fittings at each port.

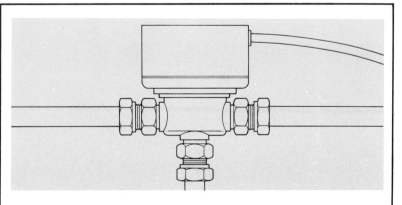

The pipework is connected to a motorised valve by compression-type fittings; a two-port valve is similar to the three-port type, but minus the bottom port. The motor is mounted on top of the valve and is wired back to the system programmer or a thermostat.

30 Fitting pumps

Circulating pumps should always be installed between a pair of isolating valves so they can be removed easily for servicing or repair. Some come complete with valves; otherwise, fit standard gate valves.

During the installation of a central heating system, it's best to remove the pump after it has been plumbed into position and to fit a plain length of pipe between the couplings. This is left in place until the system has been filled and flushed through to remove debris.

When installing the pump, check with the fitting instructions to see whether the pump motor shaft has to be horizontal. Mount it on a vertical pipe run if possible, so air that enters the pump is vented up the pipe. Straight runs of pipe about 450mm long at each side of the pump help to minimise noise.

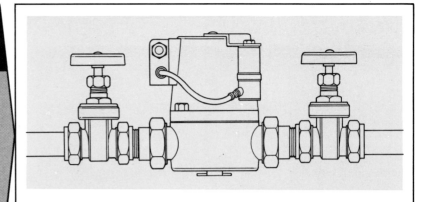

Always mount a pump between isolating valves so it can be removed easily for servicing or repair. Some pumps have integral valves. Avoid siting the pump at the lowest point of the heating circuit return pipe, since sludge may collect in it.

31 Making up circuit pipework

It's best to start by positioning the major components of the system – the boiler, radiators, tanks and cylinders – before starting to make up any of the pipework. If any of the connections are likely to be awkward to make up with the equipment in position, connect short stubs of pipe to which the circuit pipework can then be linked at the appropriate time. This is often essential for hot cylinders in awkward recesses.

Plan the pipework installation to minimise the amount of disruption to the household. For example, pipework to the bathroom radiator and the bathroom appliances can be run in at the same time, avoiding two separate lifts of floorboards. Similarly, flow and return pipes between boiler and cylinder and pipes to and from the loft should be installed at the same time. Label pipes as you fit them.

Divide the installation up into areas so you can tackle pipe runs within any part of the house in one session. Fit all the major components before running in the pipe circuits.

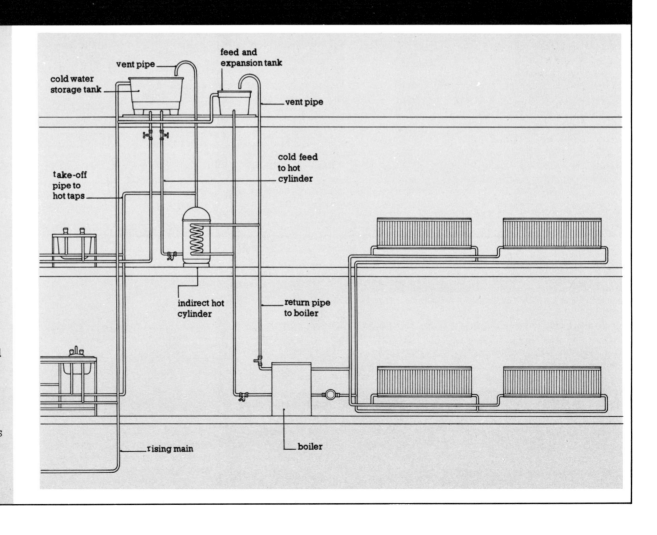

32 Gas and oil pipes

The supply of gas to the boiler should be teed off other pipes close to the meter. Soldered joints must be used on the pipe run; leave the final connection to a qualified fitter.

Oil storage tanks supply the boiler by gravity feed, and should be installed on brick piers with a slight slope towards a sludge valve so condensed water or rust particles can be removed.

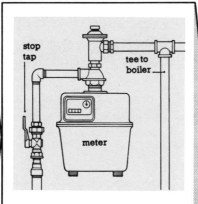

1. A new supply pipe for a gas boiler is teed off existing pipes close to the meter. Soldered fittings are used throughout.

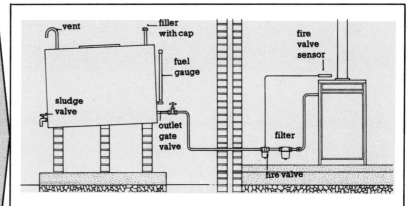

2. Oil storage tanks are sited out of doors on stout brick piers. The filler pipe has a screwed cap, while the vent pipe is designed so rain cannot enter. A filter catches debris in the supply pipe, and a fire valve and sensor is fitted near the boiler.

33 Working with microbore pipe

Microbore pipe is mostly 8, 10 or 12mm in diameter, and is soft enough to be bent easily by hand. This means that installation is much easier than with small-bore (15mm) pipe, since the pipes can be threaded through floor joists or behind skirtings rather like electrical cables. However, to avoid kinking on all but the shallowest bends, a bending spring – slipped over the pipe rather than inside it – should always be used.

The main flow and return pipes for the heating circuit on each floor are run in 15 or 22mm pipe to manifolds, from where the microbore flow and return pipes run to each radiator. These are usually connected by twin-entry valves, which incorporate a long tube to carry flow water to the far end of the radiator. The other end of the radiator is sealed with a plug.

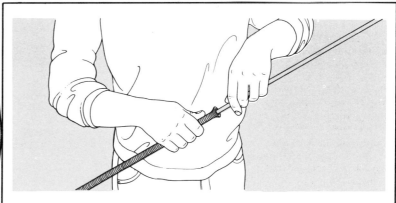

Although microbore pipe is flexible enough to be bent easily by hand, kinking will occur on all but the gentlest bends. To avoid this, always use an external bending spring of the appropriate size for the pipe being bent.

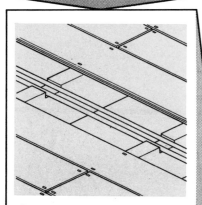

1. Pipe runs beneath floors can be set in shallow notches cut in the joists, or can be threaded through holes in the joist centres.

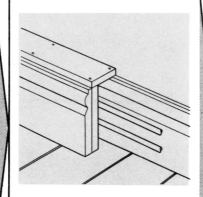

2. Because of the small diameter of microbore pipes, they can be concealed easily behind false skirting boards.

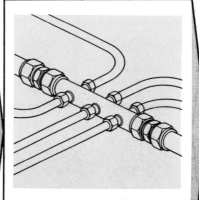

3. Manifolds distribute water to each radiator on the floor. The main flow and return pipes are 15 or 22mm in diameter.

4. With microbore pipework, radiators are usually fed by means of a twin-entry valve at one end of the radiator.

A central heating system is only as good as its controls, and most modern systems have quite an impressive array.

At the heart of the controls is the system's programmer, which is mounted somewhere convenient so its settings can be checked and altered easily if necessary. It is generally surface-mounted, but flush-mounting types are available. The various cables linking it to the other controls can be run on the surface in mini-trunking, or can be buried in conduit.

The room thermostat is also wall-mounted – on an inside wall at least 1.5m (about 5ft) above the floor in any convenient position where air can circulate freely round it. However, it must be out of draughts and away from any heat sources – radiators, pipework, even TV sets – which could encourage it to give false readings. Flush and surface-mounted types are available.

The cylinder thermostat is usually strapped to the side of the hot cylinder, about a third of the way up and in contact with the metal walls.

The system's circulating pump and any motorised valves are usually concealed, but it is sensible not to make them too inaccessible in case they need maintenance or repair work.

All the various components are connected together via a multi-terminal junction box; wiring instructions supplied with the programmer indicate how the various connections are made. Power is supplied to the box from a fused connection unit fitted with a 3-amp fuse.

A typical control set-up involves some quite complicated wiring using a junction box and special multi-core cable. Detailed instructions are supplied with the programmer.

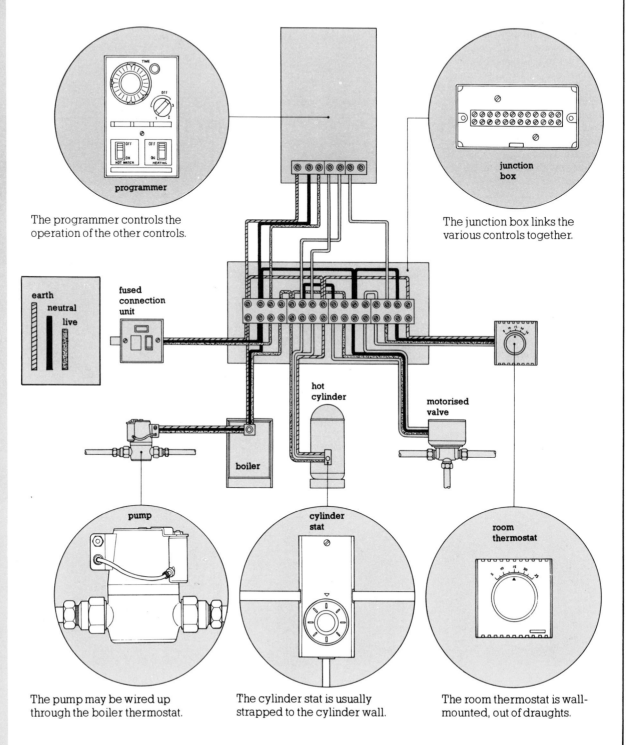

The programmer controls the operation of the other controls.

The junction box links the various controls together.

The pump may be wired up through the boiler thermostat.

The cylinder stat is usually strapped to the cylinder wall.

The room thermostat is wall-mounted, out of draughts.

programmer

junction box

earth
neutral
live

fused connection unit

hot cylinder

motorised valve

boiler

pump

cylinder stat

room thermostat

With all the installation work completed on the system, the final stage is to fill it with water and get the system running – known as commissioning.

To fill the system, open the gatevalve to allow the header tank to fill. Then open all radiator handwheel and lockshield valves, and close all drain cocks and radiator air vents. As the system fills, check carefully for leaks – it's a good idea to leave floorboards loose until this has been done. Once the header tank begins to fill up, indicating that the system is full, bleed any trapped air out of radiators and other vent points, starting at the lowest radiator on the system. Then check the water level in the header tank; it should be about 100mm above the take-off pipe. Adjust the level if necessary by moving the float or altering the float arm angle.

It's a good idea at this stage to flush the system through so any debris in the pipework is washed out. Attach a hose to the lowest drain cock and let the system drain and refill.

Now it's time to fire the boiler (see below), set the controls and bring the water temperature up to the lowest setting on the boiler thermostat and with the pump running at full speed. This helps to shift any remaining dirt and debris from the pipework that wasn't shifted by the previous cold flushing. Drain the system one more time while it is still warm, opening the radiator air vents one by one as the water level drops, and refill.

During the final refilling, remember to add a corrosion inhibitor via the header tank. Follow the manufacturer's instructions concerning quantities and dilutions.

Now the actual balancing of the system – the setting of pump speeds and lockshield valves – can take place – see below.

Solid fuel boilers

1. Check the manufacturer's literature for instructions on preparing the fuel. Light some newspaper in the base of the flue to warm it, then light the fire. Check that the hopper lid is closed securely.

2. Open the damper fully or adjust the boiler thermostat to a high setting to encourage the fire to 'take' quickly. Close down the damper or reduce the setting progressively as the fire becomes fully established.

3. Check that flue gases are being drawn properly up the flue, and are now blowing back.

4. Regulate the boiler controls as recommended in the manufacturer's literature.

Gas and oil-fired boilers

Both gas and oil-fired boilers must be commissioned by the appropriate expert – the gas board or the oil company – since special equipment is needed to set them up properly. In the case of gas boilers, this can be done at the same time as the gas supply is connected. Then set the boiler thermostat to its highest setting.

Checking system flows

With the boiler running, the next job is to check the progress of water round the circuit in case there are any blockages anywhere.

1. If you have a gravity circuit to the hot water cylinder, monitor the progress of the water by feeling the flow pipe from the boiler, and check that the cylinder itself becomes warm.

2. With the pump on, check the progress of warm water along the circuit pipework and into each radiator.

3. When the cylinder and all the radiators are warm, run the system for half an hour or so and then bleed each radiator to get rid of any dissolved air given off as the water heated up.

Balancing the system

Since different areas of the system will, all things being equal, receive differing amounts of hot water depending on how much resistance they present to its flow, the next job is to increase the flow resistance in 'greedy' areas so that the heat is evenly distributed. This is done by balancing the system using the lockshield valves fitted to each radiator.

1. Start by running the system up to its normal running temperature, with the pump speed on its middle setting (if it's variable) and all the radiator handwheel and lockshield valves fully open.

2. Check the radiator temperatures by hand, and close down the lockshield valve slightly on those that feel hotter than average – usually those nearest the boiler. This will create a rough balance in the system, ready for the fine tuning.

3. Hire a pair of clip-on radiator thermometers, which are fitted to the flow and return pipes below the radiator being checked. Clip them on to the radiator furthest from the boiler and check that the flow temperature matches the design temperature – usually about 82°C. If it doesn't, check the boiler thermostat and other controls (you may need to turn the room thermostat up fully to keep the system running while you carry out the balancing).

4. Now check the temperature of the return pipe is correct – a typical drop will be about 11°C, giving a return temperature of about 71°C. Gradually close the lockshield valve until the correct drop is achieved. The actual temperatures may fluctuate once the boiler is up to temperature, because the boiler thermostat will be cutting in and out; this doesn't matter so long as the actual drop is correct.

5. Repeat the process for the other radiators, working back towards the boiler. Then check them all again; setting one can unbalance the others, and you may need to make a series of fine adjustments.

6. If you cannot achieve a temperature drop of 11°, you may have to adjust the pump speed; raise it to increase the temperature drop, lower it to decrease it.

Checking the controls

Finally, check that the controls are operating properly.

1. Turn the room thermostat from maximum to minimum and back again; check that this makes the pump stop and start.

2. Check that the heating options selected on the programmer switch on and off at the pre-set times, and test the manual over-ride.

3. Check that thermostatic radiator valves are operating correctly.

36 Adding an extra radiator

Most central heating systems have enough spare capacity to allow at least one extra radiator to be added to the system, although if the system is to be significantly extended it may be necessary to upgrade the boiler.

The job involves cutting into the existing flow and return pipes at a convenient point and connecting in tails that will be linked to the new radiator. This means that the heating system will have to be drained – a good opportunity to flush out sludge, descale the boiler or incorporate a corrosion inhibitor – unless a pipe-freezing kit can be hired. This forms plugs of ice in the pipes on either side of the point where the tee is to be connected, and saves the tedious job of draining and refilling the entire system. Once the tees have been connected in, the new radiator is hung and connected up.

1. Start by deciding on the radiator position in relation to the existing circuit pipework, and hang it on the wall on its bracket.

2. Make up or bend the sections of pipework that will run from the radiator valves to a convenient below-floor connection point.

37 Draining the heating system

You will need to drain down your heating system to carry out repairs or alterations to the system, and you may also have to drain it in a hurry if a leak develops or a pipe bursts. It's therefore essential that you know how to stop water entering the system, and where the main drain cock is situated.

The first step is to turn off the boiler, and an immersion heater if one is fitted in a direct system. Allow solid fuel boilers time for the fire to die down before draining the system.

Then stop water entering the header tank by turning off the stop tap feeding it, or by tying up the ballvalve arm, and attach a length of hose to the lowest drain cock. Lead this to an outside gully. Then undo the drain cock and open radiator vents as the water level drops. Reverse the sequence to refill the system.

38 Getting rid of airlocks

Airlocks occur when air enters the plumbing or heating system and becomes trapped – usually at a high point in the system. There are several possible causes.

Among the most common are faulty pipework design and wrong pipe sizing. For example, the pipe taking hot water from the hot cylinder should slope downhill slightly from the cylinder; if it slopes the other way, any air that collects is trapped and cannot escape up the vent pipe, causing an airlock. Similarly, if the cold supply pipe to the hot cylinder is too small, air can be drawn into the system through the vent pipe when the bath is being run. Such faults should be cured by altering or replacing the pipes, since the problem will keep on recurring.

An airlock can usually be cured temporarily by using water at mains pressure to drive it out.

1. Start by turning off the stop tap on the branch from the rising main which feeds the header tank. Use penetrating oil if it's stuck.

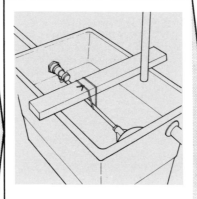

2. If you don't have a stop tap, stop water entering the tank by tying up the ballvalve arm to a batten laid across the top of the tank.

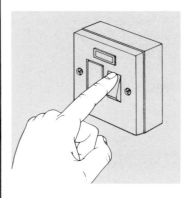

3. Before starting to drain the system, turn off the boiler. Also switch off the immersion heater on a direct system.

4. Connect a length of ordinary garden hose to the main drain cock, which is situated at the lowest point on the system.

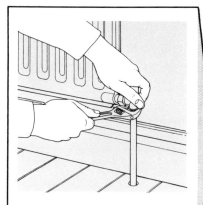

3. Connect the upper end of these sections to the radiator valves, tightening the compression fittings carefully with a spanner.

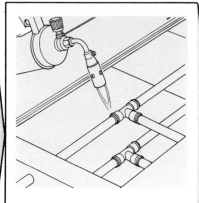

4. Run the new flow and return pipes back below the floor to meet the main circuit pipework and connect them in using two tees.

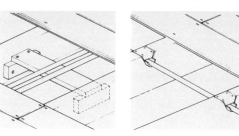

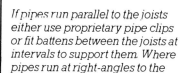

If pipes run parallel to the joists either use proprietary pipe clips or fit battens between the joists at intervals to support them. Where pipes run at right-angles to the joists, cut a notch for the pipe and replace a piece of the waste material to hold the pipe firmly in place. Mark the floorboards above pipe runs.

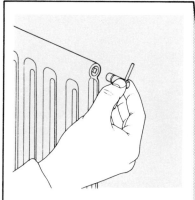

1. Air in the heating system usually collects in the highest radiator on the system. Bleed it by opening the air vent with a special key.

2. To clear an airlock in the hot pipework, link the hot tap to the kitchen cold tap with hose and open the hot tap, then the cold one.

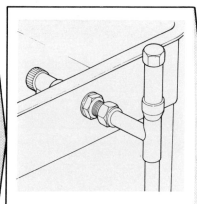

3. If air persistently collects at a high point in the system, it may be worth installing an automatic air vent at that point.

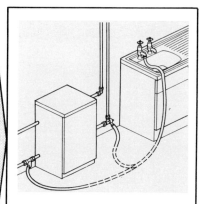

4. Avoid airlocks after draining heating systems by filling from the bottom using a hose between kitchen tap and drain cock.

5. Lead the hose to a gully or drain outside the house. Check that the indoors end is securely pushed on to the drain cock.

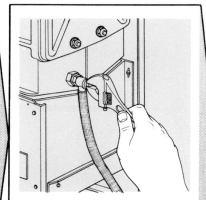

6. Open the drain cock by turning its square spindle with a spanner. Check that water is flowing into the gully.

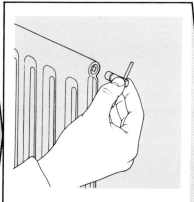

7. As the water level in the system drops, open the air vents on all the radiators to encourage all the water to drain out quickly.

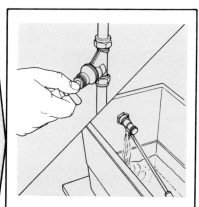

8. Refill the system again by closing the drain cock and restoring the water supply to the header tank.

40 Curing boiler problems

Modern central heating boilers generally give little trouble, especially if they are regularly serviced, but there are a number of simple repairs that you can carry out yourself – on gas-fired boilers. Work on oil-fired boilers should be confined to cleaning oil filters twice a year; servicing should be left to an expert. With solid fuel boilers, sluggish output could be due to soot in the flueways and ash clogging the grate; occasional cleaning should solve the problem.

On gas-fired boilers, the commonest problems involve the pilot light, the thermostat and the automatic ignition system. The illustrations here show a typical boiler; if you're unsure how they relate to yours, leave the work to an expert.

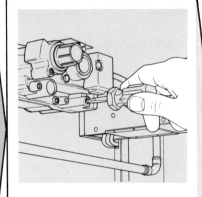

1. If the pilot light keeps going out, try adjusting the flame height by turning the small screw situated on the gas valve.

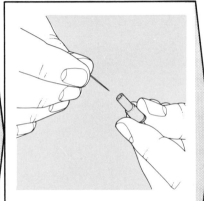

2. If this doesn't work, suspect a blocked nozzle. Clear it with a pricker. You may have to remove the main burner assembly to get at it.

41 Types of thermostat

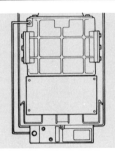

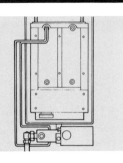

Electric thermostats have a sensor that is inserted in a dry pocket in the boiler's water jacket; a capillary tube links it to the boiler's control unit. With non-electric types two capillary tubes run from the water jacket to the boiler's gas valve.

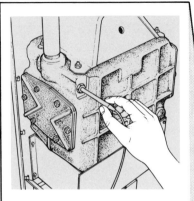

1. To replace a thermostat, undo the retaining screw or remove the split pin that secures it in its housing within the water jacket.

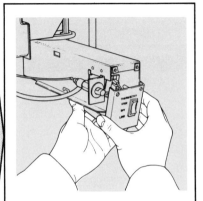

2. Remove the control panel cover to get to the capillary connections. Disconnect the old thermostat and fit the new one.

42 Cleaning the boiler

It's a good idea to clean out a gas boiler annually to keep it working properly. First of all, switch off the gas and electricity supplies and allow the boiler to cool down. Then remove the boiler casing to give a clear view of the heat exchanger, and clean it with a stiff-bristled flexible wire brush. If the gas valve and thermostat are directly beneath, cover them with a cloth to keep dirt and soot out.

Next, remove the flue cover and clean inside the flue with a brush. Check the condition of the gasket between flue and boiler, which may need replacing. Then use a vacuum cleaner with a nozzle attachment to clear out all loose debris from the boiler surfaces, including the inside of the boiler casing.

Finally, remove the burner unit, brush it down and clean the gauze filter if one is fitted.

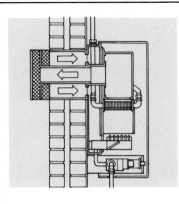

1. Most balanced-flue gas boilers have a similar internal layout, with the burners beneath the heat exchanger.

2. Remove the boiler casing and use a stiff-bristled flexible wire brush to clean all the accessible surfaces of the heat exchanger.

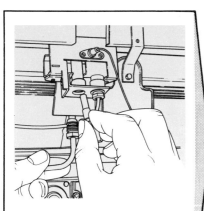

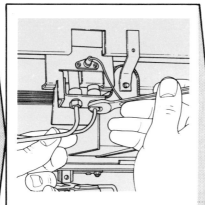

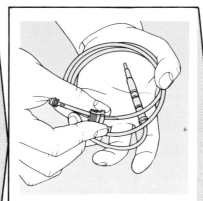

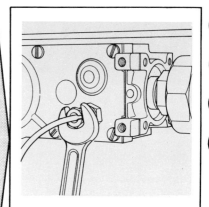

3. If the nozzle is completely blocked and cannot be cleared with a pricker, or it is showing signs of wear, replace it.

4. If the thermocouple is faulty the pilot will not light. To replace it, unscrew its fixing nuts – one by the pilot, one at the gas valve.

5. Straighten the new thermocouple, slide on the two split nuts at the flattened section and slide one along to each end.

6. Reconnect the new thermocouple, tighten the nuts at the pilot light and gas valve positions. Test its operation.

43 *Checking the ignition device*

Piezo-electric spark generators are used on most boilers that are fitted with permanent pilot lights. When a fault occurs it is usually either in the unit's high-tension lead or its generator. You can test the generator unit by unplugging the lead and holding an insulated screwdriver with its tip nearly touching the piezo terminal. If the generator is working, you will see a spark when the device is fired. If it isn't, unscrew the spark unit from its bracket and fit a replacement by reversing the disconnection sequence.

Check the lead itself by disconnecting it and holding its tip close to the boiler's water jacket. Fire the device; if the lead is undamaged you will see a spark between the tip and the boiler casing. Replace it if it's faulty. Make sure the lead is kept well away from the burners.

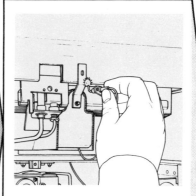

1. Check the high tension lead by disconnecting it and holding it close to the boiler casing. Fire the device and look for a spark.

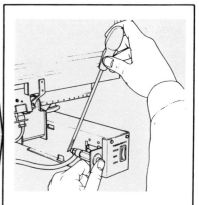

2. Check the spark generator by disconnecting the lead and holding a screwdriver near to the terminal. Fire it and look for a spark.

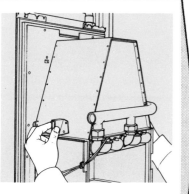

3. Next, unscrew and remove the flue cover and clean out soot and debris from inside the flue itself, again using a stiff brush.

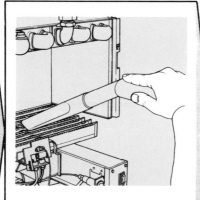

4. With all the soot and dirt loosened, use a vacuum cleaner with a nozzle attachment to clean all the internal surfaces.

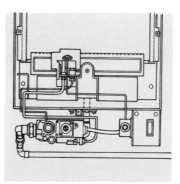

5. To clean the burners, turn off the gas supply and disconnect the gas supply line. Then remove the cover plate at the bottom of the boiler.

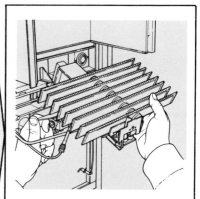

6. Slide out the burners and clean them. There is usually enough play on the electrical cable to the gas valve to allow this.

44 Curing pump problems

The circulating pump is the heart of a central heating system, and modern pumps generally perform for years without giving any trouble. However, there are several minor faults which can occur, and which you can easily put right yourself.

The first is air collecting in the pump; getting rid of this is simply a matter of opening the air bleed screw on the pump casing with a screwdriver. The second is faulty electrical connections; vibration can make these work loose, and removing the inspection plate on the pump body to check them is a straightforward task. The third is a blockage, caused by sludge – the by-product of corrosion – and other debris within the pipework fouling the pump's impeller.

It's often cheaper and simpler to completely replace an old pump than to try to repair it.

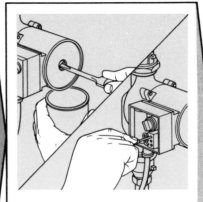

1. Cold radiators, noise in the system or overheating indicate a pump fault. Try bleeding off air; check electrical connections.

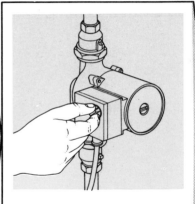

2. Try adjusting the pump speed to help clear sludge that may be clogging up the impeller. Drain the system for a permanent cure.

45 Replacing a radiator valve

You may have to replace an existing radiator valve which has developed a fault, or you may want to fit a thermostatic valve (TRV) in place of an ordinary handwheel type. The procedure is the same in either case.

Start by shutting off and draining down the heating system. Then disconnect the existing valve from the radiator coupling and the pipe tail, and set it aside. Carefully cut through the olive on the pipe tail so you can remove it and the old capnut.

Now you can connect the new valve to the radiator coupling and join in the pipe tail, taking care not to kink it as you tighten the capnut. Finally, fit the thermostatic sensor head.

Note that you shouldn't replace all your radiator valves with thermostatic ones; leave one manual one as an open circuit for the boiler if the others shut down.

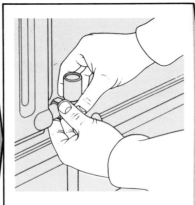

1. Drain the heating system so you can disconnect the old valve from the radiator coupling and the supply pipe.

2. Connect the new valve body to the coupling and the pipe tail, and fit the sensor head. Refill the system and test the valve.

46 Patching a radiator

Most panel radiators are made from sheet steel, and this can corrode away from the inside as time goes by, especially along seams and at corners, because of electrolytic corrosion within the system. The result of a leak can be a highly unpleasant mess, with black, sludge-laden water spoiling floorcoverings.

If a pinhole leak appears, it may be possible to effect a repair by soldering the leak or patching it with a plumbing repair putty. If solder is to be used the radiator should be drained; repair putties can usually be applied if the surface is wet, but check the instructions first. Use wire wood or emery paper to remove surface rust from round the pinholed area, and treat it with a rust inhibitor before attempting to patch the leak. In the long term, aim to replace the radiator.

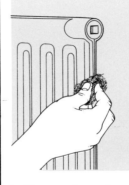

1. Clean up the surface of the radiator in the vicinity of a leak, using wire wool or emery paper to expost bright metal.

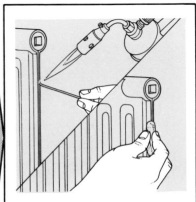

2. Either solder the leaky seam after draining the radiator, or use two-part epoxy plumbers' repair putty to patch it.

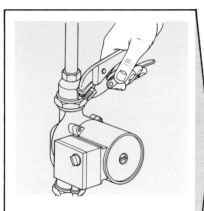

3. If the pump is completely blocked, it will be necessary to disconnect it from the circuit. First turn off the isolating valves.

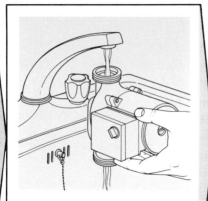

4. Flush the pump through with clean water to remove as much of the sludge as possible from the impeller chamber.

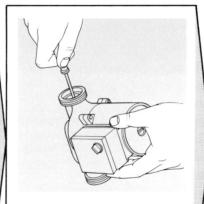

5. If the impeller is actually jammed, try to free it by inserting a screwdriver and locating it on the impeller blade.

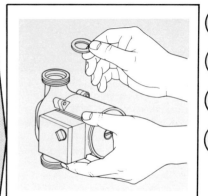

6. Once you have cleared the blockage, fit new seals at each end of the pump and replace it between the isolating valves.

47 Faultfinder

If you have problems with your central heating system, it helps to know what is wrong even if you are unable to put the fault right without professional help. Here are the causes of some of the commonest problems, and their cures.

Top of radiator stays cool
*This is usually caused by air (or corrosion by-products) collecting in the top of the radiator and stopping the water from circulating freely. **CURE** Vent the radiator by opening the bleed valve with a special key. If corrosion is the cause, add a corrosion inhibitor at the feed-and-expansion tank.*

Centre of radiator stays cool, top and ends are warm
*A build-up of sludge (caused by corrosion in the system) along the bottom of the radiator is preventing the blocked area from heating up. **CURE** Shut off the radiator valves, disconnect the radiator and flush it out with water. Replace and reconnect. Add a corrosion inhibitor to the system.*

Radiator remains cold
The likeliest cause is the closure of the handwheel valve or the malfunctioning of a thermostatic radiator valve, but the problem

*may also be caused by incorrect setting of the lockshield valve or a simple blockage in the radiator inlet or outlet. **CURE** Open a closed handwheel valve, reset or replace a thermostatic one. Check that the lockshield valve is open, and adjust it so the radiator is as warm as others on the circuit. Remove the radiator (as above) to clear inlet or outlet blockages.*

Several radiators remain cool
*If radiators in one part of the house remain cool, the usual fault lies in the zone valve supplying that part of the circuit, or in the timer or thermostat controlling the valve's operation. **CURE** Drain the system and clean or replace the faulty valve. Check the control settings and the wiring between control and valve (with the power off). If the fault persists, call an engineer.*

All radiators remain cool
*Assuming that the boiler is working properly, the fault probably lies in the pump or its controls. **CURE** Bleed the pump via its bleed valve to clear an airlock if the pump is running. If it has stopped, turn off the boiler and remove the pump for cleaning or replacement as necessary. Check control settings and connections. Call an engineer*

if the fault persists.

Water leaks
*Water can leak from faulty connections or damaged pipework anywhere on the system. The hardest job is tracking the fault down. **CURE** Try tightening leaking compression or threaded joints slightly with a spanner. If this fails to work, turn off the boiler, drain down the system and remake the joint from scratch. If pipework is damaged, make a temporary repair with epoxy putty or waterproof tape; then drain the system and fit a new piece of pipe.*

Drip from feed-and-expansion tank overflow pipe
*This is caused by a faulty float or ballvalve. **CURE** Replace the float if it is punctured. Turn off the water supply and dismantle the valve, fitting a new washer and lubricating the piston before reassembling it. Replace the valve completely if it's badly worn.*

Noises in pipes or boiler
Banging or hissing noises are usually caused by overheating of one type or another. Causes include:
● *a build-up of scale in the system **CURE** Shut down the system and*

treat with descaler before flushing through and refilling;
● *a lack of water caused by an empty feed-and-expansion tank **CURE** Lubricate the jammed ballvalve piston, or fit a new valve;*
● *a faulty boiler thermostat **CURE** Shut down the boiler, but leave the pump working to circulate water and cool the system down. Check the thermostat, call an engineer if it fails to click on and off;*
● *pump failure on solid fuel systems **CURE** Check wiring connections to pump, clear airlock via bleed valve, remove pump for cleaning, replace pump if all else fails.*

Boiler not working
*If the boiler simply does not come on when it should, the fault may lie with the controls; with gas boilers, the pilot light may have gone out. **CURE** Check the setting on the room or boiler thermostat, and the connections to the programmer. If this has failed, check its power supply, and replace the programmer if necessary. Call an engineer if the boiler still won't come on. If the pilot light is out, relight it following the boiler manufacturer's instructions. If it will not light, suspect a blockage or unit failure, and call an engineer.*

48 Laying loft insulation

Around a third of all heat lost from a typical house goes literally through the roof unless insulation is used to stop it. Until 1965 there were no nationally-enforced standards for loft insulation, and the Building Regulations of that year required the use of a paltry 25mm (1in) of loft insulation in new houses. Later Regulations have now raised that level to around 100mm (4in), but this still applies only to new houses. There are many older houses around which have little or no insulation in the loft, and their owners are wasting hundreds of pounds every year on fuel that is warming the atmosphere instead of their homes. Yet insulating the loft is one of the simplest do-it-yourself jobs around, needing no special tools or equipment; just the right quantity of insulation material, which is relatively inexpensive and widely available.

The principle of loft insulation is extremely simple. A layer of the insulation material is laid in the loft, so it rests directly on the ceiling surface. This traps a layer of still air at that level which prevents the passage of heat into the roof space. The net result is that the house stays warmer, while the roof space becomes considerably colder; this in turn means that any water tanks and pipes in the roof space have to be insulated too to prevent them from freezing up in cold weather – see Projects 52 and 57. The only drawback from insulating lofts in this way is the attendant problem of condensation (see below).

Two materials are commonly used on a do-it-yourself basis: glass fibre blanket and loose-fill expanded vermiculite. The former is a mat of glass fibres which is sold in the form of a compressed roll in a width that will fit between ceiling joists set at a standard spacing of 406mm (16in). The roll length varies from manufacturer to manufacturer, and also depends on the thickness of the material; the 100mm thickness is commonly sold in rolls 8m (about 26ft) long. Loose-fill insulation is an expanded mineral called vermiculite, which is sold in bags and is poured out between the joists and levelled out to the required depth.

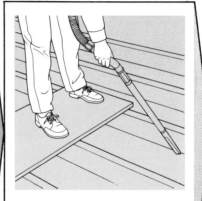

1. Clear all stored materials from the roof space. Then use a heavy-duty vacuum cleaner to remove dust and debris from the ceiling.

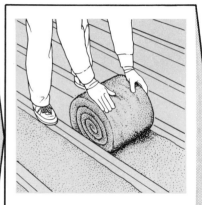

2. Unroll each length of blanket between the joists. Wear gloves and a facemask to protect yourself from loose fibres.

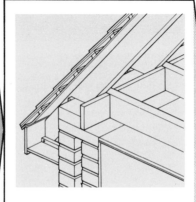

1. To prevent loose-fill material disappearing down the wall cavity, block the eaves with lengths of timber wedged between the joists.

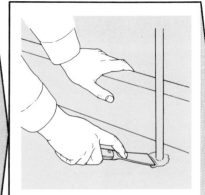

2. Fill any holes in the ceiling through which pipes pass, using quick-setting plaster or expanding aerosol filler foam.

49 Ventilation in lofts

One problem with insulating lofts using these materials is that they do not stop the passage of water vapour into the loft from the house. Unless this can escape, it will condense on the now-cold surfaces in the roof space; this will saturate the insulation, rendering it useless, stain ceilings and cause rot in the roof timbers. To prevent this, the current Building Regulations require ventilation openings at the eaves on opposite sides of a pitched roof, with an area at least equal to a continuous slot 10mm (in) wide running the whole length of the eaves. In practice this ventilation is supplied by cutting holes or short slots in eaves soffits, or by incorporating airbricks in gable walls if there are no overhanging eaves. In addition, an impermeable vapour barrier can be included below the insulation.

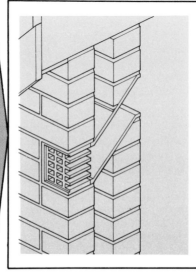

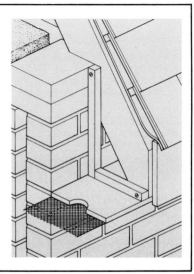

3. Form simple butt joints between consecutive lengths. Tear the rolls to length as necessary, or cut them with household scissors.

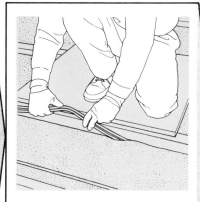

4. Lift electrical cables above the insulation wherever possible, fixing them instead to the sides of the joists with cable clips.

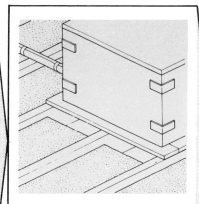

5. Don't lay the insulation beneath cold water storage tanks or feed-and-expansion tanks; warmth from below helps stop them freezing.

6. Use left-over material to insulate the loft trap door. Cut a piece of insulation to fit and secure it with loosely-knotted string.

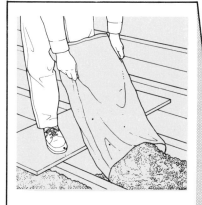

3. Standing on a stout board, empty the contents of each sack out into the space between the joists. Rake it roughly level by hand.

4. Make a simple notched spreader to level the insulation to the required depth between the joists. Draw it along each pair of joists in turn.

5. If the joists are less than 125mm (5in) deep, lay the insulation level with the top of the joists using a timber straightedge.

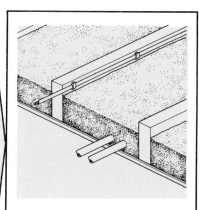

6. Pipes running across the loft can be covered, but electric cables should be lifted clear and clipped to the sides of the joists.

50 Draughtproofing the hatch

The trap doors fitted in loft hatches are seldom a close fit, and so even if the door is insulated on its upper surface warm air can still rise round it into the loft; cold draughts may also be felt at times on the landing. The answer is to draughtproof the door by fitting self-adhesive foam strip all round the reveal on which the trap door closes. Alternatively, the strip can be fitted to the edge of the trap door itself if it is less likely to be damaged by people climbing into and out of the loft.

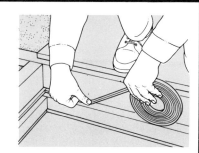

To stop heat loss into the loft and eliminate cold downdraughts, seal the hatch opening with self-adhesive foam strip.

51 Recessed lights

If you have downlighters or similar light fittings recessed into the ceiling, don't lay insulation material directly over them; this could result in overheating, and might start a fire. Instead, use offcuts of timber, plywood or chipboard to create a simple protective box and stand this over the recessed part of the fitting. Bore holes in its top to allow some ventilation, and then fit the loft insulation neatly round it. This will also protect the fitting from accidental damage.

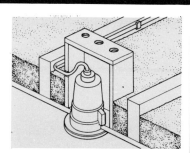

Use timber, plywood or chipboard to create a simple protective box round light fittings that are recessed into the ceiling.

Once the loft floor is insulated, the loft will be considerably colder than before the insulation was installed. It is therefore essential that any cold water storage tanks or feed-and-expansion tanks in the roof space are insulated to prevent them freezing up in cold weather.

To insulate these tanks, you can buy standard tank insulation kits. For square and rectangular tanks, rigid polystyrene sections are used, while for round tanks ready-made jackets are available; both come in a range of standard sizes. Alternatively, ordinary glass fibre loft insulation blanket can be tied in place round the tank.

The loft floor beneath such tanks should not be insulated, to allow a little warmth from the rooms below to reach them and help keep the water temperature above freezing point.

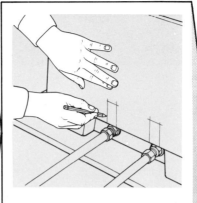

1. With rigid polystyrene boards, offer up each panel in turn and mark on it the positions of incoming and outgoing pipes.

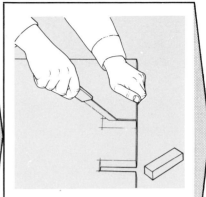

2. Use a sharp knife or a proprietary heat gun with a hot wire cutter to remove the marked cut-outs from the panels.

1. If you're using ordinary loft insulation, wrap the first length round the lower part of the tank and tie it in place with string.

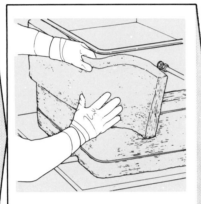

2. Wrap a second length round the upper park of the tank so it just overlaps the first length, and tie it on in the same way.

3. Fit the tank lid if it has one; otherwise make one from exterior-grade plywood (not chipboard, which could absorb moisture).

4. Finally, cover the lid with one or more lengths of blanket, tied or taped in place so the lid can still be lifted off if necessary.

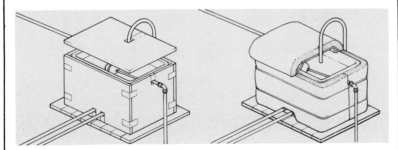

Rigid polystyrene boards are ideal for square or rectangular tanks. Make cut-outs for pipes and tape or pin corner joints.

Loft insulation blanket can be used to insulate tanks of any shape. Tie lengths round the tank sides, then cover the lid.

It's just as important to insulate your hot water storage cylinder as it is to tackle cold water tanks, but for a different reason. In this case the object of the exercise is to stop unnecessary heat loss from the cylinder and to keep the water hot for as long as possible, thereby reducing heating bills.

If your cylinder is unlagged, buy a proprietary jacket for it; various sizes are available to suit standard cylinder sizes. Then slip it over the neck of the cylinder, tying it round the hot water draw-off pipe, and allow the plastic-covered insulated sections to fall round the sides of the cylinder. Run the tapes supplied round the cylinder to hold the panels in place, and check that there are no gaps.

If you're fitting a new cylinder, choose one with a shrunk-on foam jacket (see step 4).

3. If the panels are over-large for the tank, hold them in place and scribe the tank outline on them. Then cut them to size.

4. With all the panels cut to size and notched as necessary, offer them up to the tank and pin or tape the corner joints.

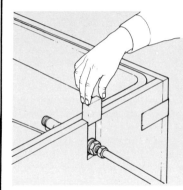

5. Fill any gaps where the panels were notched to fit round pipes by slotting in small offcuts. Tape them to keep them in place.

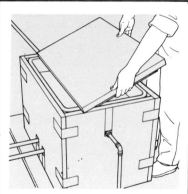

6. Stick two boards – one about 50mm larger all round than the other – together to form a lid, and fit this in place.

55 Using plastic jackets

You can buy ready-made insulation jackets to fit standard sizes of round-cold water and feed-and-expansion tanks; some are also available for rectangular tanks. They consist of flexible plastic panels containing glass fibre or mineral wool which are draped over the tank. When fitting one, align the top section first; then swivel it round so that incoming pipes line up if possible with the gaps between sections, and tape the joints. Make a hole to admit the vent pipe.

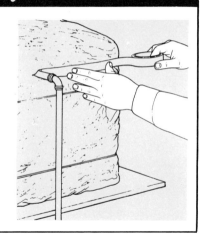

56 Using loose-fill material

It's perfectly possible to insulate a tank of any shape using loose-fill material. Start by building a simple box round the tank, using offcuts of chipboard or plywood; it should be big enough to allow about 75mm (3in) clearance all round the tank, and should rest on the platform supporting it. Then pour the insulating material into the gap between tank and box to just above the normal water level. Finish off by cutting a lid for the tank; use exterior-grade plywood so moisture doesn't affect it.

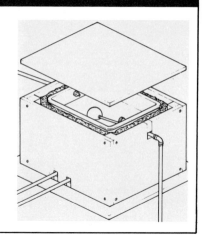

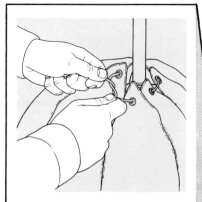

1. To fit a proprietary cylinder jacket, tie the tops of the insulated panels round the hot water draw-off pipe.

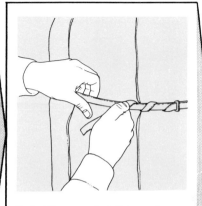

2. Let the panels fall down the sides of the cylinder and tie them in place with the straps provided. Pipes can pass through the gaps.

3. Check that all the panels are straight, and that there are no gaps anywhere. Tuck their lower ends underneath the cylinder.

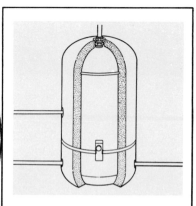

4. Replacement cylinders are now available in a range of sizes complete with shrunk-on foam plastic insulation.

Pipework is more prone to freezing in cold weather than any other part of the plumbing system. Once lofts have been insulated, any pipework in the roofspace is particularly at risk. So also is pipework beneath suspended timber floors, which will be very cold in winter if the void is properly ventilated.

Central heating pipework should also be insulated, to prevent freezing when the system is off or the house is unoccupied and also to cut down heat losses when it is running.

The commonest insulation material is made of plastic foam. It comes in 2m and 3m lengths, in diameters to suit standard pipe sizes, and is split along its length so it can be slipped onto the pipe. An alternative is pipe bandage, which is wrapped round the pipe in a spiral and tied on.

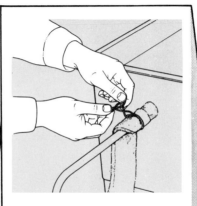

1. With bandage-type insulation, start by tying the first loop in place with string at one end of the pipe run.

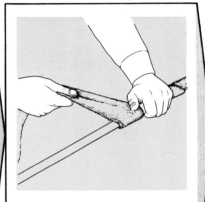

2. Work along the pipe run, winding the bandage on in a spiral with each successive turn overlapping the one before it.

1. Open up the split along a length of foam pipe insulation and slip it over the pipe at the start of the run. Squeeze the split closed.

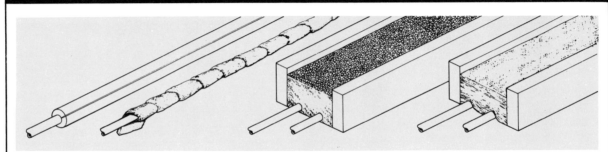

Split foam plastic sleeving (left) is the easiest type of insulation to use, since it is simply slipped into place on the pipe. Bandage types

(second left) are more tedious to fit, but may be more economical on pipe runs with lots of connections and awkward bends.

Where pipes run between joists above ceilings, it's often easier to insulate them with loose-fill or glass fibre insulation.

2. With some types, the split locks together when squeezed round the pipe. With others, it has to be taped closed along its length.

3. To insulate tee junctions, use a mitre box and a serrated bread knife to make neat 45° cuts in the ends of the insulation.

4. Insulate the straight-through section first; then offer up the last length to the tee and check that the mitres fit closely.

5. Tape all joins between lengths on straight runs, and at tees (see 4), using waterproof adhesive tape. You'll need to tape bends too.

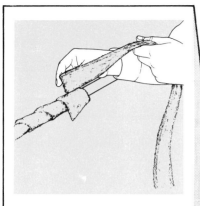

3. When one length runs out, overlap the start of the next one by one turn and tie the join securely with string or tape.

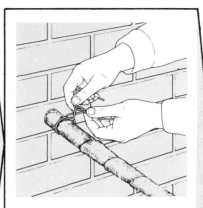

4. At the end of the run, cut off any excess bandage and tie up the final overlap neatly. Check that no gaps have opened up.

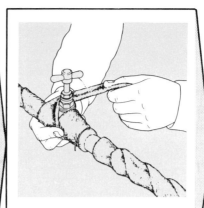

5. If stop taps and gate valves are encountered along the run, wrap the bandage tightly round the tap body to protect it.

6. Where pipes pass through openings in walls, pack the bandage into the gap or fill it using an aerosol of expanding filler foam.

59 Draughtproofing door bottoms

Draughtproofing is an essential part of any home insulation programme. The average non-draughtproofed house contains enough gaps round its doors and windows to add up to the equivalent of a hole 225mm (9in) square in an outside wall, and these gaps are responsible for up to 10 per cent of the total heat lost from the house as well as for causing uncomfortable cold draughts. Fortunately, there are now dozens of products on the market to enable these gaps to be draughtproofed easily.

One of the first places to tackle is the gap underneath exterior doors. This can be draught-proofed in a number of ways. The simplest is by fixing a rigid strip excluder containing a flexible seal to the bottom of the inner face of the door so the seal is compressed against the floor surface. Automatic versions of this type rise as the door is opened and drop as it is closed. Threshold strips contain flexible seals which press against the door bottom, while interlocking types have door and threshold sections which lock together to keep both draughts and rain out.

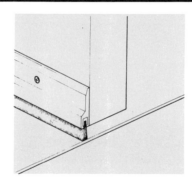

1. The simplest door bottom excluder consists of a rigid strip carrying a flexible seal which is compressed against the floor.

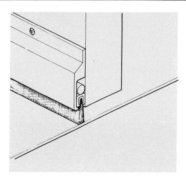

2. Automatic draught strips raise the flexible seal as the door is opened and lower it when it closes, minimising floor wear.

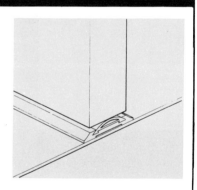

3. Simple threshold strips contain a flexible seal which presses against the bottom edge of the door as it is closed.

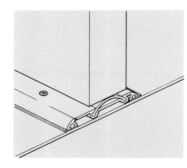

4. Some threshold strips also incorporate a replacement sill section – more durable for main entrance doors.

5. Interlocking types consist of two parts – a special threshold strip and an overlapping section fitted to the outer face of the door.

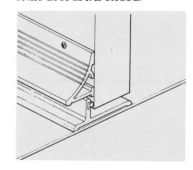

6. For exposed doors, a special interlocking type with a shaped weatherbar will throw rainwater clear of the door bottom.

60 Fitting door bottom excluders

Draught excluders for door bottoms come in a wide range of types (see previous page). Whichever type is chosen, care must be taken when fitting it to ensure that it works efficiently without impairing the operation of the door.

The first stage is to read the fitting instructions carefully, since precise positioning of the excluder is always important. Then make sure that you can identify all the components correctly, and that all the fixings are included.

Make all measurements carefully to avoid mistakes; then cut the components to length to suit your door width. Note the positions of fixing screws, and if necessary cut off surplus material from both ends so keep them centred. Then fit the excluder and check its operation.

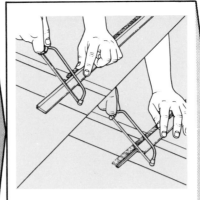

1. To fit a simple brush excluder, measure the door width and then slide back the brush. Cut the rigid strip first, then the insert.

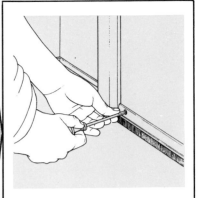

2. Check the fit of the excluder, and mark the position of its top edge on the door. Hold it in place and drive in the fixing screws.

1. To fit an automatic rise-and-fall excluder, first screw the main body to the door at the correct height. Note the inset ends.

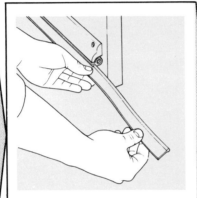

2. Next, cut the flexible seal strip to the correct length and slide it into place within the main body of the excluder.

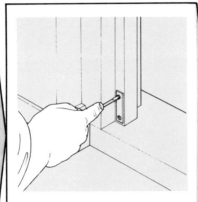

3. Check the instructions concerning the positioning of the striker plate. Then screw it in place to the door frame.

4. Close the door and check two points: the excluder body must just clear the door stops, and the seal must press against the floor.

61 Threshold strips

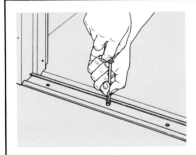

1. To fit a compression-type threshold strip, remove the flexible vinyl insert. Then cut the strip to length and screw it in place.

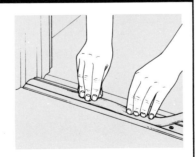

2. Then cut the vinyl insert to the same length and press it into place in the base strip. Check that it is compressed when the door closes.

62 Two-part excluders

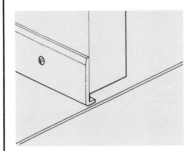

1. Check the instructions regarding the relative positioning of the two components. Then cut the door section to length and fit it.

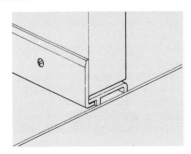

2. Next, cut the sill section to length, position it carefully so it interlocks with the door section and screw it to the threshold.

63 Draughtproofing doors and casement windows

Hinged casement windows, their opening top lights and the sides and heads of door openings are all virtually identical as far as draughtproofing is concerned. In all three cases the hinged window or door closes into a rebate in the frame, and so if a flexible sealing strip is fitted into the side or face of the rebate any draughts will be stopped.

The most popular material for draughtproofing these rebates is self-adhesive plastic foam. This is sold in rolls, and is designed to be stuck onto the face of the rebate so it is compressed against the frame when the door or window is closed. Modern types are much more durable than earlier ones. An alternative type is the sprung-seal excluder, a metal or plastic strip which is pinned or stuck to the side of the rebate and presses against the door or window edge.

1. To fit self-adhesive foam strip round door and window rebates, simply unroll the strip and press it firmly into place.

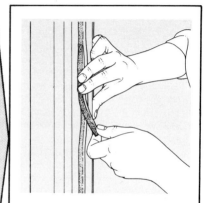

2. If the gap between frame and rebate is especially wide or uneven, stick a second layer of the strip on top of the first one.

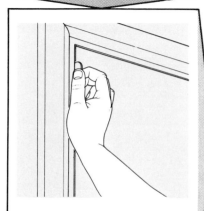

1. Sprung-seal draught excluders need about 2mm between door and frame. Check that you have it all round using a coin.

2. Measure the length of each section of the door or window rebate carefully using a steel tape measure. Write down the figures.

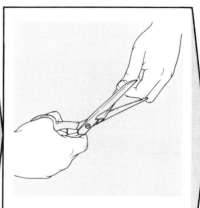

3. Unroll the excluder and cut the lengths you require. Plastic ones can be cut with scissors; use tin snips on metal types.

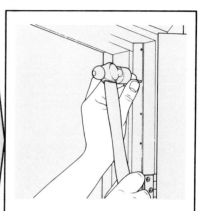

4. Offer up each strip to the side of the rebate and pin or stick it into position. Make sure the sprung edge is facing the right way.

64 Using mastic excluders

Mastic-type draught excluders are particularly useful for ill-fitting windows. Precise instructions vary from brand to brand, but fitting sequences are similar. Start by opening the window. Next, pipe a bead of mastic round the rebate into which the window closes, and smooth it off with a moistened finger. Then apply a release agent or special tape to the window to stop it sticking and close the window. Leave to set for a time, then trim off the excess.

1. Open the window, clean the rebate thoroughly and then pipe a generous bead of mastic all round the face of the rebate.

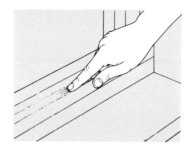

2. Smooth it off with a moistened finger, apply release agent or tape to the window and close it. When the mastic has set, trim the excess.

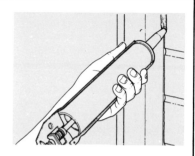

3. Don't forget to tackle gaps between window and door frames and the masonry. Seal them with a non-setting exterior-grade mastic.

65 Fitting brush strip excluders

Brush strip excluders consist of a rigid plastic moulding into which a continuous length of fine bristle (or sometimes wool pile) is inserted. It is designed for use round doors and windows of all types, and is pinned or screwed in place so that the bristles are deformed slightly to create a draught seal. They are particularly effective for use on doors and windows which do not fit well in their frames, since the bristles can cope with any gaps. They can also be used on sliding doors and windows.

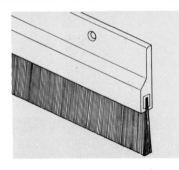

1. Brush strip excluders have a strip of fine bristles set in a slim plastic moulding which is fitted to door or window frames.

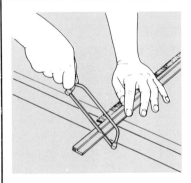

2. Measure the length of strip required. Then slide the bristle strip out, cut the moulding and trim the bristle to match.

3. Test-fit the strip to find the optimum fixing position. Then pin or screw it into position round the door or window frame.

66 Draughtproofing sash windows

Sash windows are particularly difficult to draughtproof well. Firstly, they slide, so many window draught excluders cannot be used. Secondly, they are often a poor fit within their frames.

On the inside, fit foam strip or spring-seal excluder to the top of the outer sash and the bottom of the inner one. Fit spring-seal excluder to the frame sides (this involves taking out the sashes first). Seal the gap between the meeting rails with a simple flap-type excluder. On the outside, fit a brush-type excluder to the outer sash only, and seal gaps round the frame with mastic.

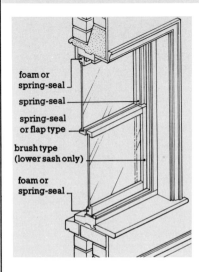

foam or spring-seal
spring-seal
spring-seal or flap type
brush type (lower sash only)
foam or spring-seal

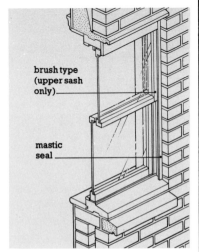

brush type (upper sash only)
mastic seal

Tackle different parts of a sash window in different ways. The top and bottom can be draughtproofed with foam strip or spring-seal excluder (which can be used on all other surfaces). You can use brush-strip types outside on the outer sash, inside on the inner one.

67 Letterboxes and cat-flaps

Letterboxes can cause noticeable cold draughts in the hallway — even more so if the outside flap sticks in the open position after a delivery. Fortunately, it's a quick and easy job to fit a proprietary draught excluder to the inner face of the door. There are two types: one is a simple flap; the other is a variation on the brush strip excluder used for doors and windows, with two rows of bristles set within a plastic frame. Excluders of the first type are also used for cat-flaps.

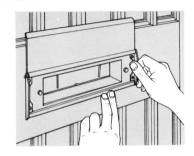

1. An interior flap works rather like the outside one, but in reverse. Offer it up, mark its position and screw it in place.

2. The brush strip type contains two rows of bristles to exclude draughts. It too is simply screwed to the inner face of the door.

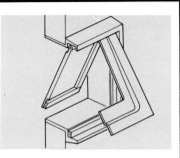

3. Draughtproof cat-flaps by fitting an inner flap. Add self-adhesive draughtproofing strip round the actual opening.

Many homes contain fireplaces and flues that are seldom or never used, and considerable amounts of heat can escape unless the flue is restricted or blocked off.

The simplest measure to take, ideal if the fireplace is used occasionally, is to fit a throat restrictor across the angled throat above the fireplace itself. It's a simple matter to install one, by extending the retaining screws at each side once the restrictor is in place. Because the restrictor is adjustable, it can also be used to regulate the burning of the fire.

If the flue is no longer needed, it's better to remove the fireplace and surround and block it off completely. You can do this in two main ways. The first involves fitting a timber frame round the inside of the fireplace opening, nailing a sheet of plasterboard to it and giving the board a skim of plaster. The second involves using bricks or blocks to fill in the opening, and then plastering over them. Note that an airbrick should be included in either case. At the top of the flue the chimney pot should be removed and the flue capped with a paving slab. Again, an airbrick should be included.

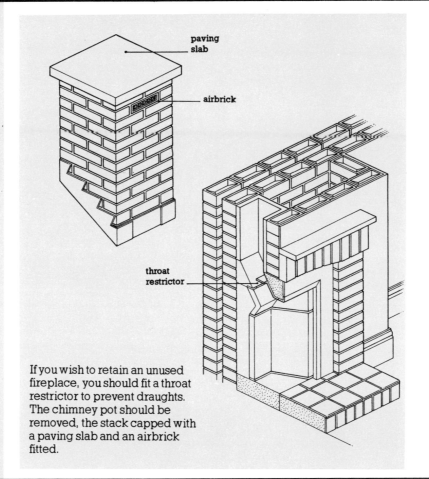

If you wish to retain an unused fireplace, you should fit a throat restrictor to prevent draughts. The chimney pot should be removed, the stack capped with a paving slab and an airbrick fitted.

If a fireplace is no longer needed it can be removed and the opening blocked, using bricks, blocks or plasterboard on a timber frame.

69 Insulating used flues

An old flue that is still in use can be given an insulated lining that helps stop condensation within the flue and also improves the passage of smoke. The job, which must be carried out by professional installers, involves lowering a flexible 'sausage' down the flue, inflating it with compressed air and then pouring insulating concrete into the gap between sausage and flue. The sausage is then removed.

1. The chimney pot and flaunching is removed and the flexible sausage is lowered carefully into the flue from the top.

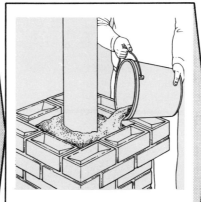

2. It is then inflated, and lightweight insulating concrete is poured into the resulting gap between sausage and flue.

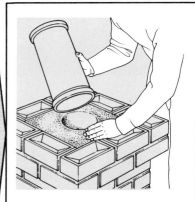

3. When the concrete has set, the sausage is deflated and removed to leave a smooth circular flue, and the chimney pot is replaced.

Almost all modern homes are built with wall insulation included in the structure – either within the cavity if it's of traditional construction, or as part of the inner wall panels in timber-frame houses. However, many older homes would benefit enormously from having their exterior walls insulated, since as much as a third of all heat lost from a typical house is lost here.

With cavity walls, the least disruptive form of insulation to have is cavity filling. The gap between the inner and outer leaves is filled through holes drilled in the outer leaf. The insulating material may be urea–formaldehyde (UF) foam, mineral fibres or special insulating pellets. All have to be installed by professional contractors, to ensure that the job meets the requirements of the Building Regulations (approval is needed).

Alternatively, the inner faces of outer walls can be lined with insulating plasterboard, known as dry lining, or with plasterboard over slab insulation. This method is also ideal for solid walls; the only other treatment suitable is the application of exterior insulating rendering, which can be expensive.

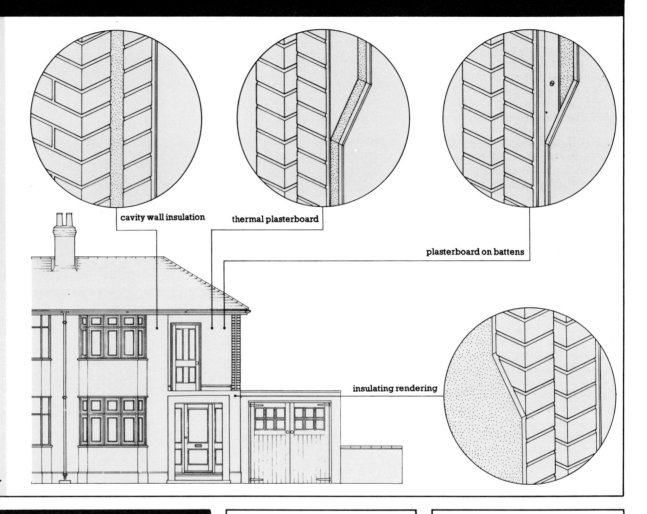

cavity wall insulation

thermal plasterboard

plasterboard on battens

insulating rendering

Dry-lining the inner face of exterior walls is an effective and relatively inexpensive way of cutting down heat losses through the walls. However, it is rather disruptive, since the walls concerned are being completely resurfaced. There is, however, negligible loss of space.

The job can be carried out using either insulating plasterboard or ordinary plasterboard fixed over slab or blanket-type insulation.

The insulated type has a layer of foam insulation on the back, and incorporates a vapour barrier to prevent water vapour from reaching the wall itself and causing harmful interstitial condensation within it. The boards can be fixed to battens or simply glued directly in place. If ordinary plasterboard is used, a vapour barrier of polythene sheeting must be incorporated between boards and insulation.

1. Unless the walls are flat and true, start by lining them with battens at 610mm (24in) centres. Frame openings as shown.

2. Measure up and then cut the boards to size using a panel saw or power jig saw. Work with the plasterboard side uppermost.

72 Cavity wall insulation

Cavity walls in existing houses can be insulated most easily by injecting insulation into the cavity through holes drilled in the outer leaf. Urea-formaldehyde foam is the most widely used material; this is pumped in under pressure and sets hard as it dries out. Alternatives are mineral fibres and specially-coated insulating pellets, both of which are blown into the cavity and allowed to settle. Installing either of these types requires rather larger holes than the foam type; all three types have to be installed by skilled professional contractors, and Building Regulations approval has to be sought from your local authority before the job is carried out to ensure that only approved materials and methods are used.

In new houses, the cavity can be filled as the walls are built, using insulating batts.

1. With all types, the insulation is injected into the cavity through holes drilled in the outer leaf of the walls.

2. After installation, it's important to check that airbricks are clear and that insulation has not got into switch and socket boxes.

73 Insulating behind radiators

If your central heating system has conventional wall-mounted radiators, there will be some heat loss through the walls on which the radiators are mounted. Although this is not a major factor in the house's overall loss of heat, it is worth preventing simply because the remedy is relatively inexpensive. It involves fitting a layer of reflective material to the wall surface behind the radiator. This can best be done before the radiators are fitted, simply by sticking self-adhesive foil to the wall surface. On an existing installation, it is easier to hang the foil behind the radiator on the radiator brackets; in this case a more rigid material is used. Both types are widely available and extremely easy to fit; they should be cut to a size slightly smaller than the radiator, so they are not noticeable when fitted.

1. With self-adhesive types, mark the radiator position on the wall; then cut the foil to size and press it into place.

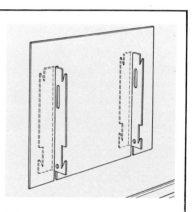

2. Loose-fitting types are simply hung over the radiator brackets. Note that ordinary cooking foil is not suitable, since it tarnishes.

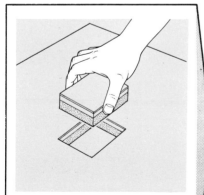

3. Offer up each board and mark the positions of any cut-outs that will be needed. Make internal cut-outs with a padsaw.

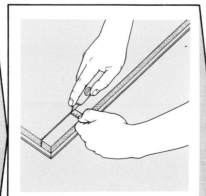

4. At external corners, cut away the foam layer to allow the cut edge of the next board to butt up to bare plasterboard.

5. Fit the first board at the corner, its edge protruding by an amount equal to the thickness of the foam. Then offer up the second board.

6. Nail the boards in place with plasterboard nails. If the walls are flat, you can stick them in place with panel adhesive instead.

Where lofts are being converted into habitable rooms, there is obviously no point in having insulation across the loft floor since the benefit of heat rising from rooms below would be lost. Instead, the roof slope has to be insulated.

The simplest way of insulating the underside of the roof slope is to use insulating plasterboard nailed directly to the underside edges of the rafters. However, you may want thicker insulation than this type of board can provide, and in this case you can use either rigid polystyrene boards or glass fibre blanket instead. Whichever is chosen, it must be installed so that an air gap is left between the upper surface of the insulation and the underside of the roof decking. This is easy to achieve with rigid polystyrene, simply by pinning it to battens run down the inner faces of the rafters. With glass fibre blanket, it is best to use the type which is covered with waterproof building paper; this comes in widths to suit standard joist spacings, and has tongues at each side which are stapled to the rafters.

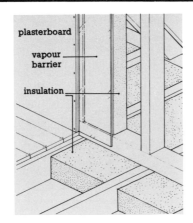

Above: Walls within the loft are insulated using rigid boards or blankets set between the studs. Note the vapour barrier between plasterboard and insulation. The loft floor outside any loft rooms is insulated in the usual way.

Right: The underside of the roof slope is insulated by fitting rigid boards or insulating blankets between the joists. A vapour barrier is fitted between the insulation material and the plasterboard lining.

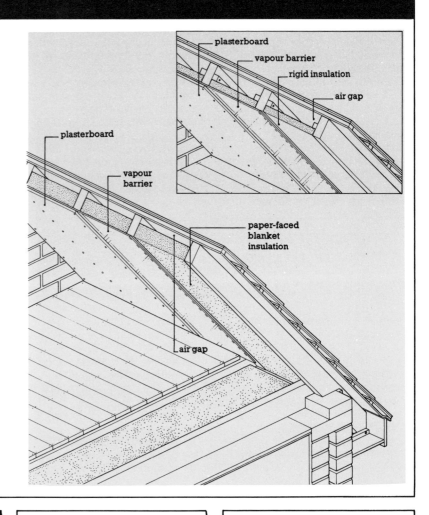

Ground floors can also benefit from some insulation, although the heat losses through them are generally far less than through uninsulated walls and roofs – perhaps 10 per cent of the total heat lost from the house. Solid floors will feel warmer under smooth floorcoverings like vinyl and tiles, while timber floors will be a lot less draughty.

With solid floors, the simplest technique is to lay polystyrene boards over the existing floor, cover this with flooring-grade chipboard and then lay the floorcovering on top. However, this does have the disadvantage of raising the floor level by about 50mm (2in), if this is unacceptable the only alternative is to dig up the floor.

With timber floors, the best method is to fit either rigid foam or paper-faced blanket between the floor joists.

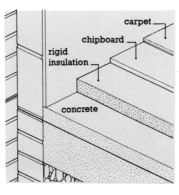

1. On solid floors, lay rigid polystyrene sheets over the concrete and put flooring-grade chipboard on top.

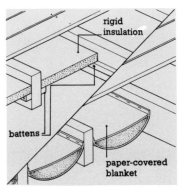

2. On suspended timber floors, either rest polystyrene strips on battens or fix paper-covered blanket between the joists.

Insulating flat roofs

Flat roofs are a popular way of roofing home extensions, but unless adequate insulation is incorporated into the structure when it is built, considerable heat losses can occur and the rooms below tend to be very cold. Unless you are prepared to pull down the ceiling to insert extra insulation, you will have to tackle the problem another way.

On the outside, the answer is to lay rigid polystyrene boards over the existing felt (after removing any mineral chippings used as a surface dressing) and to top these with lightweight slabs. Check with your local Building Inspector that the roof can take the weight.

On the inside, the solution is to line the ceiling with rigid boards or blankets set between battens, and then to put up a vapour barrier and a new plasterboard ceiling.

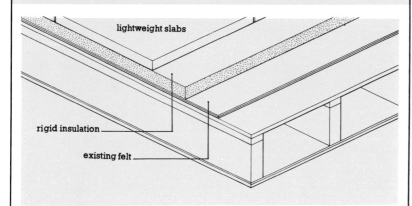

Insulate a flat roof from above by laying rigid polystyrene boards on top of the existing felt. Then lay lightweight slabs over the top. Check first that the roof is strong enough to take the weight.

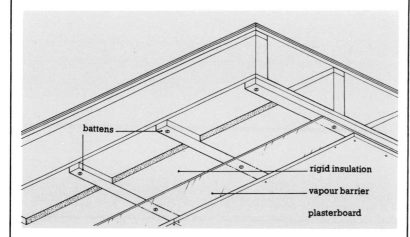

Insulate from below by nailing battens across the lines of the ceiling joists at 400mm (16in) centres. Then fit insulation between the battens and put up a vapour barrier and a new ceiling.

Double glazing

Double glazing is the only effective way of cutting down on heat losses through windows, which can be considerable if they are large and there are a lot of them. It works by trapping a layer of still air between two panes of glass; to create this gap you can either install a manufactured sealed double glazing unit in place of the existing single pane of glass or fit what is known as secondary double glazing – a separate inner 'window' mounted on the existing frame or within the window reveal.

Sealed units are now widely used in new houses and replacement windows, but for many homes secondary double glazing is the only option. The inner panes can be fixed, hinged or sliding, and a wide range of do-it-yourself systems are available to suit any window.

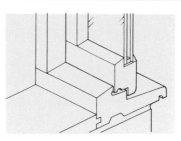

1. A sealed double glazing unit is fitted into the frame rebate.

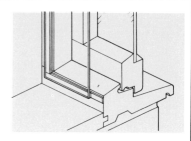

2. Rigid plastic sheeting can be secured with magnetic strips.

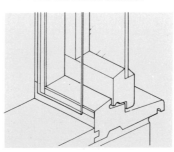

3. Plastic film is held in place with double-sided tape.

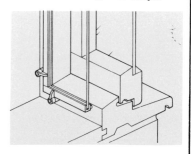

4. More substantial fixed panes are secured with special clips.

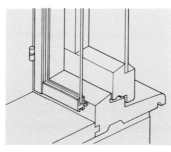

5. Hinged panes allow windows to be opened for ventilation.

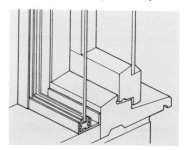

6. Sliding panes run in tracks fitted in the window reveal.

78 Fitting sliding secondary glazing

Sliding secondary glazing units are generally the most satisfactory type to use. They are fairly unobtrusive, especially if the sections are aligned with the uprights in the existing window; they can be opened easily for ventilation (and for escape in a fire), yet don't protrude into the room when open as hinged types do. However, they are generally the most expensive type.

To install them, the first stage it to fit the track within the window reveal (or, with some systems, to the window frame itself). This must be fitted level and square; if it isn't the panes will not run or close properly and gaps will reduce the efficiency of the installation.

Once the track is in place, the panes are edged with plastic or metal trims and are lifted in. It is a simple job to remove them for cleaning or for summertime storage.

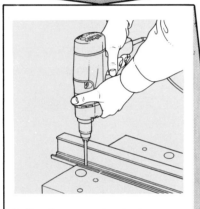

1. Start by measuring the height and width of the opening. Then cut the track to length and drill fixing holes at regular intervals.

2. With some systems, the track sections are assembled using small corner joints; in others, they are fixed in place separately.

79 Fitting sealed units

Sealed double glazing units can be fitted in place of single panes of glass in most types of window frame, although special 'stepped' units may have to be used if the rebate is shallow. Unless the window is a modern one for which the manufacturer offers off-the-peg glazing units, you will have to order the unit made to measure from a glass merchant. The unit can incorporate obscured or coloured glass if this is specified

when the order is placed. Take the measurements carefully, at top, bottom and each side of the opening, and remember to subtract a clearance allowance of at least 6mm (¼in) from each measurement.

In replacement windows, the units can be held in place with putty or glazing beads. In new windows, special flexible glazing gaskets are used to lock the units into the frames.

3. Offer up the track and use small wedges or shims to ensure that the bottom track is level and the frame is square. Mark the fixing holes.

4. Fix the track in position to the window frame or the reveal as appropriate. Check once more that it is level and square.

80 Using flexible plastic film

Flexible plastic films offer an inexpensive way of double-glazing fixed windows (or any that won't be opened in cold weather). They resemble the clear food wrapping film widely used in the kitchen nowadays, and are held in place with double-sided adhesive tape. Then the film is positioned across the window, stuck in place all round, and heat from a hair drier is used to shrink the film slightly and pull out any creases. The film is discarded at the end of the winter.

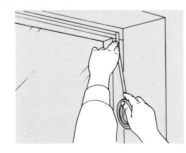

1. Stick the double-sided tape all round the surface of the window frame. Then peel off the release paper at the top only.

2. Position the top edge of the film on the tape. Then peel the release paper from the sides and bottom and stick the film in place.

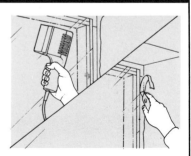

3. Use a hair drier to shrink the film and pull out any creases. Then cut off excess film all round with a sharp knife.

1. To fit a sealed unit, remove the existing pane and line the rebate with putty. Then set smaller spacer blocks in place to support the unit.

2. Offer the unit up, resting its lower edge on the spacer blocks. Then raise it to the vertical and bed it in all round.

3. Secure the unit within the frame using glazing sprigs at 300mm (12in) intervals; these aren't needed if glazing beads are used.

4. Either apply facing putty as for ordinary glazing, or cut and fit glazing beads on a thin bed of putty all the way round.

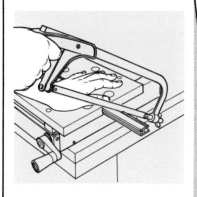

5. Next, follow the instructions on measuring for glass, and order the panes. Then cut the edge trims and gaskets to length.

6. Fit the nylon gaskets to all edges of each pane. In most cases you need a mallet or soft-faced hammer for the job.

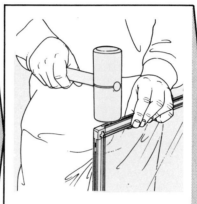

7. Fit the edge trims on top of the gaskets, again using a mallet. Don't forget to include the small corner jointing blocks as you do this.

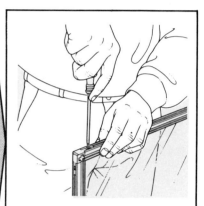

8. Lock the corner joints by tightening up the small screws, and check that all the trims and gaskets are properly seated.

(81) Hinged and fixed secondary glazing

In cost terms, hinged and fixed secondary glazing fall between the inexpensive film type and the more expensive sliding versions. Metal and plastic kits are widely available, and both are easy to install, but hinged types protrude into the room when they are open for ventilation, and fixed types could be a safety hazard in the event of fire. Whichever type is chosen, it is important that the seal between the inner pane and the window frame is effective or condensation will result.

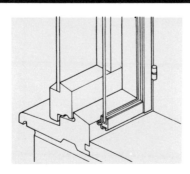

Hinged panes are hung on small side hinges, and are held closed by small catches. Fixed panes may

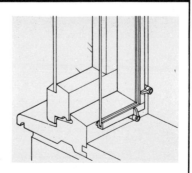

also be held by catches, or may be screwed directly to the window frame itself.

9. Complete the job by lifting the completed panes into place in the tracks. Engage the top edge first, then drop the bottom into place.

Condensation is caused by warm, moist air meeting a cold surface. When this occurs, the temperature of the air drops and so does the amount of moisture it can hold; the result is that the moisture condenses onto the cold surface in the form of minute water droplets. When severe condensation takes place, the surface can literally run with water. Quite apart from the nuisance of steamed-up windows, condensation can encourage the growth of unsightly black mould on decorations, may saturate insulation materials and can lead to rot and structural damage.

The main problem areas in most homes are the kitchen, where cooking and washing up create lots of steam, and the bathroom where baths and showers have the same effect. The cure involves striking the right balance between heating, ventilation and insulation. More heating means that air temperatures are higher, so the air can carry more water vapour. Better insulation means fewer cold surfaces on which condensation can occur. More (or controlled) ventilation means that steam is exhausted before it condenses.

AFFECTED AREAS	CAUSE & SYMPTOMS	CURES
Exterior walls and ceilings beneath lofts and flat roofs	Lack of insulation, leading to condensation on walls and on ceilings between joist lines	Install cavity wall insulation or dry lining (solid walls). Cover ceiling with insulating tiles
Exterior walls where lintels and cavity closures link the leaves of cavity walls	Direct structural bridge to the outside causing condensation round door and window openings	Dry-line the affected areas with insulating plasterboard, or use 'warm' wallcoverings (eg cork)
Single-glazed windows and doors or uninsulated metal door/window frames	Glass is a poor insulator, and metal an excellent conductor, so condensation forms readily	Double-glaze windows. Bond thin timber linings to affected metal frames, or replace with thermal-break frames
Exposed pipework and uninsulated cold water storage cisterns	Cold water in pipes and cisterns chills metal and ceramic surface, on which condensation then forms	Insulate pipes and loft cisterns, box in WC cisterns and back with loose insulation
Chimney breasts in rooms where flues are disused and blocked off	Lack of ventilation in disused flue allows condensation to form, causing damp patches on plaster	Fit air bricks in block-up fireplace and at the top of the chimney stack if it is capped
Roof linings, structural timber, loft insulation and goods stored in insulated lofts	Lack of ventilation in loft space following installation of loft insulation, causing damp and rot	Fit air bricks in gable walls or use soffit and ridge vents. Replace sodden insulation
Hard floorcoverings laid over concrete floors	Cold floors attract condensation just like cold walls, so feel damp	Lay carpets, or re-lay floor screed over polystyrene boards
General condensation	Low air temperatures combined with poor insulation and ventilation	Increase heating levels, improve insulation all round, install an extractor fan or dehumidifier

An electric extractor fan can go a long way towards eliminating condensation in problem rooms such as kitchens, utility rooms and bathrooms, by delivering the moisture-laden air to the outside before condensation can occur and replacing it with air drawn from the rest of the house. Such controlled ventilation is far more cost-effective than opening a window, which simply wastes heat. Fans can be installed in a hole cut in a window or an outside wall, or can be ceiling-mounted.

It's important to choose a fan that is powerful enough to provide the necessary number of air changes. A kitchen or bathroom needs around 10 air changes per hour, so the fan must have a quoted extract rate of 10 times the room's volume (length × width × height). Manufacturers' literature always quotes this, usually as cu m/ hr.

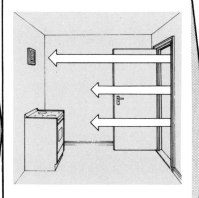

1. Extractor fans should be sited as close as possible to the main source of steam, and opposite the main source of replacement air.

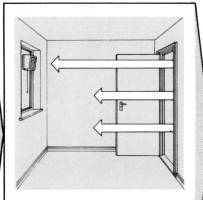

2. Arrangements such as this should be avoided, since the fan will not exhaust the room as it is too close to the air source.

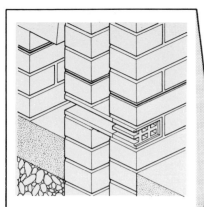

1. Air bricks are essential for ventilating the void beneath suspended timber floors. Ducts should be used in cavity walls.

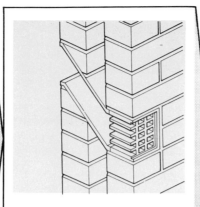

2. Inclined ducts prevent rainwater penetration where airbricks are installed in gable walls to ventilate lofts.

3. For extractor fans and tumble driers, ducts leading to the outside are fitted with cowls to prevent backdraughts.

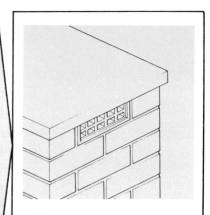

4. When unused flues are sealed, an airbrick must be included to prevent the formation of condensation within the flue.

84 *Sound insulation*

It is extremely difficult to improve the level of sound insulation in an existing building, whether you want to prevent noise getting in from outside or to contain noise levels inside. As far as external noise is concerned, tackle the obvious weak spots first of all. This means fitting acoustic double glazing to windows, setting the two panes of glass set at least 200mm apart and lining the window reveals with acoustic tiles. Replace hollow-core external doors with solid ones, and make sure that

draught-proofing is efficient too, since sound travels through any small gaps in the building's envelope.

Contain sound within noisy rooms by using sound-absorbent materials in the room concerned. This means fitting acoustic ceiling tiles, lining the walls with thick cork or soft fibreboard and laying thick carpets over underlay.

Noise transmission through the structure is the hardest of all to eliminate, specially when it passes through party walls or travels

between floors in flats and maisonettes. Noise coming through party walls can be reduced somewhat by building a stud partition wall in front of it, and fitting absorbent insulation material in the space behind. The stud wall should be fixed to the floor, ceiling and side walls, but should not touch the party wall itself at any point. Line the room side with a double layer of plasterboard.

You can tackle noise transmission through floors and ceilings in a similar way. For floors,

lay a new 'floating' floor of joists and chipboard on top of the existing floor over a layer of insulation material. For ceilings, put up a false ceiling below the existing one, clad with a double thickness of plasterboard as for party walls, and pack the space above it with insulation to help absorb the sound.

If noise in the home is too serious to be helped by these means, it may be worth consulting an acoustic engineer.

3. To fit an extractor fan in a prepared window opening, offer up the gaskets that line the hole and fit the outside grille.

4. Attach the inner mounting plate to the outside grille, following the manufacturer's instructions. A helper outdoors may be useful.

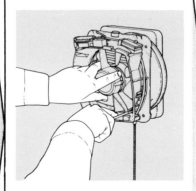

5. Fit the fan body to the inner mounting plate, and check that all the fixing screws are properly engaged and tightened.

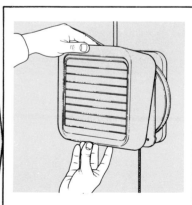

6. Finally, fit the motor casing. Then plug the fan in or connect it up to the mains permanently and test that it works properly.

Glossary

Air vents are special valves fitted to radiators and at other points in the system to allow trapped air to be removed.

Back boilers have a boiler fitted behind a room heater, and may work on gas or solid-fuel. They require a conventional flue.

Balanced flues are specially-designed flues which pass through outside walls. They supply air to the boiler or heater as well as getting rid of combustion products.

Ballvalves are float-operated valves used to fill storage and WC cisterns automatically. High and low-pressure types are available.

Cylinder thermostats are controls attached to the hot water cylinder to control the temperature of stored hot water.

Direct cylinders do not contain a heat exchanger, so water heated by the boiler or immersion heater is supplied directly to the taps.

Draincocks are special valves fitted at low points on heating and plumbing pipework to allow the system to be drained for repairs.

Dry-lining means lining walls with a layer of insulating plasterboard to improve the insulation.

Feed-and-expansion tanks are small storage tanks used to top up losses in vented heating systems, and to accommodate expansion in the water volume as the system heats up.

Flues take away the combustion by-products from boilers and heaters. They may be conventional or balanced.

Froststats are low-level thermostats used to bring heating systems on when exterior temperatures drop to freezing point.

Gatevalves are isolating valves used on low-pressure sections of plumbing systems – for example, on pipes running from the cold water storage tank to cold taps and the hot cylinder. They have round handles, and can be fitted either way round in the pipe run.

Handwheel valves are fitted to the inlet of a radiator to allow the flow of water to be turned on and off.

Indirect cylinders contain a heat exchanger; water in the primary circuit from the boiler heats the water in the cylinder, and this is supplied to the hot taps.

Lockshield valves are fitted to the outlet of a radiator to regulate the amount of hot water it receives. Once set, it should not be altered or the system balance may be upset.

Microbore pipe has a diameter of 10mm or less, and is used in conjunction with special distribution manifolds on microbore heating systems.

Motorized valves are used on heating systems to divert the flow of hot water to individual parts (or zones) – the hot cylinder, the upstairs heating circuit etc.

Programmers are the main controls on heating systems, governing heating periods and zonal control.

Rising main is the incoming mains-pressure cold water supply pipe, rising up through the house to the cold water storage tank.

Room thermostats switch the boiler on and off as room temperatures vary. They are linked to the programmer.

Stop taps are fitted on mains-pressure pipe runs to allow them to be isolated if necessary. They must be fitted with the arrow on the body pointing in the direction of flow, and have bar handles.

Storage cisterns hold the domestic cold water supply and fill the hot cylinder on indirect systems.

Thermostatic radiator valves (TRVs) are fitted to individual radiators in place of the handwheel valve, and allow rooms to be heated to pre-selected temperatures.

Vent pipes are fitted as safety devices on heating and hot water systems; they discharge overheated water back into the storage cistern or feed-and-expansion tank.

Index

Indoor repairs

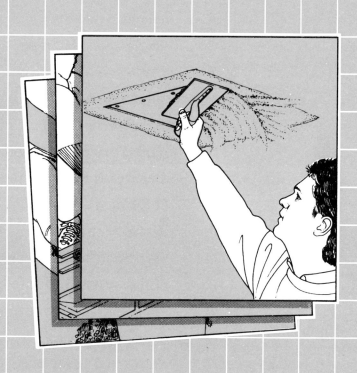

Indoor repairs

Indoor repairs

Safe in the knowledge that the walls, roofs, doors and windows on the outside of your home will keep the weather at bay, you might feel that once inside you can relax and enjoy a little comfort. Unfortunately, it doesn't always work out that way. Like everything else in this world, the various bits and pieces that make up your home's interior don't last forever. They do wear out. They can break. Or they may simply succumb to one of their many active enemies such as woodworm, fungi, even burglars.

Whatever the cause, though, when things go wrong you need to know how to put them right – fast, because little faults left to their own devices have a nasty habit of growing into big ones. In most cases, you won't find it difficult. Given a few fairly basic tools and techniques, the majority of indoor repairs require nothing more than a little commonsense and a certain amount of elbow grease.

Given the complexity of a modern home, you might think that keeping its interior in good order was a truly Herculean task. But don't worry – most of the internal structure is quite capable of looking after itself. There are, though, certain items that are particularly prone to problems, and it is on these that you should concentrate most of your effort.

Top of the list is the interior joinery – the doors, stairs, floor-boards and joists, plus all those sundry pieces of wood such as skirting boards, architraves, and so on. Quite apart from being vulnerable to both mechanical damage and general wear and tear, wood's tendency to shrink and swell as the weather changes can lead to joints opening up, cracks appearing between woodwork and masonry, doors failing to fit their openings, creaking floorboards, and a host of other headaches.

You must also be on your guard against wood-devouring insects (such as woodworm) and fungi (wet rot, dry rot, and so on). Do all you can do to stop them gaining a foothold, and treat any localized outbreaks that do occur as quickly and as thoroughly as possible, calling in professional assistance if necessary where the infestation has got out of hand.

Your home's floors, whether of wood or concrete, are another potential trouble spot – not surprising really when you consider what they have to put up with. Dampness, unevenness, creaks and groans are very common, but fortunately not that difficult to put right.

Walls – or at least the plasterwork – may also suffer, particularly when exposed to young children and clumsy furniture removers. Small cracks and dents can, of course, be safely left until the time comes to redecorate, but more substantial damage should be attended to straight away – not always easy with hollow partition walls.

And what about the fireplaces and flues? Some may need attention simply because of old age, while others may have suffered from the changes in heating fashion, having been alternately blocked up and reopened, perhaps several times since they were first built.

Finally, remember that perhaps the most important indoor jobs you can undertake are those designed to keep out unwanted visitors – burglars. Locks and alarms may not be cheap, but they are nothing like as expensive as having your home ransacked and valuables stolen.

① Adhesives – types and their uses

Modern adhesives are fussy about what they do, so choose with care. Our table gives the main options, but there are a few points to remember. Firstly, specialist adhesives bond better than general ones — 'super-glue' will not stick wood as well as woodworking adhesive. Secondly, allow for the conditions in which the adhesive will be used. Some need a perfect join and clinically clean environment to form a bond. Finally, always follow the instructions.

General-purpose	*Clear household adhesive (solvent: acetone / nail varnish remover)*
Wood	*White PVA adhesive or hot-melt glue gun indoors, urea-formaldehyde or two-part resin type outdoors (solvent: water). Use two-part acrylic adhesive (solvent: meths) to bond wood to other materials*
Metal	*Epoxy-resin, cyanoacrylate (superglue) or two-part acrylic adhesive (solvents are meths, acetone or special solvent, meths respectively)*
Laminates	*Contact adhesive (solvent: acetone). Use with care; emulsion type is safer*
Wallboards	*Panel adhesive (sold in cartridges), contact adhesive*
Floorcoverings	*Special rubber (solvent: petrol) or synthetic latex types (solvent: water)*
Ceiling tiles	*Special adhesive for polystyrene tiles*
Ceramic tiles	*Special tiles adhesive; waterproof types for wet areas (solvent: water)*
Glass, china	*Epoxy-resin, cyanoacrylate or acrylic types (see Metal for solvents)*
Rigid plastic	*Cyanoacrylate or two-part acrylic types (see Metal for solvents)*
Soft plastic	*PVC adhesive for vinyl, polystyrene cement for polystyrene*
Carpet, fabrics	*Latex-based fabric adhesive (solvent: water)*

Unfortunately, you cannot drive an ordinary screw, nail, or bolt into a wall and expect it to hold. It almost certainly won't. Instead, you need a proprietary fixing device, but with so many on the market, how do you decide which? The main factors to be taken into account here are the required fixing strength and the type of wall.

In solid masonry, screws and plastic wallplugs are normally adequate for all but structural building work, where the great strength of expanding metal bolts is a must. There are alternatives, though — notably chemical fixings which virtually glue the screw or bolt in place. Look out, too, for special plastic plugs designed for use in breeze blocks and lightweight concrete blocks too crumbly for ordinary types.

Hollow partition walls and ceilings pose more of a problem. For light fixings use a plastic cavity plug (there are special versions for plasterboard) or a metal toggle fixing (better on lath and plaster). Their strength is, however, limited by that of the plasterboard or lath and plaster skin, so for heavy loads screw directly into timbers supporting the wall or ceiling.

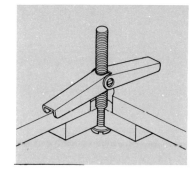

1. This toggle's machine screw braces sprung, folding metal arms against the wall or ceiling's skin when it is tightened.

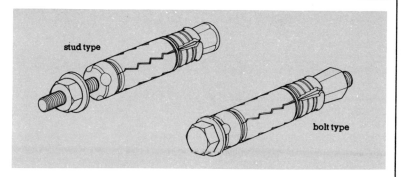

stud type

bolt type

2. Expanding bolts provide fixings of great strength (mainly used for heavy structural work). Some have normal headed bolts,

whilst others have threaded studs which accept a washer and nut. Both are usually supplied with the fixing.

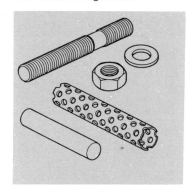

3. A typical chemical fixing consists of threaded stud and nut, perforated metal sleeve, plus a capsule of bonding chemicals.

4. Drill a hole in the wall, push in the perforated sleeve, then carefully slide in the capsule containing the chemicals.

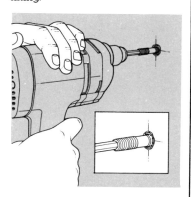

5. Finally, drive the threaded stud home with a drill and wait for the chemicals released from the broken capsule to harden.

③ Fixings in solid walls

To make a fixing in a solid wall, basically just drill a hole, pop in a wall plug and drive home an ordinary screw. But take care. Choose a good plug. In general, the more serrated the outside, the better the grip. Check, too, on the size compatibility of plug, masonry drill and screws. Carefully drilling is also essential. Be sure the hole is deep enough, and don't let the drill bit enlarge it by wandering. Finally, don't overtighten the screw as you drive it home.

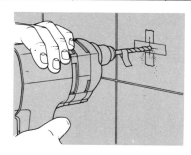

1. Drill a hole deep enough for both plug and screw. Tape round the drill bit as a depth guide. Tape on tiles helps the bit bite.

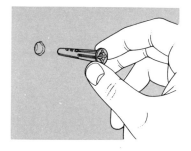

2. Push the wall plug into the hole until the end flange is level with the surrounding plaster. Check that it is a snug fit.

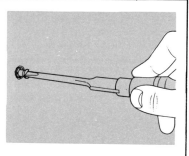

3. Drive the screw into the plug to complete the fixing. If the plug fails to grip, fit a slightly larger one in its place.

4 Undoing stuck fixings

Stubborn old screws can turn the simplest repair jobs into nightmares — unless you know how to remove them. If the screw head is in good condition, scrape away any old paint around it, then turn the screw as if to tighten it before attempting to remove it. If this fails, heat the screw by applying a soldering iron to the head. Once cool it should come out easily. And if the old screw head is badly 'chewed'? Here you must resort to a more drastic solution shown on the right.

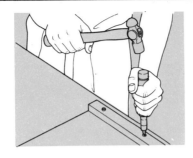

1. An impact driver — a spiral ratchet screwdriver you hit with a hammer — should work if the screw head is not too damaged.

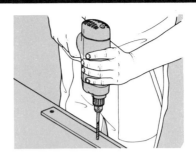

2. Badly damaged screws are best drilled out completely. Plug the resulting hole in the wood with dowel ready for a new screw.

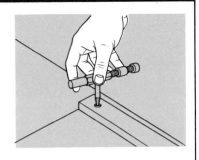

3. Alternatively, use a screw extractor — try hiring one. This bores into the screw to provide enough grip to unscrew it.

5 Tool kit – general repairs

The best way to assemble a tool kit for home repairs is to buy only the most basic items at first; then add to it as the need arises. Don't get anything too outlandish, though. It is more economical to hire rather than buy a tool you may use only once or twice.

As a start, get a good electric drill (with an extension lead and a set of bits), a hammer (a claw or cross-pein design is best) and a selection of screwdrivers. These together with a tape measure, some screws, nails, and wall plugs will cope with most fixing jobs. A saw (the tenon saw is a good general-purpose type), plane (or rasp-type shaping tool), and sanding block (with abrasive paper in a choice of grades) are equally good buys for wood shaping, and here it is worth adding a craft knife, a set of chisels, and a mallet.

And for metalwork? Pliers, an adjustable wrench, and a junior hacksaw will cope with most jobs around the house. Similarly, a couple of cold chisels, a club hammer, a small trowel, and a steel float will enable you to tackle simple masonry jobs.

Finally, get a robust, good quality torch so you can see what you are doing in dark corners.

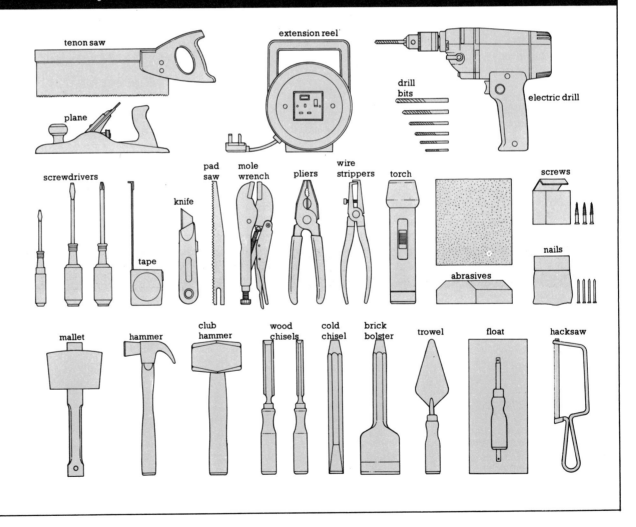

Nails, pins and tacks offer one of the simplest ways to join things together, but despite their outward simplicity they are actually quite cunning pieces of engineering, and to make the most of them, it is important you choose the right type for the job.

For general rough carpentry, round and oval wire nails are best — the latter are less likely to split the wood. For finer work use panel pins (or hardboard pins, both for fixing sheet materials), moulding pins or lost head nails. And to fix sheet materials there are various tacks (for carpets, upholstery, and so on), and clout nails (mainly for roofing felt). There are highly specialized nails too, such as glazing sprigs to hold glass in rebates, masonry nails for fixings to soft masonry, and annular nails (ideal for fixing hardboard underlay to floors because their ribbed shank stops this type of nail working loose).

In addition, you may come across a variety of old-fashioned 'cut' nails, the most common being the cut flooring brad used to nail down floorboards.

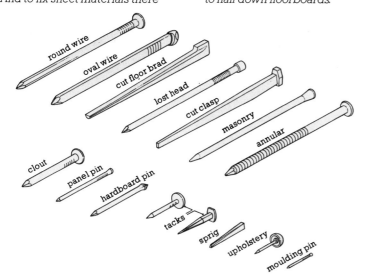

1. Getting very small pins started can be hard on the fingers, so try holding them by pushing them through a piece of stiff card.

2. Pincers are best for removing most nails, but you can also use a claw hammer. Protect the timber's surface with scrap wood.

Screws are not as easy to use as nails, but they do provide a much stronger fixing, and one that is easier to undo if necessary.

For woodwork, the most useful is the countersunk screw — its flat-topped, tapered head is made to finish flush with the surface of the timber. Sold in a choice of lengths, finishes and thicknesses (denoted by a gauge number, Nos 8, 10, and 12 being most common), you'll find countersunk screws with either conventional slotted heads or one of the more modern cross-head patterns (Phillips, Pozidriv, and Supadriv). Cross-headed types generally afford the screwdriver better grip. To fix hardware to woodwork there are the raised-head and roundhead screws, the former a cross between the roundhead and countersunk types.

In addition, you will find several specialist screws such as the sturdy coach screw with its square bolt-like head, the mirror screw with its screw-on decorative head cover, and the self-tapping screw for light metalwork and the like. There are even double-ended dowel screws, plus a variety of screw hooks and screw eyes.

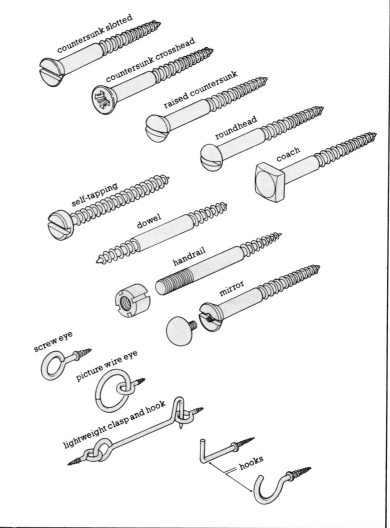

Although you can tackle repair work with a hand drill, power drills make the work much easier. In general, the more powerful and versatile the drill, the more you have to pay.

The wattage is the normal measure of power, and for diy drills this will be from 250 to 550W. A better guide to drilling power, though, is chuck capacity. Ranging from 10 to 13mm, this represents the largest drill shank you can use. Note this is not the maximum hole size (drilling capacity). With suitable bits, much larger holes are possible.

As for versatility, start with speed. Single-speed drills are cheapest, but two-speed models —high for wood, low for masonry —give better results. Better still are variable-speed drills whose trigger acts as a throttle, letting you adjust the speed to your needs. Next consider hammer action —where the bit goes in and out as well as turning —for easier penetration in masonry. And if you want to use the drill as a powered screwdriver you need reverse action. You may also find torque (turning power) adjustment useful for some jobs.

Finally, look at the drilling aids on offer as extras.

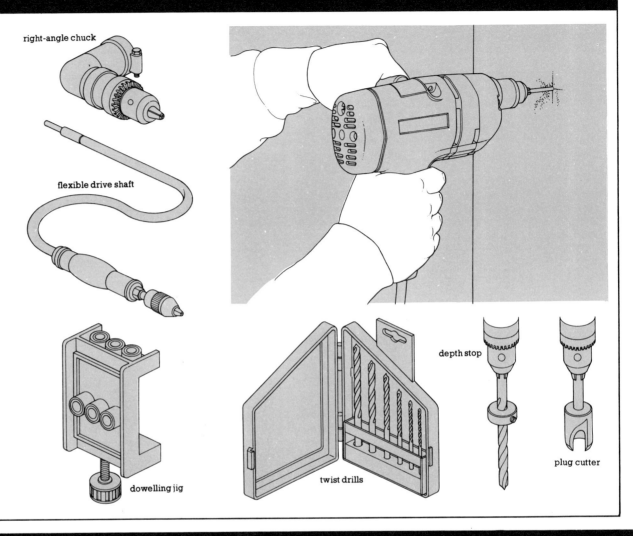

right-angle chuck

flexible drive shaft

dowelling jig

twist drills

depth stop

plug cutter

The simplest power sander is the disc sander. Widely sold as a drill accessory (a rubber backing plate to which you clamp sheets of abrasive), it is good at shaping but does not give a good finish.

For that, the orbital sander is the tool to choose, the rectangular sole plate working the abrasive with a sort of scrubbing action. Like the disc sander, it is sold as a drill accessory; however, integral versions are better, offering speed adjustment and a choice of sizes.

Orbital sanders are very slow, though. To remove waste quickly while still producing a good finish a belt sander (so called because it drives a continuous belt of abrasive between two rollers) is a much better buy. Many are fitted with a bag to collect the dust.

And for still faster waste removal (say, smoothing sawn timber) there is the power planer —the power tool equivalent of an ordinary bench plane. This uses, not abrasive, but rapidly rotating cutter blades.

1. For the best results, orbital sanders should always be worked in the direction of the wood grain, never across it.

⑩ Jig saws

When it comes to taking the hard work out of home repairs, the jig saw is almost as useful as an electric drill. Available as either a drill accessory or an integral power tool (the latter is better), it was originally designed for making shaped cuts in relatively thin materials. However, modern jig saws are far more versatile, and armed with a selection of blades (for metal, plastic, and wood) you will find it an ideal general-purpose power saw.

The main thing to look for when buying is speed adjustment. Although single-speed models are cheapest, you will find two-speed and variable-speed saws much easier to use, and the higher the top speed the better. Weight and quality of manufacture are also important. Cheaper, lighter models tend to vibrate too much to be accurate.

In addition, there is a variation on the jig saw worth considering — the scroll saw. This allows the blade to rotate independently for intricately shaped cuts.

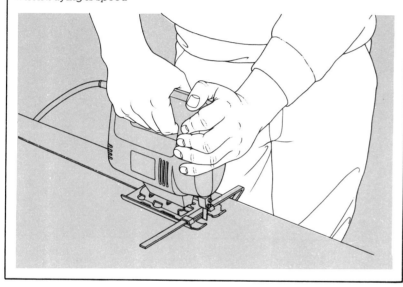

⑪ Circular saws

Circular saws are used mainly for heavy sawing operations — for example, sawing large boards to size. However, they are also capable of more delicate work such as slicing waste joints.

Available as integral power tools and drill accessories, most diy versions are fitted with blades 140 or 184mm in diameter, giving a maximum cutting depth of 40 and 62mm respectively. All normally allow the depth of cut to be adjusted, and can be set with the blade at an angle.

⑫ Routers

Consisting of a base plate, electric motor and interchangeable cutter (available in a choice of shapes and sizes), the router is used to cut grooves, rebates, and housings in timber. There are two types. The standard router has a fixed cutter; once you have set the depth of cut and switched on, no further adjustment is possible. With the plunge router, the cutter can be raised or lowered at will (though there is an adjustable depth stop), allowing the tool to cut mortices and the like.

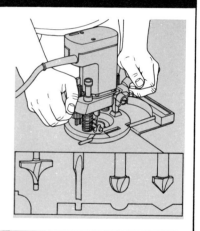

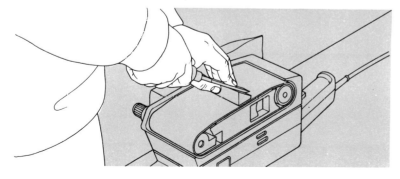

2. Fitted with a suitable abrasive and held upside down in a safe bench support, belt sanders can do simple grinding jobs.

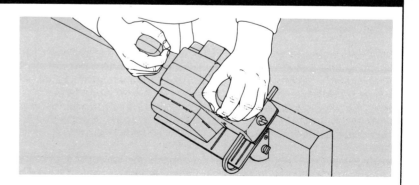

3. Power planers can do anything a bench plane can, including chamfering. Built-in guides make for greater accuracy.

There are dozens of different hinges available — so many that whatever your needs, someone almost certainly makes a hinge to meet them. The most widely used, though, (certainly for internal doors) is the butt hinge — the rising butt being designed to raise the door clear of carpets as it opens and then to shut it under its own weight. Other hinges worth remembering are sprung 'lay-on' hinges (found on modern kit furniture), mortise and cylinder concealed hinges, the various flap hinges, and hinges designed specially for glass doors.

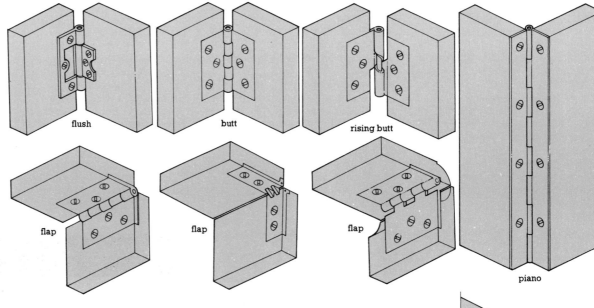

flush

butt

rising butt

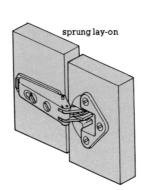

flap

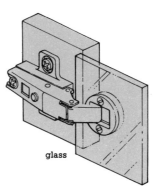

flap

flap

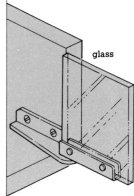

piano

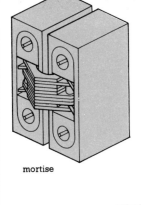

mortise

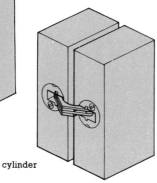

cylinder

sprung lay-on

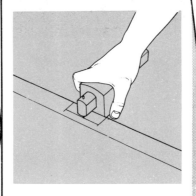

glass

glass

Butt hinges must be fitted with care if the door is to open and close smoothly – and only when required. The basic idea is to set them in rebates which leave them exactly flush with the surrounding timber, while at the same time leaving the door absolutely vertical. The hinges themselves are also important – they must be able to take the door's weight. For most internal doors a pair of 75mm butts is about right. Add a third mid-way between the two for heavier doors, and increase the hinge size if the door is very heavy.

Finally, be sure to position the hinges correctly. On a flush door, set the bottom hinge about 230mm from the bottom of the door, the top hinge about 150mm from the top. On panelled doors fit the hinges 25mm above and below the bottom and top rails respectively.

1. Mark out the hinge rebate on the door with a marking gauge, try square and knife. Darken the cut lines with a pencil.

2. Carefully chop out the waste with a sharp chisel, constantly using the actual hinge to check rebate's depth and general fit.

Stays are used to hold lids, together with top- and bottom-hung cupboard doors, in the open position, and as with so much furniture hardware, there is no shortage of choice when it comes to styles, designs and materials. In fact, though, most are just variations on three basic types.

There are the lid stays (for lids), lift stays, (for bottom-hung doors and flaps), and flap-down stays (for top-hung doors). Most of the better designs incorporate some form of damper to ease the lid or door into the open or closed position.

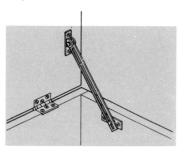

1. A simple, yet very sturdy traditional lid stay design.

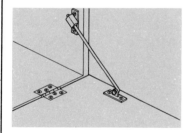

3. Another lid stay, this time with an 'anti-slam' friction brake.

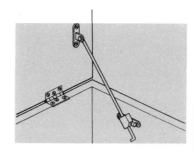

2. This lift stay uses friction to stop the door slamming down.

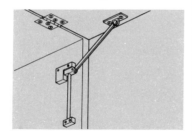

4. The flap down stay — stronger and more complex than the rest.

Joining pieces of wood together, either to mend a break or make good an existing joint that has weakened with age, is perhaps one of the commonest of all indoor repairs. Unfortunately, it is rare that you can manage using neat, conventional woodworking joints and techniques. And it's here that the various angle irons, repair brackets and corner brackets come in. All you do is screw them in place over the join. For neatness, either set them into the wood to leave them flush with the surrounding surface, or choose brass versions and make the plates a decorative feature.

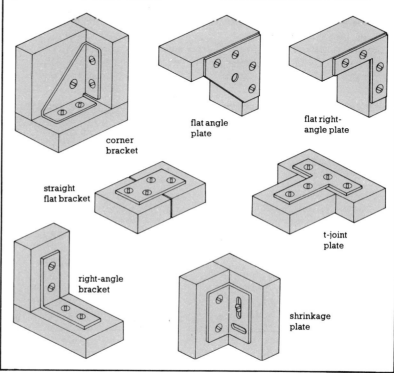

corner bracket

flat angle plate

flat right-angle plate

straight flat bracket

t-joint plate

right-angle bracket

shrinkage plate

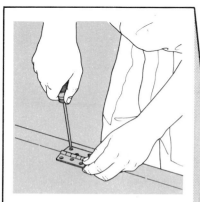

3. Having marked and drilled pilot holes for the screws, fix the hinges securely in place and offer the door up to the opening.

4. Stand the door on scrap wood to give the correct clearance (6mm) at the bottom, then mark the hinge positions on the frame.

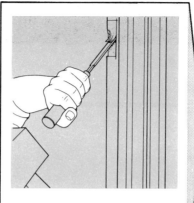

5. Tidy the marking out with knife, try square, and marking gauge, chop out the waste, then hang the door with one screw per hinge.

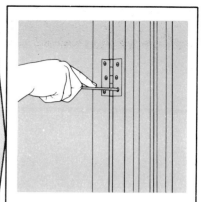

6. Add the remaining screws, easing or tightening them (packing out gaps with card) until the door closes smoothly.

17 Curing sticking doors

Poorly fitting hinges are a common cause of sticking doors. With use, screws work loose, and the hinge rebate distorts. The solution is simply to remove the door and deepen the rebate or pack it out with scrap wood glued and pinned in place.

The introduction of a new and thicker flooring into the room is another possible cause. Here either plane a little off the bottom of the door (the clearance under the door should be about 6mm), or, in the case of a thick carpet, fit rising butt hinges.

The most common reason for sticking, though, is that the door or door frame has swollen or shrunk. Here the door must be planed down to fit, but don't do so at once – wait a few months. The problem may be temporary, due to very wet or very dry weather. Lubricate the door edges with talc or candle wax.

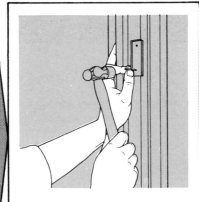

1. If an existing hinge rebate is too deep, pack it out with a thin card, or a piece of scrap wood glued and pinned in place.

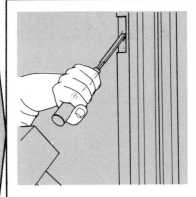

2. If the hinge rebate is too shallow, deepen it with a chisel, using the hinge itself to check that you don't cut too deep.

18 Floorboards – repairs and relaying

Floorboards are prone to a number of problems, but few are more annoying than draughty gaps between boards. How you fill these depends on how neat a finish you want. If looks don't matter at all, push filler between the boards, allow to dry, then sand smooth. Alternatively, fill the gaps with fillets of timber glued in place. For a perfect job, though, you must lift every board and relay the entire floor.

Floorboards also need attention due to old age and general wear and tear. If a board is in reasonable condition, you can merely relay it with the old underside on top. Where the damage is more extensive, however, you must replace it completely. But there is no need to replace an entire board if only part of it is damaged. Simply cut out the affected section and replace that.

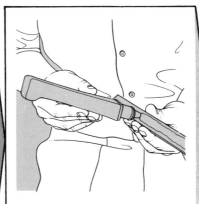

1. Plane down a timber fillet so it is slightly thicker than necessary to fill the gap. Smear with woodworking adhesive.

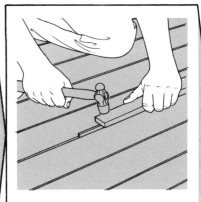

2. Tap the fillet firmly into the gap until just proud of adjacent boards, protecting its edge from the hammer with scrap wood.

19 Tool kit

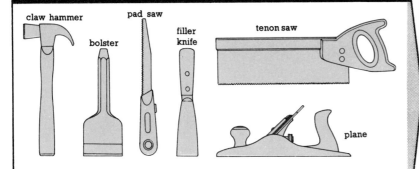

claw hammer *pad saw* *bolster* *filler knife* *tenon saw* *plane*

The floor fixer's tool kit — a tenon saw and pad saw for cutting boards; a bolster (or flooring chisel) for lifting them, a hammer to nail them down, and a plane plus filling knife to fill gaps.

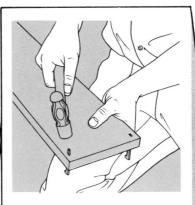

1. You may be able to re-use the old flooring brads, so knock them out straight away – before you accidentally kneel on them.

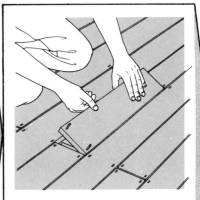

2. If the old board is sound, just turn it over and drop it into place. If not, cut a section of new floorboard to fit the gap.

3. Where the door has swelled, mark the places where it rubs by holding carbon paper against the frame and closing the door.

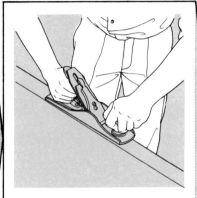

4. Plane off the excess timber, taking care not to remove any more than necessary – you cannot make the door bigger again.

5. If you need to fit new hinges, hammer dowels into the old screw holes so that the new screws will grip properly.

6. Rising butt hinges come in two parts. Screw one half to the door; the other to the frame, then drop the door into position.

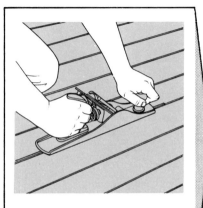

3. Once the glue has set hard, plane off the excess fillet to leave it perfectly flush with the surrounding floorboards.

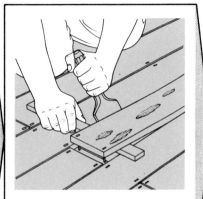

4. Starting at one end, lever up the board with a bolster chisel. Use a batten to stop it springing back as you work along it.

5. If only part of the board is to be replaced, saw off the damaged section of board flush with the side of a joist.

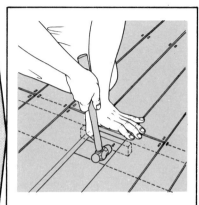

6. Nail a batten to the side of the joist against which you made the cut in order to support that end of the replacement board.

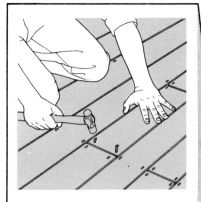

3. In most cases, it's simplest to nail the repaired section of board to its support batten and joist, using cut flooring brads.

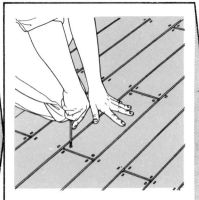

4. If the repaired section of board is warped, refix it with woodscrews. Tightening these should straighten floorboard out.

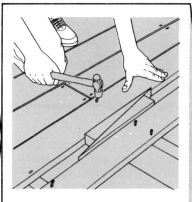

5. When relaying several boards to close gaps, use wedges to butt each one hard against its neighbour before nailing it down.

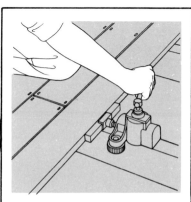

6. Alternatively, you may find it more convenient to hire a flooring cramp – a sort of horizontal jack clamped on to a joist.

20 Levelling solid floors

Before laying a floorcovering, make sure the floor itself is smooth and level or it may spoil the new flooring's appearance and shorten its life.

With most modern solid floors this isn't difficult. Simply skim the surface with self-smoothing flooring compound. But do check for rising damp first. Lay a small sheet of clear plastic on the floor, tape it down round the edges to form an air-tight seal, then leave it for a few days. Any condensation in the plastic 'bubble' indicates rising damp.

Where damp is present, a damp-proof membrane must be provided and linked to any dpc in the house walls. Liquid sealers can be used for this, but may have to be protected with a 50mm thick concrete screed. If the resulting loss of room height makes this impractical, the floor must be dug up and relaid.

1. Start by scrubbing the floor clean with warm water and detergent, aiming to remove all traces of dirt and grease.

2. Next, mix the self-smoothing compound with water to a creamy smooth consistency, following the manufacturer's instructions.

1. Before laying a damp-proof membrane, lever off old skirting boards and so on with a bolster chisel, and remove room doors.

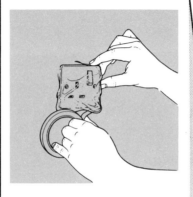

2. Having repositioned them higher up the wall where necessary, protect power sockets with polythene taped in place.

3. Now brush on the sealer to form the damp-proof membrane. Apply two coats at right-angles to each other to avoid pin-hole gaps.

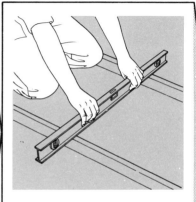

4. The next step is to divide the floor into manageable bays with 50 x 25mm battens. Check that their top edges are level.

21 Levelling wooden floors

Floorboards may also need levelling ready for a new floorcovering. The simplest method is to cover them with 1220mm square sheets of hardboard laid smooth side up. It's not difficult and there is no need to be too fussy about trimming the hardboard to fit. But there are a couple of important points to remember.

Firstly, fix the boards with annular nails. These will not work loose as the floor springs. Drive them in 230mm apart across each board's surface; 150mm apart round the edges. Secondly, be sure to condition the new hardboard. Brush water into the sheets' mesh sides and stack them back to back in the room in which they are to be used for a few days. If you don't do this the hardboard may distort after you have laid it, as it adjusts to the room's humidity.

1. Saw standard 2440 x 1220mm sheets of hardboard in half (a step ladder makes a handy saw horse) and set aside to condition.

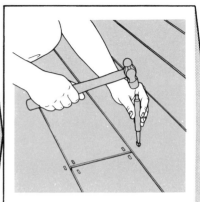

2. Check that all the existing floorboards are securely nailed in place, and punch any protruding nail heads below the surface.

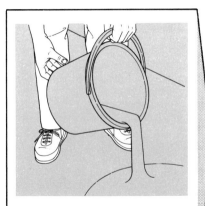

3. When the mix is ready, start in one corner of the room and pour a little on to the floor – enough to finish about 1 square metre.

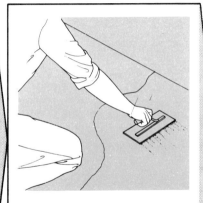

4. Spread out the compound fairly roughly with a steel float to a thickness of about 3mm, then leave to settle flat and harden.

1. Self-smoothing compound can be used to cover old ceramic floor tiles, but their glaze must first be sanded to provide a key.

2. The compound won't stick to dusty concrete. If there is cement dust on the surface, seal it with stabilizing primer.

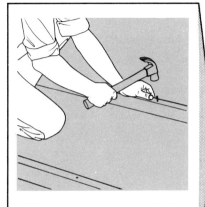

5. When you are satisfied, fix the battens temporarily to the floor with masonry nails. Wear goggles – the nails sometimes shatter.

6. Tackling one bay at a time, shovel fine concrete over the membrane and tamp down using the batten edges as a guide.

7. Give the concrete's surface a final smoothing with a steel float. When all bays are filled, leave the concrete to harden.

8. To complete the floor, lever out the guide battens, retouch the nail holes with bitumen, and fill the vacant slots with concrete.

3. Strike a chalk line between mid-points of opposite walls to find the room's centre, and lay the sheets working out from there.

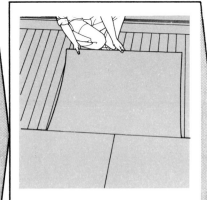

4. For the best results, position the hardboard so that the joins between sheets are neatly staggered brick-fashion.

5. Lay narrow strips of hardboard over floorboards providing access to pipe and cable runs so these can be reached for repairs.

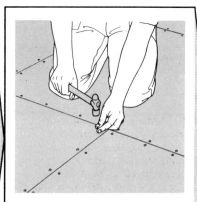

6. Secure the hardboard with 25mm annular nails driven in at 150mm centres along the board's edges, flattening it out as you go.

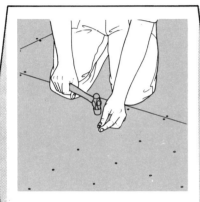

7. With the edges of the board fixed in place, nail it down across the centre, driving the nails in at roughly 230mm centres.

8. To cut a sheet to fit against a wall (which may be irregular), first line it up squarely with a sheet you have already fixed.

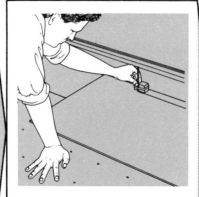

9. To allow for irregularities in the wall, 'scribe' the hardboard by running a pencil and wooden spacer block along the skirting.

10. Cut along this line for a perfect fit with the wall, then cut the sheet's other edge level with those already in place.

(23) Repairing skirtings

Skirting boards are very vulnerable to accidental damage and attack from rot, so it is well worth knowing how to patch them. The basic technique is quite straightforward – cut out the damaged section, cut a new length of skirting to fit, and then nail this in place. But there are a few practical complications.

To begin with, sawing through skirting boards in situ is not easy. Levering them away from the wall with wedges helps but it is still a time-consuming job. Secondly, you must find new skirting to match the old. Modern designs should be readily available, but you may well have to hunt for some ornate older styles. If all else fails, try to make up your own replacement using a mixture of plain softwood and decorative mouldings. Glue and pin these together in situ, fill any gaps before redecorating.

1. Lever the skirting from the wall, secure with wedges, then saw out the damaged section, mitring the ends.

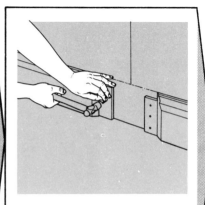

2. To secure the replacement section, slip wooden blocks partly behind the existing skirting, fix with masonry nails.

(24) Repairing architraves

Architraves – the decorative mouldings around doors, windows and so on – are not normally worth patching. Instead, replace them completely. Architrave mouldings in softwood are available from most good timber yards, though as with skirting boards, you may have difficulty in matching old, ornate designs.

As for the work itself, both the old and new mouldings are simply nailed to the door or window's structural wooden frame, so it is a straightforward job. In fact, the only complication is that, for appearance's sake, it is usual to mitre the architrave at the corners – not difficult given a good mitre box and a reasonable ability with a tenon saw, but a job needing care, since any mistakes here tend to be glaringly noticeable and difficult to disguise effectively with filler.

1. Clear away any paint, plaster, wallpaper, and so on from the edge of the architrave and lever it away with a bolster chisel.

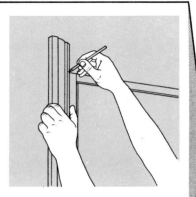

2. Offer up a length of moulding to the door frame, and mark the position of the inside of the mitre cut on its edge.

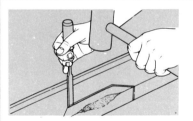

1. To repair damaged timber – say, a window sill – saw and chisel out the offending wood, tapering the cut-out's ends.

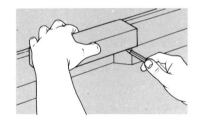

2. Using the cut-out as a guide, mark up and cut a replacement piece of wood accurately, leaving it slightly oversize.

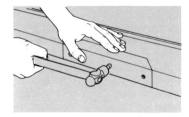

3. The 'patch' can be glued and screwed in place. Countersink the screw heads and cover with filler or glued dowel plugs.

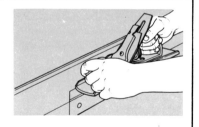

4. When the glue has dried, plane the 'patch' accurately to match the size and profile of the surrounding timberwork.

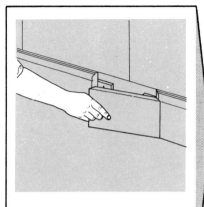

3. The new skirting can now be cut to fit and pinned in place to the support blocks. Punch the pin heads below the surface.

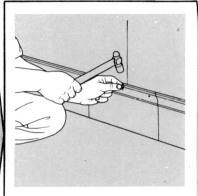

4. If suitable replacement skirting cannot be found, build up the repair from plain softwood and assorted timber mouldings.

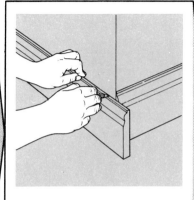

5. External corners are normally mitred. Use the skirting on the one wall as a guide to marking up the patch on the other.

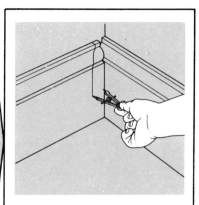

6. Internal corners are not mitred; use a pair of compasses to transfer the skirting's profile to the end of the new piece.

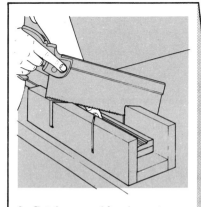

3. Cut the new side pieces to length, mitring them accurately at the top, then check them for fit against the door frame.

4. When you are happy with the fit of the side pieces, pin them in place against the door frame. Punch in the pin heads.

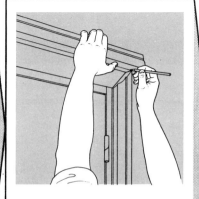

5. Using the side pieces as a guide, cut the top section of architrave to length, mitring both ends, and nail this in place.

6. Finally, reinforce the mitred corner joints with a nail driven into the top section's ends through the side pieces.

26 Replacing a stair tread

A badly worn stair tread can be dangerous as well as unsightly, so it is well worth replacing. The exact method depends on the stair's construction, and in some cases the job is very difficult; the main problem is to extract the old tread without causing too much damage. However, take a look at your stairs and see how they are put together. With some the tread can be removed from above, while with others you must remove the retaining wedges and blocks, and slide it out from the underside of the stairs.

Having got the old tread out, you will in most cases have to make up a replacement yourself using the original as a pattern – preferably from preservative-treated softwood. Where it cannot be fixed in place in the same way as the original, support it on wooden blocks.

27 Curing creaking stairs

Stairs generally creak because a tread is loose and is rubbing against neighbouring components when you step on it. It is therefore often possible to effect a temporary cure by puffing chalk or talc into the joints, lubricating the edges of the timber causing the creak. However, the only permanent cure is to refix the stair tread.

On the underside of the stairs you will probably find that a block reinforcing the tread/riser join has come loose or fallen off completely. Alternatively, check the hardwood wedges holding the tread in the strings (the stair's sides). These too may have loosened or disappeared. In either case, it's a simple matter to put things right. But if you cannot get at the stair's underside, you must simply do what you can to fix the tread as neatly as possible from above.

1. Lever off any mouldings covering the ends of the treads and tap out any inset balusters, taking care not to damage them.

2. The treads and risers are often held together by a tongued-and-grooved joint. Use a thin pad saw to cut through the tongue.

3. The tread should now be held in place with nothing but glue, so lever it out with a crowbar or something similar.

4. The next step is to make a replacement tread. Use the original as a model but check its fit on the stairs from time to time.

28 Repairing balusters & hand rails

Because of their importance to safety, handrails and balusters (the vertical members of the balustrade) should always be repaired as quickly and thoroughly as possible.

Handrails are obviously the most important, though if these break it is best to replace them completely rather than attempt to fix them – repairs are seldom strong enough to be trusted.

Broken balusters, on the other hand, are eminently suitable for do-it-yourself replacement. If they have broken cleanly, you can simply dowel-joint the two halves together. Removing them for repair can be tricky, though, and normally you will have to saw through them – at least at the top. Refixing balusters securely can also be a problem. The best options are to skew-nail or screw them to the rail's underside.

29 Baluster breaks

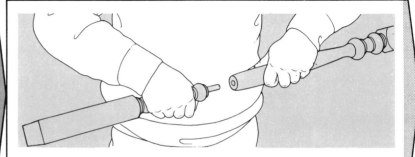

If a baluster has broken cleanly in two, tidy up the broken ends, bore a hole into each ready to receive a dowel, then glue the two halves back together. Finally, make good with wood filler.

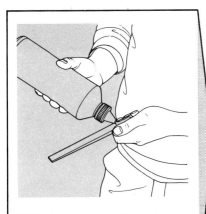

1. Tap loose wedges back into place. Cut replacements for any that are missing, gluing the sides before hammering them home.

2. Similarly, reglue any triangular softwood blocks that reinforce the tread/riser join. If there are none, make some.

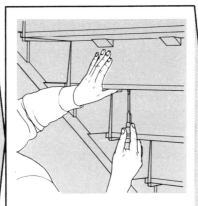

3. If the creak persists, reinforcement can be provided by screwing up through the tread into the riser's bottom edge.

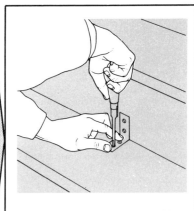

4. If you cannot get at the stair's underside, fix the tread's rear edge with a bracket, and screw the front edge on to the riser.

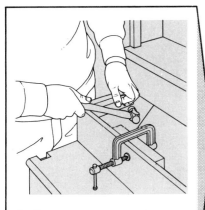

5. Since you cannot use the original joints, the new tread is supported on blocks glued and nailed to the riser and strings.

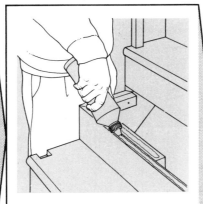

6. You are now ready to fit the tread so smear adhesive over the upper edges of the riser, strings and support blocks.

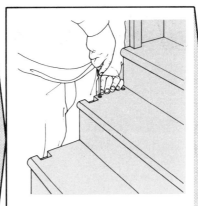

7. Carefully slide the tread into position then secure it with a couple of screws driven into the strings and wipe off excess glue.

8. Finally, glue and pin the balusters and end mouldings back in place, then prepare the stairs for redecoration.

30 Fixing balusters to hand rails

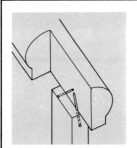
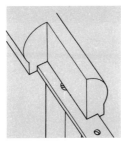

Balusters are fixed to hand rails in many ways. They may be skew-nailed, screwed to a secondary rail which is then covered by the hand rail proper, or secured with mortise and tenon joints. When replacing a baluster, skew-nailing is normally best

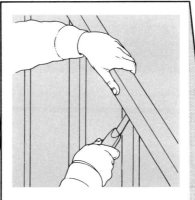

1. To remove a baluster, saw it level with the underside of the rail. Use a hacksaw if you encounter screws or nails.

2. Once the top end is free, you should be able to just knock the baluster out. Protect it from the hammer with scrap wood.

3. To refix a baluster, screw or nail through it at an angle into the rail, bracing it against a block clamped in place.

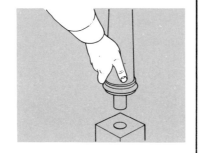

4. Glue the bottom into its recess, tapping thin wooden wedges in around its sides to hold it tightly in position.

31 Balustrade kits

If the handrails and balustrades are in very poor condition, it is worth considering having the whole lot replaced. You can now buy kits specially designed for diy installation, and containing almost everything you need to do the job. There is a choice of designs (though most have a period flavour), and because the components are to a simple modular formula, it is possible for a relative beginner to fit quite complex rails and balustrades containing curves and bends at the first attempt.

32 Replacing a newel post

1. Saw through the old newel post a little above the point where it joins the stair's string. This stub forms a base for the replacement.

2. Most replacements have a stud which you glue into a hole bored into the 'plinth' formed by what is left of the old newel.

33 Drawer repairs

Wooden drawers are normally supported on wooden strips fixed to their sides which locate in channels cut into the unit's carcase. The channel/runner positions may be reversed, the channel may be just one or two wooden beads, and in some cases both channel and runner may be absent, leaving the drawer to slide on its own base. But all have one thing in common: they wear out.

1. Drawer runners tend to wear out first. Prise or chisel them off and then glue and pin strips of new wood in their place.

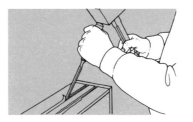

2. If the channels in a drawer are worn, cut new ones alongside them, and reposition the carcase runners accordingly.

3. If the drawer stops (which stop the drawer being pushed in too far) wear, fit small wooden plates to take over their job.

Most traditional furniture is constructed using either mortise-and-tenon or dowel joints, and both are likely to weaken as the adhesive holding them together becomes brittle with age.

At this stage, you can simply take the joint apart, clean it up, and then reglue. However, if the joint has been loose for some time, you may well find that the dowels or tenons themselves are damaged or broken and in need of replacement.

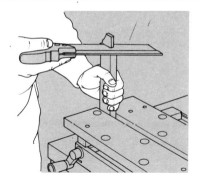

1. Saw off broken tenons flush with what appears to be the end of the rail in the assembled piece of furniture.

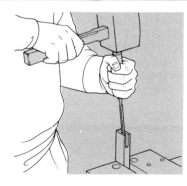

2. Next, using a tenon saw and a small chisel, cut a slot equal in width to the old tenon in the rail's end.

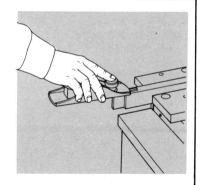

3. Into this, glue a tongue of new timber, and shape this into a tenon ensuring it is a good fit in the old mortise.

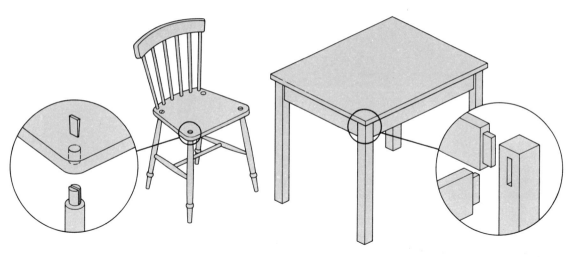

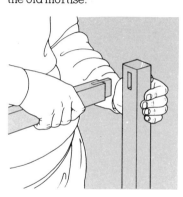

4. You now simply glue the joint back together, cramping it tightly until the adhesive is completely set.

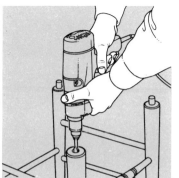

1. A similar technique is used to mend old dowel joints. Saw off the broken dowels and drill holes for new ones.

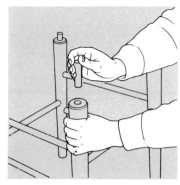

2. Select new dowels of the same size as the old, cut them accurately to length and glue securely in place.

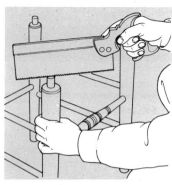

3. Test the joint for fit, and if it is loose (the old hole may be mis shapen), saw a slot in the end of the new dowel.

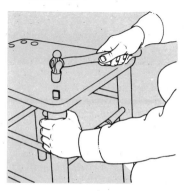

4. Having glued and assembled the joint, you can now hammer a wooden wedge into the dowel's slot to tighten it up.

35 Treating woodworm

Woodworm (the common furniture beetle) is the most common wood-boring insect and is capable of doing considerable damage in your home.

It starts life with an adult female laying eggs on some suitable exposed timber. These hatch into larvae which then bore into the wood and eat it away from the inside, before turning into adult beetles and eating their way out again. It is only at this stage that the small flight holes which are the classical sign of woodworm attack appear – after the damage has been done.

In treating woodworm, you should therefore stop newly hatched larvae from getting into wood by saturating the surface layer with toxic chemicals. If you can soak the interior (via old flight holes) to kill any larvae still active, so much the better.

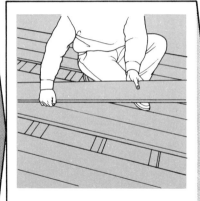

1. The beetles like to lay their eggs in quiet spots. Gaps between floorboards are ideal, so lift a few to expose the timber.

2. Lifting every fourth board should give sufficient access. Brush and vacuum out any dirt, dust, and other debris.

7. Don't forget the skirting boards. Lever these carefully away from the wall so you can spray their unpainted rear faces.

8. The loft is another favourite breeding ground. Roll back the insulation to expose the joists and any wooden ceiling laths.

9. Protect any exposed electrical wiring (including junction boxes) by wrapping it in plastic and taping this in place.

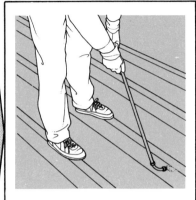

10. You can now start spraying. Treat joists, rafters, ceiling laths – every bit of exposed timber that you can find.

36 Applying preservative

Wood rot caused by fungi is another big problem, and here too, the solution is to impregnate the timber's surface with chemicals to stop rot spreading. Wood rot is far more damaging than woodworm, though, so don't wait for trouble – prevent it. Where there is a risk of dampness (fungi need moisture to gain a foothold), treat vulnerable timbers with preservative and use preservative-treated wood for repairs and improvements.

If the wood is already rotten, what you do depends on the extent of the damage and the type of rot. With wet rot, so long as the wood is structurally sound, it can be repaired rather than replaced. However, dry rot (which leaves the wood crumbly and cracked as if charred) is a more formidable enemy, best treated professionally.

1. If the wood is sound, wet rot damage can be fixed using a rot repair system. Start by applying the brush-on hardener.

2. Once that has set, make good the rest of the damage with the system's filler. Allow this to harden, then sand smooth.

3. Spray both the joists and the underside of the boards. The chemicals and equipment can be got from tool hire shops.

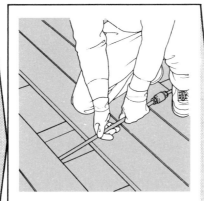

4. Be sure to spray every bit of exposed timber, right up to the edges of the room, or woodworm could gain a fresh foothold.

5. Don't forget to spray the underside of the boards you lifted to gain access to the rest of the floor.

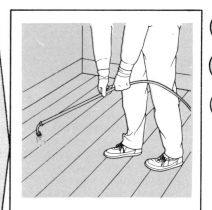

6. Finally, refix the lifted boards and spray the floor surface. Again, be sure not to miss any by working systematically.

37 Treating furniture

When treating furniture against woodworm you can afford to be rather more thorough.

The chemicals needed are available in acrosol cans for spraying, and most come with a flexible attachment allowing you to impregnate the timber via the flight holes. You can also buy woodworm killer separately to soak the wood. Concentrate your efforts on bare timber in hidden corners — especially the backs and interiors of units, the undersides, and so on.

1. Having sprayed large areas, fit the aerosol's nozzle and squirt woodworm killer into any flight holes visible.

2. After treatment, once the fluid has dried, the flight holes can be filled using a suitable wood filler ready for redecoration.

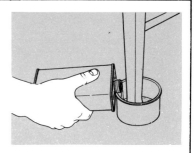

3. For a really thorough job, stand chair legs and the like in a bowl of woodworm fluid and leave this to soak into the endgrain.

3. Finally, to prevent further rot, insert pellets of preservative into holes drilled in and around the affected timber.

4. Tackle the preventive spraying of roof and structural timbers in the same way as woodworm treatment.

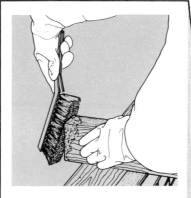

5. Timber end grain is especially vulnerable to fungi attack. Treat it by brushing on a thick coating of preservative paste.

6. Check your home's dampproofing, too, particularly dampproof membranes isolating floor timbers from rising damp.

38 Replacing a fireplace

Before pressing an old, disused fireplace back into service, you should always have the flue swept and the whole set-up checked by a professional. Flue repairs are also best left to the experts as they can be very difficult, but you can repair an old fireplace yourself.

It's a messy job, but not a particularly difficult one so long as there is no back boiler to get in the way.

Having removed the old fireback and so on, it is simply a case of bedding in a new fireback (which you can buy from a builder's merchant or fireplace specialist) and then making up the mortar flaunching that forms the mouth of the flue. That done, all that remains is to fit a grate and light the fire.

1. Set the bottom half of the fire back squarely in the opening on a bed of mortar, using a spirit-level to check that it's level.

2. To allow for expansion when the fireback heats up, slip a sheet of corrugated paper behind it. This will burn away.

39 Removing an old fireplace and choosing a replacement

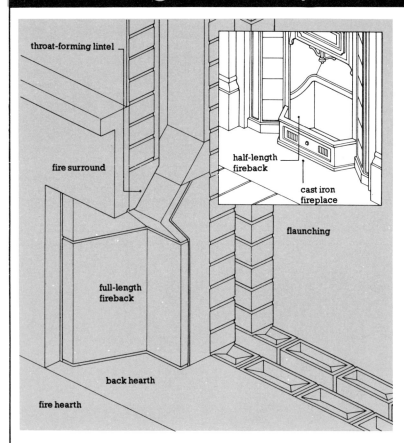

throat-forming lintel

fire surround

half-length fireback

cast iron fireplace

flaunching

full-length fireback

back hearth

fire hearth

There are two basic types of fireback to choose from. The standard 'full length' version is the one to get for an ordinary open fire. The smaller half-length type is for partly enclosed fires of the sort you get with an old-fashioned cast iron fireplace.

1. Carefully measure up the existing fireback so you can order a replacement of exactly the same size and design.

2. Starting at the top, use a club hammer and cold chisel to break up both the mortar flaunching and the old fireback.

3. Remove the pieces of fireback and flaunching, then use a shovel to break up and remove the soft lime mortar and rubble behind.

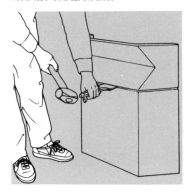

4. When you have got the new fireback, break it into two halves by tapping along the horizontal expansion joint with a cold chisel.

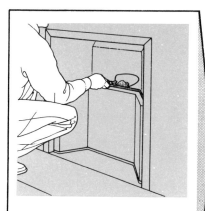

3. Next, fill behind the fireback with a fairly dry insulating mortar, made with lime (rather than cement) and vermiculite.

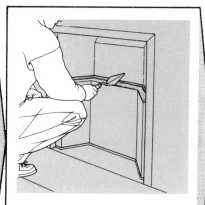

4. You are now ready to add the top of the fireback. Bed this on to the fireback's bottom half with a layer of fire cement.

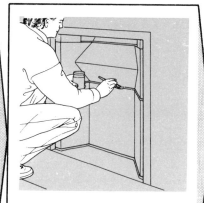

5. Finish sealing the join, then fill in behind the upper fireback with more insulating mortar, to finish level at the top.

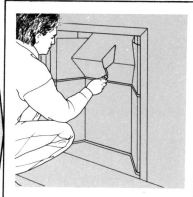

6. Finally, using ordinary mortar, complete the sloping flaunching that extends the fireback's slope up to meet the flue.

(40) Blocking a fireplace

If your home has central heating, you may decide that you no longer need fireplaces, and in this case you may decide to block them up. It looks better, and cuts out a lot of draughts.

There are three main methods to choose from. You can simply cover the opening with a sheet of plywood or something similar, leaving the fire surround in place if you wish. Or, for a neater finish, you can remove the surround, block the hole with plasterboard, bricks or concrete blocks, and then plaster it over to leave it just like any other wall.

The job must be done properly. In particular, you must ensure that the flue has enough ventilation to prevent the build-up of condensation which would eventually lead to dampness on internal walls. Incorporating a simple grille when you block the fireplace is enough.

1. First, remove the front hearth. You may be able to lever this up whole with a spade. If not, hack it out with a cold chisel.

2. Get a friend to help, remove as much of the fire surround as comes away easily – the mantelshelf itself, for example.

(41) Continuing the floor

To complete the illusion that the fireplace never existed, extend the room's ordinary floor to cover the fire's hearth. This will probably be either a single section that can be levered up with a garden spade, or an area of tiling. Beneath it there may also be a mortar screed which can be chiselled out to reveal a concrete apron. Raise this to normal floor level with either a concrete screed (for solid floors), or with floorboards nailed to slim timber battens and existing joists.

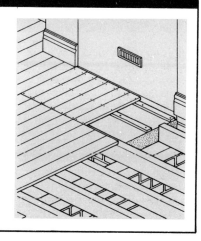

(42) Capping the chimney

Having blocked a fireplace, it is a good idea to block the chimney that served it, to stop the weather getting in and causing penetrating damp on the chimney breast walls. As usual, though, you must ensure that the flue will be adequately ventilated, so don't just seal the top of the flue. Instead, either fit it with a good weather-proof metal cowl, or remove it, and give the chimney stack a 'roof' made from a ridge tile (or something similar) securely bedded in mortar.

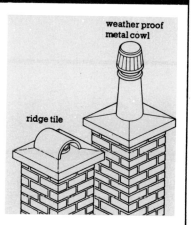

weather proof metal cowl

ridge tile

3. Chip away the plaster around the fire surround. Bedded in this at the sides will be two metal lugs screwed to the wall.

4. Unscrew the lug's fixing screws if possible. If they are stuck fast, then cut through them with a hacksaw or cold chisel.

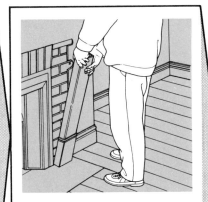

5. It may now be possible to lever away the entire fire surround. If not, remove the side pillars and the rest should follow.

6. If there is a cast iron fireplace, lift it out. Ordinary fire backs can either be broken up and removed or left in place.

43 Fireplace construction

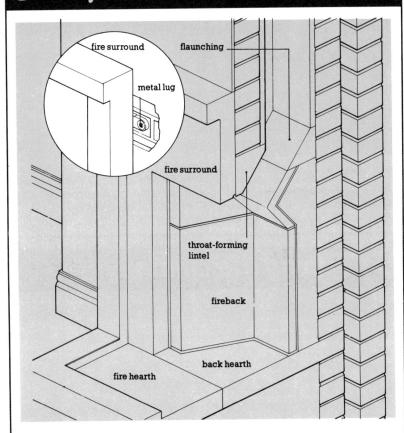

fire surround · flaunching · metal lug · fire surround · throat-forming lintel · fireback · back hearth · fire hearth

The fireplace starts as a rudimentary opening in which are fitted the fireback, flaunching, back hearth and throat-forming lintel that improve its fuel burning efficiency. To improve its appearance, the opening is framed by a decorative surround screwed to the wall, and is given a decorative hearth at the front.

44 Boarding the opening

For a neater finish, block the fireplace off with plasterboard and apply a skim coat of plaster to blend it into the surrounding wall. Clearly, this means removing both the fire surround and hearth, and for the best results it is also worth removing the fireback itself to leave a neat, square opening.

As for fitting the plasterboard, this is done in much the same way as when panelling.

Construct a wooden framework within the opening and fix the plasterboard to this with plasterboard nails. Just one point to watch: if the opening is very wide, make sure the framework gives intermediate support. Using 12mm board, ensure the timbers are no more than about 400mm apart.

With the plasterboard in place, all that remains is to skim over it with plaster.

45 Using bricks and blocks

The ultimate method of closing off an old fireplace is with bricks or concrete blocks. However, since the result is obviously very permanent, do make absolutely sure that you will not need the fireplace again first.

As when using plasterboard, start by removing the hearth and surround and then completely clear out the back of the fireplace. If you are using bricks, you must now chop out half bricks from the side of the opening so that the new brickwork can be keyed in to the old (there is no need for this when using concrete blocks). What follows is then just a fairly straightforward bricklaying job which you finish off by plastering the exposed masonry to match the rest of the wall. To provide flue ventilation just build in an airbrick. There's no need to fit a grille unless you want to.

The simplest way to block off a fireplace is just to cover it with a piece of plywood, hardboard, or something similar (perhaps a decorative variety) screwed to a wooden framework set within the opening. In fact, the technique is so simple, you can even leave the old fire surround in place, which makes it the ideal choice if you feel you may wish to re-open the fireplace at a later date. Don't forget, you must incorporate a grille into the wooden panel to ventilate the flue.

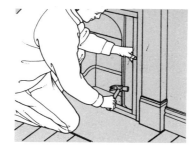

1. Line the opening with a frame made from 50mm sq sawn softwood, fixing this with masonry nails, or screws and wallplugs.

2. Cut the covering panel of board to size, and fix this securely to the frame so it finishes flush with the surrounding wall.

4. Cut a ventilation hole near the bottom of the panel (or simply bore a few large holes) and cover with a suitable grille.

1. Construct a simple frame within the fireplace opening, adding intermediate supports for the plasterboard if required.

2. Cut the sheet of plasterboard accurately to size, and fix it to the wooden framework with galvanized plasterboard nails.

3. Skim over the plasterboard and any exposed brickwork to leave the fireplace area flush with the surrounding wall.

4. To complete the job, neaten the ventilation hole cut in the plasterboard (ideally before it was fixed in place) with a grille.

1. After removing the fireback and so on, give the surrounding masonry a thorough cleaning to remove dust and other debris.

2. If you are using bricks, chop half bricks from the sides of the opening to key in the new work, and include an airbrick.

3. Allow time for the mortar to harden, then plaster over the new and old brickwork to blend it in with the rest of the wall.

4. Concrete blocks are faster than bricks, and there is no need to key them in. However, some cutting to fit may be necessary.

47 Plastering tools

For most simple repairs to plasterwork all you need is a filling knife, a paint brush, and a sanding block. However, larger jobs which involve replastering require slightly more in the way of equipment — a spot board and bucket for mixing, a hawk to carry wet plaster to the job, and a plasterer's trowel (steel float) plus a wooden float to apply the plaster and produce the required finish. In addition, an angle trowel is worth having for working into internal corners, as is a comb scratcher for keying new plaster ready for the next coat. You will also need a long straightedge to check that the new plasterwork is flush with the surrounding wall.

spot board

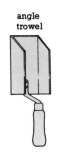
angle trowel

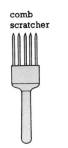
comb scratcher

filler knife

bucket

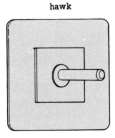
hawk

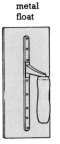
metal float

wood float

48 Surface cracks

Small surface cracks and holes in plaster are very easy to repair. Just rake them out with the corner of your filling knife, wet them and fill with a proprietary filler. There are, however, a few tips worth remembering.

Firstly, when raking out the crack, angle the filling knife so that it just undercuts the plaster, thus providing a key for the filler. Secondly, be sure to brush out the crack to remove any dust that would stop the filler sticking. Lastly, don't try to produce a perfect finish with wet filler; leave it slightly proud of the surrounding wall to allow for shrinkage during drying, and then sand it smooth once hard.

Incidentally, you will find that some cracks – notably those between walls and woodwork – re-open very quickly. Fill these with flexible mastic or caulking rather than ordinary filler.

49 Patching plaster

Although proprietary fillers are convenient, they are expensive – too expensive for large repairs. Here real plaster is much more economical, and not difficult to use on relatively small areas.

Begin by removing the damaged plaster with a hammer and bolster chisel. Stop as soon as you reach sound plaster – it's worth marking the area to be replaced before chiselling.

Having brushed down and wetted the wall, you can now apply the plaster, smoothing it on with a steel float. If the hole is deep, don't fill it all at once. Build up the repair with two or three layers, scratching each one and allowing it to dry before applying the next. On the final coat, use a batten to check that the repair is flush with the surrounding wall, and then polish the new plaster ready for redecorating.

50 Small holes in plasterboard

Plasterboard walls and ceilings are extremely vulnerable to mechanical damage; a moment's carelessness when moving furniture could leave you with a hole in the wall. What's more, when it comes to filling holes in plasterboard there is a snag – apply filler and it will simply fall through into the cavity behind the plasterboard skin.

There is a very neat solution to the problem. Cut a piece of plasterboard slightly larger than the repair, thread a piece of string through its centre, and push it through the hole so that it is left hanging in the cavity. If you now pull on the string, the plasterboard patch will block the hole allowing you to make good with either plaster or filler. You then simply cut off the string (the plasterboard should stay put), and finish neatening the repair in the normal way.

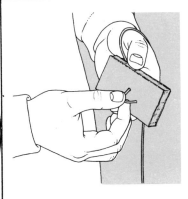

1. Cut a piece of plasterboard slightly larger than the hole to be filled and bore a small hole through the centre.

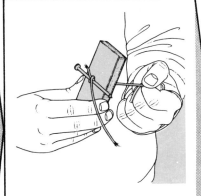

2. Thread a length of string through this hole, and tie one end to a small nail so it cannot be pulled back out again.

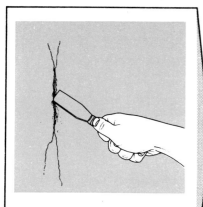

1. Rake out the crack with the filling knife, aiming to slightly undercut the surrounding plaster in order to key in the repair.

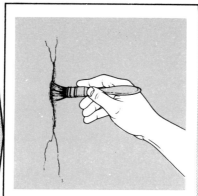

2. Brush out any dust in the crack, then wet it down to stop the filler drying out too quickly – especially in hot weather.

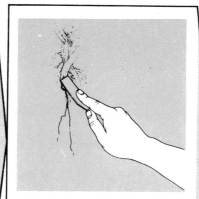

3. Force the filler right into the crack with a filling knife, then smooth it off to leave it just proud of the surrounding plaster.

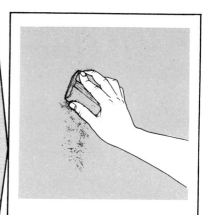

4. Leave the filler to harden completely, then rub down with fine glasspaper until smooth and flush with the rest of the wall.

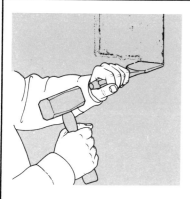

1. Hack away the defective plaster with a club hammer and bolster chisel, neatening the edges of the area to be repaired.

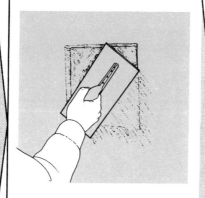

2. Brush off any dust then wet the wall and apply the plaster with a steel float. Fill deep holes in stages or the plaster may sag.

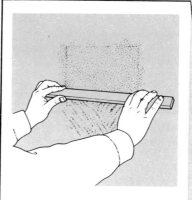

3. On the final coat, check that the repair is flush with the wall using a straightedge, sawing off excess plaster if necessary.

4. To complete the repair, wet the surface by flicking water on to it with a brush, and polish smooth with a steel float.

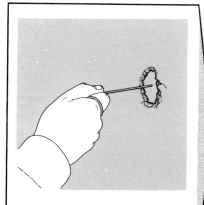

3. Push the plasterboard patch through into the wall's cavity, then pull on the string so that the patch completely blocks the hole.

4. Keeping a tight grip on the string, you can now make good with filler in the normal way. The patch will stop it falling through.

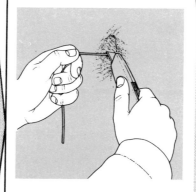

5. As the repair nears completion, stop, wait for the filler to harden sufficiently to support itself, then cut the string.

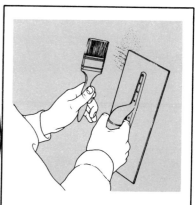

6. All that remains is to add a little more filler or plaster, and polish the repair just as you would on a solid wall.

51 Large holes in plasterboard

Even with the little trick for filling small holes in plasterboard, plaster and filler are of no use for mending holes of any size. They are simply too weak, and would soon break up and fall out. The solution is to make the repair with a plasterboard patch, fixing this to the wall or ceiling's internal timberwork.

To do this, you simply cut away the damaged plasterboard, working outwards from the hole until both ends of the resulting opening finish over the centre of a supporting timber. At the top and bottom of the enlarged hole, you then fit two new timbers (noggings), screwing or nailing these in place. That done, all that remains is to cut a plasterboard patch and nail it in place, finishing the repair off with a skim coat of plaster to disguise the joins and produce a smooth surface ready for redecoration.

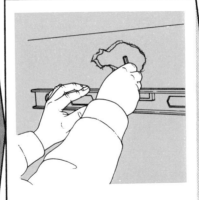
1. With the aid of a spirit-level, draw parallel lines above and below the hole to indicate the top and bottom edges of the patch.

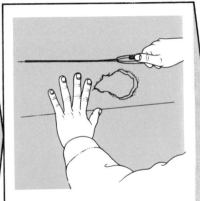
2. Using a sharp knife, cut through the plasterboard along these lines until you are mid-way over a supporting timber.

52 Holes in laths and plaster (with laths intact)

Before the coming of plasterboard, lath and plaster (plaster applied to a backing of thin wooden slats) was the normal finish for ceilings and stud partition walls. The trouble is that, with age, the plaster skin often begins to come away from the supporting laths, and may eventually fall off in lumps.

Fortunately, though, so long as the laths are intact and reasonably sound, this sort of damage looks worse than it is. In fact, all you need do to remedy the situation is to clean up the laths, picking out all the bits of old plaster stuck between them, and then apply a new plaster skin. However, this is a real plastering job, and it is therefore best to start with fairly small repairs. Applying a smooth, flat, even coat of plaster to a large area requires a certain amount of practice.

1. Cut neatly round the damaged section with a sharp knife, and remove every bit of loose plaster within this area.

2. Apply a thin base coat of plaster, using enough pressure to squeeze it between the laths in order to hold it in place.

53 Holes in laths and plaster (with broken laths)

Repairing lath and plaster is slightly more difficult where the laths are broken or rotten. In fact, if a fair proportion of the existing plasterwork is affected (or looks likely to become affected in the near future) you should consider replacing the lath and plaster completely rather than face the need for repeated repairs.

As for the repair technique, really all you can do is treat the lath and plaster as if it were plasterboard – cutting the damaged section back to the supporting joists or studs, inserting new timber noggins between these, and then nailing up a plasterboard patch. If possible, use plasterboard that is slightly thinner than the lath and plaster so that when skimmed over with finishing plaster, the repair will blend in perfectly with the surrounding plasterwork.

1. Pull away the damaged plaster and laths – carefully, because heavy chunks may come off unexpectedly.

2. With a padsaw, enlarge the hole into a neat rectangle, cutting back to the centres of the nearest joists or wall studs.

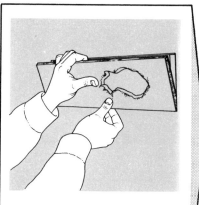

3. Having joined the top and bottom cuts with two vertical side cuts, simply remove the damaged section.

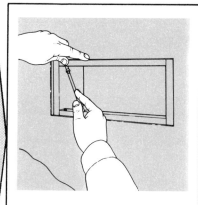

4. Fit noggins to support the patch and existing plasterboard, screwing them firmly to the vertical timber studs.

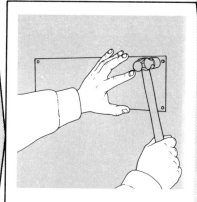

5. Cut a piece of plasterboard to fit the hole, and nail this, plus the existing plasterboard's free edges, to the studs and noggins.

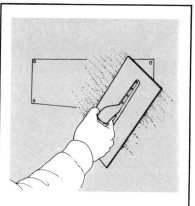

6. Complete the repair with a skim coat of fresh plaster, polishing the surface to leave it ready for redecoration.

3. As the base coat starts to harden, scratch the surface to provide a key for the next layer, and allow to set completely.

4. You can now apply a second, thicker coat to bring the repair level with the surrounding plasterwork.

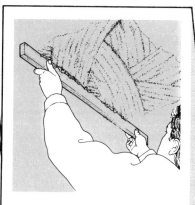

5. Draw a straightedge across this coat before it sets to ensure that it is level, flat, and flush with the wall or ceiling.

6. Finally, apply a thin finishing coat, merging this into the surrounding plaster, before polishing it smooth.

3. Continue as when patching plasterboard – fixing noggins between the joists, and nailing up a plasterboard patch.

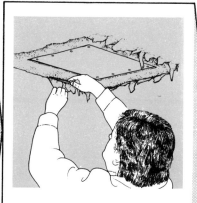

4. The next step is to remove any decoration (paper, paint, and so on) from the area immediately adjacent to the repair.

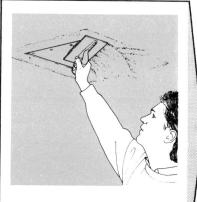

5. You can now apply a skim coat of finishing plaster to cover the plasterboard patch and merge it into the surrounding plaster.

6. As the skim coat starts to go off slightly, wet its surface and polish with a steel float, to leave it ready for redecoration.

54 Repairing plaster corners

If there is one area of plasterwork that is certain to become damaged at some time or other it is an external plastered corner; the slightest knock and it is chipped. Fortunately, where the damage is slight you can usually make a fairly invisible repair, working by eye. However, where the damage is more severe, obtaining a really clean right-angled finish in this way isn't easy. But there is a simple trick that can help: tackle the repair one wall at a time, using a batten nailed to the other wall as both guide and formwork.

There is just one further tip worth remembering: if a particular corner seems to suffer excessive regular damage, consider replastering it completely, incorporating a purpose-made metal lath as reinforcement.

1. Clean up the damaged corner, removing any loose and crumbling plaster and cutting back to sound material all round.

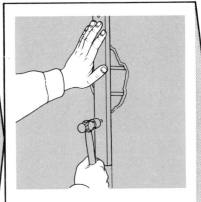

2. Nail a timber batten temporarily to one wall so that its edge lies exactly along the line of the original corner.

55 Repairing plaster mouldings

Plaster mouldings, particularly ornate period pieces, are often rather delicate, and can be difficult to repair using conventional filling techniques. If you are not careful you may actually make matters worse.

The answer is to adopt a more restrained approach, using runnier-than-normal plaster to build up the repair in stages. This has the advantage of both filling cracks and gluing them together.

As for reproducing the moulding's design, you must simply work by eye and hope, using your fingers, lolly sticks, – anything that helps mould the plaster into the shape you want. Don't forget that you can continue working the plaster once it has set using a sharp knife. In fact, 'carving' is often the only way to achieve intricate shaping and a really clean finish on ornate work.

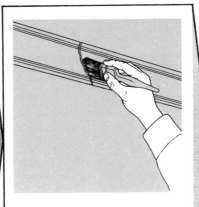

1. Faced with a crack in plaster moulding, start by carefully brushing out any dust that might stop the new plaster bonding.

2. Work a fairly wet plaster mix into the crack with your finger, shaping it as far as possible to match the moulding's profile.

56 Fixing a loose ceiling centre

General repairs to decorative plaster ceiling roses are tackled in the same way as those on any other plaster mouldings. However, plaster roses are subject to an additional problem which needs special treatment – they can come loose.

Given the weight of some roses, it is clearly advisable to get to work quickly, so start by locating the joists immediately above the rose and fix the rose to them with the broadest headed screws you can find. These should provide enough support for short-term safety, but for permanent fixing you must gain access to the space above the ceiling. Here, check the nibs of plaster protruding between the ceiling laths. Remove any that are loose, then pour some quick-setting plaster over the entire area to restore the bond between plasterwork and laths.

1. Locate the joists immediately above the ceiling rose, and drill pilot holes into these through the plasterwork.

2. You can now give the rose instant support by screwing it to the joists, using screws with the broadest heads you can find.

3. Fill the hole on the second wall in the usual way, working right up to the batten so that it moulds that edge of the repair.

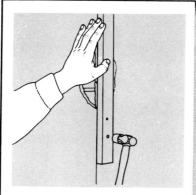

4. When plaster has set, remove the batten and fix it over the repair, again with one edge along the line of the corner.

5. You can now fill the hole on the remaining wall, using the edge of the batten as a guide just as before, and leave to set.

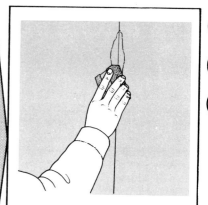

6. Lastly, remove the batten, fill in the nail holes and sand the repair smooth; lightly round off the very edge of the corner.

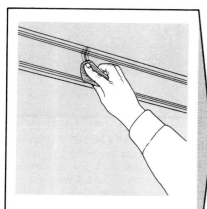

3. Once completely dry, carefully sand the repair smooth, using a knife if necessary to sharpen any detail in the design.

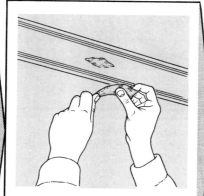

4. Use gauze to cover small holes. Soak the gauze in a slurry of runny plaster, and gently smooth it into place.

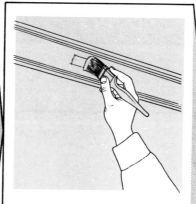

5. Gradually build up the repair by brushing on successive coats of slurry, allowing each to set before applying the next.

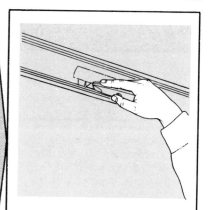

6. Finally, use a sharp knife to scrape off any plaster that may have dribbled down from the repair, and clean up the finish.

3. Check the nibs of plaster protruding through the ceiling laths above the rose. Remove any that are loose or broken.

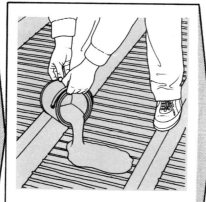

4. Pour quick-setting plaster over the laths so that it flows between them and bonds to the plaster covering the ceiling.

5. The rose should now be secure, so make any necessary repairs to the surface and plaster over exposed screw heads.

6. Lastly, run a bead of plaster round the rose, smoothing it off with your finger to fill any gap between rose and ceiling.

57 Boxing in pipework

Unless you are keen on 'high-tech' interior design, you will probably regard exposed pipework as unsightly. So how can it be disguised? The answer is, of course, to box it in, and you should manage this given the most basic diy skills.

But make sure everything fits together neatly and check that the runs are true so they really look part of the house. Allow, too, for the fact that plumbing can go wrong. You must be able to unbox the pipes quickly and easily for repairs and maintenance, particularly where the run includes stop taps and drain cocks. To achieve this, the pipe enclosure's 'lid' should simply be screwed into place – don't glue it or use nails. And leave the screw heads exposed. Fit them with decorative cups and/or covers if you wish, but don't conceal them with filler.

1. Mark the positions of battens that support the boxing in, and ensure they are vertical or horizontal with a spirit-level.

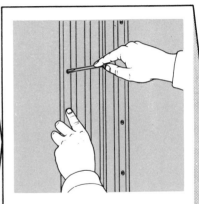

2. Fix the battens (50 x 25mm sawn softwood) to the walls with screws and wallplugs set at intervals of 300 to 450mm.

58 Proprietary pipe covers

A still simpler way of boxing in most pipe runs is to use a proprietary pipe cover. Made from rigid PVC, these consist simply of backing plates that you screw to the wall behind the pipes, and a cover that you snap on over it. Both come in single and multiple pipe versions, and in most cases the backing plates incorporate built-in pipe clamps. This obviously makes them ideal for new plumbing, allowing you to tackle both the pipe fixing and boxing-in as a single operation, but you can use them on existing installations as well.

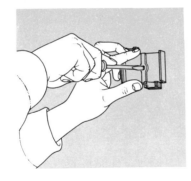

1. Fix the backing plates to the wall behind the pipes with screws and wall plugs, setting them about 1.2m apart.

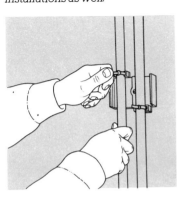

2. Fix the pipes into the backing plates' built-in clamps, tightening these up until the pipes are held really firmly in place.

3. Finally, clip on the pipe covers. For neatness, make mitre joints with a fine-toothed saw when turning corners.

59 Boxing larger pipes and fittings

Boxing in larger pipes – waste and soil pipes, for example – is more complicated, for the simple reason that the boxing-in is larger and therefore needs more support. In fact, in most cases you are faced with building the same sort of carcase as you would for a piece of built-in furniture, though here, because its appearance is not important, you can assemble it using simple butt joints, glued and screwed or nailed together.

Size affects the construction in another way, too. The larger the 'lid' the harder it is to lift on and off to gain access to the pipes. For this reason, it is a good idea to cover the enclosure with a series of smaller, more manageable sections. Those you are likely to open most often for maintenance (over stop cocks or at rodding points) can be hinged to make access easier still.

60 Boxing ideas

Of course, the boxing-in shown above does not suit every style of decor, but there are alternatives. Pipes in corners, for example, can be hidden by a panel fixed at 45 degrees across the angle, while those near ceiling level may be covered by coving. Built-in furniture can also be pressed into service, and since some boxing-in is on the scale of furniture making, you could also incorporate some simple shelves. Cupboard-style doors can also neaten access to stop-taps.

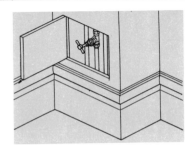

1. Where stop taps have been boxed in, fit a hinged inspection hatch. It's neater and more convenient than a screw-on panel.

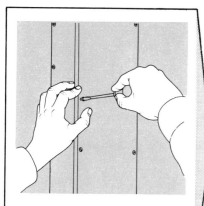

3. All that remains is to screw the boxing-in (12 to 19mm plywood or chipboard) into place, leaving screw heads exposed.

4. To box-in pipes in the middle of a wall, put up one side of the enclosure, then mark out the other side as in a corner.

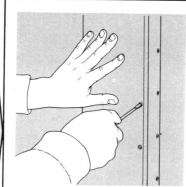

5. With one side in place, it is a simple matter to complete the boxing-in by screwing the rest firmly into place.

6. For pipes at the base of a wall, face the enclosure with skirting board so as not to interrupt the skirting run around the room.

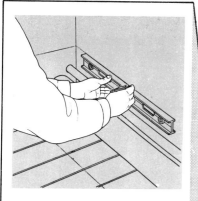

1. Mark the outline of the boxing-in on the walls and floors using a spirit-level. Don't take levels from pipes: they may slope.

2. Now begin building the carcase using 50mm sq sawn softwood. Start by screwing the members to walls and floors.

3. Next, give the carcase a front rail, add intermediate vertical and horizontal supports every 500mm or so and begin cladding.

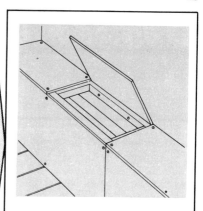

4. In general, the chipboard or plywood cladding panels should be screwed in place, but hinge those at used access points.

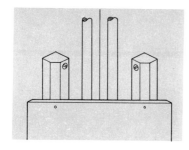

2. Pipes in corners can be hidden by a single panel fixed at 45 degrees across the angle to a pair of suitably shaped battens.

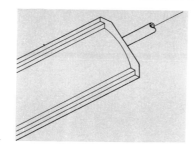

3. Where pipes run almost at ceiling level and instant access will not be needed, cover them with coving.

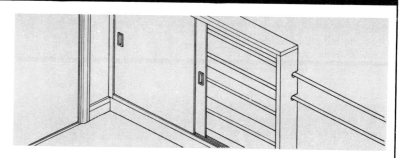

4. Built-in furniture can be used to conceal pipes and also provide storage space. Here, where space is limited, a shallow cupboard with sliding doors takes up very little room. If it conceals hot water pipes it will give you extra airing space.

61 Fitting knobs and handles

Despite the great number of different door and drawer knobs, pulls and handles on the market, in terms of the way in which they are fixed there is very little to choose between them. In fact, there are just three options in common use.

With the first, the fitting is screwed (sometimes nailed) to the face of the door, drawer or whatever. Alternatively, a semi-concealed fixing may be used – normally a bolt or screw driven through the door or drawer front into the back of the fitting. Finally, you will occasionally see fittings set into the furniture – mainly 'military chest' fittings. In this case, the rebates are normally quite simple to cut (though you need a hole saw for some round inset pulls) and once inset, the fitting is normally held in using one of the methods given above.

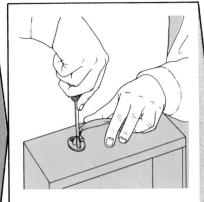

1. Simple surface-mounted handles are normally just screwed in place with matching countersunk screws.

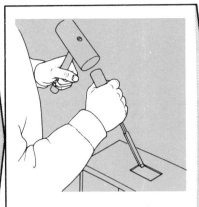

2. Some fittings are inset into the wood. Using the fitting itself as a guide, mark out the rebate and chop it out with a chisel.

62 Bolted and multiple fixings

Whether you are renovating furniture or building new, the handles, knobs and other fittings play a major role in determining the overall look of the piece.

There are quite a number to choose from. You will find handles, knobs and pulls in styles ranging from more or less ornate period reproductions, through the purely functional, to what some might think so modern as to be avante garde. There's a choice of materials, too, with old favourites such as brass, wood, stainless steel and porcelain still holding their own against the newer, more colourful plastics and enamelled steel.

However, there are a few tips on buying to remember. If you cannot find what you want locally, get a catalogue from a specialist supplier — most do mail order. Better still, visit a specialist shop so you can see what you are paying for. Photographs are seldom to be trusted, particularly with brass where quite subtle colour variations can mean the difference between liking and hating a piece. And talking of brass, don't be misled by the huge differences in price between apparently identical items. Cheap fittings are plated, not solid.

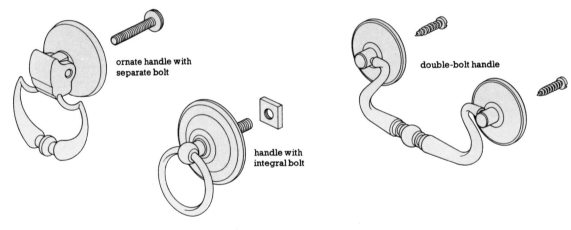

ornate handle with separate bolt

handle with integral bolt

double-bolt handle

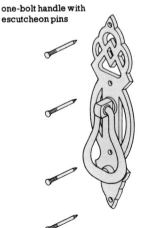

one-bolt handle with escutcheon pins

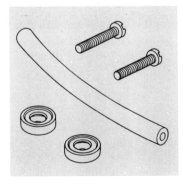

Most knobs and handles for furniture have concealed fixings of one kind or another — bolts or screws threaded through from

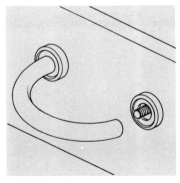

behind, or integral bolts held on with nuts. Modern plastic handles can be made up from lengths of flexible plastic tubing.

3. Set the fitting into its recess, then secure permanently, usually simply by driving matching screws through the face plate.

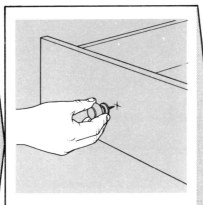

4. Some knobs have a built-in screw. Just bore a hole and twist them in. Dip the thread in adhesive to help stop them twisting out.

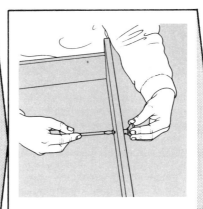

5. Others are held by a separate machine bolt driven through the furniture. Hold them steady in one hand; tighten up with other.

6. Wooden knobs are usually secured by means of ordinary countersunk wood screws. Glue thread for a permanent fixing.

63 Fitting a letter flap

Technically, fitting a letter flap to your front door is a fairly simple job. However, since cutting a sizeable chunk out of any door is a very final step, it is worth taking special care over the marking out.

Start by deciding where the flap is to go in general terms, bearing in mind that anyone delivering post and papers may not use it if it is awkwardly placed. Make sure, too, that the spot you have chosen won't weaken the door. A central horizontal rail is the best choice, but on glazed doors you may be forced to use one of the uprights.

That done, mark out the flap's slot accurately using the hinged flap itself as a guide to size. And if the flap is to be fitted in the central rail, measure up to make sure it will be accurately centred vertically and horizontally or it will look odd.

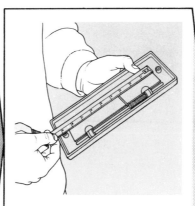

1. Mark up door as accurately as possible ready for the slot to be cut out. Measure the hinged flap to find out how big this should be.

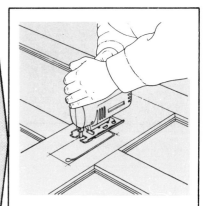

2. Starting at a hole drilled at one corner, saw round the slot's outline, then clean up the corners with a rasp.

64 Draught excluders and baskets

A good letter flap should keep out the wind, but it won't stop draughts. That takes purpose-made draught-proofing; the most common design consists of two rows of bristles mounted in a plastic or aluminium frame. Simply screw this to the door's inner face to cover the slot. Something else letter flaps won't do is stop letters falling on to wet and muddy doormats, so fit a box to catch them. You can buy these in wire or plastic, and here, too, fixing is simple.

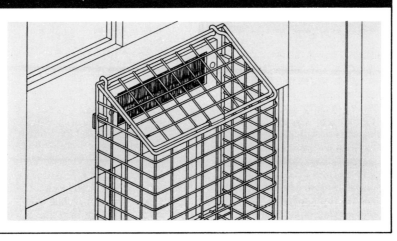

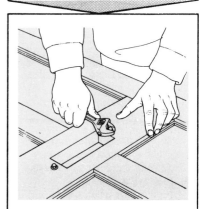

3. To fix the flap itself, drill a hole at each side of the slot, hold it in place, then push through the retaining bolts and tighten up.

65 Repairing carpet

Carpets are fairly durable, but they can be damaged by cigarettes, excessive wear, and so on. Obviously, if the carpet in question is expensive, then leave mending to experts, but with humbler types there is no reason why you should not do it yourself.

The method depends largely on the scale of the damage. Frayed edges, for example, need only a little adhesive and fabric tape, while small holes can be disguised using tufts taken from inconspicuous edges. Large areas of damage, however, need patching. If you don't have a suitable piece of spare carpet for this, cut the patch from a stretch of carpet that never shows – say, from under the sofa – matching any pattern. Even then the repair won't be 'invisible' because of colour differences caused by fading, but thorough cleaning should help the repair blend in.

1. If the area of damage is small – say, a cigarette burn – trim off the ruined tufts using a pair of small, sharp nail scissors.

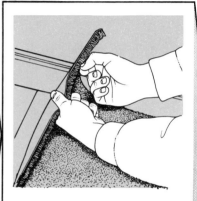

2. Next, pull or clip a few tufts from an edge where they will not be missed. Pop them straight into an envelope – they are easily lost.

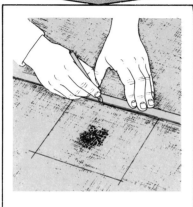

1. If the damage is more extensive, turn the carpet over and draw a neat rectangle to enclose the area to be repaired.

2. Spread latex adhesive over the guide lines and when dry, cut out the damaged section of carpet with a sharp knife.

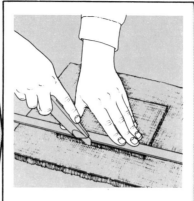

3. Use the damaged section as a pattern for a repair template. Working on the back, cut round it, guiding the knife with a rule.

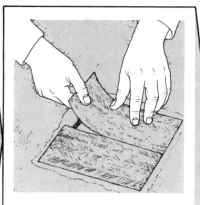

4. That done, carefully stick strips of hessian backing over the hole, allow to dry and then turn the carpet back right side up.

66 Repairing floorings

Although the precise technique for repairing 'hard' floorcoverings such as wood blocks, vinyl, cork tiles and so on depends on which of these you are dealing with, in principle the strategy is the same.

Faced with a minor defect – a small stain, scorch mark, or dent, for example – first try to remove it by rubbing down the surface with glasspaper or wire wool. If this works, then simply reseal and/or repolish the floor as appropriate. If it doesn't then all you can do is treat the floor as if it was more seriously damaged. Remove the affected section and replace it with a patch, a new tile or a new wood block – a good reason for keeping a few left-overs after laying a new floorcovering. Obviously, if the damage is more extensive still, consider replacing the floorcovering completely.

1. On a true wood block floor (as opposed to one made with veneered plywood), chisel out the damaged 'fingers' of wood.

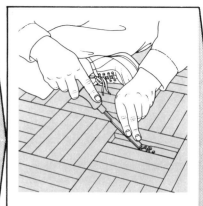

2. Next, use an old chisel to scrape away the old adhesive. Black bitumen can be softened first with white spirit.

3. Use the tufts to cover the now bald area, sticking them down one by one with latex adhesive, using a cotton wool bud.

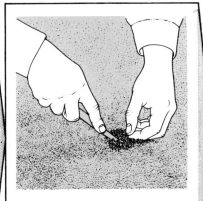

4. To make sure the tufts stick, press them firmly into the carpet's backing with the point of a knife or a sharp stick.

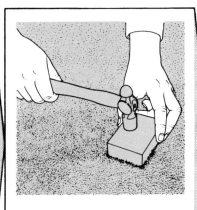

5. When the damaged area has been completely filled, tap down with a wooden block to ensure the tufts are bedded into the adhesive.

6. When the adhesive is dry, comb the carpet to raise the pile before trimming transplanted tufts that are too long.

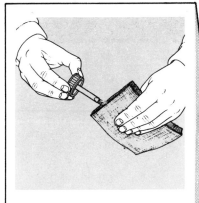

5. Having checked that the patch is a perfect fit, coat the back and the edges of its backing ready to stick it in place

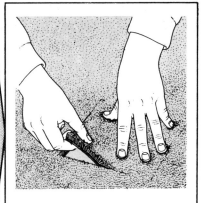

6. Press the repair patch firmly on to the hessian backing, tapping it down with a wooden block to make sure it beds down flat.

67 Mending edges

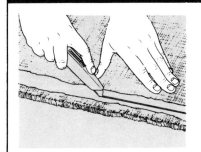

1. If the carpet's edge is frayed, seal it with latex ahesive, then trim it when dry with a sharp knife, following a straightedge.

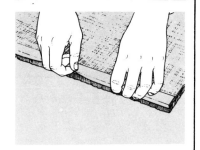

2. To prevent further fraying, bind the carpet's edge with fabric tape; stick this down so a 3mm strip turns over the edge of the backing.

3. Plane a new wooden 'finger' to fit (use stained softwood if you cannot get the right hardwood) and stick it firmly into place

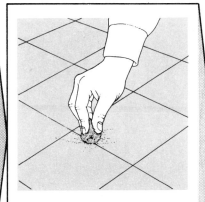

4. Stains can often be rubbed off with wire wool, though on cheap sheet vinyls this may remove the vinyl surface and some pattern.

5. To patch vinyl, lay a spare piece over the damaged section, match the pattern, then cut through both layers of vinyl in one go.

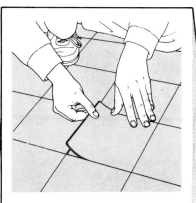

6. Lift out the damaged vinyl and stick the patch cut from the spare sheet in its place, using flooring adhesive – it should fit exactly.

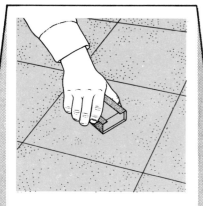

7. Cork tiles should be rubbed down with glasspaper to remove marks and smooth out dents to make them less noticeable.

8. When you are satisfied with the results, wipe over the surface with a damp cloth to remove dust, and allow to dry.

9. Re-seal with three or more coats of polyurethane varnish. Let each dry, and rub down before applying the next.

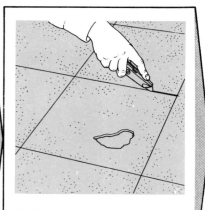

10. To remove a damaged hard vinyl tile, start by running a sharp knife around its edge to break bond with its neighbours.

68 Security

Home security is a major problem these days, yet it takes only a modest amount of hardware to deter the would-be thief.

Start with the door by which you normally leave your home. Fit this with a cylinder lock (with lockable handle if near glass) plus a mortise lock and a door chain. Mortise locks are also advisable on other external doors that can be worked on with little risk of the burglar being disturbed. For the rest, with the exception of patio doors (hook bolt mortise locks are best for these), bolts should be adequate.

Windows, too, need good locks. More burglars get in through windows than doors. Secure all those on the ground floor, plus any on upper floors that can be reached by climbing. On casement windows, use either a separate lock or a lockable cockspur handle, plus a lockable stay allowing the window to be fixed partly open for ventilation. Fit sliding sashes with separate locks designed for them.

And don't forget to protect sheds with a padlock, hasp and staple — the average thief won't steal ladders and garden tools, but he may well use them to help him break into your house.

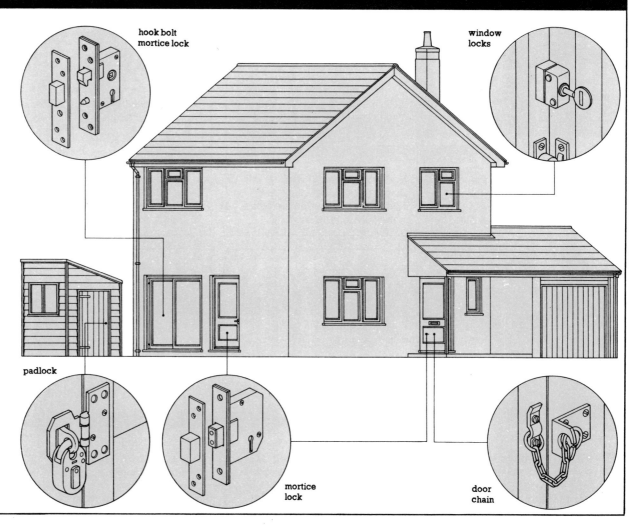

hook bolt mortice lock

window locks

padlock

mortice lock

door chain

11. Now, soften the tile by warming it using a hair drier or hot air stripper. Never use a blowlamp or you might start a fire.

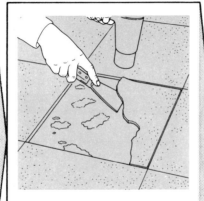

12. You should now be able to scrape the old tile away. Use a fairly hot wide-bladed scraper for this, and keep the tile warm.

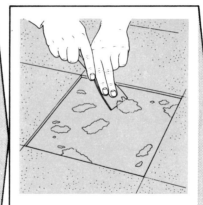

13. When you have finished, some old adhesive will be left stuck to the floor and this should be scraped off before continuing.

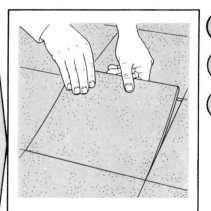

14. Once the floor is clean, simply stick a new tile into place, bedding it down on a layer of suitable flooring adhesive.

69 Fitting a mortise lock

Mortise locks may not be the easiest of security devices to fit, but at least once you have them in place they tend to stay there – burglars or no.

This is partly because most are very well made and very well designed. You certainly need have no worries about them being picked or having the bolt sawn through. However, the main reason for their success is the way in which they are fitted. As

their name suggests, they are actually set into a mortise cut in the edge of the door. The keep – the bit into which the bolt slides as you lock the door – is also very secure. It is set into a mortise cut into the door frame.

To install a mortise lock, you must therefore cut two mortises plus a key hole – not really that difficult, the key to the whole operation being really accurate marking out.

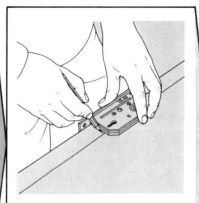

1. Mark the length of the mortise that will receive the body of the lock on the edge of the door, using the lock itself as a guide.

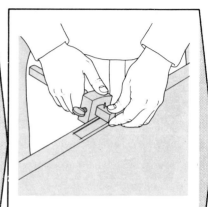

2. Mark the width of the mortise, again using the lock as a guide, with a marking gauge, centring it on the thickness of the door.

70 Types of lock

For front doors, the usual choice is a cylinder rim latch — simple to fit and use, but with several weaknesses, not least its tendency to yield to brute force. It should therefore always be backed up by a mortise lock. Set right into the door, this is very strong indeed and can be opened only with a key. However, mortise locks are not very convenient on doors subject to a lot of coming and going. Here, a combined mortise lock and handle-operated latch gives the best of both worlds.

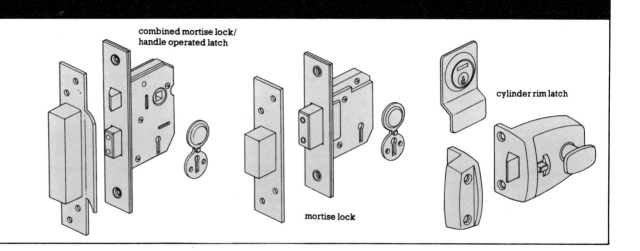

combined mortise lock/handle operated latch

mortise lock

cylinder rim latch

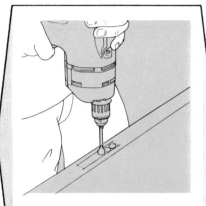

3. Remove the bulk of the waste from the mortise by boring a series of holes side by side so that each just runs into the one before.

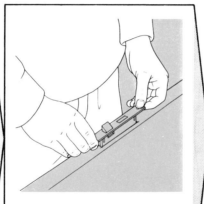

4. You can now pare away the waste from the sides and corners of the mortise with a sharp chisel until the lock is a snug fit.

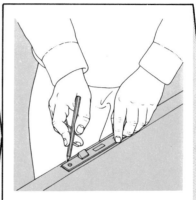

5. The next job is to mark out the recess for the lock's edge plate. Just drop the lock into the mortise and draw round it.

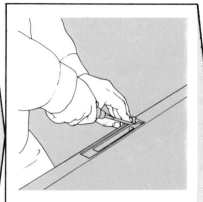

6. Taking care not to go too deep, chisel out the recess, frequently testing the fit by actually slipping the lock into place.

71 Mortise lock

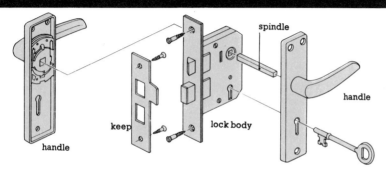

spindle

handle

keep

lock body

handle

handle

Mortise locks come in two parts — the lock itself and the keep, often just a shaped metal plate.

The handles needed to operate the latch built-in to some models are normally sold separately.

72 Fitting a cylinder lock

One reason why cylinder locks are so popular is that they are very easy to install. In fact, since the bulk of the lock and its keep are surface-mounted, most of the work involves no more than the use of a screwdriver. For the rest, all you do is chisel out a couple of shallow rebates – one in the edge of the door; one in the door frame – and drill a hole to take the cylinder.

This last can be tricky, though, if you don't have a bit large enough to accommodate the body of the cylinder mechanism. But don't worry. Simply bore the biggest hole you can, then enlarge it to the required size using a half-round wood rasp or similar tool. It doesn't matter if the result is not perfect, so long as it is completely covered by the cylinder and its surround – otherwise a burglar could prise the cylinder out.

73 Fitting a peep-hole

Security peep-holes, with their wide-angle lenses, are designed to let you take a good look at callers without revealing your own presence, and the fact that this gives you a distinct edge over any shady customers and other undesirables on your doorstep makes them worth considering in addition to a door chain, particularly for flats which don't have windows near the door. Even a conveniently

placed window doesn't offer the same degree of one-way observation as a peep-hole.

Fitting one could hardly be simpler. Having decided where the peep-hole is to to go – at eye-level in the centre of the door is the most efficient choice – just drill a hole through the door, slip in the tubular assembly, and then tighten up the threaded collar that holds it in place on the inside.

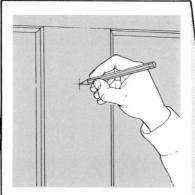

1. Mark the position of the peep-hole – normally at eye-level in the middle of the door – with a cross at its centre.

2. Bore into the door until you are almost right through, then drill in from the other side to complete the hole – this gives a neater finish.

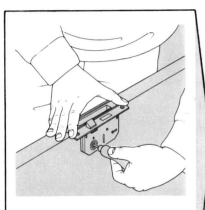

7. When you are satisfied, hold the lock against the face of the door and mark the key and handle hole positions with a bradawl.

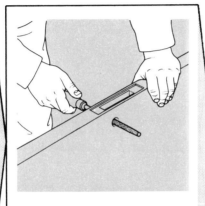

8. Drill out both holes using the appropriate bits, then use a padsaw to extend the one for the key into a keyhole shape.

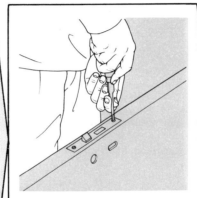

9. That done, slip the lock into its mortise and secure permanently by screwing it to the door through the recessed edge plate.

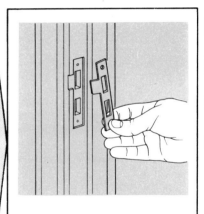

10. Lastly, mark out and cut the recess and mortises for the keep. If this is just a plate, size the mortises to suit the bolts.

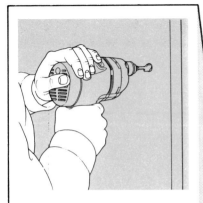

1. Mark out and drill the hole for the cylinder. Many locks come with a paper template to help here. If not, use the backing plate.

2. Screw the backing plate in position, ensuring that it is as sufficiently firmly fixed to resist burglary by brute force.

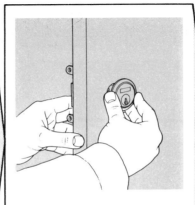

3. Slip the cylinder mechanism into its hole from outside, passing the long tail through the slot in the backing plate.

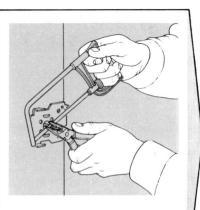

4. Remove the excess tail by snapping it off at one of the break lines stamped into it. Alternatively, use a hacksaw.

3. From the outside of the door, push the peep-hole through the hole. Ensure the lens surround lies flat on the door's surface.

4. Fit the threaded collar to the end of the peep-hole from inside your home, and tighten up to hold the assembly firmly in place.

74 Cylinder locks

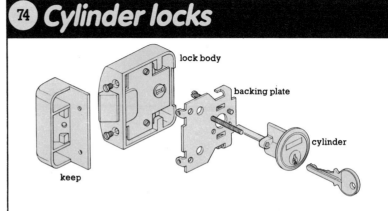

Cylinder locks consist of a keep, and an enclosed latch mechanism fixed to the door via a backing plate. From the outside, the latch is operated by a separate unit — the cylinder lock.

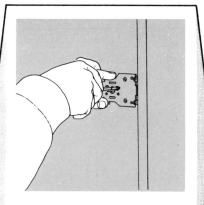

5. Secure the cylinder with the machine screws provided, driving these through the backing plate into the cylinder lugs.

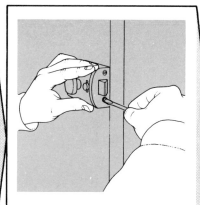

6. Screw the body of the lock on to the base plate. On some locks a rebate may be needed where it turns onto the door's edge.

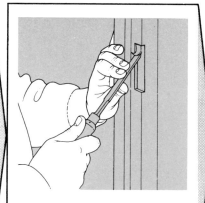

7. Shut the door, mark the position of the keep on the door frame, then cut a shallow rebate ready to receive this.

8. Screw the keep into place as securely as possible. Any weakness in the fixings here will render the lock virtually useless.

(75) Window locks

There are three main factors to take into account when choosing a window lock.

First, there is the type of window. With casement windows the options are to fit either a locking cockspur handle (in place of the existing catch) or a separate lock that shoots a bolt into the window's fixed frame rather like a miniature door lock. Locks for sliding windows (some of which are suitable for patio doors), on the other hand, are almost invariably fitted in addition to the ordinary catch.

Next, think about ventilation. If you want to be able to lock the window while it is partly open, on casements the only way is to fit a separate locking stay. Most sliding window locks, however, offer this facility as standard — simply bore an additional suitably placed hole for the bolt.

Finally, decide how easy the lock should be to use. On windows you open fairly often, the easier the better. But on rarely used windows normally inconvenient devices such as dual screws (which literally screw the movable part of the window to the frame) are acceptable — and cheaper than locks.

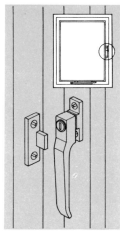
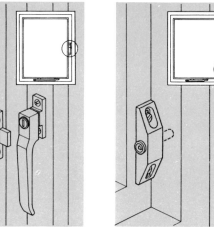

locking cockspur handle

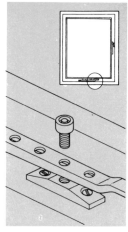

window bolt

casement stay lock

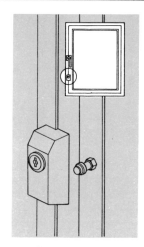

self-locking bolt

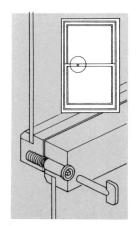

dual screw

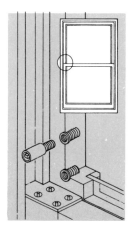

acorn stop

patio door lock

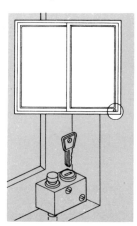

patio door lock

76 Security light systems

Another way to deter burglars is to convince them that you are at home even if you are not, and this is where security light fittings come in. Fitted in place of ordinary light switches in much the same way as a dimmer switch, they turn room lights on and off automatically. There are two main types to choose from. The first operates on a programmable time clock which you can set before you leave, while the second has a sensor which turns the lights on when it gets dark.

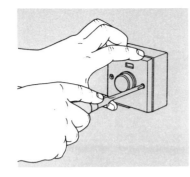

Programmable light switches are controlled by a time clock.

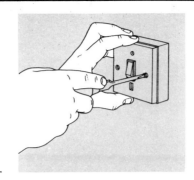

Automatic systems have sensors to turn them on when it's dark.

77 Door devices

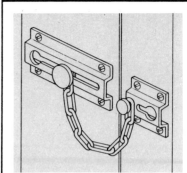

Door chains are designed to prevent unwelcome visitors bursting into your home as you open the door to talk to them.

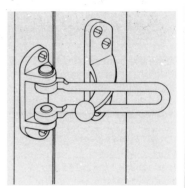

Alternatively, fit a sliding hasp to achieve the same effect. These are normally stronger than chains but not as widely available.

78 Entryphone systems

Door chains and peep-holes are all very well for checking the identity of callers, but they are not very convenient in large buildings where answering the door may entail a lot of walking and climbing stairs. The answer here is to fit an entryphone system. Basically, this consists of an intercom which allows callers to announce themselves, and lets you talk to them without going to the door. In most cases, this is used in conjunction with an electrically operated lock.

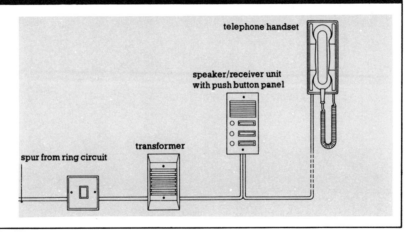

telephone handset

speaker/receiver unit with push button panel

transformer

spur from ring circuit

79 Home alarm systems

It's unfortunate but true that, no matter how good your home's locks, if a burglar has enough skill and enough time he will probably still get into your home. So consider fitting a burglar alarm as an additional deterrent. There are many diy alarm kits available, and though generally not as good as professionally installed systems, they are a lot cheaper and still give a good level of protection. They are fairly easy to install, too. Basically it is just a question of fitting likely entry points with suitable sensors, and linking them to the system's control unit – a simple wiring job. But there is one golden rule – by all means use the bell or siren casing on the outside of the house to advertise the system's existence to potential intruders, but do all you can to disguise the actual sensors, wiring, and so on.

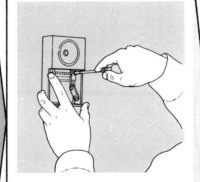

1. Start by fitting the system's control unit (normally containing a siren and on/off switch), following the maker's instructions.

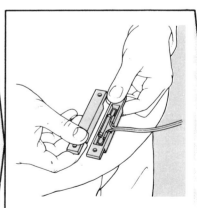

2. That done, wire up the reed switch sensors ready for fitting to doors and windows (some come pre-wired, ready to fix).

3. Screw the reed section of each sensor to the door or window frame, preferably in a top or bottom corner.

4. Now, shut the door and using the reed section as a guide, mark the position of the switch's magnet, and screw this in place.

5. Finally, run the wiring between sensor and control unit as neatly and inconspicuously as possible, fixing it with cable clips.

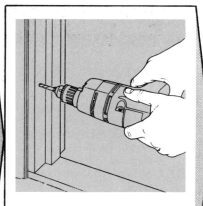

6. For a concealed switch, drill a hole in the door frame for the switch body, then drill into this from the side of the architrave.

80 *A typical alarm system*

The alarm system's most essential components are its sensors, and there are two basic types. The first is the reed switch designed to detect the opening of a door or window — if you are wise you will fit one to every external door and window in the house. It does this by means of a magnet fixed to whatever it is that opens. Held against the switch, this keeps the switch's thin metal 'reed' contacts apart. Remove it, and the switch reverts to its natural 'on' position, letting current flow round the system to raise the alarm. The second type is the pressure pad. This switches the alarm on if anyone steps on it.

The next most important component is the control unit containing the key-operated on/off switch which de-activates the system — place it somewhere handy so you can reach it quickly to turn off the alarm when you come home. It also houses the electronics that interpret the signals (or lack of them) from the sensors, and should be capable of resetting the alarm after a short time, to allow for sensors tripping accidentally — say due to traffic vibration, or heavy-footed pets. It may also contain the siren that actually sounds the alarm.

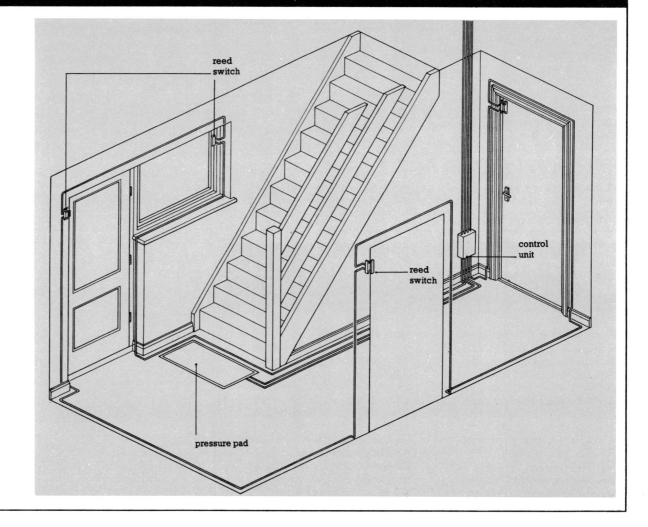

reed switch

reed switch

control unit

pressure pad

7. Fit the cylindrical switch into the main hole, and connect to the control unit via the hole in the architrave.

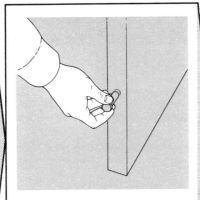

8. With this type of switch, the magnetic section is located in a hole drilled in the door edge. Ensure magnet and switch line up.

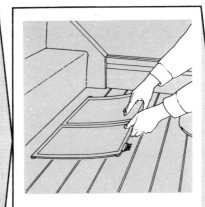

9. To trap burglars who get past the reed switches, place pressure pads at strategic points in the house – say, at the foot of the stairs.

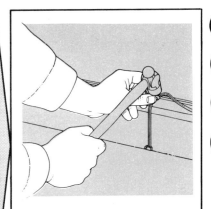

10. To complete installation, tidy up the wiring runs, concealing them as far as possible, and check that the system works.

81 Alarm kit

There are many diy alarm systems available, which are fairly straightforward to install.

Ensure that the kit contains all the components that you will need for your size of house. The key-operated on/off switch may be housed in the control unit, if so ensure that it's located in a convenient place.

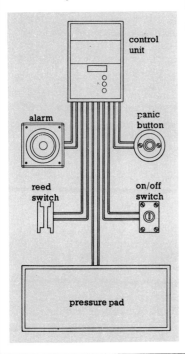

control unit

alarm

panic button

reed switch

on/off switch

pressure pad

82 Window alarms

Smashing a pane of glass to get at locks and any alarm system's reed switches is a favourite burglar's trick. To prevent it, fit windows with an alarm sensor that registers such attempted break ins. There are two types. The traditional variety consists of a foil strip stuck to the glass; anyone breaking the pane will break the foil and trigger the alarm. The more reliable alternative is triggered by vibration, but must be adjusted to stop high winds and passing cars setting it off.

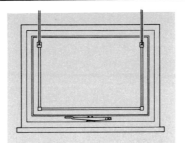

A foil strip is stuck to the glass round the edge of the window, providing a circuit. If the strip is broken the alarm is triggered.

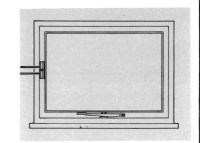

A vibration sensor is much neater and less obtrusive than the foil strip. Its sensitivity can be adjusted to suit the location.

83 Passive alarms

One of the most recent developments is the passive alarm system designed to detect movement in a room. This is achieved in one of two ways. With the first, the area is crossed by a number of thin beams of invisible infra-red light. If one is interrupted, the alarm goes off. The alternative fills the space with sound at a frequency too high for human ears. Any movement within this wash of ultrasonic sound triggers the alarm.

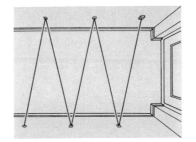

An infra-red alarm system uses an invisible beam of light, which is bounced from source to receptor, via a series of mirrors.

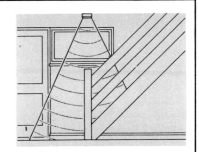

An ultrasonic detector picks up breaks in the sound waves, which trigger an alarm. Neither system is suitable if you have pets.

Glossary

Architraves are decorative timber mouldings fixed to the edges of door and sash window frames to disguise the join between frame and wall. They are mitred at corners, and are nailed in place.

Air bricks are special perforated bricks built into exterior walls to ventilate underfloor voids and lofts, and to provide air supplies for fuel-burning appliances.

Balusters are decorative vertical posts used to make up a balustrade on staircases and landings. The posts are set into the treads or attached to the staircase string at the bottom, and carry the handrail.

Coving is a decorative moulding (often called a cornice) made from plaster, plasterboard or plastic and fixed in the angle between walls and ceilings to conceal the join.

Cylinder locks are operated by a key inserted into a cylindrical barrel, and are usually fitted to surface-mounted rim locks. The cylinder passes through a hole drilled in the door stile.

Damp-proof courses (DPCs) are built into all walls just above ground level to prevent rising damp. They were often of slate in older houses, but modern houses have bituminized felt or plastic DPCs. Faulty DPCs can be repaired by injecting special chemicals into the brickwork.

Damp-proof membranes (DPMs) are damp barriers incorporated in solid floors to prevent rising damp.

Fillers are powder or ready-mixed products used to make good minor cracks and holes in plaster and plasterboard surfaces.

Firebacks are shaped fireclay mouldings that form the back of fireplace openings. They sit on the hearth and are linked to the flue above by shaped mortar flaunching.

Flaunching indoors means the shaped mortar that links the top of the fireback to the flue above.

Hearths are solid concrete areas beneath fireplace openings, designed to support the fireback and grate and protect the structure from fire.

Lath and plaster consists of thin timber laths nailed across the underside of floor joists (to form ceilings) or the face of stud partitions walls, and covered with a layer of plaster to form a hard surface. It was widely used until about 1945, when plasterboard took its place.

Mortise locks are set into the edge of the door stile, and are operated by a key inserted into a keyhole drilled through the door. They may be combined with a door handle and latch mechanism.

Newel posts are the main vertical supporting timbers in staircase construction, supporting the handrail at corners.

Plaster is a cement or gypsum-based mixture applied to wall and ceiling surfaces in a plastic state; it then hardens to form a durable solid surface layer. Various types are available for base coats (browning and bonding are the commonest) and for top (finishing) coats.

Plasterboard consists of a plaster core sandwiched between two layers of stout paper to form a rigid board that is used to line ceilings and stud partition walls. Boards are usually either 9 or 12mm thick, and come in standard 8 x 4ft sheets as well as a range of smaller panels. Different facings are available, according to whether the boards are to be plastered over or decorated directly.

Repair plates are metal plates with pre-drilled holes, available in a range of shapes and sizes and used to strengthen and repair damaged frames and other constructions.

Self-smoothing compound is a cement-based screeding material used on concrete floors to provide a smooth, hard surface prior to laying floorcoverings. It is mixed with water and trowelled out onto the floor surface, and smooths itself out as it hardens.

Index

Outdoor repairs

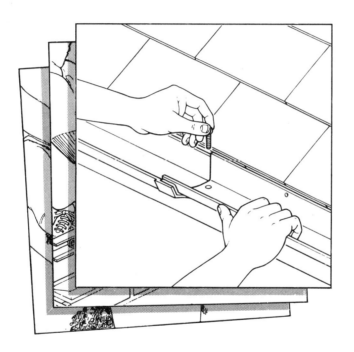

Outdoor repairs

Outdoor repairs

No matter what type of property you live in, inevitably you will be faced with the prospect of carrying out repairs outdoors – either to the property itself or to structures in the garden. The cause of practically all outdoor problems is the weather. Rain, frost, snow, strong winds and even strong sunlight all take their toll on the fabric of your property. And their attack is ceaseless, so making those repairs as soon as they become necessary is essential.

A lot of repair work can be prevented by carrying out sensible preventative maintenance on the vulnerable parts of your home. Regular painting of exposed timbers, or treating them with preservative, for example, will prevent serious damage occurring by stopping rot getting a hold. Cleaning out the gutters regularly will prevent overflowing water soaking the walls. Without doubt, a strict schedule of outdoor maintenance will save pounds in the long run.

Sooner or later an outdoor job will require the use of concrete or mortar; the former for paths, driveways and foundations, and the latter for brickwork or rendering. Both are made from cement, an aggregate and water. The strength of the concrete or mortar depends on the proportions of the ingredients and the rate at which the mix dries out.

Portland cement is used for concrete and mortar, although masonry cement is also used in the latter. Lime or a plasticiser is often added to improve workability by preventing the mixture from drying out too quickly. It also makes the concrete or mortar less likely to crack.

Aggregates are crushed stone, being graded according to the size of the stone particles. Coarse aggregate has particles up to 20mm in size; fine aggregate has a maximum size of 15mm.

Sand is also an aggregate. Sharp sand is used for concrete, soft (or builder's) sand for mortars. Silver sand is also used in mortars if a light colour is required. An all-in aggregate (or ballast), which is a mixture of sand, gravel and crushed stone, is also available for concrete work.

The proportions of cement and aggregate vary with the job, and are given opposite. The amount of water needed is difficult to quantify since it depends on how damp the aggregate is (it will never be completely dry). As a guide, water equal to half the volume of cement should be added, but only in small quantities until the mix has a buttery consistency. Too much water weakens the mix.

Concrete and mortar will stay workable for about two hours, but in hot weather may go off much quicker. After laying, protect concrete with damp sacking or polythene for about a week to prevent it drying out too quickly and protect against frost damage. After a week, the concrete will be strong enough to walk on, but it won't reach full strength for about a month.

Cement and aggregate can be bought dry-mixed for various concrete and mortar mixes in 10, 25 or 50kg bags. This is ideal for small jobs. The volume of the finished mix is printed on the bag.

Dry-mix ingredients are expensive for a large job, however, and in this case, it is cheaper to buy the materials separately. Cement comes in 50kg bags; aggregate and sand by the cubic metre (cu m) or part thereof.

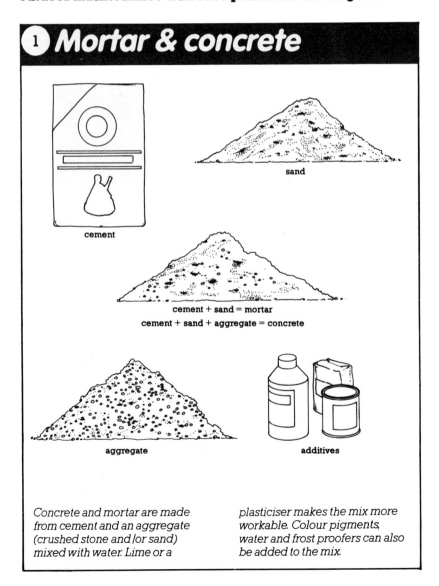

① Mortar & concrete

cement

sand

cement + sand = mortar
cement + sand + aggregate = concrete

aggregate

additives

Concrete and mortar are made from cement and an aggregate (crushed stone and/or sand) mixed with water. Lime or a plasticiser makes the mix more workable. Colour pigments, water and frost proofers can also be added to the mix.

② Mixing by hand

Small batches of mortar and concrete can be mixed by hand. Work on a hard, flat surface (a sheet of plywood is suitable). Measure out the quantities of cement and aggregate in a bucket, carefully levelling it off each time.

Mix the dry ingredients well by turning them over and over with a shovel until the colour is uniform. Even dry-mix ingredients should be treated in this way. Make a depression in the pile and begin to add water, mixing it in a little at a time until the correct consistency is achieved.

1. Mix all the ingredients dry first, even if from a ready-mixed bag. Make sure the colour of the mixture is uniform.

2. Adding a plasticiser to the water before mixing will make the mortar or concrete more easily workable.

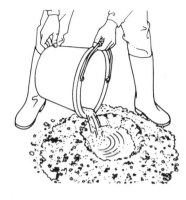

3. Form a hollow in the centre of the mix and pour in a little water. Then feed the mix in from the edges.

4. Turn the pile to mix in the water fully. Continue mixing, adding a little more water at a time.

5. Check the consistency by forming ridges with the shovel. They should hold their shape and not slump.

6. The mix should have a buttery consistency; if it is too dry, sprinkle on more water from a watering can and mix in.

7. If only a small quantity of concrete is required, use a bag of dry-mix ingredients and mix them in a bucket.

③ Mixes – ratios for various jobs

		cement	masonry cement	lime	sand
MORTAR/General purpose		1	0	1	6
	OR	0	1	0	5
MORTAR/Strong		1	0	½	4
	OR	0	1	0	3
		cement	sand	aggregate	ballast
CONCRETE/Less than 75mm (3ins) thick (paving)		1	1½	2½	0
	OR	1	0	0	3
CONCRETE/Over 75mm (3ins) thick (large slabs)		1	2	3	0
	OR	1	0	0	4
FOUNDATIONS		1	2½	3½	0
	OR	1	0	0	5

4 Concrete mixing in a mixer

Mixing concrete by hand can be hard work, so for any large job it is a good idea to hire an electric or petrol-driven mixer. Before beginning work, read the operating instructions carefully and make sure the mixer stands on firm, level ground.

Add the ingredients a little at a time, starting with half the aggregate and water, followed by the sand, cement and the remaining aggregate. Add water slowly until the correct consistency is achieved. Do not put hands or shovels into the moving drum or lean over it.

1. Add half the quantity of aggregate needed for the mix to the machine. Measure it out with a bucket.

2. Then add half the water required, followed by all of the sand, turn the machine on and mix for a few minutes.

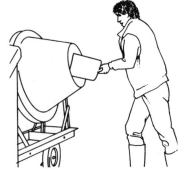

3. Add the cement and the remainder of the aggregate and mix, adding just enough water for a workable mix.

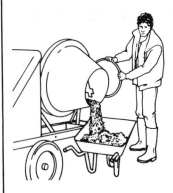

4. When the concrete is of the right consistency, leave the machine running and tip the concrete into a barrow.

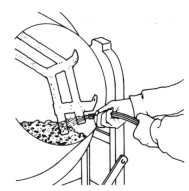

5. To clean the drum between mixes, or when the job is complete, run it with aggregate and water inside.

Bricklaying is a skill that must be practised if good results are to be obtained. However, it is not impossible for the amateur to do an excellent job, provided the work is not rushed and the correct techniques are used.

Successful bricklaying begins with the right kind of bricks. They come in three basic types, common, facing and engineering.

Common bricks are intended to be hidden by render, plaster etc. Consequently, they have no special finish. They are not suitable for load-bearing applications.

Facing bricks (or stocks) are intended to be seen and have a variety of textured and coloured finishes. They are suitable for supporting heavy loads, but if of ordinary quality should not be used outdoors unless protected from rising damp by a dpc and from rain above by a coping. Special-quality facing bricks can be used outdoors and are very strong.

Engineering bricks are very strong too. They absorb very little water and are ideal for load-bearing walls or as a dpc in garden walls etc.

Bricks are nominally 215mm long by 102.5mm wide and 65mm deep. However, the 'format size' is needed for calculating the number required for a particular job. This makes allowance for the mortar joints. The format size is 225 by 113 by 75mm, allowing for a 10mm mortar joint all round. There are also many special shapes and sizes of brick available.

The parts of a brick are known by special names; the end is the header face; the side is the stretcher face; the underside is the bed face. The top face may be flat or have a depression in it called a frog. This provides a key for the mortar joint. A single row of bricks is called a course, and courses are laid so that the bricks have an interlocking bonding pattern for strength. The two main bonds for use in the garden are English garden wall bond and Flemish garden wall bond. They both produce a strong decorative bond (see project 14).

Bricklaying also requires special tools: a bricklayer's trowel for laying mortar; a long builder's spirit level for checking that courses are horizontal and vertical; a stringline and steel pins for setting out the line of the wall; and a gauge rod for checking the spacing of courses. The last should be made from a timber batten marked off at 75mm intervals, equal to the height of one brick and its mortar joint. A bolster chisel and club hammer are also essential for cutting bricks.

5 Storing materials

If materials have to be stored before use. they should be protected from rain. This is important with cement, which is supplied in sacks. Once the cement becomes damp, it is of no use. If possible, store it in a dry outbuilding. Otherwise, make sure it is off the ground and covered with a waterproof sheet. Bricks, sand and aggregate should be stored near the site and kept covered.

1. Store aggregate and sand on a hard surface and cover with polythene. If necessary, separate them with a board.

In addition to normal rectangular clay bricks, there are vast numbers of special shapes and sizes for doing particular jobs, such as forming coping, building shaped plinths, rounding corners and providing ventilation in the form of airbricks. Some bricks have perforated centres to act as a key for mortar or to accept reinforcing rods.

Calcium silicate bricks are the same size as clay bricks but are made from sand or flint and lime in a range of colours. There is also a huge range of precast concrete walling blocks and screen blocks, some of which have the appearance of split stone, with matching coping stones and pilaster blocks for building decorative garden walls.

Bricks can be used for paving, too, although unless they are engineering bricks, they may suffer from frost damage. Concrete bricks are better and come in a wide range of colours and shapes, often with moulded-in spacers.

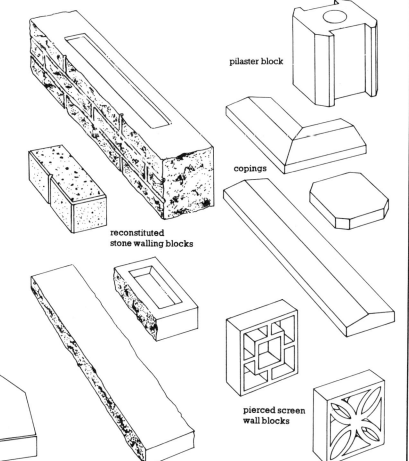

pilaster block

copings

reconstituted
stone walling blocks

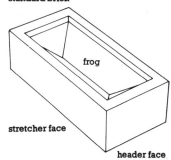

standard brick

frog

stretcher face

header face

A standard brick is 215mm (8½in) long, 102.5mm (4in) wide and 65mm (2⅝in) deep. For estimating purposes, add 10mm to each dimension for the mortar joint.

pavers

pierced screen
wall blocks

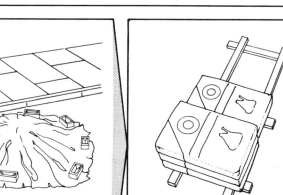

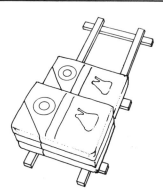

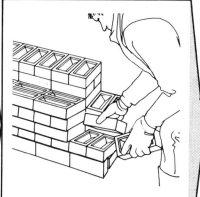

2. If sand or aggregate is left in the road, cover it with weighted-down polythene and mark with lamps at night.

3. If bags of cement cannot be kept in the dry, stack them on a wooden platform and cover with weighted-down polythene.

4. Store bricks on a stable, level surface near the work site, stacking them neatly so that they will not fall.

5. Stack concrete paving slabs against a convenient wall, standing them on battens to protect their edges.

⑦ Laying bricks — the basics

One of the most important skills in bricklaying is the ability to use the bricklayer's trowel. It is larger than all other trowels, one side of its blade being slightly curved, while the other is straight. The curved edge is for tapping bricks into place on the mortar.

Practise picking up mortar with the trowel before laying any bricks. Have the mortar on a board and slice off enough to cover the trowel blade, working it into a blade shape. Lift it from the board with a sweeping action. Lay the mortar by drawing the blade back and tilting it at the same time. One trowel full should be enough to lay two bricks.

Before beginning work, lay out the bricks dry to see if any need cutting to fit.

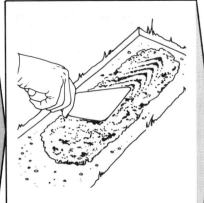

1. Load the trowel with mortar and spread it on the foundation, using the trowel to furrow the surface.

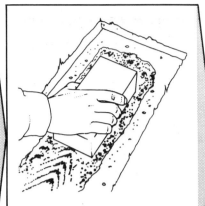

2. Bed the first brick on the mortar, making sure it is aligned correctly. Tap it down level with the trowel blade.

⑧ Building up the wall

Accurate spacing of bricks in a wall is essential if the last bricks in each course are to align. One of the ways this is achieved is to build about six courses of the ends first, forming a series of 'steps'. A line is stretched between the ends of each course while the centre is filled in. If the wall will eventually be higher than six courses, build up the ends again when this level is reached.

As work progresses, make frequent checks with the spirit level and gauge rod to ensure that the courses are horizontal and correctly spaced, and that the face and ends of the wall are truly vertical and not bulging or twisting.

Mortar that oozes from the joints should be scraped off with a vertical movement of the trowel blade.

⑨ Stretcher bond wall

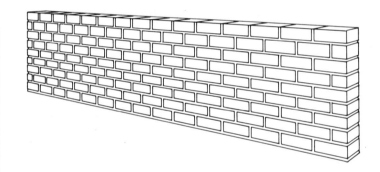

Stretcher bond is the simplest bricklaying pattern. Bricks in each course overlap those below by half a brick's width

1. Build up the first five or six courses of bricks at the ends of the wall to begin with, stepping, or racking them back.

2. As each course is laid, check that the bricks are vertical and in line by holding a spirit level across the wall face.

3. Use a home-made gauge rod, marked off at the height of a brick plus one mortar joint, to check the course spacing.

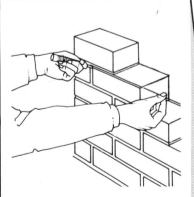

4. When filling in between the racked back ends, pin a line between the ends as a guide for each course.

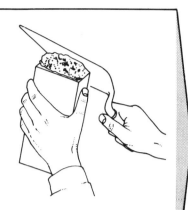

3. Before laying the next brick, spread a 10mm (in) layer of mortar on to its end to join the two bricks together.

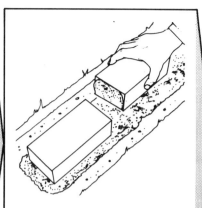

4. Position the brick, making sure it is aligned with the first. Scrape off any mortar that oozes from between them.

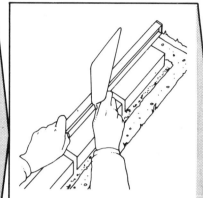

5. After laying the first course, check that the bricks are level. Tap down any 'high' bricks with the trowel blade.

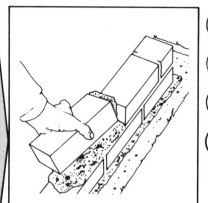

6. Repeat the procedure for the second course, starting with a half-brick to provide the necessary bonding pattern.

⑩ Setting up profile boards & string

When setting out the footings for a wall, use profile boards nailed to stakes in the ground just beyond the ends of the wall's position. Strings stretched between nails in the tops of the boards indicate the width of the trench to permit accurate digging. Extra lines can also be used to mark the position of the wall on the footings. Remove the lines for digging, but replace them for setting up shuttering or laying the first brick course.

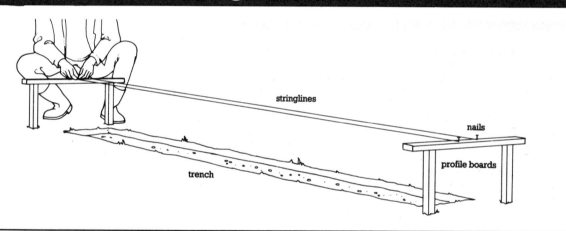

stringlines

nails

profile boards

trench

5. Lay the bricks to the line, checking frequently with the spirit level that they are horizontal and vertical.

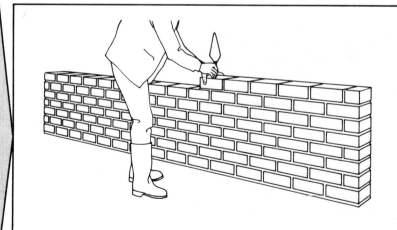

6. Lay the bricks for the last course to complete the wall. Then make a final check that faces and ends are truly vertical.

11 Forming piers — stretcher bond

The end of a freestanding wall should be reinforced by increasing its thickness by half a brick, forming a pier. Piers are also needed to reinforce long runs of brickwork – space them at 1.8m (6ft) intervals in a half-brick thick wall and at 2.8m (9ft) intervals in a one-brick thick wall.

Piers must be tied into the structure of the wall, which means altering the bonding pattern slightly, using bricks cut to various sizes. To cut bricks, 'score' a cutting line all the way round by gently tapping with a bolster chisel. Lay the brick bottom up on sand or grass and give it a sharp blow with the bolster chisel.

Remember to allow for the width of piers when digging out the wall's footings.

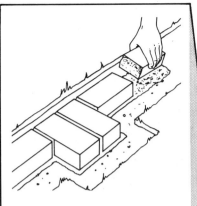

1. In a stretcher bond wall, the first course for a pier is made by laying two bricks header on to the wall's face.

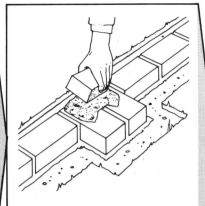

2. Begin the second course by cutting half a brick and laying it so that it bridges the joint between the two below.

12 Forming corners — stretcher bond

It is essential that any bonding pattern is maintained when forming a corner in a wall, otherwise the faces may be forced apart.

Corners are simple to make with stretcher bond, since at the end of each alternate course a brick is laid header on to begin the course of the wall's adjacent face. With more complex bonding patterns, considerably more thought is required, and bricks must be cut to maintain the bonding pattern.

It is important to mark out the footings so that corners are perfectly square, and a large home-made builder's square will ensure that they are. This should be nailed together from timber battens so that the sides are 450mm (18in), 600mm (24in) and 750mm (30in) long.

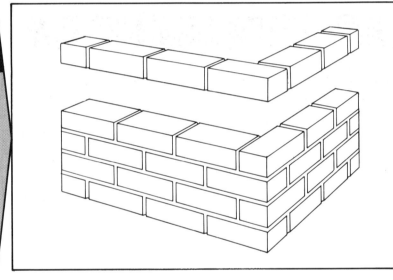

13 Pointing

Joints between bricks should be finished off neatly to prevent rainwater soaking between the bricks and damaging the wall. This is called pointing and should be done when the wall has been completed, but before the mortar has ceased to be workable. There are various styles of pointing, but struck and rounded joints are most common.

1. Point the vertical joints first. For a struck joint, press down along one side of the joint and then the other.

2. Follow with the horizontal joints, pressing in along the top of the joint to bevel the mortar so that water runs off.

3. Rounded joints can be made by shaping the mortar with a piece of bent metal tubing or plastic garden hosepipe.

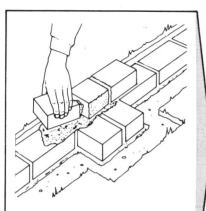

3. To maintain the bonding pattern of the wall, two three-quarter bricks are laid on each side of the half brick.

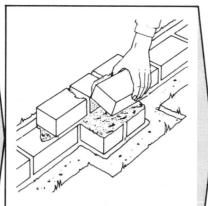

4. The pier's second course is completed by laying a brick stretcher-fashion across the two header bricks below.

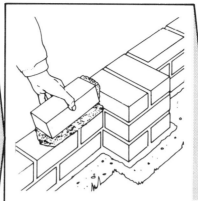

5. Lay another two bricks header on for the third course and continue the stretcher bond for the rest of the wall.

6. Use a half brick to complete alternate courses in an end pier, with two parallel stretchers above and below.

14 Garden wall bonds

Although stretcher bond is the simplest bonding pattern for a brick wall, there are several other patterns which are stronger and offer greater visual appeal. Two common bonds are English and Flemish.

In English bond, one course of bricks comprising two rows of parallel stretchers alternates with a course of bricks laid header on. This provides great strength since there are no continuous vertical joints inside the wall to weaken it.

In Flemish bond, parallel pairs of bricks, laid stretcher on, alternate with bricks laid header on in each course.

In both English and Flemish bonds, the bonding pattern is maintained at corners by the insertion of half bricks cut lengthways to continue the overlapping arrangement.

English and Flemish Garden Wall bonds are variations of these patterns.

English and English Garden Wall bonds (top), and Flemish and Flemish Garden Wall bonds (below), provide strength and an attractive appearance.

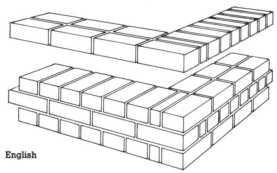

English

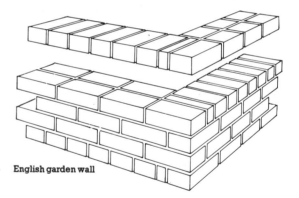

English garden wall

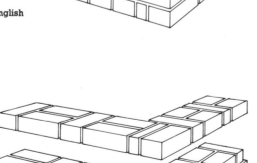

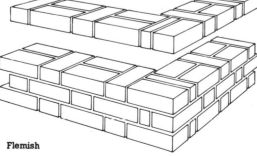

Flemish

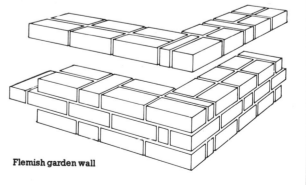

Flemish garden wall

Concrete slabs have many uses – patios, driveways, bases for sheds, garages etc. The thickness will vary with the job and the soil conditions. As a guide, patios and shed floors should be 75 – 100mm (3 – 4in) thick, and if the soil is soft, the concrete should be laid over an equivalent thickness of well-compacted hardcore. Driveways and garage floors should be 100 – 150mm (4 – 6in) thick, laid over hardcore.

Clear the site and remove the top soil. Mark the corners of the slab by driving nails into pegs set in the ground. Then outline the slab with strings stretched between pegs outside the work area. The strings should cross at the corner nail positions and meet at right angles.

Mark the string positions on the ground by sprinkling sand beneath them. Remove the strings and corner pegs, and dig out the site to the depth required. Leaving the other pegs in place allows the strings to be replaced for setting out the formwork.

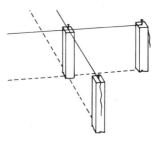

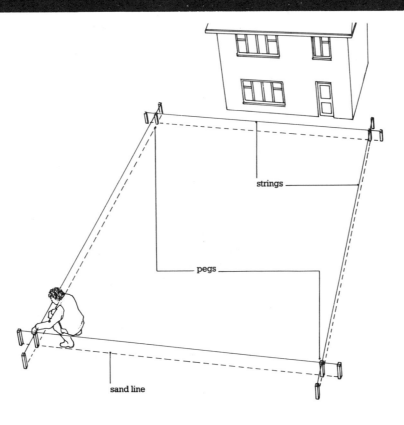

2. The strings should intersect at the nails driven into the pegs that mark each of the corners of the slab.

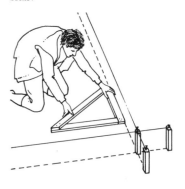

1. Mark out the position of the slab by stretching strings between pegs placed outside as the work area so that they will not

be disturbed as work progresses. That way, the strings can be easily removed and replaced at will.

3. Check that the strings cross each other at right angles, using a builder's square. Make adjustments as necessary.

Trench foundations for a wall can usually be made without the need for formwork, unless the sides of the trench are very soft and crumbly. A series of pegs, 600mm (2ft) apart, down the centre of the trench act as depth guides for digging out and allow the surface of the concrete to be levelled off. Profile boards and strings are used for setting out (see project 10).

The concrete should be laid on

firm subsoil, being 100mm (4in) thick for walls up to seven courses high, and 150mm (6in) thick above that height. The width of the footing depends on the thickness of the wall, but the amount of concrete on each side of the wall should be at least equal to the thickness of the concrete – allow more on soft soils.

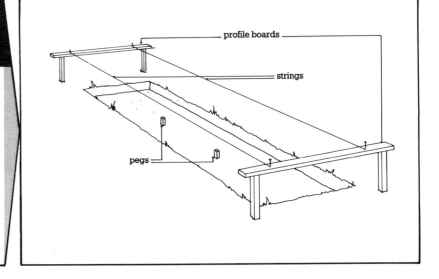

17 Setting up formwork

In most cases, formwork will be needed to contain the concrete while it sets. Sawn softwood planks are ideal and should be at least 25mm (1in) thick and as wide as the concrete is thick. The planks should be nailed to 50mm (2in) square pegs driven into the ground around the outside of the site and carefully levelled to the finished height of the slab.

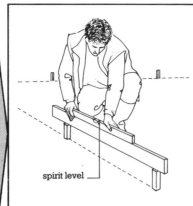

1. Space pegs for formwork at 1m (3ft) intervals around the site. Level their tops carefully to match the slab height.

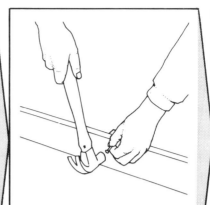

2. Nail the formwork to the pegs, making sure the boards are level with the peg tops. Make butt joints where needed.

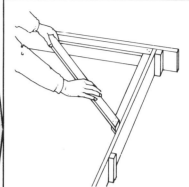

3. Make sure boards are butted together tightly at corners and check that they make right angles with a builder's square.

18 Checking levels

It is essential that the site for a concrete slab is dug out to a level uniform depth to avoid shallow areas that might weaken and eventually the concrete. In addition, if the slab is required as a base for an outbuilding, its surface must be perfectly level; if it is to be a patio or some other exposed surface, it should have a drainage fall to prevent water collecting on the surface. That fall should be away from any adjacent buildings at a gradient of about 1 in 60.

The depth of excavation is obtained by setting a series of pegs at 1.5m (5ft) intervals over the intended area of the slab. The first peg, known as the prime datum, is driven in until its top is level with the finished height of the slab, and all the other pegs levelled to it with a long straight edge and spirit level. Mark off the depth of concrete (and hardcore) on the pegs, and either dig out or fill to that level. Pegs for formwork, and the formwork itself, can also be set level with these pegs.

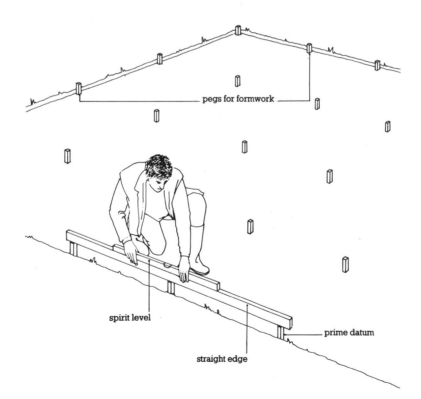

1. Control the depth of excavation by using a series of pegs driven into the ground. All the pegs should be levelled carefully so that their tops match the finished height of the concrete. Use a long straight edge and spirit level.

2. To set formwork for a drainage fall of about 1 in 60, place a wooden block beneath one end of the straight edge.

3. Over long distances, use clear hose filled with water. Drive pegs in until their tops match the water levels.

19 Laying concrete

After setting the formwork, add any hardcore (broken bricks, rubble etc), levelling it to the marks on the depth pegs. Ram the hardcore down well with a heavy timber, or use a garden roller.

Spread out the concrete, working it into the corners of the formwork. Cover half the area, leaving the concrete just above the formwork. Tamp it down with a timber beam, using a chopping action, then a sawing action to level it with the formwork. Continue in this way until the slab is complete.

Slabs over 3m (10ft) wide or long should be cast in equal-size bays with a softwood expansion joint between them. Hold this in place temporarily with extra formwork or piles of concrete until both bays are completely filled.

1. After levelling the site and laying the hardcore, tamping or rolling will compact the material fully.

2. Sprinkle the hardcore with water to dampen it, then mix the concrete and tip the barrow-loads on top.

20 Using ready-mixed concrete

For really large areas, such as driveways, the job will progress much quicker if ready-mixed concrete is used. Delivered in bulk, it is ready to be laid immediately.

Ready-mixed concrete is normally supplied in minimum quantities of about 3 cu m (4 cu yd), and the supplier will need to know the use it will be put to so that the correct mix can be supplied. It will be necessary to arrange access for the mixer truck and somewhere for the load to be dumped if it cannot be emptied directly on to the slab's foundations. Several helpers will be needed to spread and compact the concrete before it becomes unworkable, and if it cannot be dumped directly on the foundations, several stout wheelbarrows will also be needed.

1. With ready-mixed concrete, several barrows and helpers will be needed to convey the concrete from truck to site.

2. If possible, arrange access for the truck so that the concrete can be discharged directly on to the site.

21 Finishes for concrete

There are various ways in which the surface of a concrete slab can be finished, depending on the use to which it will be put. For a driveway, the rough, ridged finish left after tamping will provide good grip for car tyres in wet weather. Dragging a stiff-bristled broom across the wet concrete will also produce a non-slip surface. However, if a finer finish is required, the surface can be 'polished' with wooden or steel floats.

wooden float

stiff broom

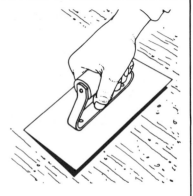

steel float

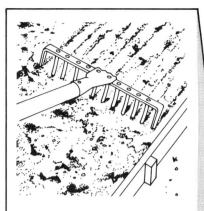

3. Use a garden rake to spread out the concrete, working it well into the corners of the formwork with a shovel.

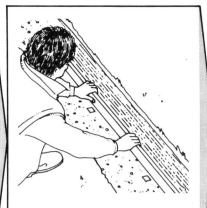

4. In a trench foundation, use a long piece of timber to level off the concrete until the tops of the pegs are just visible.

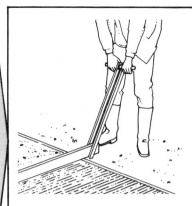

5. With a slab, work a timber tamping beam across the top of the formwork, chopping and sawing to level the concrete.

6. Very long or wide slabs should be cast in bays. Remove the temporary formwork before casting the second bay.

19 20 21 22 23

22 Using reinforcement

Concrete that will be subjected to heavy loads should be reinforced with steel mesh, which is available from builder's merchants. The mesh comprises rods about 6mm ($\frac{1}{4}$in) in diameter formed into 150mm (6in) squares. Support the mesh on pieces of brick and make sure the ends do not project beyond the edge of the slab. Make sure the concrete covers the mesh completely, working it underneath by rodding it with something like a broom handle.

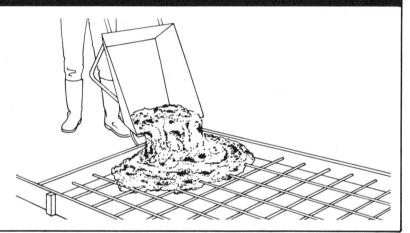

7. After laying the concrete, protect it with a polythene sheet for about a week so that it dries out slowly.

23 Breaking up old concrete

There may be occasions when it is necessary to break up old concrete, either because it is beyond repair or because it is in the way. Just how easy this job is will depend on the condition of the concrete. If it is soft and crumbly, it can be broken up with a pickaxe or a sledge hammer, or even a cold chisel and club hammer if there is only a small area to remove. If, on the other hand, the concrete is very hard, it will be quicker and much less tiring to hire an electric breaker.

When breaking up concrete, try to keep the lumps to a manageable size, otherwise they will be too heavy to carry away. Wear old clothes, stout gloves and boots, and safety goggles as protection against flying fragments.

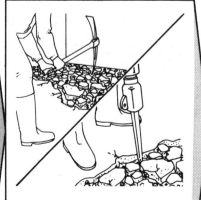

1. Soft concrete can be broken up with a pickaxe; otherwise hire an electric breaker to deal with hard material.

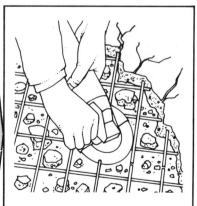

2. If the concrete has been reinforced with steel mesh, use an angle grinder to cut through the rods and remove it.

Mastics are flexible fillers that are suitable for use where some movement is expected; they are also waterproof and are used extensively for sealing gaps that might otherwise admit water. Movement occurs where timber and masonry meet, as timber expands and contracts with changes in temperature and humidity.

Typical applications are sealing round window and door frames, filling expansion gaps in walls and repairing cracks in roof flashings or roofing felt and leaking joints in gutters.

They form a dry skin that can often be painted, although many are pre-coloured. Mastics are applied by trowel, or from a tube, syringe or cartridge gun. The latter can be bought or hired. Keep mastics off your skin, as many contain harmful chemicals.

Mastics may be acrylic, bitumen, oil or silicone based and, depending on the type, may dry in days or minutes. Their useful life ranges from 10 to 20 years. Bitumen-based mastics (for roofing and guttering repairs) must be treated with bitumen-resistant primer before painting.

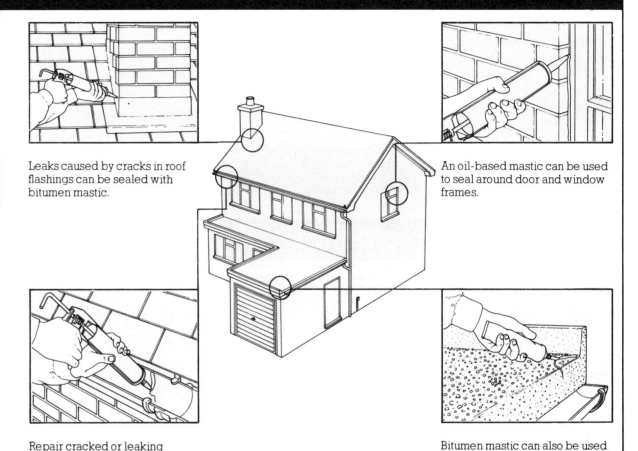

Leaks caused by cracks in roof flashings can be sealed with bitumen mastic.

An oil-based mastic can be used to seal around door and window frames.

Repair cracked or leaking gutters by applying a bead of mastic to the joints.

Bitumen mastic can also be used to repair minor cracks in roofing felt.

Rot and insect attack can cause severe damage to any timber used in the house or garden. Therefore, it must be protected from both by being treated with preservative. After installation, exterior woodwork will also need regular treatment with preservative or paint to maintain the protection.

It is possible to buy timber that has been pressure-treated with preservative. If this is not available, however, treatment will have to be done at home.

Various preservatives are available. Creosote is cheap, but stains the wood, is strong smelling and takes several days to dry. A wide range of clear and coloured wood preservatives is also available, although they are more expensive.

1. Preservative can be brushed on to fences. Starting from the bottom will prevent runs staining the surface.

2. A trellis can be treated more effectively and more quickly if spraying equipment is used to apply the preservative.

When heavy frameworks need fixing to a wall or a solid concrete floor, screws are often not up to the job. In this case, a much stronger bolt is required. A wide range of expanding bolt fixings is available in a selection of sizes. Some provide a threaded stud for a nut, while others receive a bolt, hook or eye.

All work in the same way: as the fixing is tightened, its sleeve expands in the pre-drilled hole to provide a strong grip.

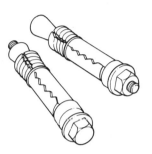

1. Expanding bolts may provide you with a nut or bolt fixing. Both expand in the hole as they are tightened.

2. Drill a hole for fixing in accordance with the manufacturer's instructions, using a masonry bit.

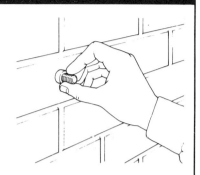

3. After blowing dust and debris from the hole, insert the fixing and tighten it by hand to set the sleeve in place.

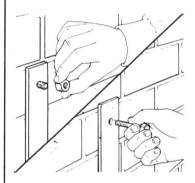

4. Remove the nut or bolt. Then offer up the item to be fixed and replace the nut or bolt so that it is finger-tight.

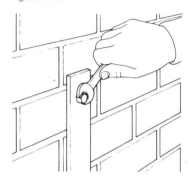

5. Tighten the fixing with a spanner, taking care not to over-tighten it in case the pressure damages the masonry.

6. Fixings can also be made in concrete by inserting a rag bolt while the concrete is still wet. Make sure it is upright.

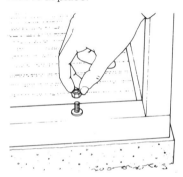

7. When the concrete has set, the frame can be assembled on top, dropping it down over the bolts and adding the nuts.

3. The ends of fence posts are particularly vulnerable. Stand them in a bucket of preservative for a day or two.

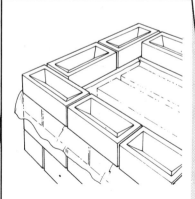

4. An alternative is to assemble a preservative 'bath' from bricks and polythene, laying the posts in it to soak.

5. The sawn tops of posts should be treated liberally with preservative to protect the endgrain.

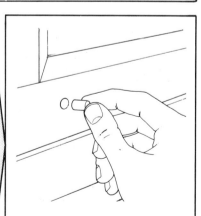

6. Vulnerable window frame joints can be protected from rot by inserting wood preservative tablets.

27 Patching timber frames & sills

Timber window and door frames can suffer from rot if they are neglected. The most vulnerable areas are where water tends to collect – that is in the lower corners of frames, on sills and at the foot of door frames.

Rot will travel beneath a painted surface, so the first job is to discover the extent of the damage. Do this by pushing a knife into the wood – if the wood is sound, it will sink no more than about 6mm (¼in). However, if the wood is rotten, the blade will sink deeply.

The affected timber must be cut out and replaced with a fresh piece. Before doing so, treat the new timber and the cut faces of the old with preservative. Once the repair has been made, paint the entire frame.

1. On a rotten sill, mark out a wedge shape beyond the damaged area and make saw cuts across the sill.

2. Chisel out the rotten wood, taking care to keep the edges of the cut-out vertical to provide a sound joint.

28 Using resin filler

Where rot is only just beginning to get a hold, frames can be repaired with a resin-based filler system.

The damaged wood is scraped away and the area treated with a hardener to strengthen it, this is followed by a filler to reshape the frame. Further rot is prevented by inserting preservative tablets in the frame on each side of the repair.

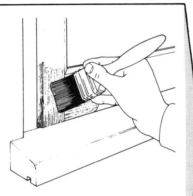

1. After scraping off all loose paint and rotten wood, a special hardener is brushed on to reinforce the damaged area.

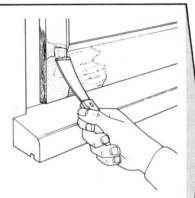

2. Once the hardener has set, the frame is reshaped to its original profile with an epoxy-based filler.

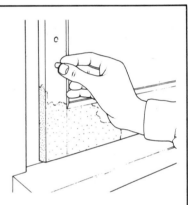

3. To prevent the rot developing again, preservative tablets are inserted in holes drilled in the frame before it is painted.

29 Re-tiling a sill

In some houses, the window may be set back in its opening with a tiled sill. Over the years, the tiles may become loose, broken at their overhanging edges or cracked by frost.

It is extremely unlikely that a match for the tiles will be found, so the entire sill will need hacking off and replacing with fresh tiles and mortar.

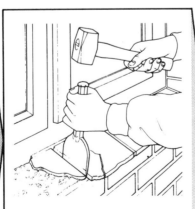

1. Chop off the tiles and mortar with a bolster chisel and club hammer. Wear safety goggles as protection from fragments.

2. Brush off dust and debris, dampen the top of the wall and spread a bed of mortar across the foot of the window opening.

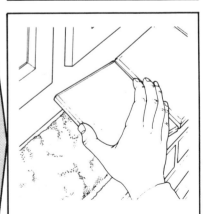

3. Set the new tiles on the mortar, bedding them carefully so that they are at the correct angle. Then point the joints.

3. Hold a new piece of timber against the sill and mark the shape of the cut-out on it. Saw it to size.

4. Fit the new piece with waterproof wood glue, reinforcing the joint with dowels driven into the old sill.

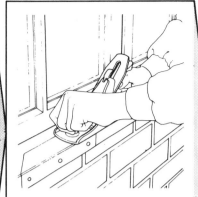

5. Finally, plane the new wood to shape so that it matches the original profile and paint the entire sill.

6. When replacing the bottom of a door frame, use an angled scarf joint, reinforcing it with glue and screws.

30 *Patching concrete sills*

Concrete sills can suffer from erosion and cracking, or may break away in places. Although repairs can be made with mortar or concrete, it is unlikely that the original concrete colour will be matched, so after repair it is best to paint the sill.

Eroded areas should be cut away to a depth of at least 25mm (1in). After treating with PVA solution, fill with cement/lime/sharp sand mortar mixed with PVA adhesive.

Open up cracks, undercut their edges and fill with an exterior-grade filler.

A broken sill can be repaired by drilling into the broken edges, mortaring in reinforcing bars and building a timber formwork around the sill. Treat the broken edges with PVA solution and pour concrete (mixed with PVA solution) into the formwork. Work the concrete with a stick to remove air bubbles and tamp it down well. Finish it off with a steel float and cover with a sack or polythene to prevent it drying out too quickly.

1. Hack off loose or flaking concrete with a cold chisel and club hammer.

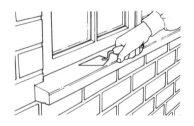

2. Fill shallow holes with mortar, trowelling it off to follow the shape of the sill.

3. After opening out a crack, brush the surfaces with a PVA solution to improve adhesive.

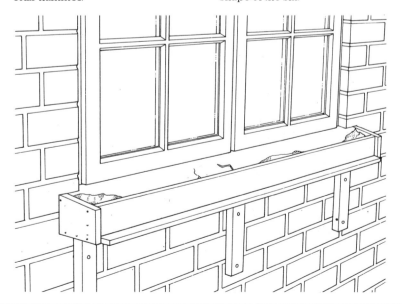

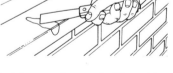

4. Mix exterior-grade filler with PVA adhesive and force it well into the crack.

5. A broken sill can be recast by building a stout timber formwork around it, adding steel reinforcement and filling with concrete.

31 Glazing a window

Cracked or broken panes should be replaced as soon as possible; they allow damp air and draughts to enter the house and are dangerous.

The glass sits in a rebate in the frame, being held by special nails called sprigs (wooden frames) or by clips (steel frames) and sealed with putty. Some wooden frames have beading to hold the glass in place. Aluminium frames use various methods, so consult the supplier before making repairs.

When ordering new glass, subtract 3mm ($\frac{1}{8}$in) from each rebate dimension to ensure clearance. Make sure it is of the same thickness as the original.

Buy the right putty for the job: linseed oil putty for wooden frames; metal casement putty for steel frames. All-purpose putty will cope with either.

1. Line the rebate with a layer of putty, after kneading it to make it pliable. Squeeze the putty between finger and thumb.

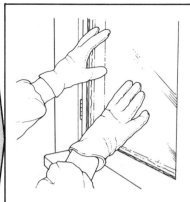

2. Fit the glass, pressing around the edges until there is 3mm ($\frac{1}{8}$in) between the pane and the back of the rebate.

32 Removing old window glass

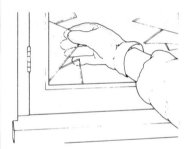

1. Remove the glass by tapping it with a hammer and pulling out the fragments. Wear thick gloves for protection.

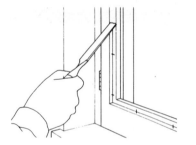

2. Remove the old putty using a glazier's hacking knife or an old wood chisel, taking care not to damage the rebate.

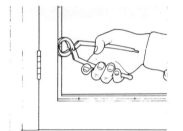

3. Use a pair of pincers to remove the glazing sprigs, or pliers to lift out the spring clips in a metal frame.

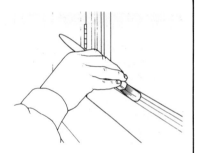

4. Prepare the rebate by sanding it with medium glasspaper and painting with wood or metal primer as appropriate.

33 Repairing a casement window

Casement windows often bind in their frames. This may be due to a build-up of too much paint on the edges of the frame, the remedy being to sand or plane it down to fit. However, it may also be caused by the wood swelling in wet weather. Allowing the frame to dry out and then applying a good coat of paint may help by preventing moisture getting at the wood. However, if that fails, the frame must be planed down where it rubs. A sheet of carbon paper slipped between the two surfaces will help you to locate the tight spots.

The joints of large casements may work loose, allowing the frame to droop. The simplest repair is to chisel a rebate for an L-shaped bracket. Treat the bracket with rustproofing paint, fit it with brass screws and cover with filler before repainting.

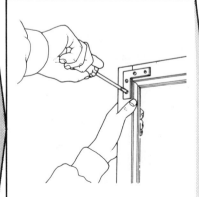

1. Loose casement joints can be reinforced with L-shaped corner brackets. Wedge the frame square first.

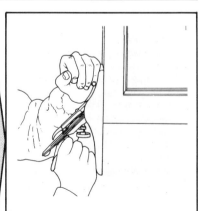

2. Where the edges of the frame rub, plane them down carefully so that the window opens and closes freely.

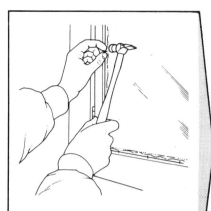

3. Tap new sprigs into place at 225mm (9in) intervals, sliding the hammer head across the glass to avoid breaking it.

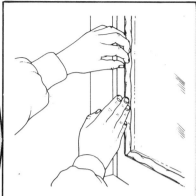

4. Add the final putty seal, smoothing it off at an angle with a putty or filling knife and mitring the corners.

5. Wetting the knife blade will prevent the putty sticking to it. Remove excess putty from the face of the glass.

6. Similarly, remove excess putty from inside the window. Leave the putty to harden for two weeks before painting.

34 *Repairing sash windows*

Sash windows are unlikely to suffer from sticking, unless they have been gummed up with paint, but they may rattle in their frames. This can be fixed by prising off the inner staff bead and central parting bead and re-nailing them to reduce the width of the window channels.

Another problem is that the cords attaching the weights to the sashes may break, so that the upper sash will not stay closed and the lower one will not stay open.

Replacing the cords means prising off the staff and parting beads as appropriate, removing the sash concerned and taking the weights from the pockets in the frame. After feeding in a new cord, it is attached to the weight at one end and nailed to the sash at the other before reassembling the window.

The sash window has two vertically-sliding sashes which are counterbalanced by lead weights concealed in the frame sides. Cords connect the weights to the sashes.

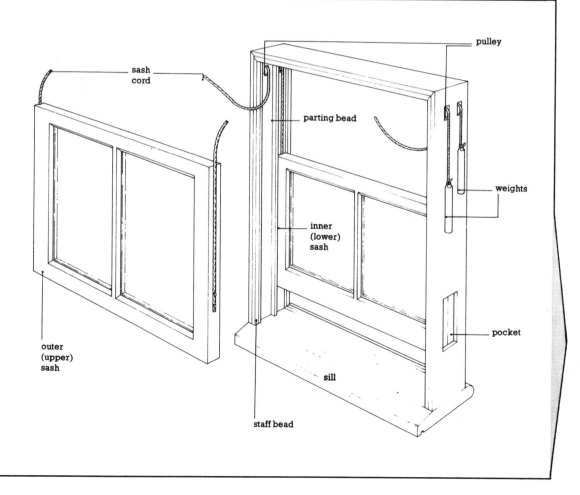

sash cord

pulley

parting bead

weights

inner (lower) sash

outer (upper) sash

pocket

staff bead

sill

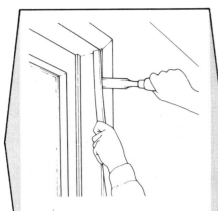

1. Use an old chisel to prise the staff bead from each side of the frame and then you can lift out the lower sash.

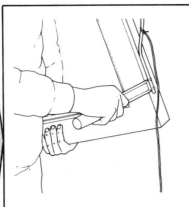

2. Tie a thin length of string to each sash cord before prising the nails from the sash or cutting it free.

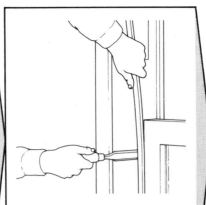

3. Prise off the parting bead, remove the upper sash and free its cord in the same manner as for the lower sash.

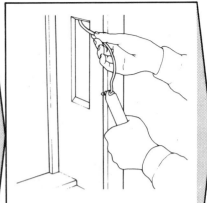

4. Prise out the pocket covers from the frame sides, lift out the weights and pull out the cords until the string appears.

35 *Soffits, fascias & bargeboards*

The exposed ends of structural roof timbers — the joists, rafters etc — are protected from the weather by soffits, fascias and bargeboards. Soffits fit below the ends of the joists and rafters where they overhang the wall. Fascias fit on to the joist and rafter ends; they provide a surface for mounting the guttering. Bargeboards provide protection to the ends of roof timbers at the gable end of a house. They may also be used with a soffit.

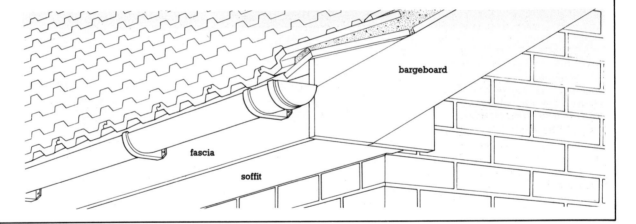

bargeboard

fascia

soffit

36 *Repairing soffits, fascias & bargeboards*

Because of their inaccessible position, fascias, soffits and bargeboards are often neglected and rot sets in. This should be dealt with quickly if it occurs.

New timber should be fitted to match the size of the old; if the exact size is not available, buy larger and saw or plane it to size. If possible, buy timber that has been pressure-treated with preservative; otherwise, coat each piece liberally with preservative before fitting.

When replacing a fascia, remember to set the guttering at a positive fall of about 1 in 120 towards the outlet.

Do not attempt to do the work from a ladder – use an access tower or scaffolding, and have an assistant ready to help manage the bulky lengths of timber.

1. Prise the old, damaged boards from the ends of the joists with a claw hammer or crow bar. Pull out all the old nails.

2. Pin a new soffit temporarily in place and mark it to length so that it ends exactly at the centre of a joist.

5. Tie the strings to new cords and pull these back over the frame pulleys. Tie the weights to the free ends of the cords.

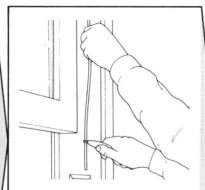

6. Mark the sash groove length on the frame from the pulley top. Cut the cord at the mark with the weight just hanging.

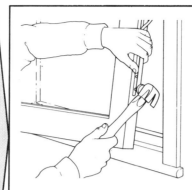

7. Fit the cords in the grooves with clout nails. Do not nail them at the top, otherwise the window won't run to the top.

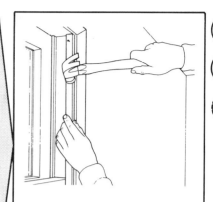

8. Replace the pocket covers in the frame and then refit the sashes, pinning the parting and staff beads back in place.

37 Repairing leaded lights

To replace broken glass in a leaded light, cut through the joints between the lead cames with a sharp knife and bend the flanges back. Work on the outside of the window so the repair will not be noticed inside, and have someone support the window inside with a flat board. Remove the broken glass and old putty.

Cut a fresh piece of glass to shape using a wheeled cutter. Fit it to the cames and bend the lead flanges back. Apply flux to the joints and resolder them with 3mm ($\frac{1}{8}$in) coreless solder. Work putty down between the cames and glass on both sides of the window, then press the flanges down. Disguise the repair by burnishing all the lead with wire wool. Colour the putty with plumber's black.

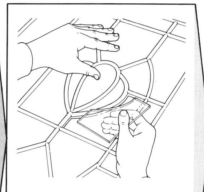

1. After lifting the flanges of the lead cames and removing the old glass, insert a new piece and bend the flanges back.

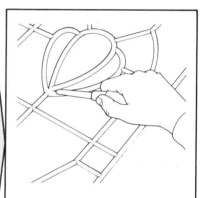

2. Solder the joints and press putty between the flanges and glass. Finally smooth the flanges with a flat blade.

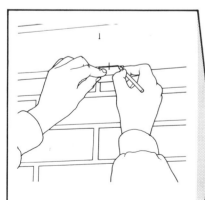

3. For a tight fit at the house wall, scribe the edge of the new soffit using a small wooden block and pencil.

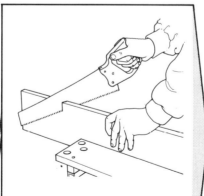

4. Remove the board and cut it to length, mitring the cut at 45°. Plane or saw the scribed edge to shape.

5. Fix the soffit in place with galvanised nails, making sure the mitred end is centred on the joist for joining to the next board.

6. Repeat the process for the next board, fitting the ends together carefully. Then add the fascia boards in the same way.

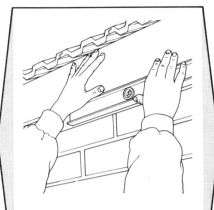

1. Cut the fascia board to length, offer it up and make sure it is level. If necessary, trim the top edge of the board.

2. When the board fits, nail it in place with galvanised nails. Finish the fascia, then paint it to match the other joinery.

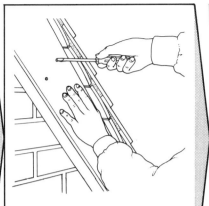

3. When fitting a bargeboard, fix it to the ends of the roof timbers with countersunk rust-proof screws.

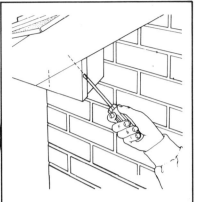

4. If the bargeboard has a tail to close off the eaves, secure it with screws driven into the edge of the bargeboard.

38 Treating rot

Unprotected timbers exposed to damp are at risk from attack by rot. Wet rot can be found indoors and out; dry rot only occurs indoors.

Wet rot makes timber go spongy, but once the source of moisture is removed, it will die out. Badly affected timber should be cut out, the area soaked in preservative and new timber installed. Slight damage can be repaired with a special hardener.

Once dry rot begins to grow, it draws moisture from the timber itself, expanding rapidly. Tiny grey strands pass through timber and masonry, often accompanied by a mass of white fibres and large fruiting bodies that throw out red-brown spores. Affected timber becomes dry and crumbles. Treatment is best left to a specialist; it involves cutting out and burning all affected timbers and treating the remainder with preservative.

Timber in and around the house can be attacked by rot. Wet rot can occur anywhere the timber is kept wet; dry rot occurs in badly ventilated spaces.

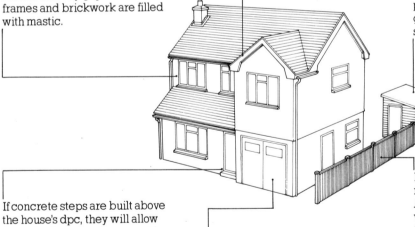

Wooden windows will soon rot unless regularly painted; also ensure that any gaps between frames and brickwork are filled with mastic.

Neglected bargeboards, soffits and fascias are likely to suffer from rot, especially if there are blocked or leaking gutters.

Cracked or badly fitted roofing felt, the lack of regular preservative treatment, or garden refuse piled against a shed will all cause rot eventually.

If concrete steps are built above the house's dpc, they will allow damp to rise up and cause rot in the door and its frame.

Garage doors are prone to rot and must be kep well protected. If side-opening, they may have to be removed from their hinges to treat the bottom edge with preservative or paint.

Fences are especially prone to rot at ground level and at the top. Apart from regular treatment with timber preservative, ensure that the panels or boards are clear of the ground and you have fitted capping rails and post caps.

39 Repairing vertical boarded fences

Close-boarded timber fences can suffer from a number of faults, which should be put right before they worsen and weaken the entire fence.

If a fence is not treated regularly with preservative (every two or three years), rot will eventually get a hold – usually along the bottom of the fence where moisture is drawn up from the ground and along the top where the endgrain of the fence boards is exposed. The rotten parts should be replaced with new pieces.

Strong winds may also cause damage, loosening boards and possibly even breaking arris rails. All loose nails should be driven back in and arris rails either replaced or repaired with special galvanised metal brackets.

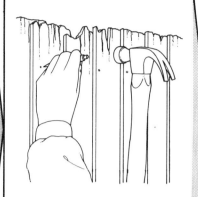

1. Rot may seriously damage boarded fences. To free rotten boards for replacement, drive the nails in with a punch.

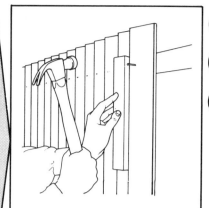

2. If replacing several boards, use a wooden offcut to ensure uniform spacing. Make sure the boards are upright.

40 Repairing fences

Timber fences come in two basic types; solid or open.

Close-boarded fences are a popular solid type. They comprise narrow vertical boards nailed to horizontal supports (arris rails) which fit between the posts. Usually, the boards are tapered in section (feather-edge) so that they can be overlapped. A horizontal gravel board protects the board ends from rot.

Other solid fences are built from ready-made panels (of horizontally-overlapping or interwoven slats) which are nailed to the posts or slotted into concrete posts.

Open fences may take the form of picket fences or ranch-type fencing. The former may have vertical spaced palings, the latter wide, horizontal boards fixed between the posts.

If a fence is to retain its looks, it must be protected from the elements. That means treating it regularly with preservative or paint, replacing rotten timber and ensuring that its posts are both sturdy enough and soundly fixed in the ground.

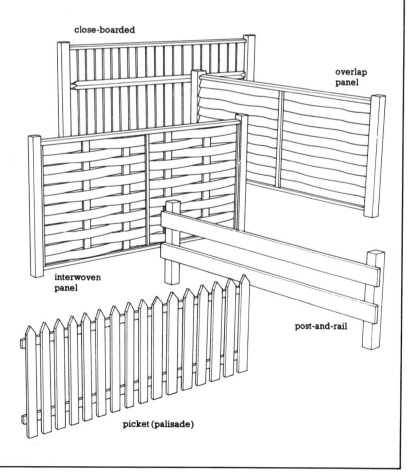

close-boarded

overlap panel

interwoven panel

post-and-rail

picket (palisade)

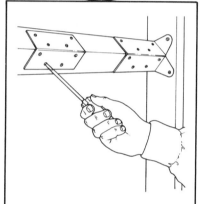

3. Broken arris rails can be repaired with galvanised brackets which should be held with rust-proof screws.

4. Gravel boards are nailed to wooden blocks called cleats. These are nailed or screwed to the fence posts.

41 Repairing woven fences

The thin slats used to make a woven fence panel are easily damaged and may pull away from their framework. The odd one or two loose slats can be refixed, but if the panel is seriously damaged, it should be replaced.

Fitting a new panel should not present too much of a problem, since all ready-made fence panels come in a standard width. After taking out the old panel, the new one can be nailed in place.

Unfortunately, not all fence runs will need an exact number of panels, and it may be necessary to cut one down to fit. To do this, the framing battens at one end should be levered off and repositioned. After nailing them together with galvanised nails, the unwanted portion of the panel can be sawn off.

1. Any thin wooden slats that have come adrift from the panel can be refixed using galvanised metal staples.

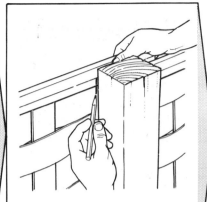

2. If a new panel needs cutting to length, stand it in position and mark where it overlaps the fence post.

42 Protecting wire fences

Wire fences need little maintenance. However, over a long period of time they may rust. To overcome this, clean off the worst with a wire brush and treat the fence with a rustproofing paint.

A sagging fence may need reclipping to the straining wire using twists of wire, or the straining wire may need retensioning by turning the tensioner at the end post.

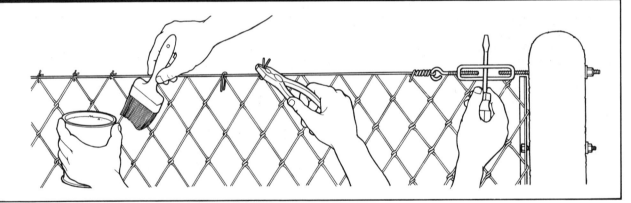

43 Repairing rotten posts

The ends of timber fence posts buried in the ground are the most vulnerable part of a fence and may rot badly. Fortunately, individual posts are easily replaced.

After cutting through the arris rails on each side of the post, lever it out and dig out any concrete or rubble in the hole. Treat the new post with preservative and insert it to a depth of about 600mm (2ft). Fill the hole with alternate layers of earth and hardcore, finishing with 150mm (6in) of concrete. once the concrete has set, the panels can be reconnected with metal arris rail brackets.

If the upper portion of the post is sound, it can be cut off and fitted to a concrete spur post or metal fence spike driven into the ground.

1. Support the fence panels with bricks and saw through the arris rails on both sides of the damaged post.

2. Lever out the old post by tying it to a stout length of timber. Long nails in both prevent the rope slipping.

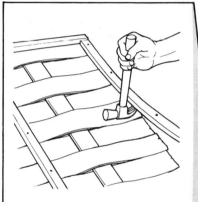

3. Use a claw hammer to lever off the framing battens at one end of the panel and pull out their nails.

4. Reposition the framing battens to align with the pencil mark and nail them together with galvanised nails.

5. Check that the panel is square by measuring the diagonals and cut off the unwanted portion with a saw.

6. Drill pilot holes in the end battens and fix the panels to the posts with 75mm (3in) galvanised nails.

44 Protecting post tops

The endgrain at the top of wooden fence posts is particularly at risk from rotting, since rain can easily penetrate the timber at this point. However, there are various ways by which it can be protected.

The simplest method of protecting the endgrain is to cut the end of the post at an angle or into a point so that water will run off quickly and not lie there. In both cases, the endgrain should be liberally treated with preservative.

Another method of protecting the top of the post is to nail on some form of cap that will keep the rain off. Shaped timber and galvanised metal versions are widely available, and should be fixed in place with galvanised nails.

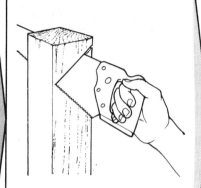

1. Sawing the top of the post at an angle will prevent rainwater seeping into the endgrain and rotting the timber.

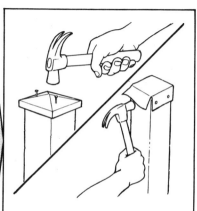

2. A wood or metal cap will also keep out the rain. Metal ones need shaping with a hammer to fit the post.

3. After ramming hardcore and earth round the post, finish off with concrete trowelled so that water will drain clear.

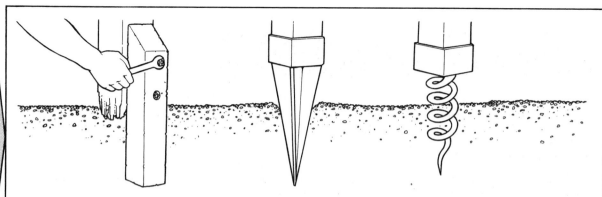

4. If the above-ground portion of the post is still in good condition, it can be bolted to a concrete spur post.

5. An alternative is to drive a metal spike into the ground and fit the post into the socket in the top.

6. A variation on this theme is a socket with a corkscrew base that is 'screwed' into the ground.

45 Replacing roof tiles

Although roof tiles are very durable, their exposed position makes them prone to weather damage; they may break, slip or fall out. Any damage should be made good immediately to prevent rain penetrating the roof.

Tiles may be of clay or concrete, and they are fixed in an overlapping pattern to timber battens nailed across the joists. Small lugs (called nibs) on each tile hook over the battens, the weight of the tiles above being enough to keep them in place. However, every third or fourth course is likely to be nailed in place for added security and strength. Modern concrete tiles are often designed to be interlocking and may be held to the battens by clips rather than nails.

46 Tile fixing methods

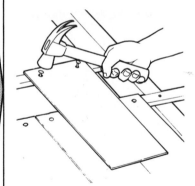

Slates and clay tiles are nailed to the battens, either at the top or in the middle.

Modern concrete tiles have projected lugs, called nibs, that hook over the battens.

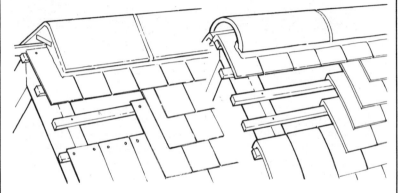

Slates and tiles are fixed to the battens in an overlapping pattern to prevent rain penetrating the

roof. At the ridge, rounded or angular ridge tiles are bedded on mortar.

47 Access- roof ladders

Safe access is essential for any roofing work. A ladder can be used to reach the roof, but it should be secured to an eyebolt driven into the soffit.

If an area of tiles is being replaced, it would be better to hire a scaffold tower. A roof ladder will be needed for moving across the roof. This has wheels so that it can be run up the roof. A hook attachment at the top fits over the ridge of the roof to hold the ladder securely in place.

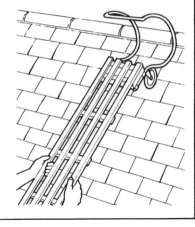

48 Replacing slates

The advent of the concrete tile has made slate too expensive for most new roofs. However, many older houses still have slate roofs which, eventually, will need repair. Replacement slates can be obtained from suppliers of used building materials. Make sure they are of the same thickness as the originals, and that they are not split, cracked or flaking. If it is not possible to find the correct size, buy a larger size and cut it down by scribing with a tile cutter and cutting with a bolster chisel. If new nail holes are needed, they should be drilled with a masonry bit.

A special tool, known as a slate ripper, will be needed to cut through the nails and allow removal of the slates. This can be hired.

1. Slide the slate ripper under the slate, hook its barbs over the nails and hit it with a hammer to cut through them.

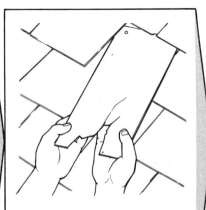

2. Remove the broken slate, using the slate ripper, if necessary, to slide it out from beneath the row above.

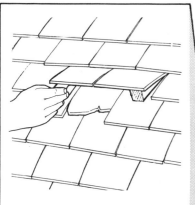

1. To remove a broken tile, lift those on either side of it with a pair of wooden wedges about 150mm (6in) long.

2. To free the tile from the batten, slide a trowel underneath and tilt it back so that the nibs are lifted clear.

3. If the tile is nailed to the batten and cannot be pulled free, use a hacksaw blade to cut through the nails.

4. Insert the new tile, hooking its nibs over the batten. If necessary, use the trowel to lift it into place.

49 Replacing ridge tiles

The top of the roof is sealed with ridge tiles bedded on mortar. Cracks or gaps in the mortar can be repointed, but if the tiles are loose they should be removed, the old mortar chopped away and fresh mortar laid.

Adding a PVA bonding agent to the mortar will make it more workable and improve adhesion. Lay mortar along each side of the ridge and butter the ends of adjacent ridge tiles, but keep the mortar clear of the timber ridge board.

At the end of the roof, the open edge of the ridge tile should be filled with mortar packed out with pieces of tile to make the end of the ridge tile tip up slightly so that rainwater runs back over the roof and does not drip on to the wall below.

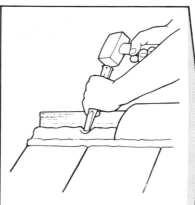

1. After lifting off the tile, chop away the old mortar, taking care not to damage adjacent tiles.

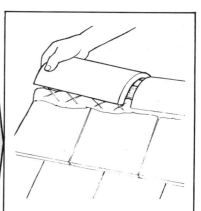

2. Bed the tile on fresh mortar laid on each side of the ridge. Trowel it off so that rain will run clear.

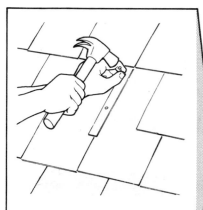

3. The new slate is held with a strip of lead or zinc called a tingle. Nail it to the batten between the slates below.

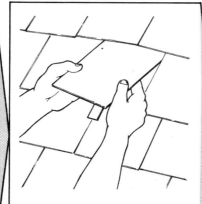

4. Ease the new slate into place, making sure the bevelled edges are uppermost to aid drainage of rainwater.

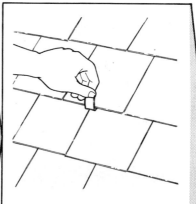

5. Bend the end of the tingle upwards to secure the slate; doubling over the end will make it stronger.

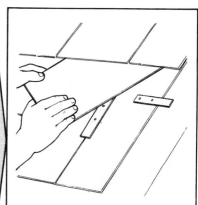

6. If a slate is being replaced at the edge of the roof, two tingles are needed to hold it in place.

50 Repairing a flat roof

The expense of building a traditional tiled pitched roof has made the flat roof a popular choice for house extensions and garages. Flat roofs are based on a timber decking (either individual boards or sheet materials like plywood and chipboard) covered with layers of roofing felt which are bonded with a bitumen compound or asphalt. A layer of stone chippings finishes it off.

Roofing felt is easily damaged and prone to cracking and blistering which will allow rain to penetrate and damage the roof. Minor damage is easily repaired, either by brushing on a waterproofing compound or by adding patches. However, if the entire roof is in a bad way, it will need recovering completely.

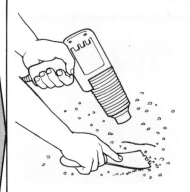

1. Soften the bitumen around a crack with a hot-air gun and scrape away all dirt and stone chippings.

2. Cut a patch of self-adhesive flashing strip and brush its bitumen primer over and around the crack.

51 Construction & flashings

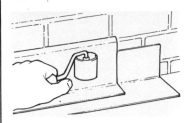

Adhesive flashing strip can be laid flat against a wall to seal the join with a flat roof.

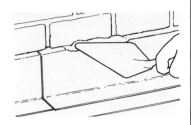

Alternatively, strips of felt can be used, the top edge being mortared into a wall joint.

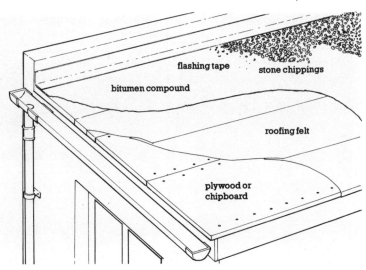

flashing tape
stone chippings
bitumen compound
roofing felt
plywood or chipboard

A flat roof is covered with at least three layers of felt, which are bonded together with bitumen compound and finally finished off with a protective layer of stone chippings.

52 Recovering a flat roof

If damage to the roof is more widespread than one or two cracks or bubbles, it can be repaired by adding another complete layer of felt.

Sweep off the roof and scrape off any moss or lichen, treating those areas with a fungicide. Slit any bubbles and allow them to dry out before pasting them down with bitumen sealer.

Brush cold bitumen emulsion over the roof and roll out the felt. Seal the edges with bitumen. Finally, spread more bitumen over the top and scatter on the chippings.

1. Clear the roof of all chippings and dirt so that it is perfectly clean and flat, ready for applying the new felt.

2. Spread out cold bitumen emulsion, working on part of the roof at a time so that it does not dry too quickly.

3. Roll out the felt in the direction of the drainage fall and overlap the adjacent strips by at least 50mm (2in).

3. Bed the patch in the bitumen primer, rolling it flat with an old seam roller. Make sure the edges are sealed.

4. Brush a further layer of bitumen sealer over the top of the patch and when tacky, scatter on the chippings.

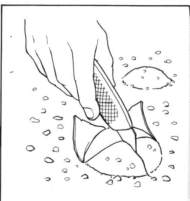

5. Cut through bubbles and bend back the felt, allowing the interior to dry out. Fill with bitumen sealer and press down.

6. Apply bitumen primer over the top of the cuts and finish the repair with a patch of self-adhesive flashing strip.

53 Patching a lead roof

Though not that common, lead roofs may be found on some older properties. Lead is very durable, but cracks and splits may occur with age.

Lead roofs can be patched with self-adhesive flashing strip or sealed completely with cold bitumen emulsion.

Where flashings are coming away from the wall, rake out the mortar joints and repoint them with fresh mortar.

1. If a lead roof is generally in poor condition, seal it by brushing on bitumen emulsion.

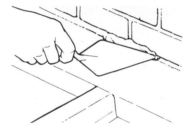

2. Refit flashings by wedging them with small rolls of lead and repointing the joints.

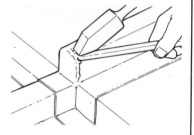

3. Splits in the joints of the lead roofing sheets may need soldering together.

54 Repairing a glass roof

Damage to a glass roof should be made good immediately, not only to prevent water pouring in but also to prevent slivers of glass falling out.

Cracked panes can be repaired temporarily with metal-backed mastic tape or self-adhesive flashing strip. Replacement panes should be toughened, laminated or wired safety glass at least 6mm (¼in) thick.

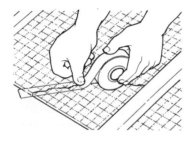

1. A temporary repair can be made with tape. Apply it to both sides of the glass.

2. Bed the glass on mastic and retain it with aluminium strips bent over the edge.

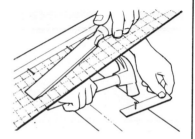

3. Drive in rustproof sprigs with a chisel and secure metal strips with galvanised nails.

Corrugated plastic sheeting is a popular roofing material for carports, sheds and other outbuildings. It is available in clear or various coloured tints, and is a much safer alternative to glass since it is less likely to be broken.

Various rounded and angular profiles are available, but the most common is 75mm (3in) round profile. Sheet size varies, but common sizes are 1.8, 2.4 and 3m (6, 8 and 10ft) long by about 750mm (2ft 6in) wide.

Corrugated plastic sheeting is easily cut with normal hand tools, and is very light, making it easy to handle. For the same reason, it must be fastened securely to the supporting rafters and purlins, otherwise the wind may lift the sheets and blow them off.

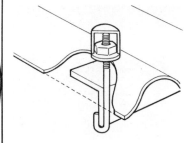

1. Special hook bolts are used to hold corrugated sheeting to angle-iron framework. They must not be overtightened.

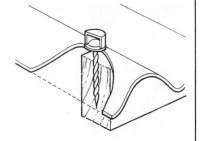

2. Alternatively, when there is a wooden framework, the sheets can be held by screws with plastic caps to keep out water.

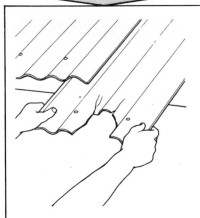

1. A damaged corrugated plastic sheet can be removed after unscrewing or pulling out its fixings. Slide it from the roof.

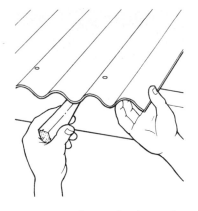

2. Set a wooden wedge beneath the overlapping sheet to lift it clear of the supporting structure of rafters and purlins.

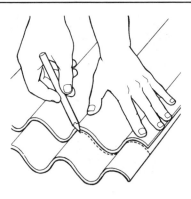

3. If the old sheet is not too badly damaged, use it to mark off the new piece, using a grease pencil or felt-tip pen.

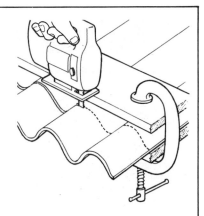

4. Clamp the new corrugated plastic sheet securely between two boards to support it and saw along the line.

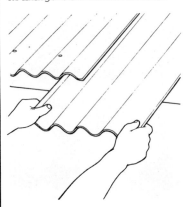

5. Slide the new sheet into place, making sure that there are equal overlaps with the sheets at each side of the new sheet.

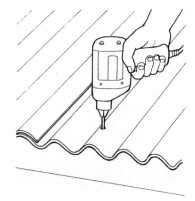

6. Drill fixing holes through the tops of the ridges, making them slightly larger than the fixings to allow for expansion.

7. Nail or screw the sheets down, using washers or plastic caps to protect the sheet. Seal nail heads with mastic.

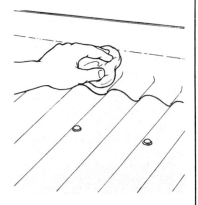

8. Finally, smooth down any flashing if the sheet meets a wall, working it carefully into the corrugated profile.

57 Fixing flashings

The junction between a roof and a wall or chimney is normally sealed with a flashing, although sometimes mortar may be used. Most flashings are made of lead which is mortared into the brickwork and laid down over the roof to prevent rain penetrating. Zinc and roofing felt may also be used in this way. An alternative is to use a self-adhesive flashing strip.

Over a period of time, flashings may come away from their joints, corrode or split. If they are generally in good condition, all that may be necessary is to rake out the mortar joints, refit the flashing and repoint the joints. Splits can often be patched with self-adhesive flashing strip, but extensive damage will probably mean replacing the flashing completely.

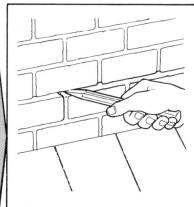

1. To fit a lead flashing, first rake out a mortar joint with a cold chisel to a depth of at least 25mm (1in).

2. Tuck the top edge of the lead into the joint and wedge it with rolls of lead. Then point the joint with mortar.

58 Types of flashing

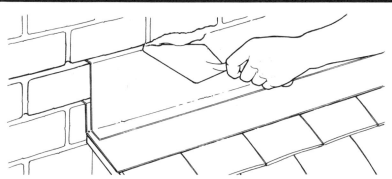

1. To get a reasonable overlap on both wall and roof, flashings may be in two pieces, the lower section being laid on to the roof itself and the section above being mortared into the joints in the brickwork of the wall.

2. Where corrugated roofing sheets meet a wall, a specially-shaped flashing strip can be laid along the top of the sheets and lapped up against the wall. A second overlapping strip is mortared into the brickwork of the wall to seal the joint.

3. Chimneys require quite complicated flashings if they are made in lead or zinc. Not only are special 'aprons' needed at the front and back of the chimney, but the side flashings must be 'stepped' so that they fit into the mortar joints.

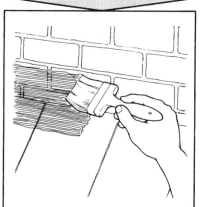

3. If a self-adhesive flashing is being used, treat both wall and roof first of all with special flashing primer.

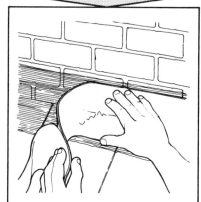

4. Unroll the flashing strip, peeling off the backing paper and pressing it down well, particularly at the edges.

59 Making good chimney defects

Because of their exposed position, chimneys suffer from considerable wear and tear that can not only allow the rain to enter, but can also weaken the structure.

Typical problems are cracked flaunching around the pots; loose, split or porous flashings; loose or damaged pots; crumbling mortar joints, and blown or cracked render.

Damp patches on the ceiling near a chimney are a clue that something may be wrong, and often this can be confirmed by looking at the chimney from ground level with binoculars. However, a close inspection may be the only answer. Use a roof ladder to reach the chimney, but if any major work is required, a scaffolding platform will be needed for safety.

61 Resetting a chimney pot

If the flaunching around the base of the chimney pot is in a poor state of repair, or if the pot itself is damaged or loose, the old flaunching will need removing and the pot resetting (or a new one fitting) before a new mortar flaunching is applied.

Hack off all the old flaunching, taking care not to damage the pot if this is reusable. In some cases, the chimney's flue may actually be wider than the pot's diameter, in which case the pot will be supported on slate strips laid around the edge of the flue. To prevent the pot falling into the flue as the flaunching is removed, tie it to the chimney with rope. Repair any damaged brickwork around the top of the chimney before replacing the pot and flaunching.

60 Chimney repairs

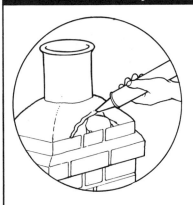

Minor cracks in flaunching can be sealed with beads of waterproof mastic.

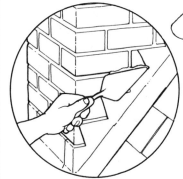

Loose flashing should be wedged back in place with strips of lead and the joints repointed.

If neglected for too long, a chimney can suffer considerably from the elements — flashings deteriorate and come loose, mortar joints and flaunching crack and crumble, bricks become porous, pots become cracked or loose and the entire structure may begin to lean.

Rake out crumbling mortar joints with a cold chisel and repoint them.

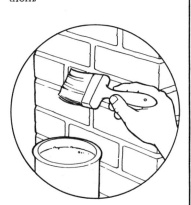

The brickwork of a chimney can be waterproofed by painting on a silicone treatment.

1. A safe working platform can be assembled from access tower components with boards to spread the weight on the roof.

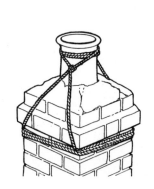

2. To prevent the pot toppling or falling into the flue, tie it securely to the chimney stack with a length of rope.

With central heating systems being installed in more and more houses, many chimneys are no longer in use, and in this situation it is a good idea to cap them at the top to prevent rainwater running down inside and soaking through the walls of the rooms below. If the chimney is particularly tall, it may also be beneficial to remove several courses of bricks to reduce its height as much as possible and prevent any possibility of it falling in the future.

There are various ways in which a chimney can be capped. Probably simplest of all is to fit a proprietary cowl to the pot, and there are several styles to choose from. Another method is to remove the pot and bed a normal half-round ridge tile in mortar to cover the top of the flue. Alternatively, both pot and flaunching can be removed and a paving slab bedded in mortar to cover the top of the stack completely. It should have a slight fall so that the rainwater will run off.

To prevent condensation forming inside the chimney and soaking through the walls indoors, the flue must be properly ventilated. A pot cowl or ridge tile will leave the flue open to the air, but if a paving slab is used, airbricks must be added to the top course of bricks in the stack. In all cases, if the fireplace has been closed off, it should also be fitted with a ventilator grill to provide the necessary flow of air through the chimney.

3. Carefully remove the old flaunching with a cold chisel and club hammer, collecting the pieces in a bucket.

3. Carefully remove the old flaunching with a cold chisel and club hammer, collecting the pieces in a bucket.

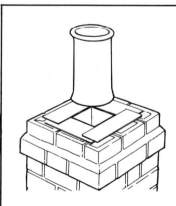

4. An old flue may be wider than the pot's diameter, in which case the latter must be supported on strips of slate.

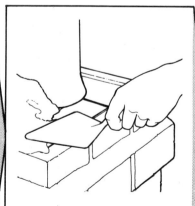

5. Moisten around the base of the pot with water and spread on new mortar made with sharp sand and a PVA additive.

6. Shape the flaunching so that it slopes down to the edges of the stack, where it should be 18mm (¾in) thick.

63 Replacing damaged bricks

Bricks that have cracked or are damaged in some other way should be replaced. However, if a large area of a wall is affected, it may indicate a more serious problem, such as subsidence. In this case, professional help should be sought.

Try to buy replacement bricks that match the originals – suppliers of used building materials should be able to help, although you may have to clean up old bricks yourself. Also make sure the mortar matches the colour of the original pointing and that the joints are finished in the same manner.

When replacing bricks in a cavity wall, take care to prevent debris and mortar dropping into the cavity where it might form a bridge for moisture.

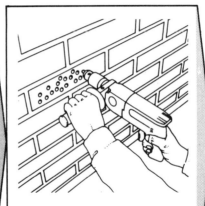

1. Begin removing the damaged brick by drilling into it or into the mortar around it with a masonry bit.

2. Use a bolster or cold chisel and club hammer to chop out the debris between the holes. Then brush out the opening.

64 Pointing profiles

There are various ways of finishing the mortar joints in brickwork, known as pointing.
*1. **Weatherstruck** joints will throw water clear of the bricks and are formed by pressing the trowel into the top edge of the joint and running it along to form a bevelled finish. The vertical joints are given a V-profile by pressing the trowel into each side of the joint.*
*2. **Rounded** joints can be formed by rubbing a length of hose or wooden dowel along the joints.*

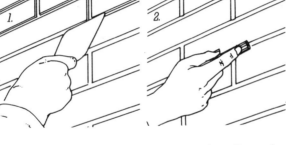

*3. **Flush** joints are used when the edges of the bricks have crumbled or are damaged. Form them by running a pad of sacking*

along them when the mortar is nearly dry.
*4. **Recessed** joints are only suitable for internal walls and are formed*

by raking out the mortar to a depth of 3mm (⅛in) with a specially shaped piece of wood.

65 Patching rendering

Damage to rendered surfaces may take the form of cracks or 'blown' patches where moisture has got behind the render and forced it away from the brickwork.

Cracks can be repaired by widening them with a cold chisel, undercutting the edges, brushing out the debris, treating with PVA bonding agent and filling with a 1:5 mortar mix.

With blown render, all the loose material should be hacked off, the brick joints raked out to form a decent key and the entire area painted with PVA bonding agent before re-rendering. This should be built up in two layers and ruled off level with the surrounding render. Finally the surface of the patch should be finished to match its surroundings.

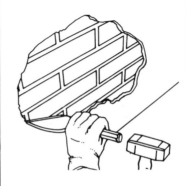

1. Use a cold or bolster chisel to cut out all the loose render, undercutting the edges so that the new render will grip well.

2. Rake out the mortar joints to form a key and moisten the wall by flicking water at it with a paint brush.

3. Moisten the surrounds of the opening and spread mortar across its bottom and on to the top and ends of the new brick.

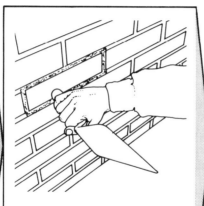

4. Tap the brick carefully into place with the trowel or hammer handle, removing any excess mortar that oozes out.

5. Once the brick is in place, tidy up the pointing with a small trowel, adding more mortar if necessary.

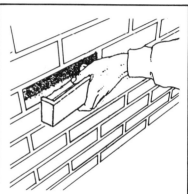
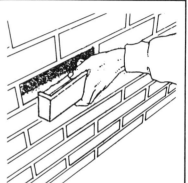

6. In a solid brick wall, chop out only half of the damaged brick and replace it with a freshly-cut half-brick.

66 Finishing touches to rendering

A large expanse of smooth render is not very interesting to look at, so various textured finishes are usually applied. Among these are pebbledash (where small pebbles are thrown at the wet render), roughcast (where the pebbles are mixed with a final coat of render) and various scraped finishes using items such as serrated spatulas or stiff brooms. For ashlar jointing, the render is scribed to resemble a wall of stone blocks.

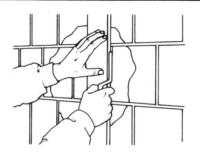

1. If the wall has an ashlar jointed finish, mark the new render to match with a piece of bent tube and a straight edge.

2. For a textured finish, stipple the render with a stiff-bristled brush after allowing it to harden for a few hours.

3. A rendered wall can also be finished with masonry paint after the render has hardened. Use a spray gun or brush.

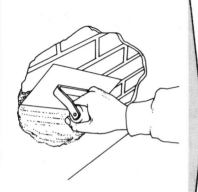

3. Apply a thin layer of 1:5 cement/sand mortar mix, spreading it evenly across the damaged area.

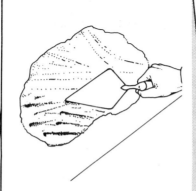

4. Scratch the surface of this first coat of render to key it for the next. Then allow to dry for about 24 hours.

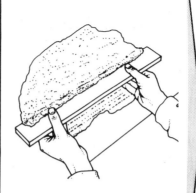

5. Apply the second coat of render so that it is just proud of the surrounding surface, then rule it off with a batten.

6. If a pebbledash finish is needed, throw pebbles on to the wet mortar and press them in gently with a wooden float.

67 Patching concrete

Athough concrete is a very durable material for paths, patios etc, cracks and even quite large holes may appear if it was not laid properly. If the damage occurs in only a few places, it can be repaired successfully, but if the damage is widespread, the concrete will need breaking up and relaying.

Cracks should be opened up with a bolster chisel and filled with a relatively-dry, 1:3 mortar mix. Treating the edges of the crack with PVA bonding agent and adding the adhesive to the mortar mix will improve the bond of the repair.

Larger holes can be filled in much the same way, but if they expose the foundations it may be necessary to add reinforcement with additional compacted hardcore.

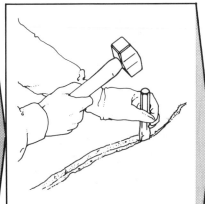

1. Open out a crack until it is about 25mm (1in) wide, removing all crumbling material. Undercut the edges.

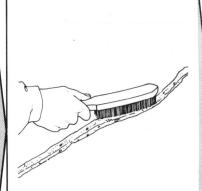

2. Brush all the dust and debris from the crack, and remove any weeds that have gained a foothold in it.

68 Patching edges

Repairing the damaged edges of a concrete path requires more effort, since the concrete must be contained while it sets. After chopping out the loose material and adding hardcore (if necessary), a 25mm (1in) thick board should be pinned against the edge of the path with stakes driven into the ground. Make sure the top of the board is level with the path surface and fill the damaged area with concrete. Leave the board in place for a week.

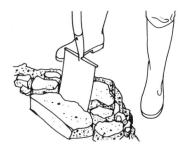

1. Remove all loose material and cut back crumbling edges with a bolster chisel. Undercut them to improve the bond.

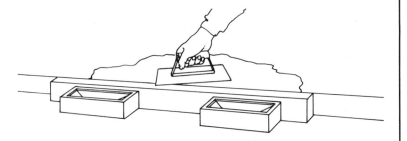

2. After cleaning out all the loose material, wedge or peg a length of board along the edge of the path to act as a formwork. Then

fill the hole with 1:3 concrete mix, tamping it down and floating it off level with the surrounding surface of the path.

69 Resurfacing a tarmac drive

Tarmac, concrete and gravel drives can be resurfaced using cold macadam, which is available in a choice of red, green or black and comes in polythene sacks. After applying a bitumen emulsion to the drive, the macadam is simply spread out, rolled flat to a thickness of about 19mm (¾in) and left to harden. A few chippings can be sprinkled over the surface before rolling it for the last time to break up the solid colour of the surface.

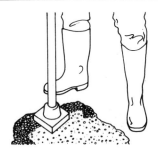

1. Holes should be brushed out, treated with weedkiller, primed with bitumen emulsion and filled with macadam.

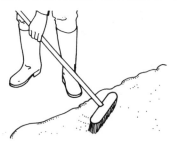

2. Pour the bitumen emulsion on to the drive and brush it out with an old broom, working on small areas at a time.

3. When the bitumen emulsion is tacky, tip out the macadam, spread it out evenly with a rake and roll it flat.

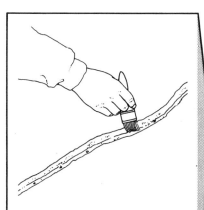

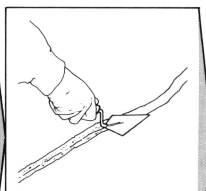

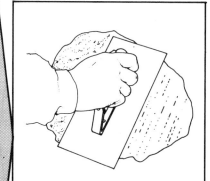

3. Paint the edges of the crack with a PVA adhesive solution. This will improve the grip of the new mortar.

4. Press the mortar into the crack with a small trowel, tamping it down well and smoothing it off.

5. If the path has been laid on bare earth, or the foundations are thin, pack in more hardcore, compacting it well.

6. After treating the edges of the hole with PVA solution, fill it with a 1:3 mortar mix and float it off level with the surrounding surface.

Resetting loose blocks & slabs

Paving blocks and slabs may be bedded in one of three ways; they may be laid on a layer of sand; they may be set on dabs of mortar on top of a layer of sand; or they may be set in a layer of mortar. The method of bedding determines the ease with which loose or damaged slabs can be reset.

If laid on sand, slabs and blocks can be levered up and more sand added to level them. If bedded on mortar dabs, it may be possible to lever them up, add fresh mortar between the old dabs and rebed the slab. However, if the slab is laid on a solid bed of mortar, it will have to be broken up, the old mortar bed chopped out with a cold chisel and club hammer, and a fresh bed laid before laying a new slab.

71 Bedding methods

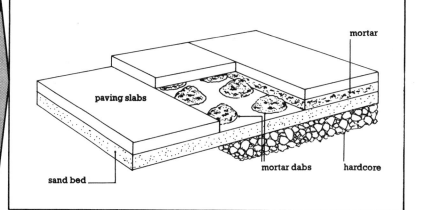

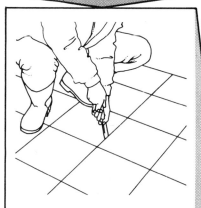

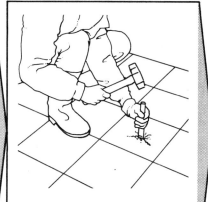

1. Loose slabs bedded on sand or mortar dabs can be levered up. Use a wide-bladed bolster chisel to prise them free.

2. Slabs set on a solid bed of mortar must be broken up. Use a club hammer and cold chisel, working out from the centre.

3. Fill any dips with fresh sand, replace the slab and tap it down level using the handle of a club hammer.

4. Alternatively, lay four or five new dabs of mortar. Replace the slab, tapping it down level as before.

Leaks from a rainwater system may be caused by blockages, sagging gutters, faulty joints, rust or other damage.

Blockages can be cleared by scooping debris from gutters or hopper heads, or by rodding the downpipes.

Sagging gutters should be dismantled and reset so that they have a fall of 25mm (1in) in every 3m (10ft).

A leaking joint between plastic gutters may mean unclipping the joint and replacing its rubber seal, or cutting out a glued joint and fitting a new piece of gutter. With cast iron, the joint must be unbolted, its putty scraped out and a layer of mastic added before bolting the sections together again.

Rusted cast iron can be repaired using a glass fibre repair kit or self-adhesive flashing strip. However, unless the damage is only limited to small area, it is probably better to fit a new plastic section. Most types include adaptors to match old cast iron systems.

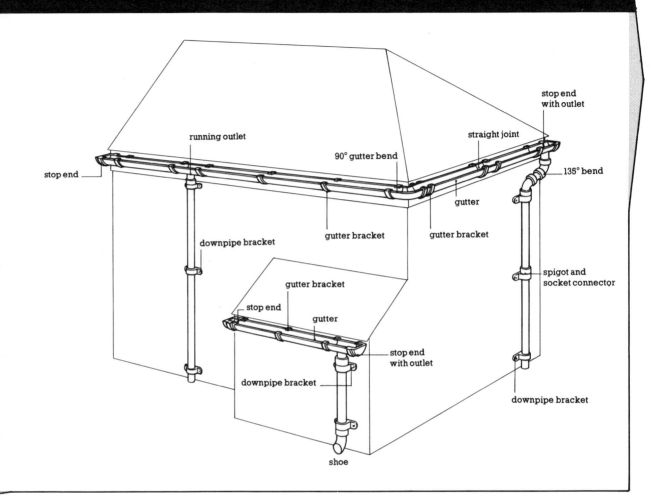

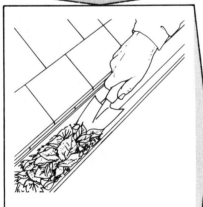

1. Scoop dead leaves and other debris from the gutter using a trowel. Collect it in a bucket suspended from the ladder.

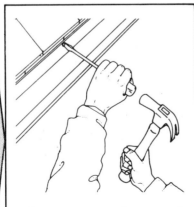

2. Some gutters may be screwed directly to the fascia. If the screws are difficult to turn, jar them loose with a hammer.

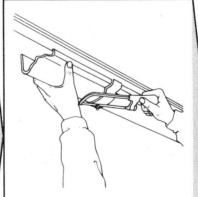

3. Unbolt the joints between cast iron gutters. If badly rusted, cut through the bolts with a hacksaw and lever apart.

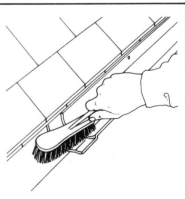

4. Scrape the old putty away from the joint and remove all old surface rust from the gutter with a wire brush.

1. To remove a section of downpipe, unscrew its bracket retaining screws or prise the nails from the wall.

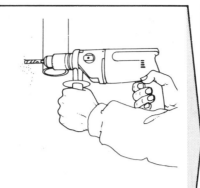

2. Remove the old pipe and bracket and drill fixing holes for the new pipe's bracket with a masonry drill.

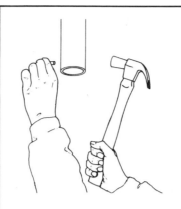

3. Drive conical wooden plugs or plastic wall plugs into the fixing holes so that they are flush with the wall's surface.

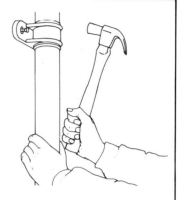

4. Fit the new pipe and secure it with galvanised nails driven into the wooden plugs. Use rust proof screws with wall plugs.

73 Cleaning downpipes

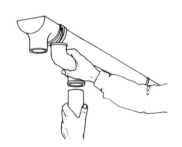

1. Remove the swan's neck connection by lifting it from the top of the downpipe then lowering it from the gutter.

2. Push a wad of rag through the downpipe with a long cane to clear the blockage. Protect the gully below with a tin.

74 Patching – glass fibre kits

Small rust holes in cast iron guttering or downpipes can be repaired with a glass fibre kit normally sold for repairing cars. In most cases, it will be easier to work on the damaged section at ground level.

After wire-brushing the rusted area back to bare metal, cut two patches of glass-fibre mat, making one 25mm (1in) larger all round than the other. Apply the mat in accordance with the kit instructions using the smaller patch first.

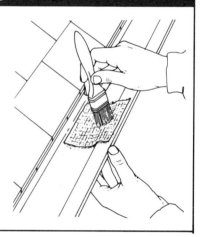

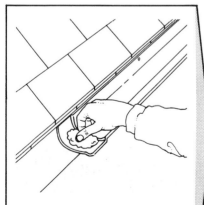

5. Press a 6mm (¼in) thick layer of mastic into the overlapping ends of the adjacent gutter sections.

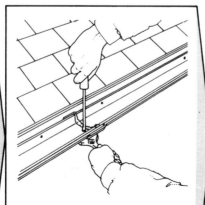

6. Refit the gutter to the fascia with new galvanised scews and reassemble the joints with new nuts and bolts.

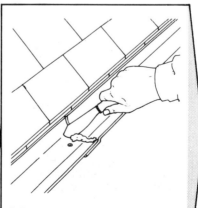

7. Trim off any mastic oozing from the joints and treat the inside of the guttering with a bitumastic paint.

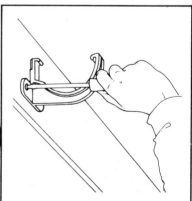

8. When fitting plastic gutter brackets, make sure they have a 'fall' towards the outlet end. Use rustproof screws.

75 Repairing manholes

Manholes, or inspection chambers, are installed in a drain run where it changes direction or joins another. Over the years, the brickwork, render or benching inside may crumble, fall into the drain and cause a blockage. Also, the cover and frame may come adrift.

When working on an inspection chamber, take care to prevent debris falling into the pipes where it might cause a blockage.

Damaged bricks should be replaced, and render made good as described in projects 63 and 65. Broken benching should be repaired with a 1:2 cement/sand mortar smoothed off well.

A loose cover frame should be rebedded on fresh mortar; take care to level it with the surrounding surface.

76 Manholes and gullies

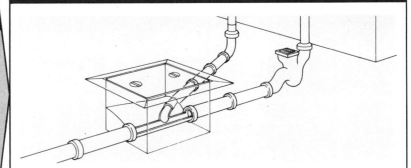

Gullies are used to connect the waste pipes from sinks, basins etc to the main underground drain.

Manholes are incorporated at the junctions of underground soil pipes.

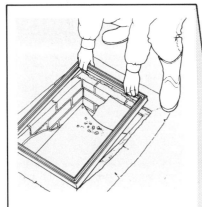

1. Chop away any mortar around the frame with a cold chisel. Lever the frame free and clean it up with a wire brush.

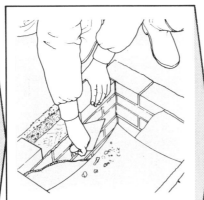

2. Clear away all the old mortar and rebed any loose bricks with fresh mortar. Patch damaged areas of render.

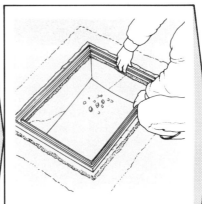

3. Set the cover frame in a bed of mortar, using a spirit level to check that it is level and flush with the surface.

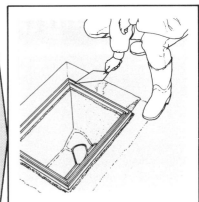

4. Add a fillet of mortar around the outside of the frame, smoothing it off neatly. Grease the cover edge and replace it.

77 Draining a waterlogged lawn

Lawns that are prone to flooding can be drained by installing a system of pipes below the ground that carries the water to a soakaway. The pipes, which are made of clay and may have perforations along one side, are simply laid end to end in a trench about 750mm (2ft 6in) deep. This is filled with shingle and covered by a layer of topsoil. As the water drains into the trench from the surrounding ground, it enters the pipes through the joints and flows to the soakaway. The pipes should be laid at a fall of about 1:250.

The soakaway should be about 1.5m (5ft) deep and 1.2m (4ft) square. It should be filled with hardcore to within 300mm (1ft) of the surface and the drainage pipe led into the centre.

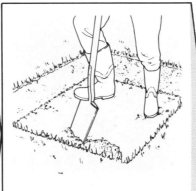

1. Dig a hole for the soakaway. If clay is discovered before the full depth is reached, make the soakaway longer or wider.

2. Filling the soakaway with hardcore will allow the water to filter away. Only half-fill it at this stage.

Old glazed stoneware gullies are easily damaged, but the wide variety of plastic gully fittings makes replacement relatively straightforward.

First, expose the gully and the joint where it is connected to the soil pipe, using a club hammer and cold chisel to break away any concrete. Cut the socket from the pipe with an angle grinder and fit a plastic connector in its place.

Fit the connector with quick-setting cement and bed the gully on a fairly dry concrete mix. Alternatively, bed a small paving slab or bricks in the concrete for the gully to stand on.

Check the height of the gully hopper, inserting a length of pipe between it and the gully if necessary. Lubricate the push-fit joints with petroleum jelly before assembly.

Make sure the hopper is aligned correctly, level and flush with or slightly below the surrounding ground. Then fill the hole with concrete, topped off with mortar.

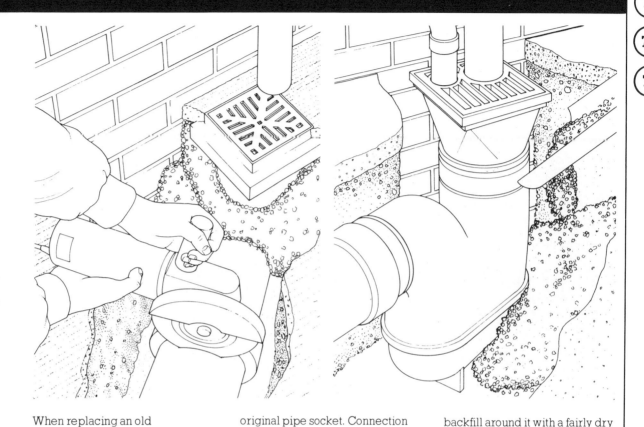

When replacing an old stoneware gully, it will be easier to cut through the soil pipe with an angle grinder than attempt to chisel out the mortar from the original pipe socket. Connection to the gully can be made with a proprietary plastic connector.

After levelling the new gully and connecting it to the soil pipe, backfill around it with a fairly dry concrete mix and finish off around the hopper with mortar for a smooth surface.

3. Lay in the main drain run to the soakaway, taking the pipe to the centre. Bed the pipes on shingle and with a slight fall.

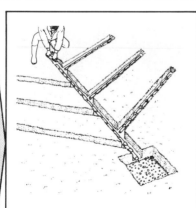

4. For a large area, run pipes in herringbone fashion to the main run. Cover the joints with slates before backfilling.

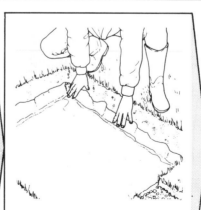

5. After adding the remaining hardcore, lay thick polythene over the top to stop soil being washed into the soakaway.

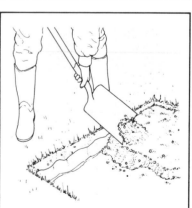

6. Finally, replace the topsoil, levelling it off and relaying any turf that was removed at the beginning.

Rising damp occurs when moisture in the ground is absorbed by floors and ground-floor walls. It may be caused by a lack of a damp-proof course (dpc) in the walls or damp-proof membrane (dpm) in the solid floors of very old properties, by the dpc or dpm becoming broken as a result of settlement, deteriorating with age or being bridged in some way.

If there is no obvious bridging of the dpc, the fault will lie in the waterproof barrier itself, which must be renewed.

Although there are other professional choices for installing a dpc (inserting new strips or using electrical conductors), the only method suitable for diy installation is to inject a waterproofing chemical under pressure into holes drilled around the base of the wall.

A new dpm can be provided by treating the entire floor with bitumastic emulsion, or laying a new polythene dpm. Both should be protected by a mortar screed laid on top.

1. Rubble piled against an outside wall may bridge the dpc.

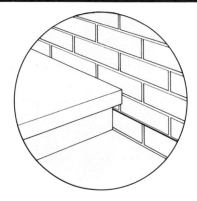

2. A step built against the wall, can have the same effect.

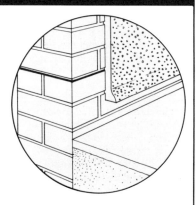

3. Render carried over the dpc provides an effective bridge.

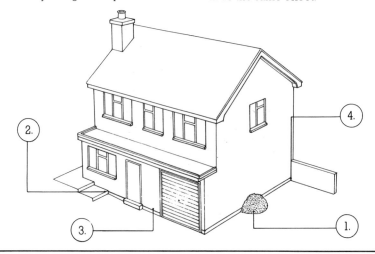

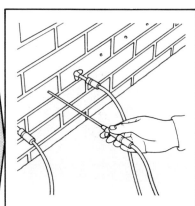

4. An adjoining wall should have a dpc linked to the house dpc.

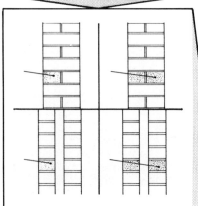

1. Walls are injected in stages. First drilling is to a depth of about 50mm, the second to 150mm in solid walls, 230mm in cavity walls.

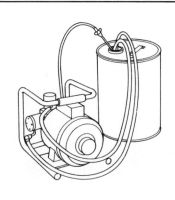

2. Insert the pump pick-up in the can of fluid and prime the machine by bleeding fluid and air from one of its nozzles.

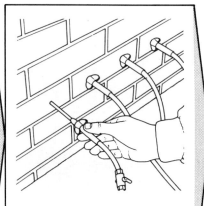

3. Insert the nozzles in the holes, tightening their nuts. Pump in fluid until it shows on the surface of the bricks.

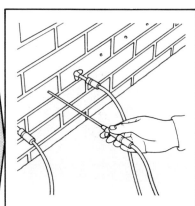

4. When injecting from one side only, drill the holes deeper after the first injection and use the longer nozzles provided.

80 Curing penetrating damp

Penetrating damp occurs when moisture finds a way into the house through the walls or roof. It will only occur during or shortly after periods of rain and will disappear during dry spells. It may come from driving rain or from water spilling down the walls from faulty gutters and downpipes.

For the water to get inside, there must be a fault somewhere in the structure, which must be rectified. This may mean sealing walls with a waterproofing liquid, repointing or re-rendering walls, sealing gaps around window and door frames with mastic, replacing crumbling putty in windows, replacing roof tiles or slates, applying new flashing to roofs, or providing new flaunching around chimney pots.

81 Trouble spots

Penetrating damp can find its way through defects in the structure of the walls and/or roof. In the main, it occurs for the following reasons:
1. Cracked or crumbling flaunching around chimney pots.
2. Torn, porous or loose flashings, or cracked mortar fillets around chimneys and where roofs meet walls.
3. Loose, broken or missing slates and tiles, or damaged felt on flat roofs.
4. Cracked or blown rendering.
5. Gaps between window or door frames and the wall, crumbling putty around window panes and clogged sill drip grooves.
6. Blocked, sagging, broken or missing guttering.
7. Leaking or broken downpipes.
8. Constantly dripping overflow pipes.
9. Wall cavities bridged by debris allowing moisture to pass through the wall or rise up past the dpc.

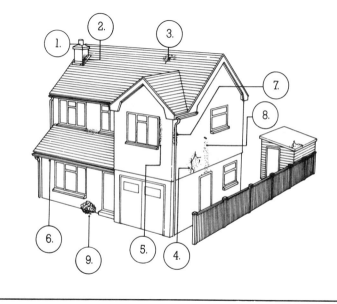

82 Damp meters

A damp meter can be hired to check for damp. The device has probes which are pressed into timber and plaster, the readings given on its scale indicating whether the degree of dampness present is acceptable or needs rectifying. By comparing several readings, it is possible to determine the extent of the dampness. Long probes are also provided with the meter for checking for damp deep inside a wall, after drilling pairs of holes into its centre.

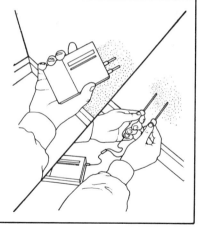

1. Damp can be prevented from penetrating the solid walls of older houses by treating them with a silicone fluid.

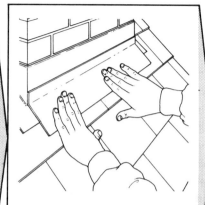

2. Torn or porous flashings around roofs and chimneys should be repaired with self-adhesive flashing strips.

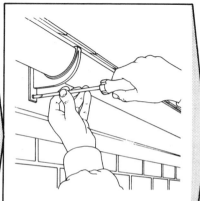

3. Repair or replace defective gutters and downpipes to prevent water spilling on to the wall when it rains.

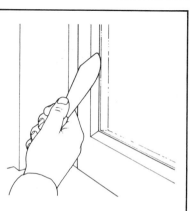

4. At windows, check that the drip grooves in the sills are clear, seal the frames to the walls and replace old putty.

Garden sheds will deteriorate rapidly if neglected; regular maintainance is the key to prolonging their useful life.

Timber buildings should be treated regularly with preservative. Cut out any rooten timbers and replace them with new pieces, soaked in preservative. Rub down painted timber or metal frames, prime them and treat them with undercoats and top coats as appropriate.

Crumbling putty should be renewed together with any broken panes of glass.

Oil locks and hinges, tightening their screws if loose. If badly rusted, remove them and fit new ones.

If the roofing felt is porous in one or two places, treat it with an overall coat of bituminous emulsion to seal it. However, if torn or leaking badly, the felt should be replaced. The new felt is held in place with extra-large-head galvanised roofing nails spaced at 150mm (6ins) centres, overlapping sheets also being bonded together with bituminous emulsion.

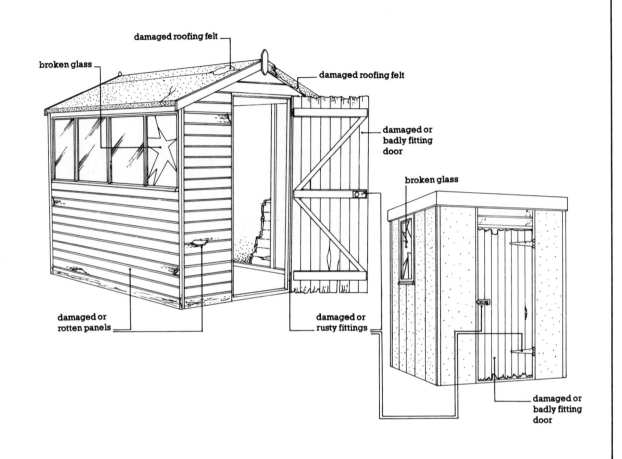

damaged roofing felt

broken glass

damaged roofing felt

damaged or badly fitting door

broken glass

damaged or rotten panels

damaged or rusty fittings

damaged or badly fitting door

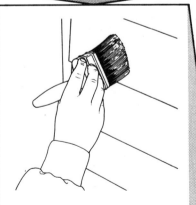

1. After cleaning the shed walls, treating them with fungicide and rubbing down, apply a timber preservative.

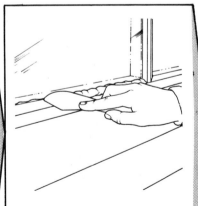

2. Old loose putty should be raked out, the rebate primed and fresh putty added. Smooth it off and mitre the corners.

3. To seal a porous roof, paint it with bituminous emulsion. Use a board to spread your weight across the roof.

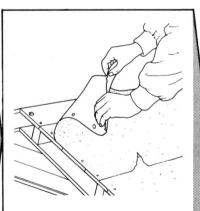

4. If the felt is in bad shape, strip it off with an old scraper, pull out the old nails and replace any rotten timber.

If a pond springs a leak, the first job is to drain the water so that a repair can be made, and if it contains fish, the water should be kept for reuse. Do this by pumping it into a holding tank made from thick polythene on a timber framework.

Cracks in concrete ponds can be repaired with quick-setting cement after undercutting the edges. Allow the cement to cure and treat the concrete with a suitable waterproof coating. Butyl rubber types are best.

Tears in pvc or butyl rubber pond liners can be patched with proprietary repair kits, but make sure the correct kit is used.

Rigid glass fibre ponds can be fixed with a normal glass fibre repair kit.

Before making the repair find the cause, which may be a sharp object beneath the liner. If so, remove it, opening up the hole if necessary, or press it down well. Then replace the sand that will have been washed away, using a funnel.

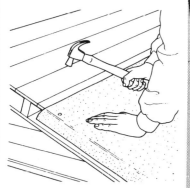

5. Cut strips of heavy-duty roofing felt to length and nail them to the roof, working from the eaves upwards.

6. Add the capping sheet. Overlap the sheets below by at least 225mm (9ins), nailing through both.

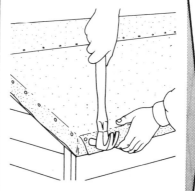

7. Rather than cutting the felt at the corners of the roof, fold it neatly so that rain cannot penetrate and nail it.

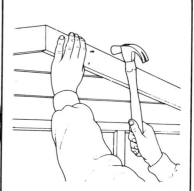

8. If the original edge battens are usable, refit them with galvanised nails. Otherwise use them as patterns for new ones.

Glossary

Additives are chemicals added to mortar and concrete mixes to improve their performance. The commonest include plasticisers, waterproofers and frostproofers.

Aggregate is sand or gravel added to cement to make mortar or concrete respectively. The term is normally used for all-in aggregate, a mixture of sand and gravel mixed with cement to make concrete.

Arris rails run between fence posts on close-boarded and picket-style fences. They are triangular in cross-section, and are usually mortised into the posts; the boards are then nailed to the rail's face.

Bargeboards are used to finish off the roof at gables, and are nailed to the ends of the roof timbers.

Builder's square is a rough wooden triangle made up from sawn timber with sides in the ratio 3:4:5, and is used to check the squareness of brickwork and concrete.

Casement windows have side-hung sashes and top-hung opening lights, and are available in a wide range of sizes and styles.

Cement is the adhesive from which mortar and concrete are made. Portland cement is the commonest type. It's usually sold in 50kg bags, although smaller sizes are also available.

Concrete is a mixture of cement, sand and gravel (all-in aggregate) plus a plasticiser (lime or a chemical additive), used to cast foundations, drives and base slabs. It can be mixed by hand from dry ingredients, or ordered ready-mixed.

Damp-proof courses (DPCs) are built into all walls rising off the ground to prevent damp from rising in the masonry. In older homes, slate was often used, but modern homes have DPCs of bituminized felt or plastic. Faulty DPCs can be cured by injecting special chemicals into the brickwork.

Downpipes carry rainwater from the gutters down to ground level, where it is discharged into a gully and runs on to a drain or soakaway.

English bond is a bricklaying bond consisting of alternate courses of stretchers and headers.

Fascias are vertical planks nailed to the cut ends of roof rafters at the eaves. Where the eaves overhang, a horizontal soffit fills the gap between fascia and house wall.

Flashings are strips of waterproof material – usually metal or felt – used to waterproof the join between a roof and another adjacent surface (usually vertical).

Flaunching outdoors means the sloping mortar fillet round the base of a chimney pot, sealing it to the stack.

Flemish bond is a bricklaying bond in which each course consists of a pair of stretchers followed by a single header.

Gravel boards are fitted between fence posts at ground level to prevent rot from attacking the boards or panels.

Gutters are metal or plastic troughs fitted at the eaves to collect rainwater and divert it into downpipes.

Manholes or inspection chambers are installed on drain runs where branch drains enter the main run or the run changes direction.

Masonry cement is ordinary Portland cement with added plasticiser.

Mastic is a non-setting filler used to seal gaps between building components such as frames and masonry.

Mortar is a mixture of sand and cement with added plasticiser, used for bricklaying and rendering.

Pointing is the finish given to the mortar courses in bricklaying. Several different profiles are used.

Soakaways are rubble-filled pits designed to help rainwater from downpipes drain into the subsoil.

Stretcher bond is a bricklaying bond consisting of a single skin of bricks 112mm thick, with bricks overlapping each other by half their length.

Index